Metamorphosis VOL.2

Cultural Metamorphoses of Korea and Hungary at the Turn of the Twentieth Century

Institute for Korean Christianity Culture HK+ Research Project, Soongsil University

보고사
BOGOSA

Metamorphosis VOL.2

Cultural Metamorphoses of Korea and Hungary at the Turn of the Twentieth Century

2024년 4월 30일 초판 발행

기획 및 편집
숭실대학교 한국기독교문화연구원 HK+사업단
https://kiccs.ssu.ac.kr
Tel. +82-2-820-0838

발행처
보고사(발행인 : 김흥국)
경기도 파주시 회동길 337-15
http://www.bogosabooks.co.kr
Tel. 031-955-9797

정가 23,000원
ISBN 979-11-6587-689-0 93300

First Edition, April 30, 2024.

Edited by
Institute for Korean Christianity Culture
HK+ Research Project, Soongsil University
https://kiccs.ssu.ac.kr   Tel. +82-2-820-0838

Published by
Bogosa Books (Publisher : Kim Heung-guk)
337-15, Hoedong-gil, Paju-si, Gyeonggi-do, Republic of Korea
http://www.bogosabooks.co.kr
Tel. +82-31-955-9797

Price 23,000 won
ISBN 979-11-6587-689-0 93300

This work was supported by the Ministry of Education of the Republic of Korea and the National Research Foundation of Korea (NRF-2018S1A6A3A01042723)

이 저서는 2018년 대한민국 교육부와 한국연구재단의 지원을 받아 수행된 연구임(KRF-2018S1A6A3A01042723)

Statement of Purpose

Metamorphosis is an occasional book series published by the Humanities Korea Plus (HK+) Project of the Institute of Korean Christian Culture at Soongsil University. It aims to adopt an interdisciplinary and transnational approach to Korean Studies from a transcultural perspective, encompassing various fields of study such as history, literature, religion, and popular culture. *Metamorphosis* includes original articles and translations of articles written in Korean or other languages to expand the perspectives and scope of Korean Studies and to promote exchanges among Korean Studies scholars in different regions.

Since 2018, the Humanities Korea Plus (HK+) Project at the Institute of Korean Christian Culture, Soongsil University, has received support from the Korea Research Foundation. This initiative is dedicated to promoting research on translation, deculturation, and cultural change in Korea from the early modern period to the Cold War era. Encouraging interdisciplinary scholarship that draws new contours in Korean studies, the project is conducting extensive research on Korean culture under the agenda of "Humanities in Transition Spaces: Metamorphosis in Culture."

Metamorphosis VOL.2

Cultural Metamorphoses of Korea and Hungary at the Turn of the Twentieth Century

Editorial Board

JANG Kyung-nam	Soongsil University
	Institute for Korean Christianity Culture
KIM Jiyoung	Soongsil University
	Institute for Korean Christianity Culture
KIM Sunghee	Soongsil University
	Institute for Korean Christianity Culture
OH Sunsil	Soongsil University
	Institute for Korean Christianity Culture
BHANG Won-il	Soongsil University
	Institute for Korean Christianity Culture

Editor in Chief, KIM Jiyoung
Managing Editor, SEO Jiae

Contributors

Authors

BHANG Won-il	HK+ Research Professor, IKCC, Soongsil University
YOON Young Shil	Assitant professor, Soongsil University, South Korea
OH Jie Seok	Assitant professor, Soongsil University, South Korea
QIAN Chunhua	HK+ Research Professor, IKCC, Soongsil University
MA Eunji	HK+ Research Professor, IKCC, Soongsil University
MECSI Beatrix	Professor, Eötvös Loránd University(ELTE), Hungary
OH Sunsil	HK+ Research Professor, IKCC, Soongsil University
KIM Sunghee	HK+ Research Professor, IKCC, Soongsil University
BLAHÓ Kata	Lecturer, Eötvös Loránd University(ELTE), Hungary
KIM Jiyoung	Assitant professor, Soongsil University, South Korea

Translators

Sarah MACK

Peter WARD

Editor's Note

The second issue of *Metamorphosis* 2 is a revised and edited version of papers presented at the joint conference of Soongsil University and ELTE in Budapest, Hungary, in October 2023. A total of 11 papers were presented at the conference, but one paper could not be published due to the author's circumstances and only 10 papers were published. Most of the articles published here have been revised, supplemented, and translated from Korean to English. Two papers by Hungarian scholars are previously unpublished works. The titles of original journal in which the article was originally published is listed at the end of the editor's note. The order of the articles is based on the theme and time period. The first section, *"the Theories,"* include three papers (BHANG Won-il, YOON Young Shil and OH Jie Seok) are related to the theories of 'cultural metamorphosis', which is the agenda of this project. The second section, *"the Aspects,"* contained five papers (QIAN Chunhua, MA Eunji, MECSI Beatrix, OH Sunsil and KIM Sunghee) that identify the aspects of metamorphosis in Korea and Manchuria as spaces of modern transition. The last section, *"the Comparison,"* have two articles (BLAHÓ Kata, KIM Jiyoung) trace the metamorphosis of cognition in the Hungary and Korea during the transition to modernity. Here's a brief introduction to each article.

BHANG Won-il examines the debate surrounding Indigenization theology since the 1960s and proposes a theory of culture rooted in the concept of transformation, using Goethe's botanical theory as a framework. Indigenization theologians argue that Christianity merges with culture like a seed sprouting in different cultural soils, leading to different expressions of Christianity, but separating the gospel from culture poses challenges and provokes intense debate. This theological perspective acknowledges the inevitable cultural change and syncretism of faith, but emphasizes the core essence of the faith. Goethe's botanical perspective explains plant development as a metamorphic process and provides a framework for change. This article aims to develop a comprehensive theory of culture by juxtaposing indigenization theology and Goethe's ideas. It is based on the principle of metamorphosis, taking into account the evolution of Christianity and the challenges of cultural integration.

YOON Young Shil critically examines the work of Im Hwa (1908-1953), especially his book A History of Korean Newspapers, through a conceptual lens. Im explores the dynamics of culture, emphasizing attributes such as universality, hybridity, and specificity, to argue for a Korean national identity in a colonial context without reducing it to a fixed stereotype. His perspective on Korean modern and contemporary literary history provides insights into cultural transformation in several ways. First, he acknowledges the introduction of alien institutions in the process of colonial transformation, yet argues for the creative blending of indigenous and alien cultural elements to enrich the colonized subjectivity. Second, he engages in debates about cultural continuity and discontinuity, emphasizing the ongoing process of monocultural creation while recognizing the structural rupture of the transition to "modernity". Third, Im's writing can be seen as a pragmatic endeavor to (re)establish the cultural identity of the Korean people, resisting the assimilation policies of the Japanese, especially in the 1940s. It can be seen as a performative act that shapes the cultural identity of a nation. Finally, Im Hwa envisions a new social imagination of the future that seeks to overcome colonial modernity during the transition to modernity, setting it up as another period of 'transformation'. This article provides a nuanced analysis of Im Hwa's contribution to understanding the cultural transformation of Korean literature and society.

OH Jie Seok examines the adopting of Christian ethics, particularly Western academic ethics and Protestant ethics, introduced to Korea by Western missionaries at the turn of the modern era. It focuses on the encounter between Korean intellectuals and Christian ethics during the transition from Confucian ideology to Western education, and analyses the reactions of late Joseon intellectuals to these ethics. While some intellectuals ignored and rejected Western academic ethics, others actively sought a new ethical framework during the Enlightenment. By examining how Christian ethics replaced Confucian values, particularly through ethics lectures in Christian schools during the opening period, this study identifies the differences between Christian ethics as transmitted by Western missionaries and Christian ethics as intended through theological or ethics textbooks. The study highlights the complex dynamics of cultural exchange and the evolving moral landscape in Korea during this transformative period.

QIAN Chunhua examines the rapid spread of socialist ideas in the Gando region, particularly after the 13 March anti-Japanese protests in Longjing (Yongjeong) and the Jingxin upheaval. The 1927 Gando Communist Party Incident in Longjing (Yongjeong) is an important event that signalled the setback of the socialist movement. This study examines the acceptance and spread of socialist ideas in Longjing (Yongjeong), focusing on lesser-known events such as the Religious Refusal Movement, the Oriental Academy Incident, and the 30 May Riots. The Religious Refusal Movement, which began in schools in the mid-1920s, was led by students who opposed religion and were influenced by socialist ideology. Their acceptance of socialist ideas was linked to their links with the Korean Communist Party, which was based in the maritime province of Siberia. The 1923 Oriental Institute Incident in Seoul, instigated by the Communist Party, fuelled the spread of socialist ideas through schooling. The 30 May Riots in Longjing (Yongjeong) drew attention to the collaboration between the CCP and the Korean Communist Party. Overall, the 1920s saw Longjing (Yongjeong) emerge as a centre for various socialist organisations, demonstrating the potential for successful collaboration with the CCP. This period, referred to as the 'Red Longjing', was a time when socialist ideology was dominant in the region.

MA Eunji explores the impact of early Bible translation in the late Joseon Dynasty within the broader context of the Reformation that swept across Western Europe. It explores how the Reformation, with its renewed emphasis on the Bible, shaped a distinct national identity and laid the groundwork for the emergence of a Protestant nation and state. Drawing on parallels with Western history, the paper examines how Protestantism in Korea sparked an intellectual awakening, fuelled Christian nationalism, shaped collective identity through biblical narratives, and contributed to nation-building. The dissemination of translated Bibles during this period combined biblical teachings with nationalist sentiments to form a more cohesive national identity, ultimately contributing to social reform and resistance to foreign domination. This convergence of biblical narrative and nationalism has been termed 'biblical nationalism' and represents an important aspect of the socio-political landscape of late Joseon Korea.

MECSI Beatrix delves into the visual documentation of Seoul, Korea, during a transformative period from the late 19th to the early 20th century, a time when Korea, traditionally known as the "Hermit Kingdom," opened its ports to the international community. The capital city of Seoul, embarking on a journey from the Joseon capital to the modern Korean Empire and through the Japanese occupation, is scrutinized through the lens of both foreign and local observers. The paper posits that earlier artistic renditions of Seoul, mainly for local consumption, contrast sharply with the photographic images introduced by foreigners in the 1880s and later adopted by Koreans. It highlights the contributions of foreign visitors, including Hungarian travelers Ferenc Hopp and Dezső Bozóky, and juxtaposes their perspectives with that of American Percival Lowell, Frenchman Pierre Loti, and Koreans such as Hwang Cheol and An Jungsik. The author underscores the symbolic restoration of Gyeongbok Palace's "woldae" as a poignant emblem of Korea's resilience and its efforts to reclaim its historical identity and cultural sovereignty after decades of colonial influence.

OH Sunsil examines the reconstruction of the Korean power system in the 1950s and raises questions about reconstruction in a resource-constrained environment. It highlights the role of Korean electricians who advocated for a hydropower-centred power system and explores the techno-political dynamics surrounding power development at the time, particularly the issue of the technological choice of primary power source. While U.S. aid officials favored the rapid construction of thermal power plants to address immediate needs, Korean engineers argued for the construction of large-scale hydropower plants, seeing geographical and resource considerations and the creation of a power system as essential to the future development of the country. While these arguments appeared to be rational technical decisions, they were influenced by Korea's colonial experience, which had seen significant growth in power infrastructure as the country transitioned from small-scale thermal power to large-scale hydropower. However, hydropower-centric development faced challenges due to the reliance on aid funding. Through negotiations, South Korean engineers embraced thermal power plants as a new option, and utilized technology provided by US aid agencies to create a strategy for rebuilding a more flexible power system that integrated thermal power alongside hydropower.

KIM Sunghee examines the efforts made by South Korean musicians during the Cold War to globalize *gayo*, a Korean popular music similar to Japanese *kayōkyoku*, by adapting it for overseas audiences. Beginning with participation in international music festivals in Asia, Oceania, Latin America, and the United States in the 1970s, South Korean musicians aimed to globalize. South Korean media companies then organized international song festivals in Seoul in the late 1970s. This study examines the impact of these festivals on the worldview of South Korean musicians in the 1970s and early 1980s, and sheds light on their role in the evolution of song into K-pop, a globally recognized form of Korean popular music. Following composer Lee Bong-jo's success at the 1970 Yamaha World Popular Song Festival, many Korean musicians participated in international music festivals in Japan. At the same time, Korean broadcasters partnered with Japanese stations to organize their own international music festivals: The Seoul International Song Festival of the Munhwa Broadcasting Corporation (MBC) in 1978 and the World Song Festival of the Tongyang Broadcasting Company (TBC) in 1979. This thesis examines the interaction between Korea and the world music scene during the Cold War, an area of research that has received little attention.

BLAHÓ Kata examines the theatrical culture at the turn of the 20th century in both the Korean Peninsula and the Hungarian territories of the Austro-Hungarian Empire, focusing on leading theater companies in Budapest and Seoul. It draws parallels between the two countries' theatrical metamorphoses, despite being separated by decades. Western-style theater, characterized by permanent buildings and canonized drama texts, emerged as a dominant form in both regions. Hungary, under Habsburg rule, saw the establishment of permanent theaters like the Pesti Magyar Theatre, while Korea's encounter with Western theater came through Japanese settlers. Despite different traditions, both regions faced censorship and the challenge of adapting foreign practices to local contexts. In Hungary, the *Thália Társaság* pioneered modern theater, emphasizing realism and literary value. Similarly, Korea's *singeuk* movement, led by student troupes, promoted realism and introduced Western drama to Korean audiences. These movements served as educational platforms, aiming to enrich societal discourse and national identity. Despite facing challenges such as censorship and lack of permanent venues, both movements left a lasting impact on their respective theater cultures. The study underscores the role of self-reliant artistic companies, like *Thália Társaság* and *singeuk* troupes, in shaping modern theater. Despite initial struggles and eventual disbandment, their emphasis on literary quality and societal relevance paved the way for future generations of theater practitioners. Ultimately, the study highlights the transformative power of theater as a medium for cultural expression and education, bridging historical and geographical divides.

KIM Jiyoung's article explores the historical relationship between Korea and Hungary, dating back to the establishment of formal diplomatic relations in 1892. Diplomatic relations between Joseon and the Austro-Hungarian monarchy. Despite diplomatic negotiations, active exchanges between the two countries did not immediately follow. However, scholars and travellers from the Austro-Hungarian royal court with a keen interest in Asia visited Joseon and recorded their observations, providing a valuable source for understanding Hungarian perceptions of Korea. This study examines how Hungarians perceived Korea by focusing on ten encyclopaedias from different periods. With limited exposure to Korea, encyclopaedias served as an important source of information to broaden the breadth of knowledge about Korea. The encyclopaedias analyzed include *Közhasznú Esmeretek Tára* (1833), *Egyetemes Magyar Encyclopaedia* (1872), *A Föld és népei, and Atheneum Kézi Lexikona* (1892), *Pallas Nagy Lexikon* (1895), *Levi Nagy Lexikon* (1915), *Tolnai Uzi Vilag Lexikon* (1927),

Catolikus Lexikon (1932), *Uj Lexikon* (1936), and *Uzi Idők Lexikon* (1939). Through this analysis, this paper sheds light on the changes in Hungarians' perceptions and knowledge of Korea during the period under investigation.

Below are the names of the journals in which each article originally appeared.

BHANG Won-il. "Indigenization and Metamophosis." *Christianity and Culture* 16 (2021): 81-112. [방원일, 「토착화와 메타모포시스」, 『기독교와 문화』 16, 2021, 81-112.]

YOON Young Shil. "Hwa Im's Writing The History of Korean New Literature and Cultural Metamorphoses." *THE DONG BANG HAK CHI* 192 (2020): 79-103. [윤영실, 「임화의 『개설신문학사』와 근대전환기 문화의 '메타모포시스'」, 『동방학지』 192, 2020, 79-103.]

OH Jie Seok. "Learning of Manners through 'Orangkae(Babarians)'! : Tracing the Active Acceptance of Western Christian Ethics beyond the Ignorance and Exclusion Against it." *Culture and Convergence* 42/10 (2020): 131-152. [오지석, 「오랑캐에게 예절을 배우다! : 서양 기독교윤리에 대한 무시·배척을 넘어서」, 『문화와 융합』 42(10), 2020, 131-152.]

QIAN Chunhua. "Red Longjing(Yongjeong): Geography of Longjing Socialist Thought at the end of the 1920s." *Korean Studies* 68 (2023): 349-373. [천춘화, 「붉은 용정: 1920년대 용정 사회주의 사상의 지리」, 『한국학연구』 68, 2023, 349-373.]

MA Eunji. "Early Biblical Translation and Biblical Nationalism in the Late Chosun Dynasty." *The Journal of the Church History Society in Korea* 44 (2016): 243-284. [마은지, 「한말 기독교의 성경번역과 성경 민족주의에 관한 고찰」, 『한국교회사학회지』 44, 2016, 243-284.]

OH Sunsil. "Reconstruction of the Electricity System in the 1950s between Colonial Heritage and Pressure on the Aid Economy." *Sungshin Humanities Research* 45/1 (2022): 251-288. [오선실, 「한국 전기기술자 집단의 형성과

1950년대 전원개발계획의 재구성: 식민지의 유산과 미국의 대외경제원조 정책 사이에서」, 『인문과학연구』 45(1), 2022, 251-288.]

KIM Sunghee. "International Song Festivals and Musicians' Sense of the World: Inter-Asian Perspective and Eurasian Imagination in the Study of Korean Popular Song during the Cold War." *The Journal of Popular Narrative* 27/1 (2021): 187-225. [김성희, 「국제가요제와 세계 감각―냉전 시기 대중음악사 연구의인터아시아적 관점과 유라시아적 상상력」, 『대중서사연구』 27(1), 2021, 187-225.]

KIM Jiyoung. "Description of Korea in Hungarian Encyclopedias: 1833-1930." *Korean Journal of German Studies* 47 (2021): 41-78. [김지영, 「헝가리 백과사전에 나타난 한국에 대한 서술: 1833-1930」, 『독일연구』 47, 2021, 41-78.]

Contents

Statement of Purpose ⋯ iii

List of Editors ⋯ iv

Contributors ⋯ v

Editor's Note ⋯ vi

Part 1. The Theories

Indigenization and Metamorphosis _ BHANG Won-il ⋯⋯⋯⋯⋯⋯⋯⋯⋯⋯⋯⋯ 3

Metamorphosis of Culture and Im Hwa's *the History
of New Korean Literature (Gaeseol Shinmunhaksa)* _ YOON Young Shil ⋯⋯⋯ 23

Cultural Metamorphosis:
From Seohak Ethics to Christian Ethics _ OH Jie Seok ⋯⋯⋯⋯⋯⋯⋯⋯⋯ 53

Part 2. The Aspects

Red Yongjeong [LONGJING]
Geographical Manifestation of Socialist Ideology
of the Yongjeong Movement in the 1920s _ QIAN Chunhua ⋯⋯⋯⋯⋯⋯⋯ 85

Korean Transformation of Western Christian Nationalism:
Biblical Nationalism in Modern Korea
at the Turn of the 20th Century _ MA Eunji ⋯⋯⋯⋯⋯⋯⋯⋯⋯⋯⋯ 107

Metamorphosis of Seoul:
Visual Representations of the Korean Capital
at the Turn of the 20th Century _ MECSI Beatrix ·· 143

Reconstruction of the Power System in the 1950s between
Colonial Heritage and the Pressure of the Aid Economy _ OH Sunsil ······ 163

How Gayo became K-POP:
International Song Festivals and South Korean Musicians' Sense
of the World, 1970-1982 _ KIM Sunghee ··· 202

Part 3. The Comparison

Parallels of Metamorphosis in the Theatre
in Korea and Hungary _ BLAHÓ Kata ·· 239

Image of Korea in Hungarian Encyclopedias:
1833-1930 _ KIM Jiyoung ··· 253

Bibliography ··· 280

Index ··· 309

Part 1.
The Theories

Indigenization and Metamorphosis

BHANG Won-il

1. Introduction

Metamorphosis is a concept that has been used to explain cultural change. This article seeks to concretize and develop this concept and find theoretical resources through a reconsideration of the South Korean indigenization theory debates of the 1960s. Furthermore, we hope to generate additional insights by connecting the theory of metamorphosis with Goethe's botany theory.

The core idea in indigenization theology is the gospel as a seed that, when implanted in the soils of a different culture, will lay down roots and form a new type of Christianity. As seeds and soils are the core motifs of this "plant growth" model, they provide many points of reference for generating a metamorphosis theory. Reexamining the major points of controversy in indigenization discussions is directly related to the purpose of this article. There is a need to organize the major areas of this debate, including how far the metaphor of the seed can extend, what is changeable versus unchangeable in religious culture, and how to address Christian identity and acculturation.

In the controversy surrounding indigenization theology, the word "metamorphosis" has very rarely appeared. Nonetheless, this article uses indigenization theology to develop a theory of metamorphosis. This is because the core of the theory is the metaphor from botany that explains cultural change. This is connected to Goethe's concept of metamorphosis within his theory of botany.

3

Goethe's ideas regarding botany are not well known but are gradually receiving more academic interest. Goethe explained the growth of plants through the gradual transformation or metamorphosis of the archetypal plant (*Urpflanze*) into its roots, stems, and leaves. He explained that single plants grow through metamorphosis and proceed to form new species of plants. This theory provides a useful point of comparison with the debates about indigenization theology and thus helps further systemize the theory of metamorphosis.

The second and third parts of this article seek to illustrate the indigenization debates, while the fourth part looks for connections between the main points of the debate and the theory of metamorphosis. In part two, the context of the debates is explained, and the major conceptual motifs of the idea of indigenization-the seed and the soil-are introduced. Next, part three considers the controversies over Christian identity and the connection between the related concepts of acculturation and indigenization. Part four begins with a brief introduction to Goethe's concept of metamorphosis and then seeks to connect it with indigenization.

Before discussing indigenization theory, however, the following should be noted about the scope of this article. First, this article analyzes the doctrinal dimensions of religious culture in detail, not its ritual and communal dimensions. In addition, indigenization discussions began with the rituals of religious culture, namely, the issue of how worship was to be carried out.[1] Moreover, beginning with such practical issues would enable a more convincing discussion. However, the controversy in itself mainly took place on the level of doctrine. This article thus pursues these points of controversy, and the main focus of analysis is its doctrinal dimensions that played out across the pages of journals and in books.

Second, this article focuses exclusively on the Protestant indigenization debates. The discussions surrounding Catholicism were distinct. In South Korea, the indigenization of Catholicism was largely made a reality through the decisions of the Second Vatican Council (Vatican II) rather than through discussions within the country. For instance, the 1984 Pastoral Council Documents included

---

1   Pong-Bae Pak (박봉배), "The Indigenization of Worship in the Korean Church [한국교회 예배의 토착화]," *Christian Ideas [기독교사상]* 35, no. 6 (1991): 54.

content designed to indigenize the decisions of Vatican II in line with South Korean realities. This was done in a variety of different ways on the ground, and some have critically reflected on what they see as the Korean Catholic Church's inability to move beyond its dependence on the Western church, including theological ideas, ceremonial forms, movements of devotion, spiritual life, and even architectural styles.[2]

Third, this article limits discussion to the 1960s and 1970s, which is considered to be the most important period of the indigenization debate. The term "Indigenization Theory" can be used in the broad and narrow senses. For instance, Kim Gwang-sik sought to understand the history of Korean theology as the history of indigenization theology.[3] His broad usage of the term has intentions to grant significance and inherit indigenization theology. On the other hand, theologians who paradoxically opposed indigenization were dependent upon the broad usage of term. Their view was that theology developed on Korean soil and in the Korean language was indigenous, and there was thus no need to go out of one's way to make use of the term.[4] To them, the broad extension of the term was a smokescreen to avoid indigenization.

This article considers indigenization theology with different intentions, which requires an alternative approach. This article looks at Korean Christianity's perception of cultural exposure. It is the view of the author that during the indigenization theology debate, such perceptions first emerged in a significant way, and these debates were the most direct manifestation of them. Given this, the term "indigenization theology" will be used in a narrower sense. Parts two and three analyze articles from Christian Ideas published in the 1960s about the indigenization controversy and the works of leading exponents of Indigenization Theology such as Yu Dong-sik and Yun Sŏng-bŏm from the 1960s and 1970s.

---

2   Sang-Tae Sim (심상태), *The Prospects for the Indigenization of the Korean Church* [한국교회 토착화의 전망] (Seoul: Sŏngbaoro Publishers), 169-70.

3   Gwang-Sik Kim (김광식), *Indigenization and Hermeneutics* [토착화와 해석학] (Seoul: Korean Christian Publishers, 1987), 7, 69-80.

4   A-Ron Pak (박아론), "Theories of Korean Theology [한국적 신학에 대한 이론]," *Christian Ideas* [기독교사상] 16, no. 8 (1973).

2. The Development of Indigenization Theology in the 1960s

1) The Context of the Debate

The 1960s were a time when the topography of the theological field was taking shape in South Korea. Immediately following liberation from Japanese colonial rule, the Protestant church lacked leaders due to the large-scale repressions mounted by the colonial government in its later period. Furthermore, the continued fracturing of the church into different sects left it in a chaotic state. The theological world did not find its vitality until more than a decade later.

In the 1960s, outside South Korea, the Second Vatican Council (Vatican II) set out the principles for indigenization, catalyzing vibrant discussions. Koreans who had studied theology overseas began to return to South Korea and form a new set of theological circles. By this point, theologians were able to seriously ask fundamental questions about Korean Christianity. They began publishing articles that asked questions about the meaning of Christianity in Korean culture.[5] In 1962, Yu Dong-sik published "Indigenizing the Gospel and Missionary Tasks in Korea" in the Methodist Theological Journal.[6] The concept of indigenization and its methods were set out concretely in this article, thus creating the beginnings of the indigenization debate. In response, Chŏn Gyŏng-yŏn published a rebuttal in New World magazine and broadened the contours of the debate from within the Methodist church to include the world of theologians and the academy.[7] After the two had criticized each other's positions, the debate moved to the pages of Christian Ideas, and many scholars subsequently joined the discussion.

First, Yu's response to Chŏn's arguments and Chŏn's retort to the response were published on consecutive months.[8] The fierce tone that Chŏn's writings

---

5   Kim paid attention the articles that were published on similar issues to those written about in Yu Dong-Sik's work by Ch'ae P'il-Gŭn and Chang Byŏng-Il. Kim, *Indigenization and Hermeneutics*, 69-80.

6   Dong-Sik Yu (유동식), "Traditional Culture and the Indigenization of the Gospel [전통 문화와 복음의 토착화]," in *The Way and the Logos [도와 로고스]* (Seoul: Korean Christian Publishers, 1978), 40-66.

7   Gyŏng-Yŏn Chŏn, "Can Christian Culture Be Indigenized?" *New World*, Mar. 1963; *Lectures on Christian Ideas Volume 3* (The Christian Literature Society of Korea, 1963), 207-13.

8   See the following: Dong-Sik Yu (유동식), "Research on the Indigenization of Christianity [기독교

sometimes exuded also incited many supporters of the indigenization position to participate in the discussion. For instance, Chŏn made the following claim:

> The problem of indigenizing Christian belief is not a question of whether you keep alive customary forms of religious beliefs or unique forms of national artistic tradition. It is a question of how all of those things shall be committed to the flames by the gospel and what new shoots shall sprout forth from the pile of ashes left behind.[9]

Chŏn's assertion was sufficient to push scholars who supported indigenization to join the discussion. First, Lee Jang-sik published an article supporting the legitimacy of indigenization, and he was followed by a number of other scholars who offered their own arguments for indigenization, including Hong Hyŏn-sŏl, Chŏng Ha-ŭn, Lee Gyu-ho, D. T. Niles (Nailsŭ), and Han T'ae-dong.[10]

On the one hand, this controversy included the continued theological efforts of Yun Sŏng-bŏm. He published his "discourse on the method of Korean theology,"[11] and he went on to publish additional articles and then a book that brought together Christianity and Korean Religion. He organized the indigenization theory in the book, assessed indigenization work in the history of the Korean church and the Tangun myth as an example of an indigenous idea of God.

국화에 관한 연구]," *Christian Ideas [기독교 이데아]* 6, no. 4 (1963): 64-8; Gyŏng-Yŏn Chŏn, "Indigenization Means Primitization," *Christian Ideas* 6, no. 4 (1963): 22-8.

9   Chŏn, "Can Christian Culture Be Indigenized?"; *Lectures on Christian Ideas Volume 3*, 207-13.

10   See the following: Jang-Sik Lee (이장식), "The Indigenization of Christianity is a Historic Task [기독교 토착화는 역사적 과업]," *Christian Ideas [기독교사상]* 6, no. 6 (1963): 36-44; Hŏn-Sŏl Hong (홍헌설), "The Possibilities and Impossibilities of Indigenization [토착화의 가능성과 불가능성]," *Christian Ideas [기독교사상]* 6-8, no. 9 (1963): 14-8; Ha-Ŭn Chŏng (정하은), "The Origins of Theological Indigenization [신학의 토착화의 기점]," *Christian Ideas [기독교사상]* 6, no. 7 (1963): 14-21; Gyu-Ho Lee (이규호), "The Philosophical Basis of Indigenization [토착화의 철학적 근거]," *Christian Ideas [기독교사상]* 6, no. 10 (1963): 10-20; D.T. Niles (나일스), "The Writings of the Saints and the Indigenization Problem [성서연구와 토착화문제]," in *Lectures on Christian Ideas Volume 3 [기독교사상 강좌 3]* (The Christian Literature Society of Korea, 1963), 279; T'ae-Dong Han (한태동), "Types of Thought and the Indigenization Problem [사고의 유형과 토착화 문제]," *Christian Ideas [기독교사상]* 6, no. 7 (1963): 14-21.

11   This was published in Bulletin, a periodical published the Methodist Theological University's Student Union, in December 1961. It was printed again as the introduction to Christianity and Korean Religion, (The Christian Literature Society of Korea, 1964).

Yun Sŏng-bŏm continued to develop his theological positions, and in 1972, he published Korean Theology: *The Hermeneutics of Genuineness* (誠). This work was a monumental study in Korean indigenization theology, declaring it to be a separate theological framework. He sought to understand the concept of theological revelation through Yi I's (李珥) concept of genuineness (誠). Here, he applied traditional cultural concepts to the pre-understanding of Christianity.

In the mid-1970s, minjung theology became dominant. Insofar as it began with an understanding of the Korean situation, this form of theology can be seen, to some extent, as the spiritual successor to indigenization theology. Minjung theologians, centeredcentred around An Byŏng-mu and Sŏ Nam-dong, noted that indigenization was unrelated to social realities and sought to understand the meaning of the scriptures from the perspective of the masses (*minjung*). Indigenization theology was swept away by Minjung Theology, but important issues remain for future scholars to consider.

Current discussions among theologians regarding indigenization theology tend to note commonalities between it and other theological schools. Yu Dong-sik studied shamanism and developed a new form of theology, the so-called p'ungryu (idyllic) theology. His view of the Korean religious psyche was of a "great life," from which he developed the task of pursuing Christianity.

Overall, the modern descendants of the indigenous theology tradition have deepened their understanding in discussion with new trends in theology, including minjung theology, religious theology, cultural theology, and hermeneutics, seeking to resolve problems it raised. However, the problem of cultural contact that indigenization theology sparked discussion of remains unresolved, and if anything, it appears to be being dissolved through fusion with different conceptualizations.

Now, let us consider how indigenization theologians understood the situation in the 1960s. The problems raised by indigenization theology were due to Christianity being unfamiliar to Koreans. It began with the thought that "Christianity cannot become a Western religion [in our country]; it must become our religion and the gospel that saves us."[12] The indigenization theologians saw their era as the problem. Protestant missionaries had been working in Korea for more than 80 years, yet Christianity seemed awkward when described as a Korean religion. They thought that such awkwardness meant that it could not be an authentic faith even for them. Yu Dong-sik noted in his own voice that he had not formed a faith and had simply followed Western voices. This is how he put it: "Even faith in Christianity, which must be the most subjective and autonomous, has lost its identity and seems to just cling to the west."[13] Yun Sŏng-bŏm also raised the issue of subjectivity and autonomy (chuch'e); he noted, "if the Korean Church is to receive the gospel, then it must first become a church with independence," and went on to argue that the Korean church had been unable to become a 'new wineskin' to hold the wine of the gospel."[14]

Conversely, the claims of theologians who argued against indigenization provided grounds for optimism. Their positive appraisal of the situation was driven by the miraculous results of missionary work in Korea. Chŏn Gyŏng-yŏn highlighted the deep, arguably indestructible, roots that the Christian faith laid in South Korea.[15] He argued that where indigenization was interpreted as meaning the "laying down of roots," Christianity could be said to have already done so. This positive assessment gathered growing support with rapid increase in the total number of Christians in South Korea. With the population of South Korean Christians approaching ten million in 1990, there was nothing left to argue against. As Pak A-ron put it, "before there was an indigenization theology, the early Korean church had ministry, and are we forgetting that its ministry is what made the massive development of the Korean church today possible?"[16]

The growth of the church thus was taken as evidence for the view. In light of the church's history of growth, it became possible to assert "what American missionaries brought to this land was not 'western theology' but

---

12 Dong-Sik Yu (유동식), "Special Sit-Down: Assessing the Major Debates of Korean Indigenization Theology and Its Prospects [특집좌담: 한국 토착화신학 논쟁의 평가와 전망]," *Christian Ideas [기독교사상]* 35, no. 6 (1991): 80.

13 Dong-Sik Yu, "Understanding the Indigenization of Christianity [기독교 토착화에 대한 이해]," *Christian Ideas [기독교사상]* 6, no. 4 (1963): 65.

14 Sŏng-Bŏm Yun (윤성범), *Christianity and Korean Thoughts [기독교와 한국 사상]* (Seoul: Korean Christian Publishers, 1964), 90, 94-6.

15 Chŏn, "Indigenization Means Primitization," 23.

16 Pak, "Theories of Korean Theology," 85.

the 'gospel of Christ.'"[17] The task that remained was to recognize reality: "Saying that the stronger the Paulian method of declaring the gospel of Christ as the gospel itself is, the faster the 'gospel's indigenization' through the pioneering and new churches missionary activities, then what are we supposed to make of Korean realities!"[18]

The external success of the church became a powerful riposte to discussions about indigenization and provided a unique backdrop to indigenization theology. In India, Japan, and China, Christianity has remained a minority religion. In these countries, Christianity needs to find ways to communicate with the existing culture in its missionary work. The South Korean situation is very different. Here, the indigenization issue is not raised by missionary work. If it were, then as those who opposed indigenization have said, with the success of Christian missionary work, indigenization lost its usefulness. In Korean indigenization theology, overcoming the logic of the power of realities on the ground (expanding congregation numbers) was the task given, and this unavoidably demanded the posing of more fundamental questions. For example, how Christianity can wholly settle within a culture? What are the cultural clashes that the introduction of Christianity may face having been accepted within a culture or the issue of acculturation?

2) Seeds and the Soil

The basic formula for indigenization can be explained through the relationship between a seed (the gospel) and the soil (culture). Christianity is the synthesis of the gospel and culture. The gospel's growth in the soil of western culture resulted in the Western church, but for the gospels to settle in Korea, they needed to grow in Korean soil. "Western missionaries took the flower of their church in pots filled with western soils that it had grown in and brought it here. We broke those flowerpots and planted them in our own rich soil, so it could not but rather grow energetically."[19] Yun Sŏng-bŏm's view was

---

17 Ibid.

18 Ibid., 86.

19 Niles, "The Writings of the Saints and the Indigenization."

that indigenization was the task of encouraging the seeds of the gospel so that they could take root. Hence, the major issue was the soil. If the soil is right, then seeds can sprout and grow. In this sense, indigenization theology was a type of theology that required a geological survey of the religious mentality of Koreans.[20] A survey of the soil is required for the seed of the gospel to grow. Potential impediments to the growth of the seeds of the gospel had to be rooted out. "If the base of people's hearts are gravelly fields, then we must first remove the stones before we can plant the seed of the gospel. If the fertilizer is lacking in nutrients, then we ensure that we have enough of it for the land to be rich in nutrients, and only then can we sow good seeds of the gospel."[21]

A basic precondition for indigenization was separating the gospel from culture. This work required that Christianity, as a living organism, and the gospel be severed from Western culture. Surgical suturing of the gospel onto Korean culture could be attempted. Severing the gospel from Western culture was not easy, hence why those who opposed the overall project raised objections at this point. Nevertheless, this amputation was the priority. "Here, there is one principle for indigenization. That is, to distinguish between the gospel itself and non-essential ancillary forms. And one must not mistake the non-essential, i.e., that world's distinct forms, with the gospel itself."[22] Yu Dong-sik found an example that he believed demonstrated the possibility of this in how the gospel spread throughout the Greek world. The ideas of the "Messiah" or the "Second Adam" used to explain Jesus to Jews were unfamiliar to the Greeks. Therefore, the Greek concept of "logos" was used to explain this to them. In this process, the gospel shed its outer skin of Judaism and donned the clothes of Greek culture.[23] Rudolf Bultmann's theological influence here is undeniable. From an existential point of view, the removal of nonessential elements from the gospel can be seen as a form of demythologization, and

20 Kim, *Indigenization and Hermeneutics*, 13-6.

21 Yun, *Christianity and Korean Thoughts*, 101.

22 Dong-Sik Yu (유동식), "Indigenizing the Gospel and Missionary Tasks [복음의 토착화와 선교적 과제]," in *The Way and the Logos [도와 로고스]* (Seoul: Korean Christian Publishers, 1978), 48.

23 Ibid., 49-50.

the same way of thinking was applied in indigenization theology. The scalpel used in demythologization was used to de-Westernize, i.e., remove nonessential western elements.

Chŏn Gyŏng-yŏn strongly argued against this view and made the two following claims: religion cannot be separated from culture, and Christianity is distinct from Christian culture. As he put it, "Christianity could be separated from culture, but it does not rely on culture; it relies on the scriptures and the confession of faith.[24] His argument that Christianity came from the confession of faith and was not a cultural phenomenon was a consequence of his narrow conception of culture. For him, culture was composed of activities such as literature and the arts, and this enabled him to contend that "to Christians, there is nothing to be mindful of when it comes to what is called culture."[25] However, one need only note the commonsensical notion that language is a part of culture for the foundations of this argument to become very precarious. Based on this assumption, he argued that Christianity is the world's religion and stressed that it is a complete product: "Christianity as a historical fact has been growing in the soils of the west for two millennia, doing battle with wrongful beliefs, and taking on a particular form before it came to Korea."[26] Hence, "there is no need for it to take on a new incarnation in Korea."[27]

Discussion of the possibility of separating culture and religion from one another is unavoidably difficult. Religion only makes itself known through cultural phenomena. In spite of this, the growth of a religion apart from a culture and in my view, the attempt to set up a single "pure thing" itself is a consequence of theological intentions. The attempt to preserve the essence of religion without the influence of culture is a type of devotional expression. This will be addressed below, but indigenization theology began from efforts to minimize the possibility that the seeds of the gospel were corrupted. This was part of an endeavor not to accept the acculturation of Korean Christianity but to prevent it.

---

24 Chŏn, "Christian Culture Be Indigenized?"; *Lectures on Christian Ideas Volume 3*, 209.

25 Ibid., 208.

26 Chŏn, "Indigenization Means Primitization," 25.

27 Ibid., 26.

3. Indigenization and Acculturation

1) Acculturation

When Christianity is accepted into a new culture, the process through which it influences and is influenced by other religions rooted in that culture can naturally be called "acculturation." A religion that manages to squeeze itself into a different culture will struggle to find its place within the existing religious culture. This process is not unusual; in fact, it can be considered necessary. Moreover, the struggle between religions and the dialogue that arises during such struggles can even be positive by inciting dynamism in religions, which helps sustain their vitality.

However, the problems facing the existing religions in a culture are far from simple. In Christian theology, maintaining the purity and absoluteness of the gospel is a priority, so allowing acculturation would be perplexing. Instead, theology provides an alternative, devotional term: syncretism. When Plutarch first used this expression, it was used simply to connote the combination of religious doctrines or rituals. However, when theologians have used the term, they have infused it with the derogatory overtones with terms such as "crossbreed" and "hybrid," to indicate a departure from principle or attempts to find a compromise but in doing so forsaking the truth.[28] In the Korean theological world, a number of terms were used in this way, including syncretization (Sŭphap; 習合) and four-character sayings: "widely said mess" (chesŏrhonhyo; 諸說混淆), "doctrinal mess" (Kyo-rihonhap; 教理混合) and syncretism (Hanhapju'ui; 混雜主義). Syncretism became enmeshed in the bitter criticisms of conservative theology and was used as a term of condemnation.[29]

Moreover, syncretism became one of the major phrases used to condemn indigenization theology. "Indigenization? Isn't that syncretism?" would be a way that the issues raised by indigenization were summarily dismissed. Syncretism

---

28 Don-Gu Kang, "Prelude to New Religious Research [신종교연구 서설]," *Religious Studies Research* [종교학연구] 6 (1987): 202-3.

29 For the history of Korean protestant syncretist discourse, see the following: Won-Il Bhang (방원일), "Theoretical Consideration on Syncretism: Toward the Description of Religious Encounter [혼합현상에 관한 이론적 고찰]," *The Critical Review of Religion and Culture* [종교문화비평] 33 (2018): 55-89.

is still treated this way, and such attacks have existed since its inception. Chŏn Gyŏng-yŏn stressed the point that "the process of syncretization is not the indigenization of Christianity.[30]

Paradoxically, this criticism of indigenization with the "slur" of syncretism was actually the starting point for indigenization theology. Indigenization theologists of the 1960s stressed the idea that their work was fundamentally distinct from syncretism. Yu Dong-sik wrote, "Indigenization should be distinguished from simple syncretism. Indigenization is not syncretism, which has lost its agency; it is an adaption to the circumstances of agents."[31] Yun Sŏng-bŏm criticized Matteo Ricci's work as syncretism and contrasted his work by claiming, "By connecting the truth of Christianity with Chinese Confucian ideas, one [must] distinguish clearly from the attitude of trying to find some kind of 'Analogia Entis' between the two".[32] When taken in isolation, this claim is no different from that of indigenization theology's critics. For instance, Lee Gwang-sun criticized indigenization theology from the point of view of missionary studies. He distinguished between indigenization and syncretism:

> Indigenization is concerned with what indigenous forms are used and how they are absorbed, whereas syncretism considers how content is transformed and fused with religious belief in order to adapt it. Indigenous forms are combined with the Christian meaning to realize indigenization, and Christian forms are combined with the indigenous meaning to yield syncretism. Syncretism must be distinguished from indigenization, and it must be rejected.[33]

What should be emphasized here is that indigenization is not distinguished from syncretism by merely indigenization theologists defending their position. They diagnosed the Korean church with syncretism and argued that indigenization was an alternative, the latter being a cure for the former. Their

---

30 Chŏn, "Can Christian Culture Be Indigenized?"; *Lectures on Christian Ideas Volume 3*, 212.

31 Yu, "Indigenizing the Gospel and Missionary Tasks," 42.

32 Yun, *Christianity and Korean Thoughts*, 97.

33 Gwang-Sun Lee (이광선), "Missionary Work and Cultural Acceptance [선교와 문화적 수용]," *Christian Ideas [기독교사상]* 35, no. 6 (1991): 71.

views were based on the claims of Chŏng Dae-wi, who argued that the major force behind the growth of the Korean church was the combination of Christianity and folk religion.[34] Yu Dong-sik accepted Chŏng's claims but also sought to ascertain why the Korean church had failed as a result. Yu took the view that Korean Christianity was intertwined with existing religion as a consequence of syncretization. Korean Christianity had become a materialistic faith due to shamanistic beliefs with a formalistic and legalistic nature derived from Confucianism and excessive mysticism from Buddhism.[35] Yun Sŏng-bŏm's view was almost identical: the Korean Church had "was a fruit that emerged as it was without going through a process of indigenization."[36] He demanded vigilance in the face of realities stamped by syncretism: "Despite expressions of shamanism arising in the church, there appears to be no interest paid to the issue. These shamanistic phenomena foretell the growth of non-Christian elements amidst such shamanistic forms. Confucianism and Buddhism are the same."[37]

Thus, syncretism is a sensitive topic for indigenization theologists. Although commonly misunderstood, attempts to indigenize were not a form of syncretism; rather, they were the most radical of attempts to break away from syncretism. The theological argument for defending the purity of the gospel was actually advanced by the claim that gravelly soil must first be cleared before the gospel can be planted.

2) Methodological Syncretism

The arrival of Christianity in Korea gave rise to acculturation, and in theological terms, this was considered to be syncretism, which was rejected to preserve the purity of the gospel. This was the unique context in which Christianity took shape in Korea. On the one hand, as indigenization theologians noted,

34 Dae-Wi Chŏng (정대위), "Religious Syncretism in Korean Society [한국사회에 있어서의 종교혼합]," *World of Ideas [사상계]* 80 (1960).

35 Yu, "Indigenizing the Gospel and Missionary Tasks," 54-7.

36 Sŏng-Bŏm Yun (윤성범), "'Cur Deus Homo' and Indigenization of the Gospel ['Cur Deus Homo'와 복음의 토착화]," *Christian Ideas [기독교사상]* 9, no. 12 (1966): 30.

37 Yun, *Christianity and Korean Thoughts*, 100.

the reality was that Korean Christianity was formed in reaction to existing religious culture. On the other hand, there was a view that cultural exposure was merely the disease of syncretism and should be stopped and the purity of the truth should be preserved. For instance, Harvey Cox termed the movement of the Holy Spirit in Korea as a "shamanist Christian movement." He asked, "Is this a particular successful, non-Catholic example of...the so-called indigenization of Christianity in an Asian culture? Or is it merely the continuation of the most salient forms of previous Korean folk religion wearing a Christian mask?"[38] and Korean theologists are actively fighting against this claim.

Part of this was driven by Korean theologians' aversion to syncretism. However, rejecting and ignoring the reality of acculturation in the name of syncretism results in a cognitive block. If a religion from one culture abandons the language within that culture and is surrounded by the hypothetical concept of syncretism, then this gives rise to the risk of devolving into self-righteousness.

The challenge that faced indigenization theology was to move beyond the barrier of syncretism to acquire a cognitive horizon. The initial plan of soundly conserving the seeds of Christianity while ensuring that it settles in a different culture encountered difficulties. However, the demands of indigenization theology was to discover productivity and vitality in suffering and go beyond the conceptual barrier of syncretism. Yun Sŏng-bŏm's Korean Theology shows how indigenization theology overcame pathological approaches and rose up to new levels. He declared a theology of genuineness (誠) and declared that he was ready for the dangers of syncretism.

> The theology of genuineness completely permits the comparison of Christian truth, the close investigation and inspection of similar religious expressions. In this sense, it may take on the character of syncretism. In the relation between revelation and nature, Christianity and culture, this is impossible to avoid. It is important to ask what should be combined here. This is because the seeds of the gospel cannot be indigenized in the soils without syncretism.[39]

---

38 Harvey Cox, *Fire from Heaven: The Rise of Pentecostal Spirituality and the Reshaping of Religion in the 21st Century* (Cambridge, MA: Da Capo Press, 2001), 222.

39 Sŏng-Bŏm Yun (윤성범), *Korean Theology: The Hermeneutics of the Holy [한국적 신학: 성의*

One of the big successes of indigenization theology is taking syncretism as its method. To settle in this land, one must take a fresh approach, and indigenization theology came to realize that doing so is not a sin. As Yun put it, "the truth of the gospel, like oil floating on top of water, cannot be separated from the spiritual cultural soil of our traditions, and enters those soils, mixed in with the soils and sprouts emerge, producing 30, 60 or even 100 times more seeds."[40] This finding confirms that indigenization theology accepted the concept of cultural mixing and became the basis for constructing a theory of metamorphosis. The next section attempts to connect the insights of indigenization theory to a theory of metamorphosis from Goethe's theory of botany.

4. Theory of Metamorphosis

1) Goethe's Botany

Johann Wolfgang von Goethe (1749-1832), the world-famous German writer who is renowned for his poetry and fiction, also took a keen interest in the natural world. Goethe's botany is significant because it is an alternative to Carl von Linné's then-dominant system of botanical taxonomy (Linnaean taxonomy), which stresses the importance of metamorphosis. He influenced scholars such as Reichenbach and left romantic traces on science.[41]

In 1775, while working as a manager in Weimar, he became interested in geology and zoology. He came to the view that there was a single structure that governed the biological world and set out to discover what it was. This plan took shape while he was visiting Italy from 1786 to 1788. In 1787, when visiting a zoo in Palermo, Sicily, Goethe became certain about the fundamental

해석학] (Sŏnmyŏng Munhwasa, 1972), 15.

40 Ibid., 16.

41 See the following: Nicolas Robin, "Heritage of the Romantic Philosophy in Post-Linnaean Botany Reichenbach's Reception of Goethe's Metamorphosis of Plants as a Methodological and Philosophical Framework," *Journal of the History of Biology* 44, no. 2 (2011): 288-90; Hye Kyung Jung (정혜경), "Goethes Plant Morphology: Consideration on Its Linkage with Naturphilosophie and Romantic Characteristics [괴테의 식물형태학: 자연철학과의 밀착성과 낭만주의적 속성을 중심으로]," *The Korean Journal for the History of Science[한국과학사학회지]* 11, no. 4 (2004).

structure that ran through the biological world. This is how he recorded this certainty:

> Whether I might not find the Urpflanze within this mass of plants. Some-thing like that must exist! How else would I recognize that this structure or that was a plant, if they were not all formed according to a model.[42]

Goethe's insights were reinforced by his observations and research. In 1790, the results of his work culminated in a poem, "The Metamorphosis of Plants" (Metamorphose der Pflanze). Goethe stressed the idea that the entire structure of a plant is contained within the seed.

> Bursts from the seed so soon as fertile earth
> Sends it to life from her sweet bosom, and
> Commends the unfolding of the delicate leaf
> To the sacred goad of ever-moving light!
> Asleep within the seed the power lies,[43]

The structure within the seed becomes the different parts of the plant. As the plant takes on its form, each part adapts to its environment. This process is anything but simple, but rather one of ordered metamorphosis. The orderliness of metamorphosis occurs within a variety of different parts of the plant.

> Artless the shape that first bursts into light —
> The plant-child, like unto the human kind —
> Sends forth its rising shoot that gathers limb
> To limb, itself repeating, recreating,
> In infinite variety; 'tis plain
> To see, each leaf elaborates the last —

---

42 Johann Wolfgang von Goethe, *Italienische Reise* (April 17, 1787), in Sämtliche Werke, 15:327 cited in Robert J. Richards, *The Romantic Conception of Life: Science and Philosophy in the Age of Goethe* (Chicago, IL and London: The University of Chicago Press, 2002), 395.

43 Johann Wolfgang von Goethe, *The Metamorphosis of Plants*, ed. Gordon L. Miller, trans. Douglas Miller (Cambridge, MA: MIT Press, 2009), 1.

Serrated margins, scalloped fingers, spikes

That rested, webbed, within the nether organ —

At length, attaining preordained fulfillment.[44]

From a cursory look at the poem, it appears that Goethe is expressing admiration for plants, but actually, the object of his admiration is the process of metamorphosis. Beneath the external appearance of differences, a deep process of similarity occurs. In addition to the variety of forms, an ordered process of formation occurs. The simple expands into the complex, and after it contracts, it ultimately disappears. This is the result of the internal, logical, and teleological principles of change that Goethe called "metamorphosis."

Goethe's theory of metamorphosis can be summarized as follows. There are two basic rules of metamorphosis. First, "regular or progressive metamorphosis," which involves the simple (relatively undifferentiated) to the complete (strongly differentiated) by going through consecutive, logical stages akin to climbing up a ladder, occurs. Second, the reverse then occurs, where nature retraces its steps, logically reversing the process of differentiation in what can be termed "irregular or retrogressive metamorphosis." The leaves of the cactus regress into hard prickles (glochids), and differentiation becomes set, or else it becomes compressed with the organ being compacted or disappearing. Additionally, there is another type of metamorphosis — accidental metamorphosis — that does not fit within these two fundamental rules. This is a type of change in which an internally driven process of metamorphosis is modified or distorted by external influences.[45] In this way, Goethe set out a theoretical framework to understand metamorphosis through botany. His pioneering theory has value as a resource to be utilized in understanding rather than as a heterodox theory of biology that it has been consigned to become.

---

44 Von Goethe, *The Metamorphosis of Plants*, 2.

45 Jonathan Z. Smith, *Relating Religion: Essays in the Study of Religion* (Chicago, IL: University of Chicago, 2004), 68-71.

2) The Agent of Change and Identity

Indigenization theology is a useful theory for describing changes in Christianity in the same way that Goethe's theory of metamorphosis accounts for changes in plants and species. In developing Goethe's theory of botany into one of cultural metamorphosis, this section considers and compares the controversies surrounding indigenization theology.

The core metaphor of indigenization theology is the idea of the gospel and culture being akin to seed and soil. The essence of Christianity (the gospel) takes root and grows in the soil of another culture, forming a new Christian culture. However, the intense indigenization theology debate has many problems to address in this seemingly refreshing metaphorical explanation. Is it possible to separate the seed from the soil, i.e., the gospel from culture? This question is related to the problem of maintaining Christian identity, which was raised by opponents of indigenization theology. Both proponents and opponents will have made assumptions about the boundaries of what they considered to be the essence of Christianity, and the debates between them considered whether the concept of the seed was included within those boundaries. This point of contention connects indigenization and syncretism in a complex relationship. At first, proponents of the former sought to distance their position from the latter, but later, Yun Sŏng-bŏm asserted that it was methodologically unavoidable for indigenization theologians to advocate for syncretism. With respect to Christian identity, the initially apparently inflexible attitude of early indigenization theologians gave way to the flexibility of Yun. This finding has important implications for our analysis. When assumed as essential, the theological metaphor of the seed became an impediment to explaining change. This called for an approach that did not see the seed as solid.

Goethe's botany appears similar to the seed and soil of the indigenization theologians, but offers a differing explanation. In Goethe's theory, seeds are the structures that grow into the plant. The structures held within the seed are not the seed; they are what Goethe called the archetypal plant (*Urpflanze*). This is not a fixed entity but a potentiality (*dynamis*) that can be changed through an orderly process. According to Goethe, everything is represented by leaves, and through such simplicities, the maximal amount of variation is possible. This theory of metamorphosis calls for an archetype that becomes a matrix of change.

The core of this concept of archetype is changeable flexibility. We will not discuss this topic at length here; however, the 20th century religious scholar Mircea Eliade succeeded Goethe's theory of archetypes.[46] Eliade used this concept but expressed regret about its confusion with Carl Gustav Jung's concept of the same name.[47] He claimed that the archetype was an exemplary model and sought to avoid it being understood as a fixed idea. The concept of an archetype being fluid is not simple, but it is necessary to create a flexible theory of metamorphosis. This finding stresses that introducing the matrix of change should not be understood as the essence of change.

5. Conclusion

The indigenization debate within South Korea's theological circles in the 1960s offered an attractive metaphor to explain change in Christianity. Indigenization theologians argued that Christianity was composed of the gospel and culture and that the essence of the gospel (the seed) takes root in different cultural soils and takes on a wide variety of forms.

For Korean Christianity to succeed, it would have to flower in a Korean form in the soils of Korean culture. However, this heated debate exposed the unobviousness of the metaphor of the seed and the soil. Can Christianity be clearly divided between the gospel and culture or between the seed and the soil? Is it possible to divide a religion between its essence and nonessential, changeable elements?

---

46 This was highly credible suggestion made by Jonathan Smith in an article analyzing Eliade's Patterns in Comparative Religion. Smith, *Relating Religion*, 61-74. Eliade and Goethe are part of the same theoretical continuum. Perhaps it is not surprising that Eliade thought of Goethe's theory of archetypes when visiting a zoo in Palermo in 1951. He wrote the following in his diary that day: "In [this] public garden··· Goethe 'contemplated' not only the lemon and orange trees but all those species of palm and cacti which allowed him to 'see' what he named the Urplant." Smith, *Relating Religion*, 67.

47 Mircea Eliade (미르체아 엘리아데), *The Myth of the Eternal Return: Cosmos and History* [영원회귀의 신화: 우주와 역사] (Seoul: Hyŏndae Sasangsa, 1976) [Translated into Korean by Chŏng Jin-Hong].

When early indigenization theologians strongly denied the existence of a relationship between their views and syncretism, this controversy remained unresolved. Indigenization theologians claimed that indigenization was not a process of randomly combining religion and culture. Rather, in claiming that culture changed, they found themselves back at the defensive logic that argued the essence of belief as unchangeable. This finding exposed the limits of such a theory of change. Subsequently, Yun Sŏng-bŏm proposed that methodological syncretism would necessarily involve the combination of both faith and culture, overcoming the inflexibility of earlier scholars. This was an important theoretical turning point in determining the relationship between the gospel and culture.

Indigenization theology initially encountered theoretical difficulties because it saw the seed as a fixed reality. Goethe's botany offers a more flexible theory. Goethe's unique botanical research explored the principle of change based upon the idea that all parts of the plant grew from archetypal leaves. He called this process metamorphosis and systemized it. Indigenization theology and Goethe's theology both explain change and set matrices of change. In indigenization theology, the concept of the seed is that, and in Goethe's botanical theory, it is the archetypal leaves and plant. Goethe's archetypal plant is structurally within the seed, and in that respect, it appears similar to indigenization theology, but its structural change is free, making it more flexible conceptually than the fixed identity of the seed metaphor in indigenization theology. If we are to understand Goethe properly and build upon his ideas, then we can apply them to explain culture, not just plants.

We have sought to explain cultural change through the theory of metamorphosis. However, cultural change is not anarchic; there are agents of change, and processes of change follow an order. By reexamining the controversies that indigenization theologists faced when seeking to account for change in Korean Christianity and utilizing Goethe's concepts of archetypes and types of metamorphosis, we can provide indispensable theoretical resources to systemize cultural metamorphosis.

Metamorphosis of Culture and Im Hwa's *The History of New Korean Literature (Gaeseol shinmunhaksa)*

YOON Young Shil

1. "New Literature" during the Transition Period and the Metamorphosis of Culture

This paper sets out to shed light on the cultural transformations in Korea during the era of modernization, adopting a scholarly perspective that interrogates the "metamorphosis of culture." The central focus is on the unique insights that the term "metamorphosis" can offer in understanding the cultural shifts that took place in Korea during the transition to modernity. The primary text under examination is Im Hwa's work, The History of New Korean Literature (Gaeseol Shinmunhaksa).

While previous studies have extensively delved into various facets of the concept of culture,[1] this paper takes a distinctive approach by providing a concise overview of the term "culture" within the context of this study. In a narrow sense, culture is delineated as encompassing artistic creations such

---

[1] The most recent study that provides a broad perspective on the concept of 'culture' (文化, culture) is: Kim Hyun-Ju, *Culture: Total History of Korean Concepts 13* (Sohwa, 2019). Other useful references include: Yanabu Akira, *A Dictionary of a Word, Culture,* trans. Park Yang-Shin (Green History, 2013); Reinhardt Koselleck et al., *Koselleck's Conceptual History Line 1: Civilization and Culture,* trans. Ahn Sam-Hwan (Green History, 2010).

as literature, art, music, and architecture. In a broader sense, it extends to the entirety of daily customs, traditions, and diverse elements of popular culture. Fundamentally, culture serves as the collective intellectual creation of humanity, distinguishing itself from the natural world. It functions as a symbolic framework through which individuals perceive and structure their understanding of the world.

The exploration of culture in this context involves an interdisciplinary approach, drawing on various philosophical and theoretical perspectives. This includes Kant's notion of spatiotemporal consciousness as an intuitive form, Foucault's examination of knowledge and discourse, White's exploration of narrative forms that shape and construct historiography,[2] and Charles Taylor's concept of "social imaginaries" in the modern era.[3] By synthesizing these perspectives, this paper aims to offer a nuanced and comprehensive analysis of the metamorphosis of culture in Korea during the period of modernization, with Im Hwa's work serving as a focal point for this exploration.

The study at hand distinguishes itself within the realm of cultural studies by considering the intricate concept of "metamorphosis" across a diverse array of cultural phenomena. Specifically, when the transformative nature of culture is scrutinized in the modern Korean context, the investigation takes on the ambitious task of transcending the conventional dichotomy between internal developmental theory and colonial modernization theory. The discourse surrounding the evolution of modern Korean novels has been historically ensnared in a clash of contrasting theories: the transplanted literature paradigm as opposed to the internal development theory, epitomized by the tension between the transplantation of external influences and the organic succession of indigenous traditions. On the one hand, several scholarly endeavors have been dedicated to exploring the persistence of traditional narrative forms such as legends, fables, and biographical tales.[4] In contrast, an extensive body of

---

2 Hayden White, *Metahistory: The Historical Imagination in Nineteenth-century Europe*, trans. Chun Hyung-Kyun (Munji, 1991).

3 Charles Taylor defines "social imaginaries" as the "ways people imagine their social existence, how they fit together with others, how things go on between them and their fellows, the expectations that are normally met, and the deeper normative notions and images that underlie these expectations." Charles Taylor, *Modern Social Imaginaries*, trans. Lee Sang-Gil (Ieum, 2016).

research has also accumulated around translation activities during the early modern period in East Asia, uncovering the transnational roots of modern Korean literature.[5]

Both of these lines of inquiry have presented compelling arguments, reaching a juncture where neither side can definitively claim victory. Consequently, there is a concerted effort to move beyond the confines of binary explanations. Instead, scholars are collectively directing their attention toward unraveling the intricate interplay and relationships wherein the diversities of "tradition" and "modernity" intersect. This collaborative focus aims to explore the nuanced combinations that defy simplistic categorizations, fostering a more holistic understanding of the dynamic cultural landscape.

We delve into the intriguing convergence of perspectives as we examine two scholars who initially embarked on their academic journeys from opposing viewpoints but ultimately arrived at a shared conclusion. Seo Young-chae challenges the prevailing notion of an authentic national literature propagated by internal development theory. Instead, he introduces the concept of the "reverse cassette effect"[6] to explain the emergence of modern Korean novels. The term "cassette effect" was originally coined by Yanabu Akira, who analyzed the process of establishing translated words in Japan.[7] In this analogy, a cassette, akin to a small "jewelry box," carries an air of mystery, sparking people's imagination about the unknown contents inside. Yanabu applied the cassette effect to describe the translation of the word "society" into the unfamiliar

---

4   Some notable manuscripts that have addressed the challenge of bridging the gap between classical literature and modern literature include: Cho Dong-Il, *A History of Korean Literature Volumes 1-4* (Knowledge Industrial Publishing, 1989); Han Ki-Hyeong, *Perspectives of the Modern Korean Novel* (Somyeong Publishing, 1999); Kim Chan-Ki, *The Formation and Turn of the Modern Korean Novel* (Somyeong Publishing, 2004); Kim Young-Min, *The Formative Process of Modern Korean Novel* (Somyeong Publishing, 2005).

5   he 'problem' consciousness in recent studies that have illuminated Korean modern literature from the perspective of translation is well represented by the following books: Jo Jae-Ryong, *Translating Sentences* (Munji Publishing, 2015); Kim Yong-Kyu et al., *Translation and Crossing: The Formation and Subject of Korean Translated Literature* (Hyonamsa, 2017); Park Jin-Young, *Birth of the Translator and East Asian World Literature* (Somyeong Publishing, 2019); Son Sung-Jun, *Translated Hero* (Somyeong Publishing, 2023).

6   Yanabu Akira and Kim Ok-Hee, *Formation of Translated Language* (Maumsanchaek, 2011).

7   Seo Young-Chae, "Korean literature studies after the national study," in *Thinking Again About Literary History* (Somyung Publications, 2018).

term "社会" during the early modern period in Japan. People, lacking a complete understanding of its original meaning, attached various implications to it, thereby enriching the semantic value of the word.

Seo Young-chae extends Yanabu's concept by introducing the notion of a "reverse cassette effect" in the translation of modern language. His argument unfolds through the example of translating the term "novel" into "小說," a term deeply rooted in East Asian tradition. This translation assimilated the preexisting connotations of "小說," transforming into a third word that no longer fit neatly into either the category of a novel or a "小說." Through this reverse cassette effect, for instance, Lu Xun could write the expansive "History of Chinese Novels," spanning from ancient times to the end of the Qing Dynasty.[8] Similarly, Kim Tae-jun leveraged the reverse cassette effect in documenting the "History of Korean Novels," encompassing the transition from the era of storytelling to the era of modern Korean literature.[9] In both cases, the reverse cassette effect, as proposed by Seo Young-chae, becomes a crucial lens for understanding the dynamic and transformative evolution of modern East Asian literature, which was formed by the amalgamation of past traditions and the infusion of Western literary influences through translation.

In contrast, Bang Min-ho initiates his discussion by critiquing the transplanted literature theory. Instead, he introduces a novel model that connects "intrinsic and extrinsic elements." To elucidate how these factors converge during the genesis of modern literature, he proposes the metaphor of "engraftation" as an alternative to "transplantation." The term "engraftation" proves advantageous in illustrating how foreign cultures or literatures meld with the inherent characteristics of a culture or literature, all the while sidestepping the subtle colonial connotations associated with the term 'transplantation.' According to Bang Min-ho, analogous to the harmonious coexistence of traditional and foreign elements in Yi Gwangsu's literary concept of "jeong" (affection, 情), the evolution of Korean modern literature can be comprehended as a process wherein diverse components are affixed to the original, thereby giving rise to something entirely new.[10]

---

8   Lu Xun, *Chinese Novel History*, trans. Jo Kwan-Hee (Somyung Publications, 2004).
9   Kim Tae-Jun, *The History of Korean Novels*, trans. Lee Ju-Myeong (Pilmak, 2017).

The discussions above converge on a common conclusion that illuminates the intricate relationship between indigenous and foreign elements, laying the foundational premise for this paper. As prior research has revealed, the processes identified as "modernization" in Korea have deviated significantly from the simple replacement of old elements with new ones. Instead, they involved a nuanced interplay of mingling, colliding, and competing forces between old and new elements, which were both internally inherited and externally introduced. Such an amalgamation of indigenous and foreign cultures in the production of a new third culture may be a fundamental attribute of culture in general.

However, a challenge arises due to the unique circumstances of modernization in non-Western regions, such as Korea, where the process underwent a "colonial transformation" marked by the overwhelming influence of foreign culture accompanied by imperialist violence. This transformation was not merely an integration or assimilation of foreign elements into the existing cultural system; neither did it entail a complete blockage of their influence. Instead, it led to comprehensive upheaval and the dissolution of the entire established cultural system. As a result, the cultural changes in Korea during the shift to modernity demand a more critical examination of cultural coloniality/subjectivity and continuity/discontinuity than typical cultural transformations. The intricacies of this process necessitate a deeper understanding of how the overpowering influence of foreign culture, coupled with imperialist violence, shaped and redefined cultural dynamics during the transitional period to modernity in Korea.

Regardless of the terminology employed, it is crucial to recognize that Im Hwa's "transplantation literature theory" inherently encompasses a postcolonial perspective. Admittedly, Im emphatically addressed the unilateral flow of the transplanted culture under the dominant influence of foreign elements. However, Im Hwa's theoretical framework not only acknowledges the complexities of cultural interactions but also underscores the agency and resilience of Korean culture. By emphasizing the idea of "mutual transformation,"[11] he proposes

---

10 Bang Min-Ho, "The Logic Structure of 'What is Literature' and 'Heartless' and Modern Transformation of Korean Literature," *Chunwon Research Journal* 5 (2012).

a nuanced perspective that goes beyond a simple assimilation narrative. Im Hwa's approach recognizes the intricate negotiations and reciprocal influences at play during the transplantation of culture, ultimately aiming to reclaim and fortify the autonomy of Korean culture in the face of colonial challenges.

In this paper, my objective is to offer a more comprehensive understanding of Im Hwa's "The History of New Korean Literature" by examining the multifaceted implications of cultural "metamorphosis." This exploration begins in Chapter 2, where I scrutinize various theoretical perspectives on cultural metamorphosis, with a specific focus on Im Hwa's cultural theory. This analysis aims to highlight the general characteristics of cultural metamorphosis, including its universality, hybridity, and singularity. Additionally, I investigate the importance of conceptualizing a unit termed "national culture" within these broader attributes of culture. Proceeding to Chapter 3, I systematically expand upon the implications of cultural metamorphosis within colonial conditions, enabling a more nuanced analysis of Im Hwa's work. Within this context, I sequentially address issues such as (1) the colonial transformation (transplantation) of culture and subjectivity, (2) the dynamics of cultural continuity and discontinuity, (3) the performative subjectification of colonial nationhood, and (4) the pursuit of a postmodern and postcolonial world. This analytical exploration aims to unravel the layers of Im Hwa's thought, providing a comprehensive examination of how cultural metamorphosis operates within the complex framework of colonial circumstances.

2. Attributes of Culture and 'National Culture' in Im Hwa's Cultural Theory — Universality, Hybridity, Singularity

In the realm of intellectual discourse, the acceptance and legitimacy of a new concept often hinge on its ability to offer a clearer and more insightful explanation of a particular situation. However, the path to gaining legitimacy is not instantaneous. When a novel concept is initially introduced, it emerges not

---

11 Im Hwa, "Method of New Literature," in *Im Hwa Literary Arts Collection 3: Logic of Literature*, ed. Shin Duwon et al. (Somyeong Publishing, 2009), 657.

in a spotlight but in a state of relative obscurity. It is during moments when familiar and existing concepts fail to adequately elucidate a situation, leading to a repetitive cycle of stagnation, that new concepts are proposed. These new ideas undergo a rigorous process of testing and validation, either gaining widespread acceptance or facing rejection as potential tools to overcome the prevailing impasse. This process of introducing new concepts is analogous to the "cassette effect." Sometimes, a novel concept may emerge as the essence of innovative thinking, providing a fundamental shift in perspective. In contrast, there are instances in which an unfamiliar, not fully refined term possesses the potential to spark imagination and stimulate new ways of thinking. The conceptual landscape of "metamorphosis" today appears to align more closely with the latter case. While it may not have yet solidified as the core essence of new thinking, the term, in its current state, serves to provoke open imagination and prompt fresh perspectives.

Jürgen Schlaeger, as the editor of *Metamorphosis: Structures of Cultural Transformations*, delves into the crisis consciousness confronting cultural studies, asserting that its roots lie in the dynamic and ever-changing nature of culture. Traditional conceptual tools in the humanities and social sciences have focused predominantly on elucidating the static aspects of an object. However, Schlaeger contends that cultural change is a continuous and fluid process characterized by perpetual movement, transformation, and variability in speed, penetrability, and cultural productivity.[12] In response to this dynamic reality, Schlaeger advocates for the adoption of perspectives and terminology that can effectively capture the essence of change itself. Rather than relying on frameworks designed for stable structures, he underscores the importance of developing a structural understanding of the multifaceted dimensions of "change." This shift in focus is deemed essential for transcending a superficial description of the surface-level manifestations of change. To pursue this deeper comprehension, Schlaeger, alongside other scholars, introduces the concept of "metamorphosis" in a collaborative research project. By exploring metamorphosis, the intention is to provide a conceptual framework that not only acknowledges but also articulates

---

12 Jürgen Schlaeger, *Metamorphosis: Structures of Cultural Transformations* (Tübingen: Gunter Narr Verlag, 2005), 1-9.

the complexities inherent in the ongoing and dynamic nature of cultural change. Through this work, Schlaeger aims to contribute to a more comprehensive and insightful exploration of cultural studies, one that is better equipped to grapple with the complexities of a world in constant flux.

While Schlaeger's concept of metamorphosis is still undergoing refinement, its significance lies in its revelation of the limitations faced by existing cultural studies and its stimulation of new modes of thinking. Following the decline of classical cultural studies, which often assumed the self-identical nature of individual cultures, the following question arises: can cultural studies move beyond mere descriptions of cultural differences and microlevel transformations to engage in more profound structural analysis? Is it truly possible and necessary to categorize a culture that is constantly undergoing changes and variations as a singular entity? Given that all cultures exist in a perpetual state of change, universally interconnected and blended through hybridity, how can we effectively discuss the "singularity" of a culture, whether defined by region or nation?

Although the term "metamorphosis" may not be explicitly invoked, many studies, often prefixed with "trans," such as transnational, transcultural, and translinguistic studies, grapple with similar inquiries. Alongside these cross-border studies, critical reflections have emerged in response to a prevalent trend in previous cultural studies that predominantly focused on describing the dissolution of intrinsic, static identities and highlighting infinitely differentiated, hybrid, and multilayered differences in a culture. However, there has been concern that these studies may inadvertently obscure the "discriminative" structures of the contemporary world and, in some cases, even eliminate the subject of resistance. Consequently, an increasing focus has emerged on the material and institutional structures of modernity, the exploration of a subject's puissance for self-creation beyond mere subjectification through power, and the 'construction' of a nonintrinsic identity. The retheorization of capitalism and the nation-state, along with contemplations on confrontation and creation amid the "irreducible differences of the master language and the guest language" in translinguistic practices (translation), and heightened attention given to the performative construction of the subject all contribute to this comprehensive and evolving context. As a consequence, there is growing interest in the material and institutional structures of modernity, the self-creation of a subject beyond mere subjectification by power, and the 'construction' of a nonintrinsic identity. The retheorization of capitalism and the nation-state, contemplation of confrontation and creation amidst the "irreducible differences of the master language and the guest language" in translinguistic practices (translation),[13] and a heightened focus on the performative construction of the subject have all become integral components within this comprehensive context.

Considering the myriad issues raised in the preceding discussions, this paper aims to examine the significance of defining a cultural "unit" and articulating/arguing for its "singularity" despite the universal hybridity of all cultures. A pivotal issue regarding this point may be debates over a "national culture." Prasenjit Duara has critically examined how nation-building agents conceal external sources of sovereignty and international recognition of a "nation" by replacing them with an authentic origin of pure nationhood. In his analysis, Duara identifies two solutions adopted to alleviate the discomfort stemming from the infinite progression and rapid pace of change in modernity. One solution entails narrating linear time as a teleological history leading toward a utopian future, while the other strives to ensure unity amid change by constructing the nation, the subject of this history, as a "symbolic system of authenticity." Claims of the nation's sacred origins, the assertion of a unique national culture devoid of traces of otherness, and the establishment of a lineage based on bloodlines are elements that substantiate this symbolic system of authenticity.[14]

Duara's analysis illuminates nationalism within the framework of the sovereign nation-state system, emphasizing the development of "national culture" amid the global circulation of institutions, discourses, concepts, and norms. In doing so, it presents a more sophisticated perspective than does the classical nationalist theorists' binary classification of normal (Western) and abnormal (non-Western) nationalism. However, as Duara's analysis moves beyond specific cases such as nationalism in Manchukuo or China to a general theory of

---

13 Lydia Liu, *Translingual Practice*, trans. Min Jung-Ki (Seoul: Somyung Publishing, 2005).

14 Prasenjit Duara, *Sovereignty and Authenticity: Manchukuo and East Asian Modern*, trans. Han Seok-Jung (Seoul: Nanam, 2008).

"nation," there appears to be a tendency to overlook the diverse historical experiences of different "nations." However, grasping nations within their historical contexts is just as crucial as the task suggested by Duara's book title "rescuing history from the nation." This approach is vital because, while postnationalism critiques the homogenized identity of the "nation," it paradoxically tends to oversimplify diverse historical experiences, various subjectivities, and varied networks of meanings. It often reduces complex civilizations that existed before the nation-state to an intrinsic identity, treating them as self-evident givens and homological representations of nations.[15]

Im Hwa's cultural theory presents a compelling argument that challenges the idea that the establishment of colonial "national culture" is inherently linked to claims of cultural "authenticity." As previously mentioned, Im Hwa conceptualizes the interaction between transplanted culture and native culture as a process of mutual transformation, wherein the native culture "assimilates" the transplanted culture while simultaneously undergoing changes in its essence. It is crucial to acknowledge that the terms "transplanted culture" and "native culture" are relative concepts that vary with time. Im Hwa contends that all cultures are inherently hybrid, making the pursuit of purity in a once-established culture devoid of meaning. For instance, the "native culture" of the Three Kingdoms Period emerged from the fusion of the native culture of the Dangun lineage and the continental culture of the Gija lineage. Similarly, Goryeo culture represents a blend of inherited "native cultures" from the Three Kingdoms and external influences, including the Tang, Song, Yuan, and Indian cultures. Within this perpetual cycle of hybridization and cultural reconstruction, there exists neither a native culture that maintains a pure intrinsic identity nor a foreign culture that remains entirely external.

Despite acknowledging the inherently hybrid nature of cultures, Im Hwa goes further by emphasizing the "singularity" of culture. For him, a culture achieves "singularity" through ongoing contact and interaction with different cultures, giving rise to a novel and distinct form. The essence of cultural singularity, in his view, does not rest in inherent purity; rather, it lies in the

15 Prasenjit Duara, *Rescuing History from the Nation*, trans. Mun Myung-Ki and Son Seung-Hee (Samin, 2006).

culture's capacity for continuous "transformation" (metamorphosis) through engagement with diverse cultural influences, thereby consistently enhancing its strength.

In the late 1930s, the period during which Im Hwa developed his cultural theory marked a critical juncture when Korea's "national culture" faced the imminent threat of extinction due to the assimilation policies enforced by the Japanese Empire. Im Hwa, a prominent figure in the Korea Artista Proleta Federatio (KAPF), took a decisive stance on the revitalization of "Korean culture" in response to these challenges.

Im Hwa's commitment materialized through initiatives such as the Hak-ye Publishing's "Korean Literary Collections" project,[16] which aimed to reintroduce Korean and world classics. The republication of Kim Tae-jun's *The History of the Korean Novel*, which emphasized the fusion of traditional and translated forms in Korean novels, was a significant part of this endeavor. Im Hwa's own work, *The History of New Korean Literature*, sought to provide a thorough and objective account of the emergence of new Korean literature during a transitional period marked by the clash between the old and new eras, where the outcome remained undetermined on either side. Im Hwa's vision of the "construction of Korean culture" did not advocate for a return to primordial purity or internal homogeneity within the Korean nation. Instead, it envisioned the creative transformation of native culture through dialogue with foreign influences, fostering a renewed cultural identity in the present moment.

3. Implications of Cultural Metamorphosis:
Several Points for Understanding Im Hwa's Cultural Thoughts

In Chapter 2, we examined the overarching characteristics of culture, focusing specifically on universality, hybridity, and singularity. Additionally, we explored the nuanced significance of establishing a "national culture" as a cultural unit

---

16 See the following: Bang Min-Ho, "Im Hwa and Hagyesa," *Sanghur Hakbo: The Journal of Korean Modern Literature* 26 (2009); Jang Moon-Seok, "Publishing Coordinator Im Wha and Hak-Ye-Sa," *Journal of Korean Literary History* 41 (2009).

in colonial situations. Transitioning to Chapter 3, our objective is to comprehensively address the issues presented in Im Hwa's *The History of New Korean Literature* from various perspectives. To achieve this goal, we will leverage the rich insights provided by the etymological nuances of "metamorphosis" and its biological parallel (e.g., insect metamorphosis). Furthermore, we draw on literary examples, including the transformative narratives found in the works of Ovid and Kafka, to illuminate and expand upon the themes under examination.

1) Colonial Transformation of Culture ('Transplantation') and Subjectivity

As mentioned earlier, the shift to modernity in non-Western countries like Korea brought about swift and profound changes that cannot be adequately explained by generalized cultural change theory alone. Using Im Hwa's terminology, the enduring practice of grafting foreign and indigenous cultures, observable since the Three Kingdoms period, faced a unique challenge during the modern transition. The dominant influence of foreign cultures during this period gave the impression of a "one-sided process of transplantation and imitation" of foreign cultural elements. Im Hwa's acknowledgment of this circumstance formed the basis for the critique of his theory of transplanted literature. Critics argued that Im's theory perpetuated notions of traditional discontinuity, Eurocentrism, and a colonized unconsciousness, commonly referred to as the "Hyeonhaetan complex."

Expanding our perspective, however, the cultural transformation labeled "one-sided transplantation and imitation" emerges as a facet of colonial transformation, a universal experience for non-Western cultures forcibly thrust into the modern world through Western colonial violence. Diverse theories of modernity continue to vie on a global historical scale when interpreting this violent transformation. Colonial modernization theory perceives colonial transformation as a necessary, albeit unfortunate, step for the "civilization" or modernization of non-Western societies. In contrast, multiple alternative theories of modernity emphasize the subjective capacity of non-Western cultural traditions, denying any one-sided transplantation and imitation of Western cultures. Notably, both perspectives deny or overlook the violent historical experience of "colonial transformation." While the theory of unilateral imitation may portray the violence of colonization as part of a narrative of "civilization" and modernization, even alternative theories of modernity tend to downplay the experience of violence and defeat inflicted by external forces (empires) to underscore the subjectivity of non-Western cultures. Im Hwa took a third approach.

> The post-Gabo Reform enlightenment process was characterized not by the assimilation of new culture through the modification and organization of existing culture and heritage but rather by a unilateral transplantation and imitation of Western cultures... [omitted]. It is crucial to highlight that even within this process of one-sided transplantation and imitation of new culture, indigenous culture, as tradition, typically played an intangible role in shaping the emerging culture. In our specific case, however, tradition might have impeded the pure adoption and construction of a new culture, yet it did not nurture it or serve as a fertile ground for its creation. This adversity did not stem from the inherently inferior quality of our cultural tradition or heritage but rather from our failure to adequately modify and transform it to facilitate the formation of a new culture in the establishment of modern culture. The root cause was our weak and insufficient spirit of independence.[17]

The quoted text is extracted from a section in Im Hwa's *The History of New Korean Literature*, where he formulates the controversial "transplanted culture/literature theory." Preceding the quoted passage, Im Hwa provides a detailed exploration of the "material background" and "spiritual preparation" that set the stage for the emergence of new literature. In discussing the material background, Im Hwa scrutinizes the absence of "independent modernization conditions" in Joseon Korea, attributing this absence to "Asiatic stagnation" and the perceived "abnormality" of modern development. It is true that Im Hwa did not break free from a Western-centric and evolutionary historical view. It is essential, however, to recognize that the evolutionary historical perspective was an epistemological condition prevalent during that time, and

17 Im Hwa, *Im Hwa Literary Art Collection 2: Literary History*, ed. Im Kyu-Chan et al. (Somyung Publishing, 2009).

this same mindset remains a challenge for contemporary scholars. Moreover, some theories of the Asian mode of production, rooted in Marxist thought, have engaged in theoretical debates on how to leverage this "difference" for the liberation of colonized societies. We must extract any implicit insights from these theoretical explorations that can expand our current cognitive horizons.[18]

One plausible way to interpret Im Hwa's depiction of the material background of new literature is to view it as a factual narrative of historical progress rather than a value judgment on the inevitable direction of history. Regardless of what the "Asian difference" from the capitalist development trajectory of the West may be, difference in itself is neither inherently good nor bad, superior or inferior. However, through the historical process of the Western colonization of "Asia," the Asian difference was signified as "inferior." This stigma holds true at least to the extent that it points to the collective causes that led to Asia's defeat and colonial dependence within "material" power dynamics. The notion of defeat in the "material" power relationship primarily denotes military defeats, e.g., in the Opium War, but material defeat extends to encompass the broader spectrum of the forceful transplantation of Western institutions that ensued. This forceful inclusion in the global system involved the imposition of capitalist trade, unilateral deprivation, and constraints on sovereignty imposed by Western powers through nation-state systems and international law (extraterritoriality, unequal treaties). This process also entailed the acceptance of modern knowledge and discourses on human/racial hierarchies that upheld this Western-centric world order, presenting Western values as universal and objective "science."

In the course of historical development, however, material power relationships remain consistently susceptible to change, with the impetus for such change originating from the extensive accumulation of cultural capacity. In this context, Im Hwa's earlier quote warrants a nuanced interpretation. As explored in the preceding section, Im Hwa endeavored to identify the singularity of a

---

18 See the following study examining Baek Nam-un, Lee Cheong-won, and Im Hwa's Asian-oriented theory of production: Hwang Ho-Deok, "Theory Dis/Count, Theorizing in Asia," *Literature and Society* 30, no. 3 (2017).

culture through the creative synthesis of indigenous and foreign elements, thereby augmenting its capacity while acknowledging the universal hybridity inherent in all cultures. Korea's problem was that the assimilation of "advanced" foreign culture was delayed due to the postponement of "port opening", coupled with the frustrations of subsequent endeavors to independently modernize the country during late Joseon Korea. Most notably, the Gabo Reform, a pivotal historical juncture, fell short of achieving the monumental dual tasks of establishing an autonomous political system internally and importing advanced civilization externally. Consequently, Im Hwa diagnosed Korea's modernization as inevitably forced to follow a unidirectional course of "transplantation" in both political and cultural spheres.

Crucially, Im Hwa refrains from attributing this setback to any inherent inferiority in Korea's "cultural tradition or heritage." Instead, he contextualizes the notion of defeat within specific failures at particular historical junctures, diverging from the prevailing colonial discourse that often depicts Joseon culture as intrinsically inferior. The primary cause of this failure, according to Im Hwa, lies in the inability at a specific historical moment of the modern transition to creatively meld indigenous and foreign cultures for the "formation of a new culture." This inability, he asserts, was chiefly a result of the weakened state of "our spirit of independence" during that particular moment.

Moreover, Im Hwa did not perceive failure at this specific moment as conclusively determined. Neither did he advocate for a "retrogressive" approach solely focused on restoring and glorifying past traditions while overlooking moments of defeat. As previously noted, Im Hwa's ultimate goal in cultural theory was "the new construction of Joseon culture" within his contemporary context by enhancing colonial Korea's capacity through the innovative fusion of foreign and indigenous cultures. Im Hwa eloquently articulates how the dialectical relationship operates between cultural transplantation and creation, as well as between colonial defeat and resistance: "While the cultural exchange between the Eastern nations and the West may seem to conclude with unilateral cultural transplantation, it inherently involves a process of deconstructing the very essence of cultural transplantation. In other words, as cultural transplantation deepens, cultural creation simultaneously matures from within."[19] Therefore, the "transplantation [into] itself of advanced culture" by underdeveloped nations already assumes the form of a struggle against advanced countries.[20]

In summary, recognizing the forceful imposition of new systems during colonization and the consequential transformation of societies (referred to as colonial transformation), Im Hwa aspired to chart a course that would empower the colonized subjects. His vision involved a deliberate exploration of a transformative journey — labeled "cultural metamorphosis" — in which the subjective capacity of the colonized people could be strengthened. This transformative process hinges on a creative synthesis of cultural traditions with the elements introduced through transplantation.

2) Cultural Continuity and Discontinuity: Combinations of Elements and Changes in Arrangement

Even when we adopt Im Hwa's proposition of cultural metamorphosis as the creative fusion of cultural tradition and transplantation, conceptual ambiguity persists. Althusser's concept of "articulation" may be helpful for avoiding this ambiguity. "Articulation" is a concept that signifies structural causality in which diverse elements are combined (合) but maintain their distinctiveness (切). To attain conceptual precision concerning metamorphosis, delineating clarity between the constituent elements and the overarching structure within the articulation phenomenon becomes crucial. This differentiation is imperative because numerous debates surrounding traditional discontinuities and successions often stem from confusion at these disparate levels.

In the transition to modernity, an influx of various technical, institutional, and conceptual elements from the West occurred. However, concurrently, the components of cultural heritage did not vanish or undergo outright replacement; rather, they endured and exerted certain influences. A notable illustration of this phenomenon is the "reverse cassette effect," as proposed by Seo Young-chae. When translating the Western concept of a "novel" into the East Asian term

19 Im Hwa, "Method of New Literary History," *Donga Ilbo*, Jan. 13-20, 1940. Also in Im Hwa et al., *The Logic of Literature: Im Hwa's Literary Art Anthology 3* (Seoul: Somyung Publishing, 2009).
20 Im Hwa et al., *Im Hwa's Literary Art Anthology 4: Criticism 1* (Seoul: Somyung Publishing, 2009).

"小說," the meanings inherent in the Western notion of a "novel" intermingle with those from the East Asian tradition of "小說," giving rise to a distinct third realm of meaning. Even terms highlighted as examples of the "cassette effect" by Yanabu Akira are not exempt from this "reverse cassette effect." For instance, "right" was translated as "權利" by combining the characters "權" and "利," or the term for "nation" or "people" was rendered "民族" by combining the characters "民" and "族"; these newly formed words encompass the traditional semantic networks associated with each individual Chinese character. Even the term "文學," established as the translation for "literature," refracts its meaning by merging implications of Western modern literature with the longstanding 文 tradition of East Asia. From this viewpoint, the infusion of foreign culture is not a process of creating anew on a blank canvas but rather an overwriting on the palimpsest of culture building upon the accumulated heritage of the past.

To comprehend cultural change as a process of overwriting on the remnants of the past, it is imperative to reassess our conventional understanding of time. The past does not simply fade away and get supplanted by the present within a linear temporal framework; instead, it converges with the future within the present, existing as the "virtual past." This virtual past not only is interwoven into all the material systems and concepts constituting the present but also plays a role in defining the present, such as through the influence of past heritage. From time to time, the virtual past unexpectedly intrudes into the present moment, manifesting through involuntary memories, the recurrence of a repressed past, or what Derridean theory refers to as "specters". Simultaneously, the virtual past is deliberately summoned to construct specific meanings in the present, as seen in the "redressing" of the past or the intentional "creation" of tradition. Furthermore, the entire virtual past undergoes constant transformation as each present moment is reiterated, and the past itself "repeats," for instance, in the repetition of revolutionary traditions, for a leap of the present toward an entirely new future.[21] This reconceptualization of time as a complex interplay between the past, present, and future underscores the

---

21 For extended discussion about the temporality of the past, mentioned briefly in this paragraph, see the following: Gilles Deleuze, *Difference and Repetition,* trans. Kim Sang-Hwan (Minumsa, 2004).

dynamic and evolving nature of cultural change, challenging the linear narrative often associated with historical progression.

To grasp cultural changes during the modern transition period, it is imperative to consider not only the individual elements but also the transformation of the overarching "structure." Solely scrutinizing the layers of elements makes it challenging to move beyond the observation that both indigenous and foreign cultures coexist. The debate often circles around whether there is continuity or discontinuity in tradition when examined solely through the lens of constitutive elements. To break free from this circular reasoning, it becomes essential to consider the overall arrangement of elements, i.e., the structural dimension, in conjunction with the amalgamation of heterogeneous elements. Given the apparent influence of both traditional elements (such as folk tales and family novels) and foreign elements (including translations of literary concepts and texts) on the emergence of modern Korean novels, engaging in binary debates about the successive development of tradition and the external influences of Western literature at the elemental level perpetuates ongoing disputes.

The emergence of "modern literature" detached from the East Asian narrative tradition is an example of a form of structural transformation. For instance, when Yi Gwang-su defined "文學" as a translation of the English term "literature" and asserted that this sense of "literature" did not exist in past Joseon, it prompted us to reconsider what was severed or continued. As discussed earlier, the reverse cassette effect of genres such as literature, novels, and poetry refracts their meanings by drawing on the East Asian tradition of 文. Furthermore, when Yi introduced a new definition of literature as "writings containing emotion/feeling (情)," the concept of "emotion" encompasses not only the semantic network of "cognition, emotion, and volition" from the West but also the notion of "人情 (human feeling)," which is significant in the tradition of East Asian novels. However, when viewed from the perspective of the overall arrangement of 文 or writing, distinct from the individual elements, there was a sort of leap or disconnection during the modern transition. There was a paradigm shift from the modern enlightenment when Shin Chae-ho's "historical biographical novels" and Yi In-jik's "new novels" vied for prominence to the era of Yi Gwang-su's notion of "無情 (heartless; feeling-less)" literature in the first modern Korean novel. This aligns with what Karatani Kojin referred to as the "origin" of modern literature — the "inversion of a semiotic constellation" — which states that modern landscapes, interiority, children, and "modern literature" were "discovered" within that inversion.[22] Even within the paradigm of new modern "literature," elements from the past, such as emotion (情), persist, but their meaning undergoes a redefinition within the new semiotic constellation (structure).

The etymological roots of "meta-morphosis," indicating a change in form (Gr. morphē), shape, or style, imply a transformation at the level of structure. The concept of cultural metamorphosis denotes more than just a quantitative and continuous process of cultural change at the elemental level; it signifies a fundamental qualitative shift. This entails the reconfiguration of the overall structure (arrangement, constellation) of elements rather than a replacement of individual elements, leading to a broader transformation of the cultural form. The modern transition in East Asia transcended the mere introduction of new elements; it underwent a paradigm shift, as exemplified by debates surrounding the "Chinese body, Western use (中體西用)" policy. The distinctions between "body" (體) and "use" (用) went beyond mere differences in elements, as some misconstrued material components, such as technology and systems, as belonging to "use," while attributing spiritual elements such as culture and morality to the category of "body." In essence, the concept of the "body" encompasses more than a simple dichotomy of material and spiritual elements; it can be understood as an overarching epistemological paradigm that shapes the fundamental worldview of a society. In this vein, Qing Chinese officials such as Zeng Guofan (曾国藩) and Li Hongzhang (李鴻章) aimed to integrate Western elements ('用') into the Chinese paradigm ('體') to fortify the country. Conversely, when Tan Sitong (譚嗣同) advocated for the concept of Western-body-Chinese-use (西體中用) through the conceptual inversion that "reality (器) is the essential [body, 體] while 'the way' (道) is a mere action (用)" (道用器體),[23] he underscored the necessity of transforming the entire

---

22 Karatani Kojin, *Origins of Modern Japanese Literature,* trans. Park Yuha (Minumsa, 1997), 38.

23 Song In-jae argues that Zhang Zhidong's theory of the unity of knowledge and application cannot be narrowly understood as a theory of modernization solely focused on technology, excluding institutions or culture. He asserts that it should be seen as receptive to all aspects of Western learning. Song Injae, "The Repositioning of Chinese Learning and Western Learning in the Concept of Zhongtixiyong

Chinese worldview in response to the rapidly changing realities imposed by Western powers.[24]

Indeed, there is ample room for debate regarding the evaluation of the historical plan of the "Chinese body, Western use" as a simple failure. The recent rapid rise of China has rekindled discussions around the body-use (體用) concept, which seemed to have reached a conclusion a century ago. There is a renewed emphasis on the Chinese or Asian "body" (體), giving rise to debates advocating for various concepts such as Confucian capitalism, Asian values, and Chinese socialism.[25] These perspectives also align with theories of alternative modernity or multiple modernities. At times, such theorists assumed that acknowledging a paradigm shift in the East entails the loss of Chinese or non-Western subjectivity. However, Tan Sitong's Western-body-Chinese-use policy was fundamentally a strategic initiative aimed at "self-strengthening" (自強) through the transformation of the "body" in response to imperialist violence from the Opium War to the Sino-Japanese War. Illustrated by Tan Sitong's work "Ren Xue" (仁學, Theory of Benevolence), his doctrine did not propose the wholesale abandonment of all elements from the past. Instead, Tan's theory sought to enhance the capacity ("強") of the subject by creatively integrating foreign and indigenous cultures within the shifted paradigm.

Korea's modern enlightenment thinkers also aimed to achieve "self-strengthening" by transitioning from a Sino-centric order to an international legal system, incorporating elements from both Western civilization and indigenous culture. The pivotal question revolved around defining the unit of the "self" that required strengthening. Only after Emperor Gojong's abdication in 1907 did figures such as Shin Chae-ho begin advocating for the establishment of a "national self." In contrast, advocates of civilizational enlightenment, such as Yi In-jik, associated "self" not with a national unit but with a political

---

in Modern China," *Concepts and Communication* 6 (2010).

24 Lee Myung-Soo, *Thinker Dam Sa-Dong, Who Thought Communication and Equality* (Seongnam University Press, 2010), 68-76.

25 Shin Dongjoon, "China's Modernization Strategy and Body Usage Debate," *Culture and Politic* 5, no. 1 (2018): 75-100.

faction (the pro-Japanese civilizational faction against the conservative faction), a social class or stratum (the emerging bourgeoisie against the literati aristocracy), or the East (Japan) as a counterpart of the West. These nonnational "selves" played significant roles in the process of Japan's annexation of Korea.[26] Im Hwa's cultural diagnosis, attributing the failure to create a new culture to "our weak sense of independence," referred to this historical phase. For Im Hwa, the real challenge was not the introduction of foreign cultural elements or the cultural paradigm shift but rather the deficiency of an "independent spirit" that impeded the realization of national "self-strengthening."

3) The Repetition of Cultural Creation and the Performative Subjectification of the Colonized Nation

As Im Hwa stressed, the integration of indigenous and foreign cultures is an ongoing, iterative process. This dynamic process unfolded across various historical periods in Korea, starting from the Three Kingdoms period, when the primitive culture of Dangun melded with continental culture. This pattern continued through the Goryeo period, characterized by the blending of the Three Kingdoms culture with foreign influences from the Tang, Song, and Yuan dynasties, and the Joseon period, witnessing the fusion of Goryeo culture with Ming and Qing foreign cultures. Even during the modern transitional period, enduring attempts were made to culturally integrate Joseon culture and Western foreign cultures, even if they were not entirely successful. In this continuous process of creating a new "singular" culture, success or failure is determined only through each performative practice. Im Hwa's writing of The History of New Korean Literature in the late colonial period can be seen as one of these numerous repeated attempts.[27]

---

26 Regarding the ideological context that led Yi In-jik to move from the 'self-strengthening' theory to a 'pro-Japanese' stance, see the following: Youn Young-Sil, "The Political Thoughts of the <Silver World> and the Issue of 'Representation/Representation' of the People," *Kubo Studies* 24 (2020).

27 To learn more about the significance of Im Hwa's 'The History of Korean New Literature' in terms of the creative integration of culture, please refer to the following: Youn Young Shil, "Korean Literature, World Literature, (In)translatability of Political Novels," *Modern Literature Research* 60 (2020).

Im Hwa's *The History of New Korean Literature* aligns with Kim Tae-jun's *The History of Korean [Joseon] Fiction*, both aiming to reconcile the diversity within Korea's premodern narratives and modern novels into a cohesive history of "Korean fiction." Kim Tae-jun's approach involved organizing diverse narratives on a loose chronological timeline. Im Hwa embarked on a more ambitious undertaking, focusing on "transitional" new literature, where the discontinuity between premodern and modern forms of literature seemed to be most remarkable. Im Hwa's approach was paradoxical, objectively stating that the new literature from the transitional period had predominantly leaned toward transplantation due to the lack of independence among Koreans at that time. Simultaneously, Im Hwa aimed to performatively construct the continuity of Korean literature by meticulously documenting the history of this new literature. However, a critical question emerges: How can the practice of writing the history of new literature effectively encompass both the discontinuity (represented by transplantation and disruption) and the continuity of Korean national culture?

Examples of metamorphosis in both biology and literature provide profound insights into the contemplation of identity continuity and discontinuity within a cultural context amidst radical changes. The transformation of organisms, which entails a complete change in form, serves as a powerful catalyst for human imagination, as human reflection on transformation grapples with the complexities of difference and identity in an ever-changing world. Moreover, tales of transformation, spanning from ancient myths and legends to modern literature and mass culture, constitute a rich repository of human creativity, offering varied expressions of identity through metamorphic narratives. Using Ovid's 'Metamorphoses' as a guiding thread,[28] Christoph Bode proposes that the narrative itself plays a crucial role in ensuring identity, even in the face of formal discontinuity during transformation.[29] In numerous transformation

---

28 Refer to the following collection of transformation myths that span from Greek and Roman mythology to the foundation myth of Rome: Ovid (Publius Ovidius Naso), *Metamorphoses*, trans. Lee Yoon Ki (Seoul: Minumsa, 1998).

29 Christoph Bode, "Plus Ça Change: Cultural Continuity and Discontinuity and the Negotiation of Alterity," in *Metamorphosis: Structures of Cultural Transformations*, ed. Jürgen Schlaeger (Tübingen: Gunter Narr Verlag, 2005).

tales, such as 'Lycaon transformed into a wolf,' 'Daphne turned into a laurel tree,' and 'Ocyrhoe turned into a horse,' the narrative becomes the sole means of guaranteeing the identity of each character by narrating the process of transformation from one state to another. Christoph Bode's interpretation aligns with Paul Ricoeur's concepts of time, narrative, and narrative identity. Ricoeur underscores the significance of narratives in organizing scattered differences within the temporal flow, constructing a 'nonidentical identity' that retains traces of difference, as it is fragmented by constant change and the intrusion of others. According to Ricoeur, individual or collective identities are not inherently given but are performatively constructed through narration.[30]

The way we perceive continuous accumulations and the constantly changing flow of phenomena as 'a culture' is achieved through this performative self-construction. Bode defines a culture as 'a discursively structured introspection of a society that persistently nourishes differences and maintains them as a site of negotiation.' In this sense, Im Hwa's act of writing The History of New Korean Literature was a practical endeavor that performatively (re)constructed the identity of the Korean nation. Im's opus aimed at dual tasks: first, constructing national literature with a focus on the 'modern transitional period,' which brought significant upheaval and transformation to the identity of Korean culture; second, preserving national identity during the late Japanese colonial period, when the identity of the Korean nation faced its greatest crisis due to Japanese assimilation policies.

4) Metamorphosis as "Becoming" and the Imagination of a Postmodern/Postcolonial World

To delve further, we explore an alternative discourse on metamorphosis in Kafka's 'The Metamorphosis.' Kafka's metamorphic narrative introduces elements such as its abrupt initiation without a discernible causal connection (the sudden transformation of a sleeping person), an inherent ambiguity that resists any ultimate interpretation, the coexistence of heterogeneous identities

---

30 Paul Ricœur, *Oneself as Another*, trans. Kim Han-Sik and Kim Woong-Kwon (Seoul: Dongmunseon, 2006).

within Gregor Samsa (human-bug), and the fiction's fragmentary structure featuring conflicting themes and perspectives on identity without synthesis or integration.[31] These characteristics of 'The Metamorphosis' appear to outright reject the harmonious yet illusory solution of constructing meaning and identity through narration. Instead, they seem to usher everything back into chaos and abyss, challenging conventional notions of narrative resolution and coherence. Walter Benjamin argued that these "obscure points"—moments that frustrate readers' interpretive efforts and leave them pondering enigmatic questions—are crucial in Kafka's novels.[32]

Building upon Benjamin's perspective, Michael Levine analyzes Kafka's *The Metamorphosis* as a 'metamorphic displacement' of Ovid's 'Metamorphoses,' suggesting that the former challenges the conventional understanding of metamorphosis presented in the latter. Ovid's work organizes and interlaces numerous transformation narratives from Greek and Roman traditions, ultimately justifying the birth of the Roman Empire (as seen in the myth of Romulus and Remus) and the deification of Julius Caesar. Similarly, in 'The Metamorphoses,' seemingly disparate and unrelated small stories coalesce into a larger narrative that substantiates the birth of the Roman nation and the divine origins of the Roman empire. In contrast, Kafka's novels, particularly 'The Metamorphosis,' are often regarded as a negation of 'the father's law', which takes various forms, including horror, criticism, deconstruction, or escape.

Ovid's 'Metamorphoses' showcases a remarkable integration of Greek cultural elements into Roman culture through narrative causality. The epic establishes connections between various Greek mythological themes, including creation mythology, the Trojan War, Aeneas' adventures leading the refugees from Troy, and the founding of Rome by Romulus and Remus, who are descendants of Aeneas. This narrative strategy effectively weaves together diverse cultural

---

31 Regarding the competition of heterogeneous identity theories in Kafka's *The Metamorphosis*, refer to the following: Kevin W. Sweeney, "Competing Theories of Identity in Kafka's The Metamorphosis," In *Franz Kafka's The Metamorphosis*, ed. Herold Bloom (New York: Infobase Publishing, 2008).

32 Walter Benjamin, ""Franz Kafka: On the Tenth Anniversary of His Death" and "Some Reflections on Kafka","" in *Illuminations*, eds. Walter Benjamin, Hannah Arendt, Harry Zohn, trans. Harry Zohn (New York: Schocken Books, 1969), 131-138.

elements, contributing to the formation of a cohesive Roman cultural identity that incorporates and builds upon Greek traditions. In contrast, Kafka's novels frequently explore the persistent fracture of identity between Jewish national traditions and German modern civilization. Within Kafka's works, themes of division, hesitation, disorientation, and a sense of a 'self that is lost in metamorphosis' are recurrent.[33]

In this respect, Kafka's 'The Metamorphosis' has the most profound significance for metamorphosis. The etymological roots of 'meta' suggest meanings such as 'after,' 'beyond,' and 'beside.' Interpreting this etymology, metamorphosis is closely tied to a situation where the 'form' (morphosis) is 'out of joint.' Unlike a straightforward transition from stable form A to stable form B or the immediate creation of a new form C by blending A and B, metamorphosis introduces an 'amorphous,' monstrous 'something' that exists in the undefined space between A and B or among A, B, and C. This transitional, metamorphic state is formless and unrecognizable. When the speed and intensity of change reach a level where the established forms of reality rupture without the emergence of new forms or paradigms to replace them, individuals experience a sense of 'anomie.' This state is characterized by a lack of formative frameworks, norms, or laws that provide order to life and the world. Drawing on Thomas Kuhn's insights, anomie is a crisis in which the existing paradigm ceases to operate effectively due to a surge of anomalies, yet a new paradigm capable of integrating these anomalies has not yet been crystallized.

The term 'transformative period' (轉形期) in Japanese and Korean literary history has connotations closely tied to the implications of metamorphosis. This period marked a time when nationalism and socialism, which were dominant ideologies until the early 1930s, began to decline, giving way to the emergence of the historical task of 'overcoming modernity.' However, for those who did not readily embrace pseudo-postmodernity, such as fascism, this era was characterized as the 'century of facts' (as coined by Paul Valéry). Within this transformative period, characterized by the decline of established ideologies,

---

33 Michael G. Levine, "The Sense of an Unding: Kafka, Ovid, and the Misfits of Metamorphosis," in *Franz Kafka's The Metamorphosis (New Edition)*, ed. Harold Bloom (New York: Infobase Publishing, 2008).

the focus shifted to 'overcoming modernity' as a historical imperative. During this epoch, characterized by a decline in established ideologies, people began scrutinizing accidental and fragmentary facts, searching for new forms of life and understandings of the world. This quest for a new 'form' of life and world resulted in an unprecedented eruption of narrative desires.

In his writing of The History of New Korean Literature, Im Hwa identified the "transition period" (過渡期) of the 1900s as another 'transformative period' in this broader sense.

> The transition period is inherently challenging to define as it represents an intermediate phase between the decline of one age and the rise of another. Unlike the declining old age or the emerging new age, the transition period lacks a clear and unified personality characterized by distinct content and form. It is during this complex interval, as the old age is fading while the new one is emerging, that the characteristics of the two ages become entangled and mixed, lacking clear distinctiveness. The true nature of the transition period lies in its potential for both the birth of the new age and the demise of the old age. It is a time marked by ambiguity, where the definitive outcome of either the new or old age is yet to be determined.[34]

Im Hwa's deliberate choice of the term 'transition period' over alternatives such as the 'enlightenment period' or the 'age of literary revolution,' as used in Japanese and Chinese literary history, respectively, reveals his nuanced perspective. The term 'enlightenment period' in Japan assumes that 'old age' is 'uncivilized', focusing on the role of 'Western foreign culture' in the process of 'civilization.' On the other hand, the 'literary revolution' emphasizes China's autonomous subjectivity but neglects the significant influence of 'Western foreign culture' on 'the birth of new literature and the downfall of old literature.' Im Hwa rejects both positions: one that overemphasizes foreign culture and dismisses traditional culture as savagery and the other that emphasizes subjectivity while overlooking the overwhelming influence of foreign culture.

34 Hwa, *Im Hwa Literary Art Collection 2.*

Im Hwa's neutral term 'transition period' captures a moment when 'the birth of the new age and the downfall of the old age were all possible.' This term reflects a more balanced perspective, acknowledging the coexistence of diverse influences and possibilities during a period marked by transformation. Im Hwa's literary history, written during the 'transformative period' between 'modern' and 'postmodern' ages during the Asia-Pacific War and reflecting on the 'transition period' between 'premodern' and 'modern' styles in the 1900s, thus suggests a desire to go beyond the performative construction of Korean national identity. His aspiration extends to envisioning alternative worlds, exploring postmodern and postcolonial realms beyond the constraints of colonial modernity, which constitutionally involves coloniality as the dark side of modernity. In Im Hwa's exploration of the 'decline of Western civic culture' amidst the devastation of World War II, his aspiration to overcome colonial modernity became apparent.[35]

In the aftermath of World War II and the prevailing widespread pessimism, there has been a longstanding acknowledgment of a cultural crisis, marked by ideological unrest and concerns about the future of the spirit in Western countries...[omitted]. The third international conference for the protection of culture, despite its intentions, merely underscored the global nature of the cultural crisis. Furthermore, these endeavors brought to light a crucial reality: the cultural crisis is a reflection of a worldwide predicament. Consequently, it becomes evident that tackling the cultural crisis requires more than isolated efforts from Britain and Germany. The primary imperative is the resolution of the overarching global crisis...[omitted]. If the prevailing form of human unity that has defined Western culture—essentially a civic form or Western bourgeois civility—proves insufficient, could culture be revitalized through the emergence of a new form of human unity arising from the consequences of war? Yet, the nature of such a form remains speculative at this point, and perhaps it is premature to delve into this matter today.[36]

---

35 Refer to the following analysis of modernity accompanied by the dark aspect of colonialism: Walter D. Mignolo, *The Dark Side of Western Modernity: Global Futures and Decolonial Choices*, trans. Kim Young-Ju et al. (Hyunam, 2018).

From his perspective, the cultural crisis during the Second World War mirrors the broader crisis in the world itself. An international conference for the protection of culture, organized by European intellectuals, is perceived as a surface-level endeavor. Im Hwa contends that the fundamental challenge lies in the reformation of the global order. Within the omitted portion of the quotation, Im Hwa references Valéry's critique of fascism. Valéry distinguishes between two types of individuals in the West: the 'European' and the 'nationalist.' The 'nationalist' individual is viewed as subjective and divisive, promoting a fascist 'totalitarianism' centered on nationalism and blood lineage. In contrast, the 'European' individual is a guardian of culture and civilization responsible for the grandeur of Western civilization. Valéry aimed to defend an objective and universal culture against the nationalistic fascism of Germany and Italy, yet his envisioned culture remained inherently Western-centric.

Im Hwa astutely observes this limitation, striving for a third path that transcends both fascist totalitarianism and Western-centric cultural advocacy. If the prevailing 'form of human unity' in modern times was merely a Western-centric 'civic form,' could humanity, after the ruins of war, discover a 'different form of human unity'? However, Im Hwa asserts that the replacement for Western civic culture cannot be fascist totalitarianism, leaving 'what form will it be' in the realm of the 'not-yet-come (未-來)'. He seemed to expect that the unknown future, the 'monstrous something' that has yet to take shape, would quietly swell up in the process of the meta-morphosis of culture, within the hyphen (-) that connects 'meta' and 'morphosis,' in the quest for a new form beyond colonial modernity.

4. Conclusion

In this paper, we have specifically examined the implications of the unfamiliar term "metamorphosis" and its relevance to understanding cultural changes in modern transitional Korea, with a focus on Im Hwa's The History of New

---

36 Im Hwa, "The End of Civic Culture," in *Im Hwa's Literary Art Anthology 5: Criticism 2*, ed. In Ha Jung-Il et al. (Somyung Publishing, 2009).

Korean Literature. The longstanding debate between the theories of transplant literature and intrinsic developmentalism surrounding the formation of modern Korean novels seems to converge toward an exploration of the 'singular' way in which indigenous and foreign cultures blend. The study of cultural metamorphosis serves as a perspective from which to analyze the cultural changes in Korea during the modern transition, starting from the conclusions that emerge from this debate.

In Chapter 2, we reviewed several theoretical resources related to the metamorphosis of culture, analyzing the attributes of culture presented in Im Hwa's cultural theory as a combination of universality, hybridity, and singularity. Furthermore, based on these general attributes of culture, we examined the significance of claiming national identity in colonial history without essentializing 'national culture.' Chapter 3 delves into the multilayered implications of metamorphosis to more comprehensively reveal the problems associated with Im Hwa's cultural thoughts. Im Hwa acknowledges the violent imposition of modern institutions and knowledge through colonial power (colonial transformation) while also believing that the creative integration of cultural traditions and the transplantation of foreign cultures (metamorphosis of culture) can enhance the subjective capacity of a colonized people.

The issue of continuity and discontinuity surrounding the succession of tradition can be more clearly resolved by distinguishing the dimensions of elements and structure. In the dimension of elements, the process of continually blending heterogeneous elements of past indigenous and foreign cultures to create a unique third culture is always repeated, and in this sense, the past always coexists with the present (continuity). Simultaneously, the transition to 'modernity' involved a kind of 'disruption' in terms of a paradigm shift in perceiving/constructing the world (discontinuity). While acknowledging such structural transitions (disruption, transplantation), Im Hwa sought a path where the creative integration of existing traditions and foreign cultural elements within the new structure could lead to the enhancement of the capabilities of colonial Koreans and the decolonization process. Im Hwa's writing on the literary history of the 1900s actively reconstructed the national cultural identity fragmented by the discontinuity and disruption of the modern transition era. Simultaneously, in another 'transformation period' of the Second World War, when he wrote his literary history, he projected antimodern/anticolonial desires into the early 'transition' period, seeking new social imaginaries for the yet-to-come future.

Cultural Metamorphosis:

From Seohak Ethics to Christian Ethics

OH Jie Seok

1. Introduction: A Two-Tier Model of Christian Ethics

Korea's intellectual society is the result of an intricate interweaving of the threads of traditional East Asian values (Confucian values) and foreign thought imported from the West.[1] The intellectual society of the Joseon Dynasty distinguished the country from surrounding nations, such that the country referred to itself as the nation of ceremonial propriety in the East.[2] Western thought was foreign in this context. Occasionally, Korean intellectual of this era exhibited acceptance of such thought, but more often, they chose to ignore or reject it. After the Ming-Qing transition, Joseon intellectuals, who endorsed Sinocentrism, considered the Manchu, the new ruling power in China, the Japanese, and people from the unfamiliar West to be barbarians (오랑캐).[3]

---

1 Jie Seok Oh (오지석). "Koreans and Christian Ethical Thought [한국인과 기독교윤리사상]." In *Life Led by Value [가치가 이끄는 삶]*, ed. Kim Hyung-Min et al. Dongyeon [동연], 2013, 311.

2 Korean: "동방예의지국"

3 "Who are the barbarians?" Regarding this question, we can consider the people who have been viewed as barbarians throughout history. The term "barbarian" is not unfamiliar. Namely, our nation used this term practically throughout the Joseon Dynasty. Originally, the term "barbarian" referred to a tribe called Orangkai, which was one of the Jurchen tribes living in Manchuria, specifically those who were nomadic and living in the region of the Ussuri River tributary. The concept of the "barbarian" was developed by Chinese people, who defined all ethnic groups other than themselves as barbarians. Thus, they divided barbarians into four categories: Eastern Barbarians, Western Barbarians,

53

In particular, they referred to Westerners as *yangyi* (洋夷) or "Western barbarians" (서양의 오랑캐). This characterization was extended to the Catholic priests who lived in China beginning in the 16th century to spread Christian culture and Western natural sciences and technology as well as to Protestant missionaries who came to Joseon during the period of port opening. As such, how did Joseon intellectuals perceive and react to the ethical thought that these 'Western barbarians' (洋夷) wished to disseminate? This question led the author to research the theme "Learning Manners from Barbarians! (오랑캐에게 예절을 배우다!)."

Why should this issue be chosen as a research topic? The author's interest was sparked by reading the records of expeditions that opened the eyes of Joseon intellectuals to the world, the lineage of Northern Learning (北學) and Practical Learning (實學), the etiquette studies of the reformer Park Gyu-su (朴珪壽), and the book Geo-Ga-Jap-Bok-Go (居家雜服攷).[4] In particular, this research was strongly influenced by the following texts:

Southern Barbarians, and Northern Barbarians.
A term that was originally a proper noun indicating the "Jurchen tribe" came to be used as a common noun to express disdain for all uncivilized and ill-mannered tribes. The concept of the "barbarian" was derived from the Chinese historical experience and the desire to guard against other ethnic groups. In our country, this term was commonly used by some Confucian scholars who considered themselves to represent "Little China," and even Jurchen tribes who were derived from the same Goguryeo lineage were derogatorily referred to as barbarians. Especially when Westerners began to enter to the country en masse during the Seohae blockade, these people were specifically referred to as Western Barbarians. After the division of Korea, North Korea was also sometimes referred to as a barbarian country.
Searches for the keywords "Western Barbarians" (서양 오랑캐) and "Foreign Barbarians" (양이 or 洋夷) yielded the following results in October 2017. According to The Korean History Information System (한국역사정보통합시스템), there were 24 results from books, 3 from Document Boxes, 96 from translations of classical texts (87 from historical works and 9 from literary works, including Choe Deokjung's 1712 travelogue, Yeonhaengnok 燕行錄), 5 from Periodicals (1 from Haejo Sinmun 海朝新聞, 4 from Kungminbo 國民報), and 8 from Research Materials such as the Korean History Research Report 한국사연구회보. Additionally, 8 images were found. When searching DBpia for the keywords, such as "Western Barbarians" (서양 오랑캐) and "Foreign Barbarians" (洋夷), 52 articles were found in the Humanities, 5 in Social Sciences, 3 in Arts and Sports, and 1 in Natural Sciences. When searching the Korean Studies Information Service System (KISS) for the phrase "Western barbarians 서양 오랑캐," 340 articles were found, while for the term "Foreign barbarians 洋夷," 19 articles were retrieved. According to the Korea Citation Index (KCI), there were 12 articles including the phrase "Western barbarians 서양 오랑캐," and 12 articles containing the term "Foreign Barbarians 洋夷." The results from the Korean Database KRPia (한국의 지식콘텐츠) yielded 214 instances for the term "Western barbarians 서양 오랑캐."

4   거가잡복고 or 居家雜服攷, Geo-Ga-Jap-Bok-Go literally "A Study of Miscellaneous Clothing and Apparel in the Home."

Shin Ik-cheol's *Yeon-haeng-sa* and *the Beijing Cathedral*[5]

Lee Gi-ji's travelogue *Il-Am-Yŏn-Ki*[6]

Seo Ho-su's *Yŏl-Ha-Ki-Yu*[7]

The Collection of Hong Daeyoung's Letters from Chinese Scholars in the Late 18th Century[8]

Manuscripts written in Taiping by the missionary Rev. W. L. Swallen (蘇安論) in approximately 1901.[9]

As many studies have noted, since the 16th century, the transmission of Christian culture as well as Western natural sciences,[10] technology, and goods to East Asia has led to interactions between these factors and the intellectual traditions of East Asia. These interactions evolved gradually until the 18th century and then altered dramatically after the 19th century.[11] This trend naturally led

---

5   연행사와 북경천주당 or 燕行使와 北京天主堂, literally "Yeon-hang-sa and the Beijing Cathedral." Ik-Chul Shin (신익철), *Yeon-hang-sa and the Beijing Cathedral [연행사와 북경천주당]* (Bogosa [보고사], 2013). 연행사

6   일암연기 or 一菴燕記, literally "A Hermitage's Record of Yan". The author used the 2016 edition, translated and edited by Jo Young-hee (조용희), Shin Ik-cheol (신익철), and Bu Yu-seop (부유섭). The travelogue detailed records of his encounters and interactions with missionaries, thus rendering it a valuable source for examining how the yangban intellectuals of early 18th-century Joseon (Korea) came into contact with Western culture and how they perceived it.; Ki-ji Lee (이기지 or 李器之), *Il-Am-Yŏn-Ki [일암연기 or 一菴燕記]* Translated by Cho Yung-hee, Shin Ik-chul, Bu Yu-seop [조용희, 신익철, 부유섭] (Seongnam: The Academy of Korean Studies Publishing [한국학중앙연구원출판부], 2016).

7   열하기유 or 熱河紀遊, literally "Travel Notes From Rehe" or "The Envoy's Progress to Yenching." Ho-Soo Seo (서호수), *Yulha Giyu: The Envoy's Progress to Yenching* or *Record of Travel in Rehe [열하기유 熱河紀遊]*. Translated by Lee Chang-suk [이창숙] (Akanet [아카넷], 2017).

8   중사기홍대용수찰집 or 中士寄洪大容手札帖. English: *The Collection of Hong Daeyoung's Letters from Chinese Scholars in the Late 18th Century.*; Myung-Geun Han (한명근), *The Collection of Hong Daeyoung's Letters from Chinese Scholars in the Late 18th Century[中士寄洪大容手札帖]*. Edited by Park Kyung-shin (박경신) (Soongsil University Korean Christian Museum [숭실대학교한국기독교박물관], 2016).

9   In Korean: 소안론 선교사의 1901년경의 타이핑 원고. Hyo-Eun Park (박효은), "Regarding the Swallen Pastor's Korean Art Gallery and Related Documents ["스왈른 목사 舊藏 箕山風俗圖 Korean Art Gallery와 관련문서"]." In *Soongsil University Korean Christian Museum [崇實大學敎韓國基督敎博物館誌]* Issue 3, ed. Soongsil University Korean Christian Museum [숭실대학교한국기독교박물관] (Soongsil University Korean Christian Museum [숭실대학교한국기독교박물관], 2008).

10   Jie Seok Oh (오지석), "Christian Ethical Thought Transplanted through Western Missionaries [서양선교사를 통해 이식된 기독교윤리사상]," *The Korean Journal of Chiristian Social Ethics [기독교사회윤리]* 44 (2019): 273.

11   Seung-Hye Kim (김승혜), "The Encounter of East Asian Religious Traditions and Christianity

to the creation of two strata in Christian ethics. The Western Christian ethics introduced beginning in the 16th century were based on a combination of Aristotle's ethics (practical philosophy) with Scholastic theology, whereas the other Christian ethics that were transmitted beginning in the 19th century represented Protestant ethics. The Christian ethics introduced to this country exhibit two strata, which represent the foundation of this research.

Accordingly, what is the reason underlying this interest in Christian ethics in Korea? After Joseon opened its borders, the values of Koreans underwent a process of transition (전이 or 轉移) that led them away from Sinocentrism (중화에서 문명), and Confucian values and education, which focused on ethical propriety (예의 or 禮義) and mutual bonds (강상 or 綱常), were threatened. Lingering doubt also emerged about the cultural roots of these values. However, although Joseon and the Korean Empire aimed to embrace the values of the Confucian intellectual tradition, Western ethics (specifically Christian ethics) could not replace Confucian values. While Western values and Christian ethics were introduced, they had not yet become fully integrated into Korean culture.

Christian ethics feature two layers. The first layer can be referred to as Western learning ethics. This type of ethics represents the ethical philosophy introduced to China and Joseon based on Catholic ethical theology, which was then influenced by East Asian thought.[12] In other words, the Christian ethics that were introduced to China and Korea in the 17th to 19th centuries were influenced by Aristotle and Thomism and transformed through interactions with Neo-Confucianism.[13] These ethics were primarily transmitted to Koreans through books published in Chinese by Catholic priests who travelled to China alongside their collaborators. While scholarly terms did not necessarily require translation, the appearance of religious texts necessitated translation into Korean. Evidence of this situation can be found in the fact that many books of Western

---

[동아시아 종교 전통과 그리스도교의 만남]," *Spiritual Life [영성생활]* (1999): 20.

12 Oh, "Christian Ethical Thought," 286.

13 Refer to the following: Jie Seok Oh (오지석), *Joseon Intellectual Society and the Ethics of Christianity during the Transition Period [조선지식인사회와 전환기의 기독교윤리]* (Blue Territory [푸른영토], 2018), p. 180; Jie Seok Oh (오지석), *Western Christianity's Self-led Assimilation and Transformation: Beyond Conflicts and Criticisms [서양기독교의 주체적 수용과 변용-갈등과 비판을 넘어서]* (Blue Territory [푸른영토], 2018), 180; Oh, "Christian Ethical Thought," 286.

learning were translated as soon as they were introduced to the country.

The second layer of Christian ethics (기독교윤리학) is rooted in Protestant ethics. According to W. Beach and H.R. Niebuhr, the term Christian ethics refers to moral reflection that takes place within the Christian community. In simpler terms, this area of study addresses the following question: "How should a Christian live?"[14] After the opening of Joseon's ports, Protestant missionaries, who lived in a relatively comfortable environment, began to engage in missionary activities. They conveyed Christian ethical ideas to individuals who embraced Protestantism in Korean or Hangul, thus facilitating a closer integration of these ideas with their daily lives. Consequently, individuals who embraced Protestant ethical thought came to develop an additional layer or element within this framework.

This study is based on these notions. First, it examines the process by which Western learning ethics came to be accepted from the perspective of ignorance and rejection. Then, it attempts to analyzlyse the discourse of the social class that actively embraced Western culture or Christianity as a framework for the transition from "Sinocentrism" to "civilization." Furthermore, this paper aims to illustrate the process through which modern Korean society came to embrace the term "ethics" as a translation of ethics rather than focusing solely on ethical propriety; it also explores the traces of Christian ethics that are evident within this context.

2. Learning Manners from Western Barbarians (洋夷)!

When we refer to "Learning Manners from Barbarians!," this phrase naturally raises the following question: who are these 'barbarians'? As mentioned previously, traditionally, the term 'barbarians' referred to individuals in a manner rooted in traditional theories. However, during the era of *Sŏsedongjeom*,[15] the

---

14 Si-Young Moon (문시영), *The Story of Christian Ethics [기독교윤리이야기]* (HanDeul [한들], 1997), 30.

15 서세동점 or 西勢東漸, literally "The momentum of the West gradually permeates to the East" or "Western Powers' Penetration of the East." This phrase is generally used to describe the influence or spread of trends from the Western world to the Eastern world. It can emphasize various aspects

term was commonly used in a manner that included Catholic missionaries, including the Jesuits, who had been-active in China since the late 16th century.

TherefoteAccordingly, who were the 'barbarians' who strove to teach manners to Joseon intellectuals during the tumultuous period following the country's opening? Undoubtedly, these figures primarily included Protestant missionaries, especially those from the United States. Now, let us explore the origins of and encounters with these Western 'barbarians' (洋夷) with the goal of examining the opportunities and modes of interaction that are evident in this context. From where did the opportunity to meet these Western barbarians (洋夷) come, and how did these meetings occur? We shall start by asking these questions.

1) Meeting the West and Christian Ethics on the Diplomatic Journey

In Korean society, the concept of 'manners' (rye; 禮) is understood as an embodiment of the spirit, morality, and principles of Confucianism. Despite the origins of this framework in China, it has become an integral part (if not the entirety) of our cultural framework over the span of approximately 2000 years. The emergence of the Joseon Dynasty further solidified this cultural foundation due to the adoption of Neo-Confucianism, which was introduced during the late Goryeo Dynasty, which proclaimed itself to be a Confucian state. During this period, the emphasis shifted towards 'manners-based governance' (예치 or 禮治). The Joseon government and intellectuals exhibited a primary interest in matters related to 'manners.' The state published etiquette-related literature such as *Kyŏngguk Taejŏn,*[16] *Sejong Sillok,*[17] and *Kukcho Oryeui,*[18] and popularized *Chujakarye*[19] as a form of common courtesy for

---

of this phenomenon, such as culture, technology, ideas, or lifestyle.

16 경국대전 or 經國大典, literally "Great Encyclopedia of the Nation" or "Encyclopedia of National Classics." The foundational legal code of the Joseon Dynasty, which was compiled by integrating the original and supplementary volumes (續典) of *Kyŏngje Yukjŏn* (경제육전 or 經濟六典) alongside statutes and laws.

17 세종실록 or世宗實錄, literally "The Annals of Sejong" or "Veritable Records of [King] Sejong." A historical record that addresses the overall governance of the Joseon Dynasty during the reign of King Sejong the Great, the fourth monarch, focusing on various aspects of the nation's affairs.

18 국조오례의 or 國朝五禮儀, literally "Five Rites of the National Dynasty." A book of etiquette compiled in 1474 by early Joseon scholars such as Shin Suk-Ju (신석주) and Jeong Cheok (정척),

the aristocracy.

In the late 16th century and early 17th century, Joseon experienced two devastating wars that led to social collapse. The emergence of Jurchens, who had once been referred to as "barbarians," as the dominant power in the Middle Kingdom during the Later Jin[20] was particularly impactful. This development triggered a series of events that prompted the Joseon government and intellectuals to address the resulting turmoil swiftly and strive to promote national reconstruction by emphasizing "manners." The aristocracy considered this task to be their mission during this era and actively worked to strengthen order and righteousness through "manners." As time passed, the introduction of practical learning led to a reassessment of the prevailing rituals in the country. However, for a long time, the people of Joseon had been educated regarding their attitudes and ways of life in both the public and private spheres by the Confucian notion of "manners," and they lived their lives continually based on this process. However, the seemingly unshakable and eternal notion of Confucian 'manners' started to exhibit certain cracks, which were nevertheless faint and elusive, due to the importation of Chinese-translated books on Western learning that had been published by Jesuit missionaries in China. This situation was further influenced by interactions between Joseon envoys who visited Beijing (or Yanjing), the center of the world, and Western missionaries and cathedrals, in which context they engaged in exchanges and dialogs.

As the period of the Ming-Qing transition passed and the Qing Dynasty entered a stable period, the books that these figures brought back or that were received as gifts from missionaries led to a tremendous disruption in Joseon intellectual society during the 17th and 18th centuries.

Shin Ik-cheol's 2013 translations of *Yeon-hang-sa and the Beijing Cathedral*[21] and *The Encounter between 18th Century Travel Diaries and Western Missionaries*[22]

---

which details the procedures and rules associated with ceremonial rites.

19 주자가례 or 朱子家禮 (Zhu Xi Jiali), literally "Zhu Xi's Family Rituals." A book by Zhu Xi (朱熹, 1130-1200) from the Southern Song Dynasty in China, which discusses the rites and ceremonies of scholar-official families.

20 Later Jin (1616-1636) in Korean is 後金." Note: Later Jin is sometimes also referred to as 금국 or 金國, literally "the Golden State,"

21 Shin, *Yeon-hang-sa.*

serve as valuable resources for understanding the dynamics underlying the interactions between travel diaries and Western missionaries. The earliest mention of Catholic-related books in the 18th century appears in Jo Young-bok's (조용복 or 趙榮福) *Yŏn-haeng-il-lok*.[23] The most frequent visitor to the Catholic Church, Lee Ki-ji, recorded in *Il-Am-Yŏn-Ki*[24] that on October 24, 1720, he visited the missionaries Xavier-Ehrenbert Fridelli[25] and Joseph Suarez[26] and received *Chil-guk*[27] and *Ch'ŏnju-sirŭi*[28] as gifts.[29]

In Gang Ho-bu's (姜浩溥) *Sangbong-nok*[30] travel record from December 29, 1727, Gang describes his views on Western learning after visiting the cathedral and engaging in a conversation.[31] On October 24, 1729, Kim Soon-hyeop (金淳協) received books such as *Manmul Jinwon*[32] as gifts,[33] and in October 1732, Lee Ik-hyeon (李益賢) visited the cathedral and engaged in conversation with the missionary Bi-eun (비은), thereafter receiving books such as *Samhak Nonhakgi*[34]

---

22 Ik-Chul Shin (신익철), "The Encounter of Scholars Going to China in the 18th Century and Western Missionaries [18세기 연행사와 서양 선교사의 만남]," *Journal of Korean Literature in Classical Chinese* [韓國漢文學研究] 51, (2013).

23 연행일록 or 燕行日錄, literally ""

24 Lee, *Il-Am-Yŏn-Ki*.

25 Xavier-Ehrenbert Fridelli (1673~1743), An Austrian Jesuit also known as 費隱 (Fèi yǐn) or 비은 (Pi-ŭn)

26 Joseph Suarez (1656-1736), A Portugal-born Jesuit. also known as 蘇霖 (Sū lín) or 소림 (So-rim).

27 칠극 or 七克, literally "the seven peaks." The role of Septem Victoriis(Qike). An abbreviated form of 칠극대전 or 七克大全, "The Comprehensive Guide to Overcoming the Seven Deadly Sins." A Catholic moral guidebook written by Father Pantoja to describe the seven roots of sin and the seven virtuous acts necessary to overcome them.

28 천주실의 or 天主實義, also known as "[The] True Meaning of the Lord of Heaven." A Catholic doctrinal book by Michele Ruggieri (羅明堅, 1543-1607), which was published in 1603 and translated into Korean by the Jesuit Priest Matteo Ricci (利瑪竇, 1552-1610).

29 Ki-Ji Lee (이기지 or 李器之), *Il-Am-Yŏn-Ki or Daily Record of Ilam* [일암연기]. Translated by Cho Yung-hee, Shin Ik-chul, Bu Yu-seop [조용희, 신익철, 부유섭]. (Seongnam: The Academy of Korean Studies Publishing [한국학중앙연구원출판부], 2016) 395.

30 상봉록 or 桑蓬錄, literally "Record of Mulberries and Wormwood." A Beijing travelogue (燕行錄) from the early 18th century. The text was authored in Chinese by Gang Ho-bu (강호부 姜浩溥), who later translated it into Korean.

31 Shin, *Yeon-hang-sa*, 127-135.

32 만물진원 or 萬物眞原, literally "The Essence of All Things" A Catholic text in which Matteo Ricci, an Italian Jesuit missionary who was active in China, described the origin of all things.

33 Shin, *Yeon-hang-sa*, 145-146.

34 삼산논학기 or 三山論學記, literally "Treatise on the Studies of the Three Mountains." A catechism written in Classical Chinese by Giulio Aleni (艾儒略, 1582-1649), an Italian Jesuit missionary who

and *Juje Gunjing*[35] as gifts.[36] In his *Yeonhaeng Illok*, Jeong Gwang-chung (鄭光忠), who traveled as a diplomat, left a record of his visit to the cathedral and meeting with Liu Songling[37] on January 21 and January 24, 1756.[38]

In 1761, Lee Sang-bong, the author of *Bukwonrok*, visited the cathedral on January 8. During this visit, he became aware of Western learning through the preface of Aleni's "Zhibao Outi." On January 24, he revisited the cathedral, met Liu Songling, and observed the celestial sphere. Lee mentioned reading "Cheonhak Choham." On February 6, he made another visit to the southern part of the cathedral, where he engaged in a discussion on marital ethics with Liu Songling and Seo Seung-eun, a descendant of Seo Gwang-gye. Additionally, Lee was introduced to more than 50 pages of the geography texts *Chikbangoegi*[39]

---

worked in China. This text is a Catholic doctrinal book that focuses on the uniqueness (唯一性) of Catholicism (天主), the issue of good and evil (善惡), the question of blessings and disasters (禍福), the immortality of the soul (靈魂不滅), judgment after death(死後審判), and evidence and doubts about the incarnation (天主降生).

Note: The term "Three Mountains" (삼산 or 三山) refers to the nickname for Fuzhou (福州) in Fujian Province(福建省). Due to the presence of Jiuxianshan (九仙山) to the east of the city of Fuzhou (福州城), Minsan (閩山) to the west, and Yuewangshan (越王山) to the north, it is also called Samsan (三山).

35 주제군징 or 主制群徵, literally "The Dominance of Collective Signs." A catechism of Catholic doctrine written in Classical Chinese by Charles-Philippe Raux, a Jesuit missionary in Beijing, which was published in 1629. This book presents evidence and explanations pertaining to the existence of God, who governs and rules the world.

36 Ibid., 153-159.

37 Liu Songling (劉松齡), The Chinese name of A. Von Hallerstein (1703~1774), a German Jesuit missionary.

38 The January 21, 1756, entry in "Yeonhaengilrok" details a conversation with a diplomat from the West. The content can be briefly summarized as follows: "In general, there are large and small countries in the West, which is approximately 90,000 li away from China. The people there call China the East. The map drawn of the region was even larger than that of China, with 32 nations established within it. Each has its own ruler, and they do not govern each other. Because men and women marry and become relatives, they live harmoniously and do not fight much. Their judicial systems and laws highly respect the celestial path, and their language and writing are very different from those of China. Their writing resembles a tadpole's movement, and their spoken language follows the native tongue. When a man and a woman marry, they follow one person and do not serve two. When they mourn the death of a relative, it ends in a year. When they offer sacrifices to their ancestors, they always have a portrait. ... They are very proficient in the calendar system and excel in painting. The astronomer at the observatory is a Westerner. Among them, those who are good at painting stay in the palace and are responsible for all painting work. There are currently 25 Westerners staying here, with six living at the Southern Church (referring to the West Church) and the rest staying at the East Church or outside the West Flower Gate. One of the six people at the West Church is Liu Songling." Shin, "The Encounter of Scholars," 467-468. Shin, *Yeon-hang-sa*.

39 職方外紀, literally "Chronicles of the External Territories." A representative work of European

and *Konyeodoseol*,[40] and he received two copies of *Konyeodoseol*[41] as well as two copies of *Hwangdo Chongseongdo*[42] as gifts.[43]

Hong Daeyong (홍대용 or 洪大容, 1731-1783), a prominent figure in the *Bukhak* "Northern Learning" ideology,[44] arrived in Beijing on December 27, 1765, where he stayed until February 1766. He visited the southern wing of the cathedral on January 7, 9, 13, and 19 as well as February 2, and he visited the eastern wing on January 24. Notable cathedral visits included a dialog with Liu Songling and Antoine Gogeisl (포우관 or 鮑友管, 1701-1771) on January 9, where they observed the cathedral's wind chimes and self-ringing bells. On January 19, they engaged in a brief conversation about Catholic learning and discussed astronomy by reference to the *Yeoksanggoseong*.[45] They also

---

geography that divides the world into five continents. This text was compiled by the Italian missionary Giulio Aleni (艾儒略) in the third year of the Ming Dynasty (1623).

40 The conversation progressed as follows: Liu Songling (劉松齡): "Does your country also have a principle of justice like ours? I presume it would be more detailed. If it discusses the principle of ruling a nation and maintaining peace in the world, it is like our principle of 'great harmony.' However, among the five cardinal relationships, in the relationship between husband and wife, they only observe their propriety and do not have a practice of taking concubines. What they respect and worship is only the Lord of Creation who created heaven, earth, and all things, and they do not worship any other false gods." Lee Sang-bong (이상봉): "If they do not take concubines, does a man also observe chastity for his wife, as when a woman does not remarry when her husband dies?" Liu Songling (劉松齡): "Just as a wife can remarry when her husband dies, a husband can also remarry when his wife dies. However, the fact that they cannot take a concubine while their wife is alive is just like how a wife cannot remarry while her husband is alive."

41 坤輿圖說, literally "Explanation of the Map of the Earth"

42 黃道總星圖, literally "Complete Map of the Ecliptic and Stars." A celestial map of Western origin that was created by Western missionaries in Qing China, namely, the German missionary Ignaz Kögler (대진현 or 戴進賢) and the Italian missionary Ferdinando Bonaventuri Moggi (이백명 or 利白明).

43 Shin, *Yeon-hang-sa*, 173-209.

44 北學, literally "Northern Learning." "Bukhak" or "Northern Learning" was a pragmatic ideology that emerged during the late Joseon Dynasty in Korea. It sought to address the challenges faced by the country by incorporating certain cultural and institutional aspects drawn from the Qing Dynasty of China. As the Qing Dynasty's dominance persisted for longer than anticipated, the ruling class in Joseon began to argue that China had illegitimately appropriated the essence of "Central Civilization." In response, a group called the Yeon-am Group (연암일파 or 燕巖一派) advocated for the adoption of Qing Dynasty's systems as a means to reintroduce the lost Central Civilization. Bukhak's focus was on practical reforms such as utilizing bricks and carts, improving agricultural tools, and promoting foreign trade. However, it did not evolve into a comprehensive philosophical framework or a comprehensive plan for societal transformation.Top of Form

45 역상고성 or 曆象考成, literally "the achievement of understanding historical events and their manifestations." A 1724 book on retrocalculation compiled by Chinese scholars such as He Guoceng

observed an armillary sphere,[46] a telescope.[47] scriptures, and the cathedral's self-ringing bells.[48]

On February 2, they observed the self-ringing bells and the compass[49] and discussed the principles of the *yeokbeop*[50] calendar system.[51] Hong Daeyong compiled his experiences with the cathedral into *Yupo Mundap*.[52] Furthermore, he summarized his thoughts on Catholicism in his work *Ŭlbyeong Yeonhaengnok*.[53]

Additionally, Protestant ethics, which were introduced in the relatively open environment of human and material exchange that occurred after the opening of the port, were communicated in Korean or Hangul rather than in Chinese to ensure that they were closely related to life. Therefore, the layers or traces of the people who accepted Protestant ethical thought constitute another stratum.[54]

Park Ji-won (박지원 or 朴趾源, 1737-1805), who wrote *Yŏlha Ilgi*,[55] visited various places in Beijing and combined these visits to produce *Hwangdogyirak*.[56] This text includes a record of his visit to the cathedral. He expresses his thoughts

(何國琮) and Mei Guancheng (梅觀成). It was created to reform China's traditional timekeeping methods by introducing Western astronomy during the late Ming Dynasty, and it was revised by Chinese scholars based on the "New Western Method Calendar" (서양신법역서 or 西洋新法曆書).

46 혼천의 or 渾天儀, literally "all-encompassing sky instrument." An armillary sphere is a model used to show celestial objects in the sky. It is composed up of rings arranged in a spherical shape, which represent information such as the longitude, latitude, and ecliptic. Unlike a celestial globe, which focuses on constellations, the armillary sphere offers a detailed view of the sky. It was invented independently in ancient China and Greece and later used in the Islamic world and Medieval Europe.

47 원경(망) or 遠鏡, literally "scope, telescope."

48 자명종 or 自鳴鐘, literally "self-ringing bells."

49 윤도 or 輪圖, literally "compass."

50 역법 or 曆法, literally "calendar/almanac method." *Yeok-beop* is the lunar-solar calculation method used in traditional East Asian calendars, particularly in Korea. This method involves determining the positions of the sun, moon, and other astronomical factors to establish the dates of various events and holidays. *Yeok-beop* focuses on the interaction between the lunar and solar calendars to ensure alignment and accuracy with regard to tracking both the phases of the moon and the solar year. It incorporates complex calculations and astronomical observations to establish a harmonized calendar system.

51 Ibid., 211-247.

52 유포문답 or 劉鮑問答, literally "Liu Bao Questions and Answers."

53 을병연행록 or 乙丙燕行錄, literally "Record of Ŭlbyeong (1765-1766) Travel to Yan [China]."

54 Myung-Kwan Kang (강명관), *Hong Daeyong and 1766 [홍대용과 1766년]* (Seoul: Korean Classical Literature Translation Institute [한국고전번역원], 2017), 137-138.

55 열하일기 or 熱河日記, literally "A Record of Travel in Rehe."

56 황도기략 or 黃圖紀略, literally "Brief Chronicle of the [Chinese] Imperial Map."

on Catholicism directly in the following passage below:

"…The word 'Catholicism' (天主) refers to the great root (宗主) of all things in the universe. Westerners have made a good calendar system (曆法), live in houses built according to their country's system, and cherish truthfulness and trust in their academic development. They regard serving God brightly as the best, regard filial piety and mercy as public duties, and consider preparing in advance for the big issues of human life and death, entering the religion and not worrying about it, as the ultimate goal. This is a different doctrine from that of the Chinese saints, and needless to say, it is the teaching of the barbarians…"[57]

"…They themselves evaluate their scholarship as a study that investigates the origin and scrutinizes the fundamentals. However, the purpose is excessively high, the speech is biased and cunning, resulting in the sin of deceiving heaven and deceiving people, and they do not know that they themselves fall into the pit that violates righteousness and harms human ethics.…"[58]

In 1790, Seo Ho-su (서호수 or 徐浩修, 1736-1799) left a diplomatic record in the form of his work.[59] On July 26, 1790, Seo Ho-su visited the graves of Western missionaries, including Matteo Ricci (利瑪竇, 1552~1610, an Italian Jesuit missionary), on his way to Yuanmingyuan (also known as the Old Summer Palace)[60] in Beijing. It is difficult to find records of the visit to Ricci's tomb

---

57 Kang, *Hong Daeyong and 1766*, 137-138. "천주라는 말은 천지 만물의 큰 근본(宗主)이다. 서양 사람들은 역법曆法을 잘 만들었고, 자기 나라의 제도로 집을 지어 살며, 학술은 부화하고 거짓된 내용을 근절하고 성실과 신뢰를 귀중하게 여긴다. 하느님을 밝게 섬기는 것을 으뜸으로 삼고, 충효와 자애를 공적인 의무로 삼으며, 개과천선하여 종교에 입문하고 사람이 죽고 사는 큰 문제에 미리 준비하여 근심하지 않는 것을 궁극의 목표로 삼는다."

58 Ji-Won Park (박지원), *Yeolha Ilgi [열하일기]* 3, Revised New Edition, translated by Kim Hyeoljo (Dolbegae [돌베개], 2017). Original text: "그들 스스로는 자신들의 학문은 근원을 연구하고 근본을 따지는 학문이라고 평가한다. 그러나 뜻을 세움이 지나치게 높고 말하는 것이 편벽되고 교묘해서, 하늘을 기만하고 사람을 속이는 죄과를 범하는 데로 귀결되고, 의리에 어긋나고 인륜을 상하게 하는 구덩이에 스스로 빠지는 줄 모른다."

59 열하기유 or 熱河紀遊, literally "Travel Notes From Rehe." Ho-Soo Seo (서호수), *Yŏl-Ha-Ki-Yu or A Record of Travel in Rehe [열하기유 熱河紀遊]*. Translated by Lee Chang-suk [이창숙] (Akanet [아카넷], 2017).

60 원명원 or 圓明園, literally "Gardens of Perfect Brightness." The main imperial residence of the Qianlong Emperor of the Qing Dynasty. The 860-acre complex was known as the "garden of gardens" (萬園之園), and was "arguably the greatest concentration of historic treasures in the world, dating and representing a full 5,000 years of an ancient civilization," according to chaplain Robert McGee

in Joseon diplomatic records, but interestingly, Hong even produced a *gomun*[61] obituary document[62] mourning Ricci. Seo Ho-su was proficient in astronomy and the calendar techniques associated with Western learning and briefly described the Western culture that had been introduced to China by Western missionaries, including Ricci, in his writings.

Among the books on Western learning that were procured through diplomatic endeavors or received as gifts from priests upon visits to the cathedral, those dedicated to Western learning ethics or the Sinicized Christian ethical discourse include Matteo Ricci's *Ch'ŏnju-sirŭi (The True Meaning of the Lord in Heaven)*,[63] *Kyowuron (Theory of Making Friends)*,[64] *Ishipo-ŏn (The Book of 25 Paragraphs)*,[65] and Portuguese Jesuit Father Diego de Pantoja's (방적아 or 龐迪我, 1571-1618) *Ch'ilgŭk*.[66] Other noteworthy works include the work of the Italian Jesuit Alfonso

---

of the British Army. French and British troops destroyed the complex of palaces and gardens in 1860 during the Second Opium War.

61 고문 or 告文, literally "information document." A written notice or announcement of someone's passing. *Gomun* are used to inform others about a death and to convey condolences. It is a customary practice in some East Asian cultures, such as China and Korea, to send *gomun* to friends, family members, acquaintances, and colleagues to notify them of a death and invite them to pay their respects or attend the funeral ceremonies.

62 The inscription on Lee Seo-tae's (Matteo Ricci's) tombstone reads as follows: "Though the earth separated us by nine thousand miles, and the world separated us by two hundred years, how did we cross the mighty river and climb over the rugged mountain to find this grave in Gyeongju, where only clothes and shoes remain? Seo-tae's way was diligently serving his superiors, and Seo-tae's courtesy was faithfully following the heavens. His machine has been passed down to the country of Gi-ja, and his book has flowed into the writings of Hak-san. The fact that I added content to the "Original Text of Mechanics" can be compared to how Yang Ung dared to write the "Tycoon Classic." Carrying the book and the machine, I reveal the fulfillment, and I admire the vastness of the sky in the world." Seo, *Yŏl-Ha-Ki-Yu*, 222.

63 천주실의 or 天主實義, also known as "[The] True Meaning of the Lord of Heaven." A Catholic doctrinal text by Michele Ruggieri (羅明堅, 1543-1607), which was published in 1603 and translated into Korean by the Jesuit Priest Matteo Ricci (利瑪竇, 1552-1610). The text includes a description of Catholic ethical theology.

64 교우론 or 交友論, literally "Theory on Making Friends." A Catholic doctrinal book and catechism written by the Jesuit priest Matteo Ricci (利瑪竇, 1552-1610), which discusses the theories of friendship derived from ancient Greece in the West and Christian ethics.

65 25언 or 25言, literally "The Book of 25 Paragraphs." An abridged introduction by the Jesuit priest Matteo Ricci (利瑪竇, 1552-1610) to excerpts from Epictetus's Stoic text *Enchiridion*. This work includes 25 of the original 53 chapters.

66 칠극 or 七克, literally "The Seven Peaks." A Catholic moral guidebook written by the Portuguese Jesuit Father Diego de Pantoja to describe the seven roots of sin and the seven virtuous acts necessary to overcome them. The text represents a discourse on self-cultivation and was developed in the course of the initial encounters between Christianity and Confucianism.

65

Vagnoni (고일지 or 高一志, 1566-1640),[67] such as *Tong'yu kyoyuk (Educating Children)*,[68] *Sŏhak susin (Self-Cultivation Through Western Learning)*,[69] *Sŏhak jega (Western Learning for the Family)*,[70] and *Sŏhak chipyŏng (Western Knowledge for Social Harmony)*,[71] as well as Giulio Alenio's *Sŏhak pŏm (Western Learning as a Model)*.[72] The collection also includes catechisms (教理書), faith-related books (信心書), and similar texts.

In 2009, the scholar Shim Hyun-ju argued that Catholic ethical theology started to become detached from doctrinal theology (or organizational theology) beginning in the 16th century, establishing itself as an independent discipline. This evolution is attributed to the emphasis of the Reformed churches of the time on salvation through "faith alone", which led to a greater focus on the moral life in theological studies. Furthermore, the ethical theology of the time

---

Note: The subtitle of the book "Chilgeuk" by Panttoha, which was published in Iljo-gak in 1998, was borrowed for this research. "Chilgeuk" is a term meaning "seven peaks" or "seven regions," which can be interpreted as a metaphor for a diverse or broad perspective. This text is also known by its full title 칠극대전 or 七克大全, literally "The Comprehensive Guide to Overcoming The Seven Deadly Sins."

67 Alfonso Vagonini (고일지 or 高一志, 1566-1640)

68 동유교육 or 童幼教育, literally "The Education of Children." A text written by the Italian Jesuit Alfonso Vagnoni (고일지 or 高一志, 1566-1640) in the mid-17th century with the purpose of promoting Christian missionary work through the education of children.

69 서학수신 or 西學修身, literally "Self-Cultivation Through Western Learning." A text written by the Italian Jesuit Alfonso Vagnoni (고일지 or 高一志, 1566-1640) to offer insights into ethics and explore the transplantation of Western ethical thought into China during the late Ming Dynasty. This text presents itself as a complete Western seedling in Confucian soil, and it focuses on cultivating personal virtue and moral principles. Although the text draws on Confucian language and concepts, it seeks to engage with Aristotelian ethics and emphasizes the importance of sincerity, self-cultivation, and the pursuit of both individual and communal well-being.

70 서학제가 or 西學齊家, literally "Western Learning for the Family." A text written by the Italian Jesuit Alfonso Vagnoni (고일지 or 高一志, 1566-1640), which represents the "accommodation" approach taken by Jesuit missionaries. This text combines Christianity and Confucianism, emphasizing European family ethics, including spousal relationships and the education of children.

71 서학치평 or 西學治平, literally "The Application of Western Knowledge for Social Harmony." A political science text written by the Italian Jesuit Alfonso Vagnoni (고일지 or 高一志, 1566-1640), which presents Western "monarchical" governance, drawing upon Confucian ideals of social harmony through self-improvement and governing. Certain sections of the book, such as those examining government structure, the origin of political authority, and techniques for ruling a nation, resemble the traditional Chinese monarchist text *Di Fan* (제범 or 帝範, literally "The Emperor's Example") in certain ways.

72 서학범 or 西學範, literally "Western Learning as a Model." An exploration of the Western education system produced by Italian Jesuit Giulio Aleni (애유략 or 艾儒略, 1582-1649), an Italian Jesuit, mathematician, astronomer, and geographer who served as a missionary in China for 36 years.

highlighted the 'faith life and life norms' of Christians as well as "virtuous and evil deeds," interpreting moral life as a spiritual pilgrimage directed toward God.[73] The initial stratum of Christian ethics, i.e., Western learning ethics, evolved based on a combination of Thomistic interpretations of Aristotle's praxis with Confucianism and Yangmingism[74] (also known as the "School of the Heart").

2) The Reaction of Joseon Intellectuals to Christian Ethics: Ignorance and Exclusion

The history of ethics is typically characterized by confrontation and conflict. This claim is particularly evident when conflicting ethical theories or concepts of "ethics" encounter each other, thus necessitating competition with the preceding ethos. The clash between two distinct ethical frameworks often leads to unpredictable outcomes. In this historical context, we can identify two recurring tendencies in various cultures, both of which aim to maintain their own systems and respond to change through exclusion. These tendencies often take the form of ignorance and exclusion. One such tendency involves incorporating elements from other cultures to instigate one culture's own transformation. All ethical theories strive to uphold their own perspectives while seeking to exclude others, resulting in conflict. Every ethical framework exhibits an inherent tendency to resist and fundamentally challenge other such frameworks, especially when they initially encounter disparate systems of ethics. The concepts that each system adopts can appear alien or highly unfamiliar.[75] A notable instance of this phenomenon in our history is when the intellectuals

---

73 Sim, Hyeon-ju (심현주). *Fundamentals of Christian Social Ethics [기독교 사회윤리 기초]*. Bundo Publishing [분도출판사], 2009, p. 7-8.

74 양명학 or 陽明學, literally "The Study of Yangming." A major branch of Neo-Confucianism developed by the idealist Confucian scholar Wang Yangming in opposition to the Rationalistic School led by Cheng Yi and Zhu Xi. "Yangming asserted that the supreme principle (Li or 理) can be learned through introspection, challenging Cheng and Zhu's belief that it can only be sought in the external world. Yangmingism emphasizes the unity of action and knowledge in relation to moral concepts, with the main principle being "regard the inner knowledge and the exterior action as one" (知行合一)."

75 Oh, "Koreans and Christian," 311.

of the Joseon era first encountered Christian ethics, also known as Western learning ethics.

Christian ethics or Western learning ethics, as encountered by the intellectuals of the Joseon period, can be viewed as a challenge to the human-centric ethical approach and traditions of Confucianism.[76] In essence, Christian ethics demand a shift from a human-centric ethical perspective to a God-centric perspective. The foundation for human ethical conduct in Christian ethics is found in "God's command" and "God's reward."[77] In *Ch'ilgŭk*, the Portuguese Jesuit Father Diego de Pantoja (龐迪我) associates the necessity for human moral goodness with "rewards." In contrast, Confucian scholars believe that humaneness exists independently of "rewards"; hence, moral conduct is naturally appropriate. Pantoja criticizes Confucian scholars' disregard for rewards as inadvertently weakening people's resolve to perform virtuous deeds.

Elements that were foundational to Christian ethics, a component of Western ethical philosophy, were unfamiliar and not highly attractive to the intellectuals of the Joseon era. However, this situation does not imply that the intellectual society of late Joseon refrained from reading literature related to "Western learning ethics." In fact, "Western learning fever" (서학열 or 西學熱) was prevalent in Joseon society. This phenomenon is depicted by Joseon historian Ahn Jeong-bok (안정복 or 安鼎福, 1712-1791) in *Ch'ŏnhakgo*[78] as follows:

"···The writings from the West (西洋) had already made their way to our country during the late reign of King Seonjo (宣祖). Every esteemed scholar (名卿碩儒) had seen these texts. These works were typically held in the same regard as the writings of Confucian scholars (諸子), Taoists (道家), or Buddhists (佛家), and they became a part of [the scholar's] study room (書室). However, what they primarily adopted from these works pertained only to the disciplines of astronomy (象緯) and mathematics (句股).

---

76 Refer to the following: Oh, *Joseon Intellectual Society,* 217; Oh, *Western Christianity's Self-led Assimilation and Transformation,* 217; Oh, "Christian Ethical Thought," 289.

77 Oh, "Christian Ethical Thought," 289.

78 천학고 or 天學考, literally "An Examination of Heavenly Knowledge" An analytical text in which Ahn Jeong-bok (安鼎福, 1712-1791) investigates and critiques the origins of Catholicism as transmitted to China and Joseon.

In the course of time, some scholars (士人) who embarked on the diplomatic journey to Yanjing (燕京) brought back books related to these subjects. In the years of Gyemyo (戊午年, 1783) and Gabjin (甲辰年, 1784), gifted youths initiated the preaching of celestial learning (天), delivering their teachings as if they were divinely inspired instructions, seemingly imparted by God (上帝) Himself⋯."[79]

From this period until the end of the Joseon era, the majority of scholars ignored or dismissed works related to Western learning ethics in the canon of Western literature, while a few actively embraced them. Yi Ik (이익 or 李瀷, also known as 성호 or 星湖, 1681-1764), who is regarded as the pioneer of Western learning in Joseon, positively assessed *Ch'ilgŭk* and *Kyowuron* for their contributions to Confucian theories of self-cultivation.

In contrast, scholars such as Shin Hu-dam (신후담 or 愼後聃, 1702-1761) and Ahn Jeong-bok (안정복 or 安鼎福, 1712-1791) opined that Western learning, due to its inward, personality-driven concept of heaven, adopted an attitude of rejection toward the temporal world, thus conflicting with the human-centric ethical order. On the other hand, proponents of this new Western learning, including Kwon Cheol-shin (권철신 or 權哲身, 1736-1801), Lee Seung-hoon (이승훈 or 李承薰, 1756-1801),[80] and Yi Byeok (이벽 or 李蘗, 1754-1785), were more receptive to such ideas, particularly with regard to the possession-oriented perspectives adopted by Western studies.

Individuals who accepted the Catholic faith, meanwhile, viewed the ethical ideals of Western learning as a life model and enthusiastically accepted them. However, after 1800 and the passing of King Jeongjo, the majority of Joseon intellectuals lost interest in Western learning. Concurrently, they perceived that the Confucian civilization of Joseon, which was equipped with a robust ethical and moral framework akin to the "five ethics," was superior. In their view, Westerners lacked such moral concepts and were viewed as uncivilized. Nevertheless, the execution of Catholic believers led to unfamiliar and distant

---

[79] "Consideration of Heavenly Studies [天學考]," *Collected Works of Teacher Sunam* [순암선생문집], 17, Miscellany [雜著], Year of Eulsi [乙巳], http://db.itkc.or.kr/dir/item?itemId=BT#dir/node?dataId= ITKC_BT_0534A_0170_010_0010&viewSync=OT.

[80] Lee later became one of the first Korean Catholic martyrs.

encounters with the West.

Alfonso Vagnoni (高一志 or 王豊肅, 1566-1640)[81] was the first to use the term "Western learning" (서학 or 西學) in his writings. He understood their ethics or ethical studies as a form of *Suje Chipyŏngjihak* ("learning of self-cultivation and the governance of peace").[82] This understanding is evidenced by the fact that he named his ethical writings *Sŏhak susin* (Self-Cultivation Through Western Learning"), *Sŏhak Jega* (Western Learning for the Family), and *Sŏhak chipyŏng* (Western Knowledge for Social Harmony).

In volumes II and III of *Sŏhak Jega*, Vagnoni discussed Christian ethics concerning childhood education and family ethics under the title *Tong'yu kyoyuk* (The Education of Children).

In the book's preface, as Han Lim (한림 or 韓霖) explained, "*Aekjega*[83] can be understood as the study of *Suje Chipyŏng* (修齊治平之學), which governs one's character as well as the family and society. This field of study is viewed as one of the five areas of philosophy (logic, natural philosophy, geometry, metaphysics, ethics).[84]

A text titled *Oegyujanggak Mokrok* (Table of Contents of the Kyu Pavilion),[85] which was stored in the Oegyujanggak Pavilion library on Ganghwa Island in December 1791, shows that works such as *Tong'yu kyoyuk* (The Education of Children), *Pirok Hwidap* (Exquisite Record Collection),[86] and *Sŏhak susin*

---

81 Alfonso Vagnoni (고일지 or 高一志 (Gao Yizhi), 1566-1640.) An Italian Jesuit missionary also known as Wang Fengsu (王豊肅), who served in China. Vagnoni arrived in China in 1605 but was expelled during the Nanjing Incident in 1616. He returned to China at the end of 1624 and conducted missionary work in Shanxi, where he changed his name to Gao Yizhi due to his recognition among the local population. He passed away on April 9, 1640, in Jiaozhou, Shanxi.

82 수제치평지학 or 修齊治平之學, literally "learning of self-cultivation and the governance of peace."

83 액제가 or 厄第加, pronounced "è dì jiā" in Mandarin. A phonetic translation of the term "ethica" coined by Giulio Alleni (애유략 or 艾儒略, 1582-1649)

84 Alfonso Banoni (알폰소 바뇨니), *Child Education Theory by Banoni* [바뇨니의 아동교육론 (동유교육 or 童幼教育)], translated by Kim Gwiseong (Buk Korea Publishing [북코리아], 2015), 5.

85 외규장각목록 or 外奎章閣目錄, literally "contents of the external pavilion associated with the Kui constellation." A collection of important historical records from the Joseon Dynasty, which was previously stored in a pavilion called *Oegyujanggak* (외규장각 or 外奎章閣) that was specifically established by King Jeongjo (조선 정조 朝鮮正祖, 1776-1800) to preserve records about the royal family. During an 1866 punitive expedition (병인양요 or 丙寅洋擾) undertaken by the Second French Empire in retaliation for the execution of seven French Catholic missionaries, French troops set fire to the pavilion, and many valuable books were destroyed.

86 비록휘답 or 斐錄彙答, literally "exquisite record collection of answers [to questions]."

(Self-Cultivation Through Western Learning") as well as *Sŏhak Jega* (Western Learning for the Family) were stored in the library. However, no record exists of the texts being used—only that they were burned during the 1866 punitive expedition to Korea by the French (丙寅洋擾).

This situation suggests that *Aekjega* or *Suje Chipyŏng* Western self-cultivation theory was not very influential in Korean society at that time. Giulio Alleni (애유략 or 艾儒略, 1582-1649) defined the Western concept of 'ethica' as "observing the discipline of righteousness"[87] and coined the phonetic Chinese translation *è dì jiā* (액제가 or 厄第加) to describe it.[88]

Alleni interpreted Western ethics from the perspective of Confucian *Su'shin ch'aejagŭ chisigyo p'yŏngch'ŏngha* ("cultivating oneself, harmonizing the family, governing the state, and bringing peace to the world")[89] and viewed its content in line with Aristotle's practical philosophy: ethics (修身), home economics (齊家), and political science (治天下).

He explained *Su'shin* (修身) as "contemplating the roots of all things and naturally pursuing good and avoiding evil." Furthermore, he wrote, "Western scholars inevitably strive for virtuous actions, even in minute details, seeking meticulousness in high moral standards and correctness in handling everyday life affairs."[90]

Alleni introduced Western ethics as a counterpart to Confucianism's core tenet of *Suje Chipyŏng-ui Hak*[91] and focused on high moral standards (綱常倫理).

---

87 "The Study of 'Xiū Qí Zhì Píng [修齐治平]': A Study of Investigating Meaning and Principle [修齐治平之学厄弟加者:[譯言察義理之學]," in *Western Studies Outline [西學凡]*, *The First Compilation of Heavenly Studies [天學初函]* 1 (Taiwan Student Bookstore [臺灣學生書局], 1965), 40-41.

88 Ibid.

89 수신제가치국평천하 or 修身齊家治國平天下, literally "cultivating oneself, harmonizing the family, governing the state, and bringing peace to the world." This Confucian proverb, which was first introduced in *Da Xue* (대학 or 大學, literally "Great Learning"), is sometimes abbreviated as 修身齊家 or 修齊治平 and emphasizes the importance of personal growth, responsible family management, effective governance, and ultimately the achievement of global harmony. By focusing on self-improvement and fulfilling these roles, individuals contribute to the creation of a well-ordered society. This concept reflects Confucian teachings on personal and societal development.

90 Ilmo Yang (양일모), "A Semantic Change of the Confucian Concept of Yunli [Ethics] in Modern Korea [유교적 윤리 개념의 근대적 의미 전환-20세기 전후 한국의 언론잡지 기사를 중심으로]," *Philosophy and Communication [개념과 소통]* 64, (2017): 15.

91 수제치평학 or 修齊治平學, literally "the study of Suje Chipyŏng." An abbreviated form of *Su'shin ch'aejagŭ chisigyo p'yŏngch'ŏngha* ("cultivating oneself, harmonizing the family, governing the state,

However, this term was not a translation but rather an interpretation of *ethica*. However, this view does not actually seem to have been widely introduced or accepted in Joseon intellectual society. Namely, it was not necessary for Joseon elites to understand the all-too-obvious *Suje Chipyŏng-ui Hak* by reference to the *ethica* terminology used by the Jesuits.

This dismissive attitude toward *ethica* can be detected in the writings of Yu Kil-chun (유길준 or 俞吉濬, 1856-1914), the first Korean to study abroad in Japan and the United States. A quotation from his 1889 text *Soyugyeonmun*[92] reads as follows: "In morals (도덕학 or 道德學),[93] there are several scholars such as Socrates and Plato, and in philosophy (궁리학 or 窮理學),[94] there is Aristotle." This translation of Western ethics merely as "morals" can be viewed as dismissive.

The response of Joseon intellectual society in the late period to Christian ethics began with the evaluation of Seongho Yi Ik's (이익 or 李瀷, also known as 성호 or 星湖, 1681-1764) book *Ch'ilgŭk* (칠극, 七極).[95] He viewed *Ch'ilgŭk* as consistent with Confucius's *Kŏkki-bokŭi* (극기복예 or 克己復禮, literally "self-restraint and return to courtesy"), suggesting that it could be accepted in Joseon society.

However, Seongho Yi Ik's disciple Ahn Jeong-bok (안정복 or 安鼎福, 1712-1791) considered *Ch'ilgŭk* to be a mere commentary on Confucius's teachings and claimed that nothing could be taken from it, although it contained serious content.

---

and bringing peace to the world).

92 서유견문 or 西遊見聞, literally "Observations and Experiences From a Journey to the West." Yoon Gil-chun's travelogue, where he recorded his experiences in the West.

93 도덕학 or 道德學, literally "the study of the way of virtue"

94 궁리학 or 窮理學, literally "the study of strategic reasoning or logic"

95 칠극 or 七克, literally "The Seven Peaks." A Catholic moral guidebook written by the Portuguese Jesuit Father Diego de Pantoja to describe the seven roots of sin and the seven virtuous acts necessary to overcome them. The text represents a discourse on self-cultivation and was developed in the course of the initial encounters between Christianity and Confucianism.
Note: The subtitle of the book "Chilgeuk" by Panttoha, which was published in Iljo-gak in 1998, was borrowed for this research. "Chilgeuk" is a term meaning "seven peaks" or "seven regions," which can be interpreted as a metaphor for a diverse or broad perspective.
This text is also known by its full title 칠극대전 or 七克大全, literally "The Comprehensive Guide to Overcoming The Seven Deadly Sins."

In *Oju-yŏnmunjangjŏnsango*,[96] Lee Gyu-gyeong (이규경 or 李圭景, 1788-1856)
viewed the *anima* mentioned in *Ch'ilgŭk* as synonymous with the *Myŏngdŏk*
(명덕 or 明德, literally "bright virtue) discussed in *Taehak* (대학 or 大學, literally
"Great Learning"). Moreover, Ji Ho Mi interpreted *Chiho-mi* (지호미 or 至好美,
literally "the beauty of the ultimate good") as the *Chi-Sŏn* (지선 or 至善, literally
"supreme good") mentioned in *Taehak*. Lee meticulously analyzed *Ch'ilgŭk*
and provided an insightful interpretation thereof, ultimately responding to
the text in a manner similar to Seongho Yi Ik.[97]

In *Sŏngse-ch'uyojŭng-ui*,[98] Hong Jeong-ha (홍정하 or 洪正夏, 1684-1727)
criticized the doctrine of monogamy based on the idea of equality in Western
ethical thought. He also criticized the notion of *Ch'ŏnju Taegun Taibu Sŏl*
(천주대군대부설 or 天主大君大父說, literally "the teachings of God as the Great
Lord and Father") and *Jesamuyongnon* (제사무용론 or 祭祀無用論, literally
"the theory that ancestral rites are useless") based on "high moral standards."[99]

Hwaseo Lee Hang-ro (화서 이항로 or 華西 李恒老, 1792-1868), the
representative critic of Western learning from the nineteenth century, harshly
criticized *Ch'ilgŭk* in Volume VII of *The Collected Writings of Hwaseo*,[100] making
statements such as "Do not do the three and avoid doing the four; do not
oppose each other in argument"[101] and "The seven prohibitions [Ch'ilgŭk]
of foreigners and the eight punishments of Confucianism are argued to be
opposite."[102]

He also wrote the following: "The content [of *Ch'ilgŭk*] is all about material

96 오주연문장전산고 or 五洲衍文長箋散稿, literally "Extended Commentary on the Scattered
Manuscripts of the Proliferation of Literature Across the Five Continents"

97 Jae-Yeon Won (원재연), "Yi Kyu-gyeong's External Views and the Perception of Catholic Missionary
History in Joseon [오주 이규경의 대외관과 천주교 조선전래사 인식]," *Church History Research [교회사연구]* 17, (2001): 143.

98 성세추요증의 or 盛世芻蕘證疑, literally "Doubts and Inquiries about the Luxuriance of a Prosperous
Era"

99 See the following: Jae-Yeon Won (원재연), "Criticisms of Catholic Doctrine by Cheosa Hong
Jeong-ha during the Reign of King Jeongjo and Perceptions of Catholicism [정조대 처사 홍정하의
천주교리서 비판과 천주교 인식]," *The Dongguk Historical Society [동국사학]* 64, (2018): 183; Oh,
"Christian Ethical Thought," 290.

100 화서집 or 華西集, literally "The Hwaseo Collection."

101 "삼무망여사물상반변," or "三毋妄與四勿相反辯"

102 "양인칠극여오유팔형상반변," or "洋人七克與吾儒八刑相反辯"

wealth and pleasure, and the things it restricts are actually those pursued excessively. This indicates that Western studies fundamentally lie in punishment, wealth, and gain."[103]

3) From Zhonghua to Civilization (Toward a New Ethics)

"···How can we say that a distant barbarian has insulted Korea — the so-called land of propriety — to such an extent? People often refer to it as a land of propriety, but I believe such a claim is fundamentally unfounded. Throughout history, how could there be a country governed without propriety? This is merely the Chinese imagination, as they highly regard even the barbarians and praise them as 'the land of propriety.' It is something that should originally be considered shameful, and it is not right to boast about it in front of the world."[104]

The term *Zhonghua* (중화 or 中華, literally "central harmony") refers to the "region and culture" in which the ancient Chinese state (the Middle Kingdom) was established. Subsequently, this term expanded to encompass "the Chinese people's sense of superiority and admiration for their national culture."[105] This concept formed the basis of *Hwa'ikwan* (화이관 or 華夷觀, literally "Perception of the Chinese and the Barbarians"), which encompassed the entire civilizational consciousness of Joseon intellectuals. The transition from the Ming to Qing dynasties can be viewed as an event during which the roles of barbarians (夷) and Zhonghua (華) were reversed.

in the late 17th century, Joseon intellectual society adopted a worldview that divided the world into *Zhonghua* (중화 or 中華) and barbarians (오랑캐 or 夷). Joseon intellectuals advocated national initiatives such as seeking revenge, pursuing internal reforms and external advancements, and expanding northward.

---

103 Shin-Hwan Kwak (곽신환), "Orientation and Conflict of Scholars during the Joseon Dynasty [『조선조 유학자의 지향과 갈등』]," *Philosophy and Reality [철학과현실사]*, (2005): 387.

104 Park Gisu (朴珪壽), "Letter to Minister Wen [書牘 與溫卿]" in *Hwanchae Collection [瓛齋集]*, 8, Item 32. Original text: 所謂禮義之邦。見侮於遠夷。一至於此。此何事也。 輒稱禮義之邦。此說吾本陋之。天下萬古。安有爲國而無禮義者哉。是不過中國人嘉其夷狄中乃有此而嘉賞之曰禮義之邦也。此本可差可恥之語也。不足自豪於天下也。稍有地閥者。輒稱兩班兩班。此爲最堪羞恥之說。最無識之口也。今輒自稱禮義之邦。是不識禮義爲何件事之口氣也。Read more at https://bit.ly/48t22A2.

105 See Tae-Ho Kim, (2011), 608. "중국인의 민족 문화에 대한 우월감과 동경"

They went even further by promoting the belief that "Joseon is *Zhonghua*."[106] In the late 19th century and early 20th century, Joseon experienced significant confusion regarding the so-called "Little Zhonghua Theory."[107] This theory was to the result of the influence of Western powers encroaching upon East Asia, thus causing the traditional East Asian order, particularly the tributary system, to crumble and give way to the establishment of a new global historical order.

Due to the opening of ports and increased interaction with Westerners, the need to learn about Western etiquette became more urgent. In Volumes XV and XVI of Yu Kil-chun's (유길준 or 俞吉濬, 1856-1914) *Soyugyeonmun*,[108] the focus is more on introducing the Western way of life than on mere etiquette. Volume XVI covers topics such as "wedding etiquette,"[109] "funeral etiquette,"[110] "norms for consoling friends,"[111] "manners when entertaining women,"[112] and "attire, food, and the palace system."[113]

Other figures than Yu Kil-chun exhibited an interest in Western etiquette; even the Korean Empire's Ministry of Education, which was establishing a new education system, paid attention to this topic. In 1866, the ministry published a Chinese version and a Korean translation of the book *Manners and Customs*[114] by John Fryer, a British missionary who was active in China. In this book, John Fryer defined etiquette as something that "corrects the unruly bad habits and maintains peace among people.[115] *Manners and Customs* addressed the

---

106 Oh, *Joseon Intellectual Society*, 23-24.

107 소중화론 or 小中華論, literally "Little China Theory."

108 서유견문 or 西遊見聞, literally "Observations and Experiences From a Journey to the West." Yoon Gil-chun's travelogue, where he recorded his experiences in the West.

109 혼례의 예절 or 婚禮의 禮節

110 葬事의 예절 or 葬事의 禮節

111 붕우 상교하는 도리 or 朋友 相交하는 道理

112 여자 접대하는 예모 or 女子 接待하는 禮謨

113 의복 음식 및 궁실의제도 or 衣服 飮食 및 宮室의制度; Jae-Young Heo (허재영), "A Study of the Seoryesuji from the Point of View of Speech Education [화법 교육사 차원에서 본 『서례수지』연구]," *Journal of Rhetoric Research [화법연구]* 29, (2015): 216-219.

114 서례수지 or 西禮須知, literally "Things to Know about Western Etiquette."

115 John Fryer (프라이어, 존), *Understanding Western Etiquette [서례수지 or 西禮須知]*. Edited by Heo Jae-young [허재영] (Kyungjin [경진출판], 2015), 11.

following question: "How can customs be the same in every country around the world?".[116] This book aims to provide a detailed explanation of the differences between Western etiquette and the etiquette of the "East," whether in the context of introductions, farewells, or other customs. Furthermore, it acknowledged that etiquette can vary not only across specific nations but also over time.[117]

Beginning in the late 19th century, Joseon intellectuals began to visit Japan and America, a situation which gave rise to new intellectuals such as Yu Kil-chun and Yun Chi-ho (尹致昊, 1865-1945). Fukuzawa Yukichi's (福澤諭吉, 1835-1901) book *An Outline of a Theory of Civilization*[118] ignited a debate regarding the civilization and enlightenment of Joseon and had a significant impact. This social atmosphere was further heightened by the entry of American missionaries into Joseon in the 1880s to spread Protestantism.[119] These people formed the second layer of Christian ethics, representing Western barbarians (오랑캐 or 洋夷). During this period, new studies (新學) and old studies (舊學) coexisted, with new studies being viewed as "civilization-enlightening studies" (문명개화하는 학문 or 文明開化하는 學問) and old studies being viewed as "futile studies" (虛學, literally "empty studies") or traditional studies (傳統學問).

Another path toward the achievement of civilization and enlightenment was the acceptance of Christianity. The theory of civilization endorsed by the *Tongnip Sinmun* (독립신문 or 獨立新聞, literally "Independence Newspaper") and the *Maeil Sinmun* (매일신문 or 每日新聞, literally "Daily Newspaper"), which were founded and run by influential figures such as Seo Jai-pil (서재필

---

116 Translated from the Korean, which reads as follows: "세계 각국에 풍속이 부동ᄒ니 이 곳에서 힝ᄒᄂ 례가 엇지 다쳐에 합당ᄒ리오"

117 Fryer, *Understanding Western Etiquette*, 225.

118 문명의 개략 or 文明論之概略, literally "An Overview of Theories of Civilization." An 1875 essay in which Fuzukawa described his theory of civilization. The work was influenced by François Guizot's *Histoire de la civilisation en Europe* (1828), as well as Henry Thomas Buckle's *History of Civilization in England* (1872-1873). In *Outline*, Fuzukawa described civilization as a concept that is relative to both the specific time period and the circumstances of a society. It is also relative in comparison to other societies. For instance, at that time, China was considered to be relatively more civilized than certain African colonies, while European nations were viewed as the most advanced and civilized of all.

119 Hyun-Bum Cho (조현범), *Civilization and Barbarism - 19th Century Joseon seen from the Perspective of the Other [문명과 야만 타자의 시선으로 본 19세기 조선]* (Book World [책세상], 2005), 109.

or 徐載弼, 1864-1951, also known as Philip Jaisohn)[120] and Yun Chi-ho (윤치호 or 尹致昊, 1864-1945),[121] who were Christians in the late 1890s, were based on the recognition of Christianity as the core of Western civilization.

This interest in Christianity was the result of the perception that most civilized nations were Christian countries. In an editorial in the *Tongnip Sinmun* dated December 23, 1897 and an editorial in the *Maeil Sinmun* dated May 28, 1898, Christianity was proclaimed to be the essence of civilization, and the editorials emphasized that the Christian faith encompassed honesty, fairness, goodness, and love. The papers highlighted the Christian doctrine of equality, which deepened the level of trust between the king and the people and expanded the freedom of individuals.[122]

Newspapers emphasized the superiority of Christianity by juxtaposing it with Confucianism. For instance, they argued that although Koreans innately possess a good character, many people have lost their natural virtues and prefer to do wrong due to the corrupting influence of flawed Eastern learning. They also argued that even with respect to traditional values such as filial piety and propriety, if one genuinely believes in Christianity, this belief rectifies all wrongs and injustices. Furthermore, they claimed that core Confucian virtues such as *Inŭiyeji* (인의예지 or 仁義禮智)[123] and *Hyojech'ungsin* (효제충신 or

---

120 Seo Jae-pil, also known as Philip Jaisohn, initially attended church to learn English after escaping to the United States following the failed Gapshin Coup. However, his faith gradually deepened, and he became a devout Christian. He passionately propagated Christianity due to his belief that if the Korean people genuinely believed in Christianity, they could attain complete salvation through the power of God. Cho, *Civilization and Barbarism*, 2005, 109.

121 Yun Chi-ho was initially exposed to Christian ideas while studying in Japan and began to believe in Christianity after he was required to flee to Shanghai following the failure of the Gapshin Coup. He converted to Christianity in 1887 and traveled to the United States in 1888, where his study of Christianity solidified his Christian-centric attitudes. He believed that the power that created American civilization and democracy was Christianity. At the time, he thought that Christianity represented the only way to promote national education and restore the morale of the people, given the incompetence of the Joseon government. Dae-Hwan Roh (노대환), *Civilization, Assimilation [문명]*, 소화 (2010).

122 Ibid., 153.

123 仁義禮智 or 인의예지, pronounced "Inŭiyeji." Core values in Confucianism, such as benevolence and compassion toward others, righteousness and moral integrity, the observance of proper conduct and social rituals, and the pursuit of wisdom and knowledge. "仁" (인) refers to "benevolence," "humanity," or "compassion.", "義" (의) represents "righteousness," "justice," or "morality.", "禮" (예) signifies "propriety," "etiquette," or "rituals.", "智" (지) means "wisdom" or "knowledge."

孝悌忠信)[124] can be achieved through Christianity.[125]

In Park Hae-nam's article "A Study on the Formation and Character of Protestant Ethics during the Korean Empire," he argued that the Christian ethics imparted by the missionaries in Korea were essentially the ethical principles to which they themselves adhered. In 1897, the ethical standards stipulated by the Methodist Mission (감리교 선교부 or 監理敎 宣敎部) for their believers included compliance with family ethics, asceticism and restraint, and dedicated work. Reports from missionaries emphasized the fruits of their mission: followers ceased to engage in practices such as drinking, smoking, ancestor worship, early marriage, and extravagant celebrations, instead adhering to Christian ethics.[126]

The primary objective of the early missionaries who visited Korea was to convert Koreans into 'the citizens of God's kingdom' (하나님 나라의 백성), as viewed from the perspective of 'Christian Civilization Theory' (기독교문명론 or 基督敎文明論).[127] These missionaries perceived the process of Christianization (conversion) and the advance of civilization as identical. Evidence of their intent to preach only the Pietist faith can be detected in their positions on hygiene and laziness. The missionaries also viewed habits such as alcohol consumption, gambling, and smoking as detrimental and aimed to change these daily habits and rituals in an effort to promote a new ethical standard. In essence, the missionaries believed and put into practice the idea that the advancement of civilization is achievable through the introduction of new life orders, societal principles, and ethical standards.[128]

---

124 효제충신 or 孝悌忠信, pronounced "Hyojech'ungsin." Core ethical principles and virtues upheld in Confucian philosophy. These values emphasize the importance of showing respect and devotion to one's parents, maintaining harmonious relationships with one's siblings and peers, remaining loyal to one's superiors and country, and exhibiting trustworthiness and sincerity in one's actions and words. "孝" (효) refers to "filial piety" or "respect for parents and elders.", "悌" (제) represents "brotherly respect" or "respect for siblings and peers.", "忠" (충) signifies "loyalty" or "faithfulness.", "信" (신) means "trustworthiness" or "sincerity."

125 Roh, *Civilization, Assimilation,* 155.

126 Haenam Park (박해남), "A Study on the Formation and Character of Protestant Ethics during the Korean Empire [대한제국기 개신교 윤리의 형성과 성격에 관한 연구]," *News from the Korean Christian History Research Institute* [한국기독교역사연구소소식], no. 81 (2008): 3-16.

127 Oh, "Christian Ethical Thought," 292.

128 Refer to the following: Cho, *Civilization and Barbarism,* 114, 143, 157; Oh, "Christian Ethical

The "second layer" of Christian ethics can be elucidated in various ways, including through the examination of the practices of Protestant missionaries, the study of the books of Christian doctrine that they authored or translated, and the exploration of teachings regarding ethics or Christian ethics in Christian educational institutions. Two initial Christian doctrine books offer insight into this subject, namely, *Sŏnggyo Ch'walli* (셩교촬리 or 聖教撮理 (1890), literally "Organizing the Principles of a Sacred Doctrine") and *Kŭriseudo Mundap* (基督問答 or 그리스도 문답 (1893), literally "Questions and Answers on Christ").

However, these sources are limited in certain ways, as revealed by Lee Jang-hyung. These doctrinal books do not encompass the complex dimensions of Christian ethical teachings, such as the relationship between Christianity and the state or the political responsibilities and participatory roles of Christians.[129]

In contrast, a more comprehensive view of Christian ethics is presented in the Methodist catechism *Mi-i-mi-serye Mundap* (미이미세례문답 or 嬰兒洗禮問答, literally "Questions and Answers on Infant Baptism"). This Methodist doctrinal book incorporates teachings that span both personal and societal ethics, thereby offering a more complete perspective on Christian ethical principles.[130]

During the time of the Korean Empire and the period of Japanese rule, systematic instruction on Christian ethics and Western ethics was implemented in Christian educational institutions. At the Pyongyang Presbyterian Theological Seminary (평양장로회신학교 or 平壤長老會神學校), the missionary Reverend Charles F. Bernheisel (편하설 or 片夏薛) taught ethics in 1903.[131] Moreover, Engel (왕길지 or 王吉志) lectured in the context of a four-hour ethics course that students took during the second semester of the second year according to the 1910 curriculum of the Pyongyang Presbyterian Theological Seminary.[132]

Thought," 292.

129 Jang-Hyung Lee (이장형), *The Korean Acceptance and Establishment of Christian Ethics [기독교윤리학의 한국적 수용과 정립]* (Bookorea [북코리아], 2016), 77.

130 Ibid., 87.

131 Kwak Shin-Hwan (곽신환), "The Path of Justice and Care of Yun San-on (尹山溫; George S. McCune 1873-1941) ["윤산온(尹山溫; George S. McCune 1873-1941)의 공의와 배려의 행로"]," *Korean Christian Culture Studies [한국기독교문화연구]* 9, (2017): 54.

132 Lee, *The Korean Acceptance and Establishment*, 45.

Reviewing the 1909-1910 syllabus of Soongsil University reveals that Dr. Baird (배위량 or 裵緯良), who held doctorates in both philosophy and theology, taught ethics or moral philosophy. However, in the 1912-1913 syllabus, it appears that missionary W.E. Smith (심익순 or 沈翊舜), a Princeton alumnus, taught ethics.[133]

In the 1912-1913 Soongsil University curriculum, Reverend Charles F. Bernheisel, a professor in the humanities department, taught philosophy, logic, Christian sociology, modern history, and other subjects. After 1913, he became responsible for the ethics and moral philosophy lectures that had been handled by the missionary Smith. The modern scholar Kwak Sin-hwan speculated that *The Elements of Ethics* (1895) by James Hervey Hyslop[134] was adopted as the primary textbook for the ethics course at Soongsil University

The primary textbook used in schools within the Presbyterian Church system to teach ethics or moral philosophy was Daniel Seely Gregory's *Christian Ethics: or the Moral Manhood and Life of Duty (1897).*[135] *This text* was translated into Korean by missionary William L. Swallen (소안론 or 蘇安論) in 1915. This text is significant because it differs from the theology and ethics texts used during the transitional modern period and because it is an ethics textbook written in Korean.

Other notable works focusing on personal ethics include James Stalker's *The Ethic of Jesus: according to the Synoptic Gospels (1929),*[136] Henry C. King's *The Example of Christ* (1929)[137] and *Christian Humanism* (1934),[138] and Theodore Stanley Soltau's (소열도 or 蘇悅道) *Guidance for a Pious Life* (1936),[139] which

---

133 Jie-Seok Oh (오지석), "Metamorphosis of Philosophy Education during Korea's Modern Transition Period: Focusing on the Experience of Pyongyang Soongsil ["한국 근대전환기 철학교육의 메타모포시스: 평양 숭실의 경험을 중심으로"]," *Humanities and Social Sciences [인문사회21]* 21, (2020): 498.

134 James Hervey Hyslop (August 18, 1854 - July 1, 1920) An American professor who taught logic and ethics at Columbia University. He wrote several influential works, including the following: *The Elements of Logic: Theoretical and Practical* (1892); *The Elements of Ethics* (1895); *The Problems of Philosophy: Or, Principles of Epistemology and Metaphysics* (1905)

135 Korean title: 도덕학

136 Korean title: 그리스도륜리표준

137 Korean title: 그리스도 모범

138 Korean title: 기독교인생관

139 Korean title: 신자생활의 첩경

was written to guide believers toward a devout life.

In terms of Christian social ethics, Walter Rauschenbush's *Social Principles of Jesus* (1930)[140] and D.A. McDonald's *The Social Idea of Christianity* (1926)[141] were introduced or translated by Protestant missionaries. These books are the key Christian texts on ethics that were introduced or translated by Protestant missionaries. As a result, Christian ethics, which were believed to lie on a different level than Western ethics, began to be transplanted and developed in Korea.

3. Conclusion: The Path of Christian Ethics

This research, which originated based on Park Gyu-su's reflections on *Tongbang Yeŭijiguk* (동방예의지국 or 東方禮儀之國, literally "Eastern Land of Courtesy"), presents two tiers of Christian ethics, namely, Western learning ethics (서학윤리 or 西學倫理) and Protestant ethics (개신교윤리 or 改信敎倫理). Both types of ethics were introduced to East Asia by Western "barbarians" (오랑캐 or 洋夷), and each unfolded in different forms; in addition, an approximately 200-year gap separates these two types of ethics.

This research sought to achieve three primary objectives. First, it extended the scope of Korean Christian ethics to include Western learning ethics and the works of Protestant missionaries, examining how Christian ethics could supplant the Confucian concept of *ye* (예 or 禮, "ritual propriety") during the era of the Korean Empire (대한 제국기) or the mid-to-late 1800s (개항기 or 開港期, literally the "opening ports time period"). It also investigated interest in Western etiquette during the time of the Korean Empire, introduced ethical issues relevant to Confucian society of the time, and traced the attempts of missionaries to propose Christian ethical solutions to these issues.

Second, this research sought to investigate various writings, including travel records, that were related to Christian ethics with the goal of focusing on research in the humanities rather than strongly emphasizing the history of

---

140 Korean title: 야소의 사회훈, Translated by Go Young-hwan (고영환).

141 Korean title: 기독교사회사상

concepts.

Third, this study attempted to provide insights into multicultural issues by illustrating the process by which certain ideas can be assimilated by a heterogeneous group, even in a context in which Koreans dismissed the thoughts and practices of individuals from other cultures as 'barbaric.'

Thus, by highlighting the relevant issues of the time, this study attempted to demonstrate how certain ideas found a place within heterogeneous groups and sought to obtain insights into multicultural issues. One regrettable limitation of this research is that it failed to trace the influence and content of works such as *Todŏkhak* (도덕학 or 道德學, literally "Morality Studies") by the missionary William L. Swallen (also known as Soanron or 소안론), who played a crucial role in the modern translation of the term "ethics" into Korean and the establishment of this discipline in the modern Korean context as a distinct academic field. Omitted works include but are not limited to Volumes I and II of Pastor Ji Soowang's (지수왕 목사) *Ethics* (윤리학) and Han Chi-Jin's (한치진 or 韓稚振, 1901-Unknown) *Expanded Introduction to Ethics* (증보 윤리학 개론 or 增補倫理學槪論). All of these texts played significant roles in the establishment of the modern meaning of the term "ethics" and the identification of ethics and Christian ethics as separate fields of study is Korea's modern transitional space.

Rather than focusing on the history of concepts, future research should aim to capture the conflicts, rejections, and acceptance that occurred in everyday life when Western Christian ethics were introduced to Korea, focusing more closely on storytelling and narratives.

Part 2.
The Aspects

Red Yongjeong [LONGJING]

Geographical Manifestation of Socialist Ideology of the Yongjeong Movement in the 1920s

QIAN Chunhua

1. Introduction

The epicenter of the Korean community in Manchuria is known to be Kando (간도間島, Jiandao), and Yongjeong (용정/龍井, Longjing) is considered to be the Seoul of Kando. This is a fact that most people are familiar with. However, people are generally not familiar with the cultural and spatial characteristics of Yongjeong itself. The significance of Yongjeong can only be partially understood through a series of materials, including literary works. For instance, we can refer to a part of Park Gye-ju's book "Aeroyŏkchŏng" (애로역정 or 愛路歷程) as an example:

Indeed, at that time in Yongjeong, there were elementary schools scattered throughout the city, such as Jungang, Yeongshin, Dongheung (東興), Donga, Haesung, and Myeongshin (明信女學校), to cater to secondary schools such as the oldest Yeongshin Middle School (before Yun Heo-su 尹和洙 and Zheng Shi-bin 鄭士斌 conspired to sell Yongshin Middle School to the Gwangmyeonghui (光明會), Dongheung (東興), Daesung (大成), Eun Jin (恩眞), Myeong Shin [Girls' School] (明信女學校), and Gwangmyeong Girls' High School (光明高等女學校). Thus, Yongjeong was soaring as the cultural center of Kando.

···(redacted)···

Although Yongjeong, in terms of population, commerce and industry, or the property of its citizens, lagged far behind cities like Pyongyang, Busan, or Daegu, it could be considered the second city after the capital in terms of the number of Korean educational institutions it had at that time. Apart from the fact that Jungang School[1] was public, Eunjin Middle School and Myeongshin Girls' Middle School were mission schools run by the Canadian Mission, and Haesung School was run by German Catholics. All the other schools were operated by Koreans.

In addition, there were schools everywhere, including the Chinese-run Cheng Sheng (成盛) School, Chinese middle schools and elementary schools in the Haegwan district (해관촌), the Gwangmyeong Language School (광명어학교) and Gwangmyeong Women's School (광명부인학교) run by Hidaka Heisiro (일고병자랑 or 日高丙子郎), and the state-run Sim Sang Elementary School and the Jo Dong Special Elementary School (조동종별원학교), among others. The *Kando Daily* (간도일보 間島日報), a Korean daily newspaper published in Hangul, was operated by Sun Woo Il (선우일 鮮于日), a Korean entrepreneur. Additionally, the *Kando Shinbo* (間島新報 간도신보) was published in Chinese characters, and the Min Sheng Bao Company (民聲報社 민성보사) published a daily Korean version alongside its Chinese edition. These publications contributed to the city's cultural landscape.[2]

These passages provide an overview of Yongjeong in the 1920s, at the height of its prosperity. The aspect that stands out most notably is the abundant number of schools in the city. The educational environment of Yongjeong was exemplary because its nickname of "the No. 2 Education City after Seoul" was not unwarranted.

Yongjeong was also not considered a cultural city, as evidenced by the simultaneous publication of three newspapers in this small area. The Korean newspaper The Kando Daily (間島日報), the Japanese newspaper The Majima

---

1 Jungang School (중앙학교), literally means "the central school."

2 Park Kye-Joo (박계주), *Park Kye-joo Literature Collection 3: Love and Passion, Virgin Land* [박계주문학전집3: 애로역정, 처녀지] (Samyoung Publishing House [삼영출판사], 19756), 67-8.

[Kando] Shinpō (間島申報), and the Chinese newspaper The Min Sheng Bao (民聲報), which consisted of both Chinese and Korean versions, were all in circulation. This not only reflects the cultural atmosphere of Yongjeong but also serves as an important component in examining its diverse ethnic constituents. Despite the brevity of the abovementioned quoted passages, they sufficiently suggests that Yongjeong was a hub of education, culture, and commerce. However, Yongjeong of the 1920s was perhaps best characterized as a "city of ideology." The main objective of the current study iwas to provide a fresh understanding of "Red Yongjeong" in the 1920s, which was an era when socialist ideology was rapidly disseminated yet underresearched.

To date, studies on Yongjeong have been predominantly fragmentary and event-centric, revolving around the Yongjeong 3.13 Anti-Japanese Protest,[3] the 150,000 Won Incident,[4] the well-known Cheongsanri Battle, and the Bongo-dong Battle. Based on these studies, the year 1920 has been appraised as the zenith[5] of the North Kando independence movement, concurrently earning North Kando the moniker "the Mecca of the Korean Independence Movement." Indeed, while these significant events were the embodiment of the anti-Japanese sentiment of the Kando Koreans, they came with a harrowing cost. The storm that ensued culminated in the Gyeongsin Massacre, which commenced in October 1920. The Gyeongsin Massacre consisted of the genocide of Kando Koreans by the Japanese military, and it marked a turning point for Korean society, with a noticeable decline of armed struggle and the emerging prominence of socialist ideology.

There have been several related studies on Manchurian socialism. Notable examples include the works of Shin Joo-baek (신주백), Hwang Min-ho (황민호), and Cui Fenglong (최봉룡). Their research[6] focuses primarily on the Korean

---

3   Byung-Seok Yoon (윤병석), "The 3 - 13 Movement in Yongjeong, Yon-Byon, and 「The Declaration of Chosun Indenpendent」 [북간도 용정 3.13운동과 조선독립선언서포고문]," *Korean History Review [사학지]* 31 (1998); Jang-Won Ahn (안장원), "Exploration of the Yongjeong 3.13 Movement [용정 《3.13》 운동에 대한 탐구]," *The Korean Diaspora Journal [동포논총]* 3 (1999).

4   Byung-Ryul Pan (潘炳律), "Reinterpretation of the 150,000 Won Incident in Kangdō (Gando) [간도(間島) 15만원 사건의 재해석]," *Journal of History and Culture [역사문화연구]* 12 (2000).

5   Moon-Sik Choi (최문식), "The Peak of Armed Anti-Japanese Independence Struggle: 1920 [반일 무장 독립 투쟁의 최고봉: 1920]," *Journal of Humanities [인문논총]* (1996).

6   Ju-Baek Shin (신주백), "The Korean Socialist Anti-Japanese Move-Ment in the 'Kan-Do(間島)'

Communist Party's Manchuria Bureau from 1926-1928; the Dongman Youth Federation (東滿靑年總聯盟),[7] which was which was active prior to the establishment of the Manchuria Bureau; and the evolution of religious awareness during the socialist movement in Korean society in Manchuria.[8] Shin Joo-baek's research examines a broad range of activities and policies related to socialist movements in the Kando region in the mid-1920s; these activities were carried out mainly by youth movements, thereby offering a comprehensive overview of various factional activities within the socialist movement in the Kando region. On the other hand, Hwang Min-ho minutely reveals the formation and activities of the Dongman Youth Federation, based on Yongjeong, thereby emphasizing the significance of organizational growth within the socialist movement.

While these achievements are certainly important in the history of socialist movements in the Kando region, it was not until relatively recently, i.e., in 2017, that substantial research began to emerge on the critical Kando Communist Party Incident. With the initiation of serious research[9] into the first Kando Communist Party Incident and an overview[10] of the changes in the anti-Japanese struggle strategy of Korean socialists in Japan in the 1920s, the study of socialist movements in the Kando region has made significant strides. Recently, studies have also emerged that examine how religious people accepted socialist ideas as socialism spread in the early 1920s using the example of Cheondogyo.[11]

Region, 1926~1928 [1926~28년 시기 간도지역 한인 사회주의자들의 반일독립운동론]," *The Journal of Korean History [한국사연구]* 78 (1992).

7   Min-Ho Hwang (황민호), "Trends of Korean Socialist Movements and the Eastern Manchuria Youth Federation in the 1920s [1920년대 재만한인 사회주의운동의 동향과 동만청년총연맹]," *Journal of Studies on Korean National Movement [한국민족운동사연구]* 40 (2004).

8   Fenglong Cui (최봉룡), "Korean Social Movements and Religions in 1920~30s' Manchuria —Focused on Understanding of Religions [1920~30년대 만주지역 한인사회주의운동과 종교]," *Journal of Studies on Korean National Movement* [한국민족운동사연구] 62 (2010).

9   Byungdo Choi (최병도), "Organization of the Joseon Communist Party Manju Chongguk Dongmanguyeokguk and the Frist Round of Gando Communist Party Incident [朝鮮共産黨 滿洲總局 東滿區域局 조직과 제1차 間島共産黨事件]," *Journal of Studies on Korean National Movement [한국민족운동사연구]* 90 (2017).

10   Sun-Seob Park (박순섭), "Shifts in Anti-Japanese Struggles by Korean Socialists in the 1920s [1920년대 재만한인사회주의자들의 항일투쟁 노선 변화]," *Journal of Studies on Korean National Movement [한국민족운동사연구]* 90 (2017).

11   Kyu Tae Cho (조규태), "National Movement of Cheondogyo and Cheondoists in North Gando, 1920~1925. [1920년대 전반 북간도의 천도교와 민족운동]," *The Korea Journal of Donghak Studies [동학학보]* 57 (2020).

While these studies approach the history of socialist movements in the Kando region from the perspective of individual groups, organizations, and events, they do not pay much attention to Yongjeong, which was the epicenter of these movements. This paper aims to map the geography of socialist ideas in Yongjeong, which played a crucial role in the reception of these ideas and was referred to as "Red Yongjeong."

To this end, this paper will focus on the Religion Rejection Movement, the Dongyang Academy Incident, and the Yongjeong 5.30 Riot of 1930, all of which occurred in Yongjeong but have received little attention to date. This paper will pay more attention to the pathways and processes of the influx and dissemination of socialist ideas that can be contemplated through these events rather than an analysis of these events themselves. This will be an important task in understanding the Yongjeong locality of the 1920s, which was different from that of the 1910s, when various ideologies, including Christianity, were introduced simultaneously as Yongjeong formed its spacial identity.

2. The Influx of Socialist Ideology and the Religion Rejection Movement

The Religion Rejection Movement (종교배척운동) in Yongjeong has been mentioned in several related studies. Cui Fenglong focused on the Anti-Religion Movements 반종교운동)[12] while discussing the process of religious perception changes in the Korean socialist movement in Manchuria. According to him, the Anti-Religion Movement in Kando was systematically carried out under the direction of the Manchuria Bureau of the Korean Communist Party, and it happened primarily in schools founded by religious organizations. On the other hand, Kim Ju-yong paid attention to the Anti-Religion Movement by focusing on students' demand for the separation of religion and education while examining aspects of student movements in the North Kando region in the first half of the 1920s.[13] As seen in the preceding studies, the Religion

---

12 Bong-Ryong Choi (최봉룡), "Korean Social Movements and Religions in 1920~30s' Manchuria − Focused on Understanding of Religions [1920~30년대 만주지역 한인사회주의운동과 종교]." *Journal of Studies on Korean National Movement* [한국민족운동사연구] 62 (2010).

Rejection Movement in Yongjeong has been mentioned sporadically but has not yet been systematically treated. This paper renames the Anti-Religion Movement mentioned in the above texts as the Religion Rejection Movement" and emphasizes that this event was not a one-time episode but rather an important event that permeated the mid-1920s and was continuously carried out with a focus on each school in the Yongjeong area.

The Religion Rejection Movement was made possible in Yongjeong because many schools were established by religious groups; this was confirmed in the work of Kim Tae-guk. According to him, although the mainstream Kando region in the 1920s was focused on socialist ideology, the forces that led Yongjeong before the socialist ideology became mainstream were religious groups, as shown by the Middle School Construction Movement (중학교건설운동).[14]

As mentioned earlier in this work, the Gyeongsin Massacre in 1920 consisted of the genocide of Kando Koreans by the Japanese military; in the process, almost all the Korean neighborhoods and schools in the Kando area were reduced to ashes. However, the Gyeongsin Massacre could not extinguish Kando Koreans' passion for education; soon, the School Reconstruction Movement began.

The representative schools established during this period included Eunjin Middle School,[15] which was founded on February 4, 1920, by Canadian Presbyterian Church missionaries; Daesung Middle School,[16] which was

---

13 Joo Yong Kim (김주용), "The Characteristics of Student Movements in the Northern Gando Region in the Early 1920s [1920년대 전반기 북간도지역 학생운동의 양상]," *Journal of Korean modern and contemporary history [한국근현대사연구]* 51 (2009).

14 Taiguo Jin (김태국), "The social and cultural conditions and the movements of establishing Middle school in LongJing in 1920's [1920년대 용정의 사회 문화 환경과 중학교 설립운동]," *The Historical Association for Soong-Sil [숭실사학]* 25 (2010).

15 The Eunjin Middle School was established on February 4, 1920. It was named Eunjin (恩眞), meaning "learning the truth through God's grace," or "하느님의 은혜로 진리를 배운다" in Korean. The establishment of Eunjin Middle School cannot be separated from the missionary work carried out by the Canadian Presbyterian Church missionaries in Yongjeong. In 1913, foreign missionaries including the Canadian Presbyterian Church missionary Parker (빠카), who later took the Korean name "Park Geol" (박걸), also established the Jechang Hospital (제창병원 or 濟昌病院) to treat the diseases of their congregants and set up the Bible College (성경서원 or 聖經書院) and Myeongsin Girls' School (명신여학교) to educate the children of their congregants. They also carried out several other charitable works. See: Saeng-Cheol Han (한생철), "26 Years of Wind and Cloud Change: Eunjin Middle School [26년의 풍운변화: 은진중학교]," in *Yanbian Literature and History Materials [연변문사자료] Vol. 6* (Yanbian, China: Yanbian People's Publishing House [연변인민출판사], 1988), 45.

established on July 11, 1921, by the Daesung Confucianist group; Dongheung Middle School,[17] which was founded on October 1, 1921, by Cheondogyo believer Choi Ik-ryong; and Yeongshin Middle School,[18] which started anew on September 14, 1921, by taking over the Guangdong dormitory from the Central Church of the Presbyterian Church in Yongjeong. While most of these schools were reconstructed by religious organizations, the operation of schools by religious foundations did not last long.

Beginning in approximately 1922, the Religion Rejection Movement began to erupt fiercely in middle schools in the Yongjeong area, and the school that took the lead was Daesung Middle School. It was customary at Daesung

---

16 Daesung Middle School was a school established by the Daesung Confucian community. In the early 1920s, Seokhwa Jun (석화준 or 石華俊) of Daesung Confucianism and Changse Im (임창세 or 任昌世) of Cheonglim Church, both of whom were prominent figures in Yongjeong, proposed the establishment of a middle school. They raised funds for the establishment of the school from adherents of various Confucian and Cheonglim churches, local tycoon Nam Gun-pil 남군필 or 南君弼), various regions in Northeast China and Russian Primorsky Krai, and over 4,000 people from various parts of Korea. With the funds raised, they built a two-story brick and wood building in the 4th district of Yongjeong Village, and on July 11, 1921, they held the official opening ceremony for Daesung Middle School. At the time of the school's establishment, Kang Hun (강훈 or 姜勛) was the principal, and Lim Bong-gyu (임봉규 or 林奉圭), Hyun Ki-hyeong (현기형) and others were invited as teachers. See: Saeng-Cheol Han (한생철), "A Place of Learning Boiling with Revolutionary Zeal: Daesung School [혁명적 열의로 들끓던 배움터: 대성학교]," in *Yanbian Literature and History Materials [연변문사자료] Vol. 6* (Yanbian, China: Yanbian People's Publishing House [연변인민출판사], 1988), 28.

17 On April 15, 1921, they first established Dongheung Elementary School under the name of Cheondo Religion Institute (천도교종리원 or 天道教宗理院), and set up a middle school lecture in this elementary school. On October 1 of that year, they promoted the middle school lecture to Dongheung Middle School, and the original elementary school became an affiliated school of Dongheung Middle School. The school expenses were mainly supported by donations from within Korea and local donations, as well as students' monthly fees. See: Jong-Hong Lee (리종홍), "The Road Walked with Many Ups and Downs: Dongheung Middle School [파란곡절을 걸어온 길: 동흥중학교]," in *Yanbian Literature and History Materials [연변문사자료] Vol. 6* (Yanbian, China: Yanbian People's Publishing House [연변인민출판사], 1988), 3.

18 The predecessor of Yeongsin Middle School was Gwangdong Dormitory (광동서숙). In the fall of 1909, Yoon Sang-cheol, from Hoeryong, Korea, came to Yongjeong Sae Village (currently located near Yongjeong Station) to participate in the harvest and bought a straw-thatched house to set up as a school, calling it 'Gwangdong Dormitory'. He entrusted its management to his nephew, Yoon Myung-hee (윤명희(尹命熙), and hired Kim Yong-geun (김용근 or 金容根) as a teacher to admit approximately 30 children. Then, on September 14, 1921, they transferred the Gwangdong Dormitory to the Yongjeong Presbyterian Church Central Church and restarted as a new school, naming it 'Yeongsin School.' (영신학교) The school system was set for four years of elementary and two years of high school. See: Bong-Gu Lee (리봉구), "On the Difficult Path of National Education: Yeongsin Middle School [민족교육의 어려운 길에서: 영신중학교]." in *Yanbian Literature and History Materials [연변문사자료] Vol. 6* (Yanbian, China: Yanbian People's Publishing House [연변인민출판사], 1988), 63.

Middle School, which andwas founded by Daesung Confucianists, to observe Confucius Day on the first day of each month. On the first day of April 1922, the school prepared for Confucius Day as usual. However, not a single student attended. Following this action, the students demanded reforms from the school authorities on the condition of separating religion and education and carrying out a union sabbatical. Four days after the union sabbatical, the students' opinions were accepted, resulting in the expulsion of the Public Confucian Society (공교회).[19] Moreover, in the case of Dongheung Middle School, the transfer of school management rights was carried out legally through the organized activities of the teachers instead of through a union sabbatical. In July 1924, a group of teachers led by Lim Gye-hak was organized, and on August 11, the school management rights were received by the group of teachers in the name of the founder's association.[20] Following the Religion Rejection Movement at Daesung Middle School in 1922 and at Dongheung Middle School in 1924, the movement started at Eunjin Middle School in 1926:

> The anti-religious movement in Eunjin began in the fall of 1926 during a 4th-grade Bible class. When the pastor preached, 'Whoever rebels against authority is rebelling against what God has instituted, and those who do so will bring judgment on themselves (Romans 13:2),' a student named Yeo Chang-bin asked, 'Then, is the authority of the Japanese who invaded our country also given by God?' The pastor, struck dumb, left the classroom without finishing the lesson. The students demanded that the school authorities dismiss this pastor and threatened a union sabbatical if the request was not granted. The school had no choice but to dismiss the pastor

Next, on March 18, 1927, during the 5th graduation ceremony of Eunjin Middle School, the school authorities declared they would not award a graduation certificate to a problematic student named Choi Sung-hee. This led the 2nd- and 3rd-grade students to boycott their classes and go on a union sabbatical. Despite this, the

---

19 Han (한생철), "A Place of Learning Boiling with Revolutionary Zeal," 31.

20 Lee (리종홍), "The Road Walked with Many Ups and Downs," 7.

school authorities, including teacher Lee Tae-jun, did not comply with the students' demands. Finally, on April 25, about 150 students declared, 'We do not intend to go to heaven,' collectively dropped out, and transferred to Daesung Middle School and Dongheung Middle School.[21]

As seen from the abovementioned brief account, the organized anti-religious struggle, including the students' union sabbatical at Eunjin Middle School, did not fully develop until the fall of 1926. However, despite the union sabbatical nature of the students, Eunjin Middle School did not give in, and many students ultimately transferred en masse to Dongheung and Daesung, thereby bringing an end to the Religion Rejection Movement at Eunjin Middle School. The Rreligionus Rejection Movement by students who were relayed to several schools from 1922 to 1926 was not resistance without reason. In fact, these changes were directly related to the influx of socialist ideology:

> After the Gyeongsin Massacre, anti-Japanese sentiment surged in the village. Songs with revolutionary content, such as 'The Shipjin Song'(십진가) and the 'Peasant Liberation Song' (농부해방가) were spread throughout the village, along with songs like 'Religion is the Opium of the People', and 'Science Liberates Humanity.' Pamphlets like *Paris Commune* (빠리꼼뮨), *Criticism Theory* (매도론 or 罵倒論), *Three Thousand Miles* (삼천리), and *Criticism* (비판), and books introducing *The Story of Lenin* and Soviet pioneers were passed among students.[22]

As the newly founded socialist ideology began to spread among schools in Yongjeong, there was a growing sentiment to liberate schools from the shackles of religion. Young men from Myeongdong who were studying in Yongjeong also began to propagate this new ideology and advocated for schools to break free from the control of religion. The voices of Myeongdong school graduates and masses opposing the church's control over schools grew louder. In 1924,

21 Young-Sub Kim (김영섭), "Alliance Suspension and Anti-Japanese Movement [동맹휴학과 항일운동]," in *Eunjin 80-Year History [은진80년사]* (Eunjin Middle School Alumni Association [은진중학교동문회]. Kormadeo [코람데오], 2002), 115.
22 NO SOURCE LISTED

Kim Saguk, a famous Korean socialist, stayed in Myeongdong and advocated for new ideologies on several occasions, and Song San-woo, a graduate of the Myeongdong School, also conducted underground activities for the Korean Communist Party from Yanbian to Myeongdong. The struggle against religious control of schools became even more intense.[23]

This memoir clearly tells us that in the Yongjeong area, the influence of socialist ideology was forming a strong current. This movement can be dated as early as the immediate aftermath of the Great Kanto Earthquake and no later than approximately 1923; this timeline roughly aligns with official records. According to *The History of the Korean Communist Movement Vol. 1* by Kim Jun-yeop and Kim Chang-soon, the influx of socialism in the Manchurian region can be pinpointed around the establishment of the "Korean Communist Party Manchuria Branch" in May 1926. In contrast, Lim Kyung-suk estimates that the influx of socialism into the Manchurian region occurred from March 1921 to April 1922, stating that the earliest organized force was the group of socialists who later came to be known as the Shanghai faction.[24] This claim by Lim is largely consistent with the records in *Documents of Yanbian Literature*:

> The first Korean communist, Yi Dong-hwi (리동휘 or 李東輝), and others sent various pamphlets and copies of the underground magazine 'The Dawn Bell' to many middle schools in Ryongjeong [Yongjeong]. Between 1922 and 1923, Dongheung and Daesung, two middle schools, saw the formation of an extracurricular study group called the Gwangmyeong Association, focused on studying Marxism. Comprised of about 30 members, including some students from Eunjin Middle School, the members of the Gwangmyeong Association studied under the guidance of Lee Ju-ha (리주하), Lee Rin-gu (리린구 or 李麟求), and others, usually on nights or Sundays.
>
> (redacted)
>
> In 1922, individuals like Park Yun-seo and Ju Cheong-song came from

---

23 Lee, "The Road Walked with Many Ups and Downs," 88-9.

24 Gyeong-Seok Im (임경석), The Origins of Korean Socialism [한국 사회주의의 기원] (Goyang: *Historical Critique Publishing* [역사비평사], 2014).

Soviet-ruled Liaoning Province to [Yongjeong], uniting progressive students from Dongheung Middle School to form the Social Science Research Society and the Friendship Association. They utilized their free time to study and promote Marxist ideology. Initially, a group of ten students who shared the same intent quietly carried out their activities in a private house. This group rapidly expanded to about fifty members, conducting their activities openly in classrooms."[25]

As seen in the above records, the influx of socialist ideology generally took place between 1922 and 1923. Small groups such as the Gwangmyeong Association and the Social Science Research Society, which were centered around Dongheung and Daesung Middle Schools, were formed to study Marxism. The route of socialism's influx seems to have stemmed from the Liaoning region, which is not surprising given Yongjeong's geographic proximity to Russia. In the early to mid-1920s, students made up 38.8% of Yongjeong's population,[26] with a considerable number of students from both Korea and Russia's Liaoning Province studying in Yongjeong. Given this, it seems that the spread of socialist ideology in Yongjeong occurred quite naturally among the students.

Eunjin Middle School had a significant number of students from Liaoning Province in Russia, accounting for a staggering 10% of the total student body. Among them were individuals who had already experienced the Russian October Revolution and supported Marxist ideology. These students passed around books among themselves and actively promoted revolutionary ideas through reading groups and friendship associations. This socialist influence infused the young people of the Yongjeong area with a scientific worldview based on Marxism-Leninism.[27] In this context, religion was deemed unscientific and considered "the opium of the masses," hence something that should be rightfully rejected.

---

25 Lee, "The Road Walked with Many Ups and Downs," 4-5.

26 Taiguo Jin (김태국), "The Social and Cultural Conditions and the Movements of Establishing Middle School in LongJing in 1920's [1920년대 용정의 사회 문화 환경과 중학교 설립운동]," *The Historical Association for Soong-Sil [숭실사학]* 25, (2010): 199.

27 Han, "26 Years of Wind and Cloud Change," 47.

The Religious Rejection Movement that spread in the Yongjeong area from 1922 to 1926, with young students as the main actors, can be regarded as successful. The separation of religion and education was accomplished in most religiously founded schools, excluding Eunjin Middle School, and these schools were able to operate independently. Yongjeong, which is geographically located close to Russia, which served as the origin of socialism at the time and had an educational environment second only to Seoul in the 1920s, rapidly embraced socialist ideas and was emerging as "Young Yongjeong." However, this radical atmosphere did not last long. First, a series of natural disasters in 1924-1925 drove most schools into financial difficulty, and the suppression of socialist forces by Japanese colonial rule began to actively occur. The widespread crackdown on socialist and communist forces by Japan was most visibly manifested in the Kando Communist Party Incident in particular.

3. The Dongyang Academy Incident and the Spread of Socialist Ideas

The Kando Communist Party Incident refers to the four massive crackdowns on the Korean Communist Party that occurred in the Yongjeong area from September 1926 to May 1930. However, as seen in the review of previous related research, apart from the first Kando Communist Party Incident, no detailed or meticulous related research has been conducted. Nevertheless, one event that demands attention in understanding the geography of socialist ideas in Yongjeong is the Dongyang Academy Incident, which occurred in Yongjeong in 1923:

> In March 1923, Kim Saguk, an early Korean socialist revolutionary, came to Yongjeong from the Soviet Union's Maritime Province. In collaboration with Bang Hanmin, Kim Jeonggi, and Lee Myunghee, he established the Dongyang Academy as an affiliated school of Daesung Middle School and started the school in March with about seventy young students, primarily the first graduates of Daesung Middle School. The Dongyang Academy was the first place in Yanbian to introduce Marx-Leninist revolutionary theory as a basic subject and establish new proletarian democratic education.[28]

As described above, the Dongyang Academy was established in March 1923 by Kim Saguk, Bang Hanmin, Kim Jeonggi, Lee Myunghee, and others as an affiliate of Daesung Middle School in Yongjeong. The Dongyang Academy Incident refers to the arrest of these Dongyang Academy officials by the Kando Consulate in Yongjeong village from July 3rd to 5th, 1923.[29] According to official reports, they planned to throw a bomb at the Consulate Building on July 8, destroy the building, assassinate key officials, and distribute socialist propaganda during the ensuing chaos. Interestingly, this bomb-throwing incident is reported in slightly different ways. According to Yanbian Cultural Material VI (Page 33), the individuals planned to bury a bomb in the yard of the Japanese Consulate in Yongjeong and detonate it. Some research in Korea confirms that they intended to plant a bomb on the Cheondo Line of the Kyungp'ung Railway, which was scheduled to open at that time, thereby disrupting it. Finally, Dong-A Ilbo reported that they planned to throw a bomb to blow up the consulate and assassinate associated people. From this information, we can infer that this incident was likely a plot by Japan to dismantle the Dongyang Academy from the outset because the Dongyang Academy was the first educational institution to promote socialist ideas and train socialists.

Numerous articles related to the Dongyang Academy Incident were founddated prior to and after the outbreak can be found. As seen from these articles, the Dongyang Academy was already under close surveillance by the Japanese authorities as a propaganda agency for socialist ideas before the incident occurred. According to an article published in the Maeil Sinbo on May 25, 1923, three students of the Dongyang Academy were detained for a year starting on the 23rd for promoting communism at a lecture.[30] Furthermore, Dong-A Ilbo reported that the Dongyang Academy planned to offer courses with titles such as Introduction to Philosophy, Western History, Philosophy History, Ethics,

---

28 Han, "26 Years of Wind and Cloud Change," 32.

29 "Confidential No. 210: On the Case of the Insidious Conspiracy of Communist Koreans [機密 제210호: 共産主義 鮮人의 不逞陰謀事件 檢擧에 관한 件]," *Miscellaneous Cases related to Insurgency Group: Koreans' Part, Koreans and Radicals [不逞團關係雜件: 朝鮮人의 部 鮮人과 過激派]*, Jul. 9, 1923.

30 "Three Students of Dongyang Academy Arrested [東洋學院 生徒 三名 押送]," *Maeil Shinbo [매일신보]*, May 25, 1923, 3.

Pedagogy, Theories on Western Civilization, Theories on Business Management, Economic Development History, Social Evolution Theory, and History of Western Social Movements in seasonal lectures; however, the first lecture tour in Hoeryeong was canceled due to the arrests[31]of Kim Jeonggi and Park Wonhee.[32]

As can be seen, the Dongyang Academy in Yongjeong was recognized as a training ground for socialist factions and was identified as a faction of Bang Hanmin that planned the Korean Independence Conspiracy and promoted nationalism and communism. Furthermore, it is notable that the Dongyang Academy, while connected to the Korean Communist Party of Idonghui and Park Jinsun and the Korean National Front Korean Youth Association, was recognized as the "source of ideology" on both the Chinese and Korean sides.[33]

After the Dongyang Academy incident, Kim Saguk was released due to lack of evidence, but Bang Hanmin was identified as the main instigator of the Dongyang Academy incident and was sentenced to ten years in prison.[34] He served his sentence in Daegu prison and escaped in June 1928. However, contrary to the facts, Kim Saguk was the leader of the Seoul Communist Group; in 1923, he was elected a central committee member at the representative meeting for the establishment of the Korean Communist League. Following the conference resolution, he was dispatched to the Far East Committee of

---

31 Park Won-hee (박원희) was the wife of Kim Saguk (김사국). She married Kim on July 15, 1921, and after their marriage, she accompanied her husband on a study trip to Japan. She returned from Japan in early 1923, and after moving to Yongjeong with her husband in April 1923, she worked as an English teacher at Dongyang Academy. However, while staying in Hoeryong, Hamgyongbuk-do to promote the summer course of Dongyang Academy on July 4, 1923, she was arrested by the police. She was released on September 29, 1923, in a preliminary trial with prosecution suspended. She was a figure who practiced the women's liberation movement, and it is presumed that she was influenced by her older brother Park Kwang-hee and her husband Kim Saguk's socialist thoughts. See: Mi-Kyung Ahn (안미경), "Women's Liberation Movement and Women's Liberation Thought of Park Won-hee in the 1920s [1920년대 박원희의 여성해방운동과 여성해방사상]," *Journal of Studies on Korean National Movement [한국민족운동사연구]* 74 (2013): 176-8.

32 "Unexpected Police Arrest Interrupts Dongyang Academy's Parade [동양학원순강, 의외의 경찰에 구인되는 화로 중지]," *Dong-a Ilbo [동아일보]*, Jul 15, 1923, 4.

33 "Confidential No. 174: On the Establishment of the Third International Communist Party Propaganda Department in Korea [機密 제174호: 朝鮮內의 第三國際共産黨 宣傳部 設置에 관한 件]," in *Miscellaneous Cases related to Insurgency Group - Koreans' Part - Koreans and Radicals Vol. 4 [不逞團關係雜件-朝鮮人의 部-鮮人과 過激派 4]*, Jun. 6, 1923.

34 Myung-Hyuk Jun (전명혁), "Bang Han-Min's Media, Education Movement and National Liberation Movement under the Japanese Imperialism Occupation [일제하 方漢旻의 언로-교육운동과 민족해방운동]," *Sarim [사림]* 44 (2013).

the Comintern Executive Committee in Vladivostok to obtain the approval of the Korean Communist Party. However, Kim Saguk failed to obtain the approval of the Comintern and came to Yongjeong in March 1923 to establish the Dongyang Academy along with Bang Hanmin and others.[35] As seen from this, the Dongyang Academy was a political ideology training center aimed at cultivating revolutionaries among the Koreans in Yongjeong, which was attempted by members of the Seoul Communist Party in Yongjeong.

The establishment of the Dongyang Academy in Daesung Middle School was not a coincidence. At the time, Daesung Middle School already had a Marxist study group called the Gwangmyeong Society (광명회 光明會). The Gwangmyeong Society was a Marxist research group formed under the guidance of the communist Lee Ingoo (이인구 or 李麟求) and Lee Juhwa in 1922. Initially, the research group had only approximately ten members, but as students from Dongheung Middle School and Eunjin Middle School began to join, their membership increased to approximately thirty. Later, they openly studied Marxist theories in the classroom. This was possible because many of the students who had entered Daesung Middle School already had Marxist pamphlets, such as "The Dawn Bell" (새벽종), which was translated and published by Yi Dong-hwi in Shanghai.[36] In this way, socialist ideas were already being rapidly introduced into Daesung Middle School, and they were rapidly spreading through active study groups. The establishment of the Dongyang Academy further accelerated this learning atmosphere and the influx of socialist ideas.

The Dongyang Academy was eventually closed due to suppression; however, this certainly did not suppress the spread of socialist tendencies. On October 28, 1926, the Korean Communist Party's Dongman Regional Office was established in Yongjeong. The Dongman Regional Office not only strove to secure party members and establish subordinate organizations to expand the party but also actively participated in the establishment of the National Party, preparations for armed struggle, and the movement to establish private middle

---

35 Myung-Hyuk Jun (전명혁 全明赫), "Life and National Liberation Movement of Gyea Kwang Kim [解光 金思國의 삶과 민족해방운동]," *Journal of Korean Modern and Contemporary History* [한국근현대사연구] 23 (2002).

36 Han (한생철), "26 Years of Wind and Cloud Change," 29.

schools.[37] Under the leadership of Jo Bong-am, the Dongman Regional Office of the Korean Communist Party was established in Yongjeong, and it hads nine districts and sixteen branches, with four branches located at Dongheung and Daesung Middle Schools.[38]

In April 1927, the Daesung Middle School Youth Federation (대성중학교 청년총연맹) was established at Daesung Middle School, and on April 11, the Daesung Middle School Boys' Assembly (대성중학교 소년총회) was formed with Lee Hwan as the head. In July 1927, a joint school branch under the Korean Communist Party's Dongman Regional Office was established at Daesung Middle School, with Principal Park Jaeha appointed as the responsible secretary.[39] On September 20, 1927, the first meeting took place at the house of Jeong Jaeyoon (정재윤 or 鄭在允), with the leaders of each middle school organization and the heads of the Dongman Regional Office of the Korean Communist Party in attendance. A second meeting was convened on October 2; however, at approximately 11 pm that night, the location was unexpectedly raided by the Japanese Consulate's police in Yongjeong, and 28 people were arrested on the spot. This was the first Kando Communist Party Incident.[40] In September 1928, the second Kando Communist Party Incident occurred, resulting in 72 arrests in Yongjeong alone.

The Dongyang Academy stood out for its attempt to promote and propagate socialist ideology through direct education in a school setting rather than through the traditional method of party member development through organizational connections. The academy not only served as an organized and planned institution for the promotion of socialist ideas but also aimed to serve as an institution for the spread of socialist ideas and the training of socialist activists. Although it was short-lived, its significance had a significant impact. After the Dongyang Academy Incident, Kim Saguk sought to re-establish the

---

37 Byungdo Choi (최병도), "Organization of the Joseon Communist Party Manju Chongguk Dongmanguyeokguk and the Frist Round of Gando Communist Party Incident [朝鮮共産黨 滿洲總局 東滿區域局 조직과 제1차 間島共産黨事件]," *Journal of Studies on Korean National Movement* [한국민족 운동사연구] 90 (2017): 252.

38 Lee, "The Road Walked with Many Ups and Downs," 6.

39 Han (한생철), "26 Years of Wind and Cloud Change," 34.

40 Ibid., 34-5.

Daesung Academy in a similar way in Ningguta (닝구타or寧古塔). With the establishment of the Dongman District of the Korean Communist Party in Yongjeong, the spread of socialist ideas became increasingly rapid. However, after experiencing the first and second Kando Communist Party Incidents, the Dongman District of the Korean Communist Party was disbanded, and organized activities became increasingly difficult. However, the radicalizing activities of "Red Yongjeong" persisted.

In August 1925, news articles reported attempts to distribute propaganda in Yongjeong city to influence Kando and the surrounding areas. This included a report on the large-scale distribution of communist propaganda in Yongjeong city on August 27 by the CK Party and the Korean Communist Party, which caused major disturbances.[41] On April 1, 1927, a report announced that several influential party members had been dispatched from the Korean Communist Party headquarters in Haesamui (해삼위) to establish a branch in Kando.[42] Reports related to May Day celebrations were also frequently found in newspapers. A May Day commemorative lecture was planned by various social organizations in Yongjeong city in May 1927 but was stopped due to police prohibitions. Nevertheless, the organizers did not give up the event and changed it to a rally format, with hundreds of people gathering at the Daesung School stadium at approximately 10 am on May 2, when they were moving to the Yongjusa temple to proceed with the event.[43]

As seen from these series of articles, the socialist movement in Yongjeong was steadily maintained on a small and intermittent scale. However, with the establishment of Manchukuo in 1932, a large-scale purge of anti-Japanese forces took place, which forced most of the participants, including socialist organizations, to turn underground. The last stand in this process was known

---

41 "CK Group Members Also Participate, Kando Redness Plan, Distributing Numerous Leaflets in Yongjeong City and Turning Kando into Redness! Electric Fist Group Case Public Trial [CK 團員도 參加, 間島赤化計劃, 용정시에서 선면문 다수를 배포하고 간도 일대를 적화려든 사건! 電拳團 事件 公判]," *Dong-a Ilbo [동아일보]*, Oct 7, 1925.

42 "Korea Communist Party Sneaking Activity in Longjing, Activity in Various Places in Kando [高麗共産黨 龍井에 潛入活動, 間島 각디에 활동]," *Dong-a Ilbo [동아일보]*, Apr 1, 1927.

43 "Longjing May Day Grand, Organized by Various Social Organizations, First Large Demonstration in Kando [龍井메이데이盛大 각사회단테련합주최로 間島初有의 大示威]," *Jungwai Ilbo [중외일보]*, May 8, 1927.

as the 5.30 Riot of 1930.

4. The 5.30 Riot and the Change in Direction during the Socialist Revolution

The Yongjeong 5.30 Riot of 1930[44] was an armed uprising that unfolded over three days from May 29 to 31 to commemorate the fifth anniversary of the 5.30 Massacre.[45] The main targets of this armed struggle, which initially centered around Yongjeong, were the Japanese Consulate, the Dongchuk Company, Korean immigrant associations, and pro-Japanese landlords. What stands out about this incident is that, unlike traditional socialist organizations, this activity took the form of armed struggle. In fact, the Yongjeong 5.30 Riot inflicted significant damage on Japanese colonial rule:

> On the night of May 30, about 100 civilians, led by Kim Chul and Kang Hakje, broke into the electric company in Yongjeong carrying axes, clubs, and petroleum. They knocked down the security guard and destroyed the resistance and current meters of the power distribution board. Yongjeong and the Dudo city center were plunged into darkness. Civilians near Daebul-dong cut off telephone lines, severing communication between Hwaryeong, Daeripja, and Yongjeong. One team attempted to attack the steam locomotive at Yongjeong station but failed due to strong defense. Another team entered the city and set fire to a part of the

44 The Yongjeong 5.30 Riot is referred to in various ways such as the Gando Uprising, the Gando Incident, the Gando 5.30 Incident, and the 5.30 Uprising. However, this paper wishes to emphasize its nature as an armed riot and thus calls it the 5.30 Riot, as it was initially referred to.

45 On May 14, 1925, when workers at the No. 12 factory in Shanghai went on strike, the Japanese manager of the No. 7 factory closed the factory doors on the evening of the 15th to block the workers' support for the No. 12 factory strike. As a result, Gao Jinghong, the representative of the No. 7 factory workers and a member of the Communist Party, requested negotiations with the factory side. However, not only did the Japanese side refuse to negotiate, but they also shot and killed Gao Jinghong. In response, on the 30th, approximately 2,000 workers and students in Shanghai marched in protest, and the incident led to a tragic result where the Chinese authorities deployed police to brutally suppress the protesters, leading to 13 deaths, 15 severe injuries, and over 50 arrests. This event is referred to as the 5.30 Massacre in Chinese history. See:So-Jeon Yang et al. (양소전 외 4명 저, 김춘선·김철수·안화춘 옮김), *History of the Revolutionary Struggle of the Chosonjok in China* [중국조선족혁명투쟁사] (Yanbian, China: Yanbian People's Publishing House, 2009), 280.

102

iron factory of Dongjeom-bok and the house of grain merchant Kim Myung-hee. Kang Hakje and several others threw two explosives into the office of the Japanese East Sea Company's Kando branch, one of which exploded, leaving the office in shambles.[46]

According to preliminary statistics, nineteen pro-Japanese landlords' houses were burned, four railway bridges were destroyed (making it temporarily impossible for trains to pass), and ten telephone lines were cut off (interrupting communication). Additionally, one power plant was destroyed, causing power outages in the Yongjeong and Dudo regions, and five substations of the Japanese consulate and several offices of the Korean immigrant association were reduced to ashes. The 5.30 Riot had significant meaning as an activity jointly developed by the Chinese Communist Party (CCP) and the Korean Communist Party to revive and develop the party organization in the Yanbian region.[47]

The establishment of the Chinese Communist Party organization in Yongjeong dates back to early 1928. In February 1928, the Chinese Communist Party's Manchuria Provisional Committee dispatched Zhou Dongjiao to establish a Party organization in the Yanbian region. Zhou Dongjiao began building a Party organization based on the *Min Sheng Bao* in Yongjeong. As a result, the Chinese Communist Party's Dongman District Committee was established in August 1928, and propaganda activities focused on young people were startedpromoted through a column called *Hwang Won* ("Deserted Garden," 황원 or 荒園) in the *Min Sheng Bao*.[48] Following the announcement of the Comintern's December Theses and the proclamation of the "One-Country, One-Party" principle, the Chinese Communist Party's Manchuria Committee actively promoted the Korean Communist Party in Manchuria to join the Chinese Communist Party. The CCP Yanbian Special District Committee was established in Hwaryeong in February 1930, and on April 24, the Yanbian

---

46 Min-Sung Baek (백민성), "The May 30 Riot [5.30폭동]." In *Yuseo deep Haeran River [유서 깊은 해란강반]* (Yeongbyeon People's Publishing House [연변인민출판사], 2001), 27.

47 Chang-Soon Kim (김창순), "The May 30th Riot in Kangdō and the CCP's Manchuria Detachment [간도 5·30폭동과 중공당의 만주유격대]," *Journal of North Korean Studies [북한학보]* 13 (1989).

48 Yang et al. (양소전 외 4명 저, 김춘선·김철수·안화춘 옮김), *History of the Revolutionary*, 261-2.

Special District Committee organized the May Day Struggle Action Committee, declaring the "Red May Struggle." They placed former Korean Communist Party members Kim Hanbong (김한봉 or 金漢峰) and Kim Pyeongcheol (김평철 or 金平鐵) on the Action Committee.[49]

On May 1, 1930, approximately 400 handicraft workers in Yongjeong staged a joint strike and conducted anti-Japanese protests. Then, on May 29, Korean farmers in the Samdo district of Hwaryeong County were the first to engage in the riot, setting fire to Japanese institutions and the Korean Immigrant Association, as well as scattering flyers, which marked the beginning of the 5.30 Riot. In this way, the 5.30 Riot remained the last fortress of the dark age, showing successful cooperation between the Chinese and Korean Communist Parties; it was evaluated as an opportunity to successfully realize the incorporation of the Korean Communist Party into the Chinese Communist Party. However, this cooperation and subsequent incorporation were already underway. According to an article in the *Jungwae Ilbo* (중외일보 or 中外日報) on May 6, 1930, students from three schools (Daesung School, Dongheung School, and Eunjin School) went on a joint leave of absence and distributed propaganda in both Chinese and Korean under the name of the Chinese Communist Party.[50]

After the explosion of the 5.30 Riot in 1930, Nakamura Gento personally inspected the Yongjeong area (from January 16 to February 1, 1931) and submitted a report titled

"Inspecting the Villages of Longjing on Jiandao Island: Mourning the Weakness of Diplomacy toward China" (published by Japan of the Continent, 1931). In this report, he conducted a survey on the living environment of Koreans in the Kando region centered around Yongjeong and the economic situation in Kando. According to his statistics, of the 600,000 Koreans in Manchuria, 400,000 lived in Kando, most of whom were engaged in agriculture; it was also found that the majority were tenant farmers.[51] Nevertheless, the Kando

49 Ibid., 277-8.

50 "Communist Party Distributes Proclamations, Three School Students Take a Day Off, Numerous Subversive Propaganda Distributed [共産黨은 檄文配布 三校生은 休校 불온선전문 다수 배포]." *Jungwai Ilbo [중외일보]*, May 6, 1930.

51 Gentō Nakamura (中村玄濤), *Visiting the Villages of Longjing on Jiandao Island: Mourning the Weakness of Diplomacy towards China [間島龍井村地方を視察して: 對支外交の軟弱を悲しむ]*

region centered around Yongjeong was evaluated by Nakamura Gento as "unstable Kando." This instability primarily originated from Kando's geographical location. He reported that the geographical location of Kando, located close to Russia, and Japan's position, which was not tough in its diplomacy with China, resulted in this view of an "unstable Kando." It is clear that this was a political issue with the 5.30 Riot in mind. From Japan's standpoint, Kando was seen as unstable, and Yongjeong was seen as disorderly. In the end, "unstable Kando" and "disorderly Yongjeong" remained diplomatic issues that had to be solved through strong diplomacy.

In fact, this instability had an inseparable relationship with a series of incidents that occurred before and after the Yongjeong 5.30 Riot. Therefore, the Yongjeong 5.30 Riot was not a sudden occurrence but rather a planned armed riot based on the atmosphere and background of Yongjeong; it was also an event that signaled the incorporation of the Korean Communist Party into the Chinese Communist Party.

5. Conclusion

As explored above, in the 1920s, Yongjeong was a hub for education and culture, as well as a stronghold for socialist ideologies. This image of Yongjeong washas been confirmed through a closer look at the underexplored anti-religion movement, the Dongyang Academy Incident, and the 5.30 Riot. The Religion Rejection Movement, which occurred around middle schools located in the Yongjeong region from 1922 to 1926, sequentially erupted at Daesung School, Dongheung School, and Eunjin School. These schools became epicenterscentres because they were all run by religious foundations. In particular, the vigorous anti-religion movement during this period was directly related to the influx of socialist ideas. The Daesung and Dongheung Schools, which can be called hotbeds of socialist thought, were schools where student groups for studying socialist ideas actually existed; at the Eunjin School, it was confirmed that

(Japan: Tairiku No Nihon Hachi-Sha [大陸之日本八社], 1931).

socialist ideas were propagated mainly due to the influence of students admitted from the Yanbian Province. As confirmed through the anti-religion movement, the influx of socialist ideas in Yongjeong began approximately 1922; when this influxit was mainly affiliated with the Korean Communist Party based in Yanbian.

Moreover, the Dongyang Academy Incident, which occurred during the unfolding of the anti-religion movement, wasalso highlighted the influx of another socialist group into Yongjeong. The Dongyang Academy Incident was an attempt by the Seoul faction of the Communist Party, led by Kim Saguk, to develop an organization in Yongjeong. Although the organization existed for a short time, the Dongyang Academy Incident was noteworthy because it attempted to cultivate socialist elements through direct educational institutions, unlike the conventional method of developing party members through cell organizations.

Finally, the 5.30 Riot is a noteworthy event because, above all else, it was a successful cooperative activity between the Chinese Communist Party and the Korean Communist Party, and it symbolized ingthe event that ultimately led to the successful incorporation of the Korean Communist Party into the Chinese Communist Party. As seen from the abovementioned information, in the 1920s, Yongjeong was a region where various socialist organizations ebbed in and out; above all else, it was a region with the potential to successfully lead cooperative activities with the Chinese Communist Party. In the 1920s, Yongjeong was known as "Red Yongjeong"; it can be said that this was indeed an era of socialist ideology.

Korean Transformation of Western Christian Nationalism:

Biblical Nationalism in Modern Korea at the Turn of the 20th Century

MA Eunji

1. Introduction

The historical significance of the Reformation can be found in the rediscovery of the Bible and its influence on the formation of nationhood[1] as a precursor for the establishment of modern nation-states. Unlike in previous eras, the rediscovery of the Bible that took place in the early 16th century was a crucial catalyst for sparking and spreading the Reformation in Europe. Although the reformation was initially intended to focus on spiritual salvation, it inadvertently led to the emergence of Protestant nations and the formation of states. Biblical narratives and political models of the time did not uphold separation between church and state, so the unity of the One Holy Catholic Church was disrupted,

---

[1] The term "nationhood" signifies the status where a group acquires the qualifications to be recognized as a nation. However, it also encompasses the state where individuals and the nation are unified, and thus can be defined as 'national awareness that arises through the identification of individuals and the nation'.

See Anthony D. Smith, *Ethno-Symbolism and Nationalism: A Cultural Approach* (London & New York: Routledge, 2009).

Note: Translated into Korean by In-Joong Kim (김인중), 족류상징주의와 민족주의 (서울: 아카넷, 2016), 38.

and new national church principles were proclaimed in every country. This ultimately became the driving force for the birth of new Protestant states. Biblical ideas of liberation, covenants, chosen people, and promised land served as the basis of Reformation-era political beliefs. To a significant extent, the Bible provided a fundamental vision of a world divided into unique and sovereign territorial nations. Historical events such as those that occurred in Europe between the 1500s and 1800s laid the foundation for the phenomenon of the nation and nationalist movements of the 19th and 20th centuries.

Nationalism is a psychological state in which one feels that the highest loyalty should be devoted to the nation. Other group identities existed before the emergence of nationalism, but the sense of belonging and collective loyalty to blood lineage, family, region, dynasty, and religious groups intersected and coexisted, making them difficult to call nationalism. In contrast, true nationalism values individuals' loyalty to the nation above all other group identities and allegiances. These identities and loyalties aim to __ unify and integrate within a community and support the goal of maintaining a nation as a single political unit. Gellner described this desire for political state building as "primarily a political principle, which holds that the political and the national unit should be congruent."[2] Throughout the process of realizing this principle in the real world, nationalism became an action-oriented practical program. Nationalism has existed as both an ideology and a historical movement aimed at forming and maintaining national identity and unity. The foundation of nationalism is the consciousness and awareness of national identity and nationhood. This is because national consciousness and emotional sentiment toward the nation play a role in sustaining nationalism, which is based on very clear doctrine, commandments, and classifications.[3]

If that is the case, what is "nationhood"? What constitutes consciousness of it? What is a "nation"? These concepts are at the core of nationalism, and definitions of the nation are generally divided into two categories based on the elements that compose a nation. According to *objective factors*, the nation

---

2   Ernest Gellner, *Nations and Nationalism* (Ithaca: Cornell University Press, 1983), 1.

3   Mun-Seok Chang (장문석), *The Taming of Nationalism* [민족주의 길들이기] (Seoul: Knowledge Landscapes, 2007), 39-40.

prioritizes homogenies of cultural commonalities such as lineage, language, customs, religion, and territory. In contrast, *subjective factors* consider nation members' collective or individual sense of belonging or desire to belong to be the primary criteria. However, relying solely on either objective or subjective factors as the sole determinant is challenging because the standards used by various nations to define themselves as unified national communities can vary depending on the time period and country.

Therefore, we can identify three universal characteristics that are inherent to the concept of the nation: historicity, ideological character, and the Western origins and evolving meanings of the term.[4] Nationalism is characterized not by the fixed, unchanging essence of a nation but rather by its dynamic nature, which is itself driven by intentional changes pursued for specific purposes. The concepts of "nation" and "nationalism" are closely intertwined, but they are not entirely synonymous due to differences in their origins, historicity, and ideological nature.

The concept of a nation and national consciousness, embodying universal traits implied in the notion of nationhood, are generally believed to have emerged in the Korean Peninsula around the late Chosun period. Depending on the scholar, this timeframe was either set around the Russo-Japanese War (1904-1905) (Baek Dong Hyun)[5] or slightly earlier around the Sino-Japanese War (1894-1895) (Andre Schmid).[6] The emergence of national consciousness and the concept of the Korean nation can be notably linked to the decline of the dynastic state and the transition toward a modern nation-state.

Liah Greenfeld, in her explanation of Western modernity, says that the 'path to modernity of five countries' was each country's process of creating nationalism and moving toward a modern state. She asserts, "rather than [defining] nationalism by its modernity··· modernity [is] defined by nationalism."[7]

4 Hong-Sik Cho (조홍식), "Reflections on the Concept of Nation: A Political Sociology Approach [민족의 개념에 관한 정치사회학적 고찰]," *Korean Political Science Review* 39, no. 3 (2005): 129-45.

5 Dong-Hyeon Baek (백동현), *Discussions on Nationalism and State Ideologies during the Period of the Great Korean Empire [大韓帝國期 民族談論과 國家構想]* (Research Institute of Korean Studies, 2010).

6 See Andre Schmid, *Korea Between Empires, 1895-1919* (New York: Columbia University Press, 2002), Translated into Korean by Chung, Yeo-Wool.

Greenfield's explanation can provide valuable insights when applied to the historical context of late Chosun Korea, where foreign invasions caused the country to be thrown into existential crisis in the late 19th century. Amidst this turmoil, a new political ideal called nationalism emerged in the form of national consciousness and national movements.

This research focuses on the influence of the Reformation on the formation process of modern states and nations in Western Europe. Using this understanding as a foundation, this study examines the early Christian Bible translations made during the late Chosun period and their significance. In particular, it looks at how these translations influenced the formation of the concept of the nation and nationhood among Koreans, especially Christians. Christianity[8] introduced a modern, Western-style way of thinking to Koreans in the late Chosun era. Furthermore, it fostered a heightened sense of Christian nationalism.[9]

In this process, the Bible played a central role as a mediator, providing not only a religious identity centeredcentred around personal salvation but also a unifying narrative and discourse of nationhood as a community. Since the advent of modern books in the Enlightenment era, Christian-related texts, especially translated bibles, have made up a significant proportion of all published books. Considering this fact, one can infer that the translation and dissemination of the Bible contributed to the formation of a sense of nationhood.[10] Hence,

---

7 Liah Greenfeld, *Nationalism: Five Roads to Modernity* (Cambridge: Harvard University Press, 1992), 8.

8 Here, "Christianity" means "Protestantism."

9 The term "Christian Nationalism" is discussed in the following sources:
Kenneth Wells, *New God, New Nation* (Sydney: Allen & Unwin Pty Ltd., 1990); Chung-Shin Park (박정신), *A New Understanding of Korean Christian History [한국 기독교사 인식]* (Hyean, 2004); Ki-Young Shin (신기영), "The Emergence of Christian Nationlism in Colonial Korea [일제하 한국 기독교 민족주의의 형성]," *Tonghap Yeongu* 8, no. 1 (1995).

10 Adrian Hastings, a British historian, showcases the feasibility of this logic. He explains nationalism in relation to religion. He suggests that the translation of the universal Latin Bible into the vernacular English Bible, and its subsequent widespread use, expanded the local sphere. As a result, an 'ethnie' - a cultural and linguistic community - became a nation. In other words, a specific local language produced specific literature, and as it changed from spoken to written usage, a specific ethnie in a certain environment transformed into a nation. From this perspective, it is worth noting the role of Christianity in Korea, which significantly influenced the modernization process through Bible translations into the vernacular language. Considering that the production of various literary texts, starting with the Bible translated into the vernacular, likely had a significant impact on the development

this paper aims to explore the role of early Bible translations in shaping the notion of nationhood among Christians in the Late Period of Chosun. It further examines how this notion manifested as practical biblical nationalism in subsequent periods. Consequently, this paper seeks to establish a comprehensive definition of the concept of biblical nationalism.

2. The Bible and the Concept of the Nation

1) The Concept of the "Nation" and Biblical Nationhood

It is possible to trace the emergence of the concept of the "nation" in Korea back to a particular time in history. There is still heated debate about when the term "nation" and the concept of a national consciousness made its debut on the peninsula. However, most scholars agree that the term "nation" (민족 or *minjok* in Korean) first appeared in print on January 12, 1900, in a letter to the *Capital Gazette* (황성신문 or *Hwangsŏngshinmun*, one of the peninsula's earliest Korean-language daily newspapers). By 1904, the Korean Empire was on the brink of ruin due to foreign imperialism, and the term *minjok* could be defined as a political conceptualization of the Korean nation.

When the term *minjok* appeared again in the Capital Gazette in November 1904, "nation" meant "the population of the Korean Peninsula." However, the meaning of the idea of "nation" deepened with time. By 1908, the word *minjok* was used to describe the Korean nation as a unique cultural and ethnic community,[11] also known as an "ethnie."[12] Around the year 1908, a concept

---

of the national language, it is persuasive to regard religion and language as core elements in the formation of a nation. See Adrian Hastings, *The Construction of Nationhood: Ethnicity, Religion and Nationalism* (Cambridge: Cambridge University Press, 1997), ch. 1, 1-34.

11 Young-Sun Ha (하영선), *A History of Social Science Concepts in Korea: From Tribute to Informatization [근대한국의 사회과학 개념 형성사]* (Changbi Publishers, 2009).

12 The term "ethnie" (족류공동체) is a resident group that shares cultural identity and language, while a nation (민족 or *minjok* in Korean) is a much more self-conscious community than an ethnic community that is unified through a common language. For this reason, ethnic communities have served as the foundation for the formation of nations. For a more thorough explanation of the term "ethnic group" (족류집단). See Chan Seung Park (박찬승), *The Formation Process of 'Minjok' Concept in Korea [한국에서의 '민족' 개념의 형성]*, Concept and Communication (Hallym Academy of Sciences, Hallym University, 2008). According to this article, the term "ethnic group" (족류집단)

that translates as "national essence preservation theory" (국수보전론 or 國粹保全論) began to shift the national identity away from one of "Dan'gun – Gija succession," an idea that had persisted throughout the Chosun Dynasty. Instead, it transcended into a unified and distinct national identity known as the *Dan'gunminjok* (단군민족 or 檀君民族).[13] The representative figure of "national essence preservation theory" was Sin Chae-Ho, also known as Tanjae (단재 신채호 or 丹齋 申采浩).

In his research about the Korean "nation" amid the great political upheaval between China and Japan from 1895 to 1919, Andre Schmid discovered the original form of Korean national identity and nationalism by tracking variations in the term minjok in major Korean newspapers from that time. Early writers attempted to reconceptualize the spatial and temporal boundaries of the nation within the universalism of the modern world. Schmid especially focused on finding the origins of the Korean nation within the rise of print capitalism, which was used as a methodological framework in Anderson's *Imagined Communities,* and the emergence of newspapers written in the national language.[14]

Moreover, Shin Gi-Wook says that the emergence of the specific concept of the nation as a form of group identity is "engraved in certain social relationships and history."[15] As the 19th century transitioned into the 20th century, two ideologies coexisted in Korea, which then went through a period of change in late Chosun. One was Pan-Asianism, and the other was nationalism. Both ideologies emerged as forms of resistance against the new wave of imperialism sweeping through Asia at the time. The nationalists, unlike the Pan-Asianists, redefined Korea's national identity as something distinct from that of China

---

was used in Korea until the mid-Choson Dynasty to distinguish Koreans from foreign ethnic groups such as the Jurchens and the Chinese. Chongnyu is said to carry the meaning of "fellow countrymen." For an explanation of the concept of ethnic communities in Western contexts, see: Eun-Ji Ma (마은지), *Rediscovering the Nationalism of Maurice Barrès [민족주의의 재발견: 바레스의 민족주의]* (Seoul: Samin, 2016).

13 "Korea and Manchuria [韓國과 滿洲]," *The Daehan Maeil Shinbo,* Jul. 25, 1908.

14 Schmid, *Korea Between Empires.* As translated into Korean by Yeo-Wool Chung (정여울), *제국, 그 사이의 한국* (서울: 휴머니스트, 2007), 57; In-Joong Kim et al. (김인중 외), *The Encounter of Current Civilizations [이제문명의 조우이다]* (Seoul Economic Management, 2009).

15 Gi-Wook Shin and·Michael Robinson, *Colonial Modernity in Korea [한국의 식민지 근대성]*, trans. Do Myeon-Hoe (Seoul: Samin, 2006), 27.

and Japan and sought to enhance this identity through reinterpretation of history and the use of the Korean alphabet, Hangul (한글). The nationalists conceptualized the term "nation" from an ethnic, cultural, and racial perspective. Against this historical backdrop, the term *minjok* emerged as a reaction to the supra-international concept of race and region that took the form of pan-Asianism.[16]

The arguments above confirm that the concept of the nation was gradually emerging in the consciousness of ordinary people by the end of the Chosun Dynasty. We can also assume that the emergence of the concept of the nation was in line with the perceptions of Christians at the time. In the face of competitive invasions by Western empires, various national movements emerged in Korea as part of defensive mechanisms that came about due to the historical desire for national salvation and the establishment of an independent state. We can infer these points from the Christian national movement, which was one of these national movements.

In contrast with Korea, the origins of the concept of "nation" in the West can be traced back to approximately the 14th century.[17] If we track the preceding terms used in various Biblical texts, the Hebrew Bible uses the words *am* and *goy* to express terms corresponding to "people" and "the nation" in English. Saint Jerome usually translated both *am* and *goy* as "gens" but sometimes translated them into Latin as *nation* or *populo* (see Psalm 106, Psalm 7:4, and Isaiah 1:4, Vulgate). Meanwhile, he translated the Greek word *"ethnos"* into Latin as *natio*.

A passage from Genesis 10:31 in which Saint Jerome wrote in Latin as "cognationes et linguas et regions in gentibus" was expressed in English by

---

16 See, Gi-Wook Shin, *Ethnic Nationalism in Korea: Genealogy, Politics, and Legacy.*

17 According to Hastings, English translations of the Bible and prayer books have consistently used the term 'nation' since the 14th century. This contributed to a strong sense of community and national consciousness among the English people. The term was repeatedly used, read, and memorized, and this fueled a strong sense of being part of a nation. For further reading, see:

Hastings, *The Construction of Nationhood*, 34.

Greenfeld, *Nationalism*, 4-9.

Eun-Ji Ma (마은지), "Nationalism in France [프랑스 민족주의]," *Soongshil University Historical Society* 20 (2007): 78-80.

Chang, *The Taming of Nationalism*, 49-50.

William Tyndale (an English religious reformer and Biblical translator who lived from 1492 to 1536) as "kindreds, languages, countries and nations." Meanwhile, translators working with John Wycliffe (an English religious reformer, who between approximately 1330 and 1384, was the first person to render the Bible into English), who worked on the Vulgate in the 1380s, denoted the Latin word *gentibus* into various terms such as "folks" or "nations."

Martin Luther of the Reformation period also worked on translating the Hebrew Bible into German. He used the words *eschlechtern, Sprachen, Ländern and Leuten*. Dutch translations used the word *volken*, while Swedish and Danish versions of the text used the word *folk*. As a result of the consolidation of these linguistic developments, the old English words "genge" (from Latin *gens*) and "lēode" (from German *leuten*) became obsolete during Tyndale's time. Instead, the Old English words "leuten," "volken," "volk," "folk," "people," and "nation" were widely adopted as the translated terms.[18]

The term "nation", as it is used in biblical texts, gained universality selectively and became widely used. Based on these linguistic choices, it is important to derive the meaning that these linguistic symbols represent. In other words, there is a need to read the Biblical narrative of Israel's nationhood as an important aspect of understanding cultural and political integration, as expressed in the Bible.

In Western history, the inception of modern nationhood can be traced back to the transitional period between the Middle Ages and the modern era. For instance, the emergence of Protestant nations in 16th century Europe is closely associated with the "rediscovery" of the Bible. This is because Martin Luther's Reformation changed the essence of the Bible in several important ways.

The Reformation elevated the reading of the Bible to the heart of the Christian religious experience. Before 1517, the Bible was largely inaccessible to common people living within the Latin Catholic cultural sphere. Moreover, very few individuals had read the full text of the Bible before 1517. Latin Catholic culture of the time emphasized alternatives to the Bible, such as paraphrases,

---

18 Diana Muir Appelbaum, "Biblical Nationalism and the Sixteenth-Century States," *National Identities* 15, no.4 (2013): 323.

summaries, and annotated books, which had been edited to emphasize the Christological interpretation of the Hebrew Bible. These Bible substitutes, which are mainly composed of the allegories of Christ, often omit or obscure content about "nationhood" that can be found in full-text bibles.

Martin Luther's call to return to the Bible as a part of "salvation through faith alone" brought new discoveries to Christians, who were encouraged by reading and hearing the Bible. This was possible because new Bibles were translated into the vernacular languages of each country. Access to the Bible was no longer limited to a select group of clergymen and nobles but was granted to the common people. This became possible because of the radical new authority that granted access to all the original texts of the Old and New Testaments to both clergymen and laypeople.

Moreover, the people were granted authority to engage in a new practice of reading the full text of the Bible aloud, so even the illiterate could construct a Biblical model of intimate nationhood from the pulpit of the parish church.[19] In short, the Bible presented an external model of social and institutional nationhood to clergy and lay people alike.

The contents of the Bible also suggested an evolved model of nationhood. Let us first examine the implied meaning of the term "nation." As mentioned previously, the Bible begins with a broad description of the world arranged with words such as "kindreds," "tongues," "lands," and "nations" (Genesis 10:20). Association of the nation with terms such as "kin," "language," and "territory" was a part of contemporary biblical discourse. Scholars later confirmed these concepts as important characteristics of the nation. Moreover, the Biblical word consists of righteous nations that enjoy equal sovereignty. God established boundaries between nations and placed special nations in various territories (Deuteronomy 2:5, 9).

Within this world of nations, the Bible tells the unique story of the descendants of Israel, who are depicted as a single family tracing their lineage back to their common ancestor, Abraham. However, Israel of the Bible is not a single tribe. Biblical Israel is a community that unites warring tribes through mutual

---

19   Ibid., 321.

covenants, absorbs diverse groups of people who are not kin, and even protects the right of foreigners to reside within Israel (Exodus 12:38).[20] The Bible speaks of fair, equal nations and covenant communities.

In the same context, Anthony D. Smith's research explores how biblical beliefs influence the creation of modern nations. He discusses various aspects of biblical political beliefs in both ancient and modern times. Among these are the Covenant, the Torah, the sanctity of the election, Exodus, the Messianic role of the sacred monarchy, and the dream of reaching the Promised Land. He refers to these political contents of the Bible as "covenant nationalism."[21]

Throughout the early modern period, countries such as Germany, the Netherlands, the Czech Republic, Denmark, Switzerland, Scotland, and England followed a similar historical path in which religious and political beliefs were closely intertwined. Despite the unique historical circumstances of late Chosun, when one considers the significance of biblical translation and dissemination, one can infer that this approach contributed significantly to instilling the concept of "nationhood" and fostering national consciousness on the Korean peninsula.

2) The spread of new intellectuals and national consciousness

We have now examined the temporal situations in which the term "nation" appears. In light of this, who, why and how was the concept of the nation and consciousness of nationhood created in that specific historical context? How was the "national consciousness" that existed in the emotional and psychological realms transformed into the more tangible "practical nationalism?"

During the late Chosun period, Korean nationalists focused on elevating their cultural heritage to establish a unique ethnic-based concept of the nation as an ideology of resistance against Western and Japanese imperialism. They placed value on the unique history and language of Korea, specifically the Korean vernacular language, above the heritage that was more widely shared across East Asia or the discourse of East Asian solidarity. Instead, they forged

---

20 Ibid., 322.

21 Anthony D. Smith, "Biblical Beliefs in the Shaping of Modern Nations." *Nations and Nationalism* 21, no. 3 (2015): 403-22.

a new identity and connection based on Korean nationhood. Korean nationalists elevated Hangul, an alphabetic script that had previously been considered the language of women and the lower classes, to the status of a distinct cultural heritage that sets Korea apart from the rest of East Asia and demonstrated Korea's advancement.[22]

Sin Chae-Ho, one of Korea's most prominent nationalist historians, sought to establish the foundation of the Korean nation's historical identity. He broke away from previous dynasty-centric narratives and provided a new description of an ethnic-based national history. Sin hoped to transform Koreans' existing identities in the face of Western and Japanese imperialism during the late Chosun period. This was necessary because certain literati and intellectuals advocated for Japanese colonialism, which would integrate Korea into Japan and justify Japanese rule by claiming to spread "civilization" and "enlightenment."

Sin Chae-Ho realized that, rather than leading the nation to salvation as originally promised, "civilization" and "enlightenment" were instead leading the Korean nation to destruction.[23] Therefore, he unites various strata that had been horizontally separated in premodern Korean society under the umbrella term "nation," granting a collective identity as "Korean" to this new concept.[24] Sin's nationalist historical narrative sought to redirect people's loyalty toward a new and inclusive identity as Koreans as a unique *ethnic* group rather than toward one's king, village, clan, or family or identification with one's hierarchical status as a *yangban* (noble), *sangmin* (commoner), or *nobi* (slave).[25] He revitalized the "national spirit" and reestablished Korean history as belonging not to the dynasty but rather to the nation.

Meanwhile, Ju Si-Gyeong (one of the founders of modern Korean linguistics), who revitalized the nation and the national consciousness through Hangul, showed his strong passion for the Korean script in a statement that "I hope

22 Shin, *Ethnic Nationalism in Korea*, 57.

23 Schmid, *Korea Between Empires*. As translated into Korean by Chung, 제국, 그 사이의 한국, 258.

24 Schmid, *Korea Between Empires*, 77-8; Henry Em, (헨리 임), *The 'Nation' as a Modern and Democratic Construct: Shin Chae-ho's Historical Narrative [근대적·민주적 구성물로서의 '민족: 신채호의 역사 서술]* (Samin, 2006), 472-3.

25 Em, *The 'Nation' as a Modern and Democratic Construct*, 447.

that our people will revere, love, and use our language and our script as the fundamental assertion of our country's foundation."[26] In other words, Ju believed that Hangul should be the foundation of a new national identity and encouraged the use of the script to make Korea a stronger country.

Various textbooks published in this sociohistorical context expressed thoughts like these, reflecting nationalistic interests and efforts. Such texts emphasized the importance of the nation's language, history, customs, heroes, and identity. In the process of advancing toward a modern state, the most prominent characteristic that can be used to call for national unity and integration is a shared language. Even the historian Eric Hobsbawm, who stands in the modernist camp in regard to the concepts of nation and nationalism, recognizes that language is an important part of nation-building. Hobsbawm argued that the process of modernization fundamentally involves homogenizing and standardizing the population through the use of a literary "national language."[27]

To summarize the discussions above, figures like Sin Chae-Ho and Ju Si-Gyeong sought to establish a national identity through history and language. They did this in the face of a national crises such as foreign invasion and encroachments on Korean sovereignty. Sin, Ju and those like them were part of a group of new intellectuals and thought leaders of the era. There is no doubt that the activities of this *nouveau intelligentsia*, including the "Enlightenment Faction" (*kaehwap'a* or 개화파) and those who adhered to Christianity, played a decisive role in the spread of national consciousness. However, so-called "nations" or "nationalism" that are uniformly manufactured from the top down are impossible to sustain without strong national sentiments or nationalism that grows from the bottom up, responding from below in the grassroots of everyday life.[28]

In his research on the spread of nationalism, Hobsbawm asserts that nationalism unfolds in three stages. The first stage is primarily driven by

---

26 Peter Lee, *Sourcebook of Korean Civilization, Vol. 2* (New York: Columbia University Press, 1998), 424-6.

27 Eric J. Hobsbawm, *Nations and Nationalism Since 1780* (Cambridge: Cambridge University Press, 1990). As translated into Korean by Myeong-Se Kang (강명세), *1780 이후의 민족과 민족주의* (서울: 창작 과비평사, 1994), 127.

28 Michael Billig, *Banal Nationalism* (London: Sage, 1995).

intellectuals. In this early stage, nationalism's ideological nature is strongly emphasized. In the second stage, nationalism gradually begins to spread to the middle class, becoming the ideology of various strata such as merchants, manufacturers, craftsmen and professionals. In the third and last stage, nationalism develops into a popular movement that spreads even to communities of peasants and laborers.[29] The nationalist movement of late Chosun was no exception to this: Korean nationalism was first led by intellectuals. Then, it spread to merchants and members of the middle class, and eventually spread to the entire nation.

Here, Greenfield's assertion that all forms of nationalism share one common feature must be considered. According to Greenfield, the essence of modern national identity derives from the notion of belonging to a "people." The fundamental characteristic of this identity is the definition of one "people" as one "nation." Therefore, all members of this redefined 'people' share characteristics associated with the upper classes. Consequently, citizens of a nation-state are perceived as fundamentally homogeneous, with distinctions in class or status regarded as surface-level differences. The modern phenomenon of conceptualizations of the "nation" exhibits some facets that are profoundly democratic. The identity that late Chosun intellectuals sought to establish was one in which the hierarchical and stratified divisions among people gradually dissolved and the "people" assumed a unified identity of "nationhood." These late Chosun intellectuals proposed a conceptualization of the nation as a historical and linguistic cultural community.

3. Book Publishing and Early Translations of the Bible

1) Book Publishing and Christianity

The Korean Enlightenment period (1879-1905) began after the country's ports were opened and signified a new social transition to a society that adopted and disseminated modern civilization. The spread of books in late Chosun

---

29 Eric J. Hobsbawm, "Introduction," in *Nations and Nationalism since 1780: Programme, Myth, Reality*, ed. Eric J. Hobsbawm (Cambridge: Cambridge University Press, 1992), 1-13.

period played the greatest role in the spread of modern civilization. Like in post-Gutenberg Europe, the spread of books was facilitated by advancements in printing technology and new changes brought about by the spread of the books itself. These books provided opportunities to access knowledge that had previously been limited to the scholar class. The fact that more people became able to receive new knowledge signified a change in consciousness among members of the intellectual class.

Enlightenment-era modern printed publications can be classified into newspapers and magazines; books published as part of the "national studies movement" ("Kuk'agundong" or 국학운동); Christian documents such as bibles, hymnals, and evangelist documents that spread amid growing acceptance and faith in Christianity; and educational textbooks. Among these, Christian religious texts and textbooks spearheaded by academics composed the majority of all published works. The release of Christian texts coincided with the extensive distribution of printing technology throughout the country. This in turn stimulated the publication of a variety of books.[30]

This indicates that Christianity played a pivotal role in modern education during the Enlightenment era. This is because, once Christianity arrived in Korea, early missionary work soon became a means of enlightenment. This was particularly the case in the realm of education, where the establishment of schools centeredcentred around Christianity made a significant contribution. Accompanying this was the active publication of textbooks to meet the needs of school education. In other words, the publication of modern books during the Enlightenment era not only served the purpose of modernization through education but also included the religious purpose of spreading the gospel.

If we classify[31] Enlightenment-era books as those published between the opening of ports and 1905, we find that Christian literature comprises an overwhelming two-thirds of the total. From this detail, it is possible to infer that the Bible and Christian hymnals were indeed catalysts for significant changes

---

30 Myoung-Keun Han, "Publication of New Books and its Characteristics in the Enlightenment Era (1876-1905)," *The Historical Association for Soong-Sil* (2007): 44-5.

31 Bong Kim, *A Study on the Book Culture of the Korean Enlightenment Era* (Seoul: Ewha Womans University Press, 1999).

in Koreans' language and writing practices.[32] Further evidence supporting this claim can be found in the fact that modern printing technology was developed by Korean Christians. Even before foreign missionaries came to the peninsula, Korean Christians began reading, disseminating, and translating the Bible into Korean. Some of these were published in the form of "pocket gospel" booklets (tchokpokŭmsŏ or 쪽복음서), which were loosely bound individual books from the Bible (especially those of Matthew, Mark, Luke, or John.)[33]

The small group of Korean Protestants spontaneously translated the Bible into Hangul and published it using modern typography before foreign missionaries arrived was unprecedented in the history of global Christianity. The formation[34] of a spontaneous faith community and the publication of the Bible in their native language not only influenced Korean Protestantism but also significantly impacted the formation of modern consciousness and civilization in Korea after the Enlightenment era.

Hence, the history of translating, publishing, and disseminating the Bible in Korean serves as a significant gauge of the growth of modern Korean consciousness and civilization. In the late 19th century, attempts to spread modern knowledge through textbooks in schools faced limitations due to the absence of modern educational institutions and policies, as well as inadequate printing technology. In contrast, the acceptance and development of Christianity played a vital role in the advancement of modern publishing culture in Korea, leading to groundbreaking changes in the Korean language and script.[35] Korean-language bibles surpassed all other Korean literature not only in terms

---

32 Han, "Publication of New Books" see footnote 54; Kim, *A Study on the Book Culture.*

33 On April 18th, 2013, Professor Lee Man-Yeol delivered a lecture titled "Bible Christianity and the Growth of the Korean Church" at the Church Reformation Practice Coalition Memorial Service held to mark the 100th anniversary of the church in Korea. In his lecture, he discussed the significance of "Bible Christianity" and its impact in Korea. He provided insights into Korea's early encounters with the Bible, early translations, and their outcomes. Additionally, he emphasized the importance of Bible distribution and study. Professor Pastreich highlighted the transformative power of the Bible, stating, "As the Bible was distributed, read, and memorized, its words penetrated the very being of uninspired Koreans, breathing life into them and transforming them into new individuals." He also pointed out the emergence of a "national language study" movement within the early Korean Christian communities, as the widespread distribution of the Bible prompted a renewed focus on studying the national language for the purpose of reading the Scriptures.

34 Han, "Publication of New Books", footnote 13.

35 Han, "Publication of New Books", 27.

of volume but also in sales figures, indicating their extensive and rapid distribution across various social classes.

Christians published not only the Bible but also many other religious books in Korean. These included foreign novels such as *The Pilgrim's Progress* (천로역정 or 天路歷程) and novellar adaptations of Bible stories. Through this process, a Christian-style Korean writing style emerged. Examples of newspapers that showcase this unique style include the following:

First, we used the *Independence Newspaper* (독립신문). Although it was not directly operated by Christians, it was influenced by Christianity, much like the *Capital Gazette* (황성신문) published by Pai Chai Hakdang. Key figures involved in the newspaper's publication, such as Phillip Jaison (서재필), Yun Chi-Ho, and Joo Si-Gyeong, were all Christians, so their influence could not be ignored.

Second, publications such as "The Christian Advocate" and the Presbyterian "Christian News" were established one year after the launch of the "Independence Newspaper." Their writing style, language use, and expression methods were very similar to those of the "Independence Newspaper". The translation, publication, and dissemination of the Korean Bible hold greater significance not only in terms of modern education but also in connection with the historical situation Korea found itself in at the time. As can be verified through these examples, the wide distribution of Hangul (the Korean alphabet) was a pivotal indicator of the radical changes in late Joseon (Late Chosun) Korean society. The publication and distribution of new books brought about significant changes in the language and literacy lives of Koreans. In other words, the publication of books in both Korean and Chinese or purely in Korean was a historically groundbreaking event; as before, the dominant sphere of life was mostly in Chinese characters, which were monopolized by the ruling class. Changes in language and literacy practices led to changes in consciousness, which in turn brought about changes in the culture of Korean society itself.

2) Typography in Early Translations of the Bible: Hangul vs. Sino-Korean Mixed Script

While demand for new Western books was high during the Enlightenment period, very few authors were capable of compiling them at the time. For this reason, a significant portion of books published during the Enlightenment period were translations of Western books, which were first translated into Chinese and Japanese and subsequently translated into Korean. The widespread lack of information about foreign countries, coupled with a fervent desire to understand them, likely served as a catalyst for the translation of foreign books.[36]

Within Christianity, the situation was similar. An interesting and unique missionary phenomenon occurred where missionaries compiled Korean translations of the bible in Manchuria and Japan before ever stepping foot on the peninsula and then brought the Korean translations with them to Korea. The unique environment of the Korean mission in Manchuria, where the Ross version of the New Testament was completed, sparked a dispute among the translation authority of Ross in Shenyang and Underwood in Seoul. Eventually, the era of in-country translation to Korea began as Kenmure and Turley of the British and Foreign Bible Society (BFBS),[37] which had been supporting the translations, sided with the Permanent Bible Committee centeredcentred around Underwood, who was the de facto leader in the missionary field.

In 1893, the Permanent Executive Bible Committee (PEBC) was established, which brought all operations under its jurisdiction. Alongside the decisions of the three United Church branches, the PEBC took charge of the overall Korean Bible industry. For a period of four years, Kenmure and Miller served as cosecretaries of the joint branch. However, while formally having a joint branch, the actual administrative tasks and Bible industry activities were primarily carried out by the Korean branch of the British and Foreign Bible Society (BFBS), as had been the case before.[38]

Early Korean translation of the Bible can be divided into stages. The first began in 1877 and lasted until 1939, when the translation of the Korean Revised

---

36 Kim, *A Study on the Book Culture.*

37 John Ross, *John Ross to BFBS ESC (November 4 & 22, 1890)* (London); Sung-Il Choi, "John Ross (1842-1915) and the Korean Protestant Church: The First Korean Bible and its Relations to the Protestant Origins in Korea" (doctor of philosophy thesis, University of Edinburgh, 1992).

38 Dae-Young Ryu et al. (류대영 외), *The History of the Korean Bible Society I & II [대한성서공회사 I·II]* (The Korean Bible Society, 1994).

Version of the Bible (KRV or 개역 성경전서) was completed and published.[39]

Figure 1 Periods of Early Biblical Translation Classification

Location	Year	Translation Era	Works Produced
Overseas Translation Period	1877-1887	The Ross Edition (1877~1887)	John Ross and Lee Eung-Chan, biblical translation (Manchuria, 1877)
			The Gospel According to Luke (1882) (예수셩교누가복음젼셔)
			The Gospel According to John (1882) (예수셩교요안니복음젼셔)
			Christian Interpretations of the Gospel According to Luke (1883) (예수셩교셩셔 누가복음데쟈 힝젹)
			The Gospel According to Matthew (1884) (예수셩교셩셔 맛듸복음)
			Christian Interpretations of the Gospel According to Mark (1884) (예수셩교셩셔 말코복음)
			Christian Interpretations of the Gospel According to John (1885) (예수셩교셩셔 요안니복음 이비쇼셔신)
			Christ's Teachings in The New Testament (1887) (예수셩교젼셔)
		Lee Soo — Jeong Translation (1883~1885)	The Gospel According to Mark in the New Testament (1885) (신약마가젼복음셔언히)
Domestic Translation Period	1885-1939	Revising overseas translations (1885~1890)	
		Old Testament Translation (1890~1911)	The New Testament (1900) 신약젼셔 The Old Testament (1911) 구약젼셔
		New Testament Translation (1911~1939)	

39 Deok-Ju Lee (이덕주), *A Study on Early Translations of the Korean Bible: With a Focus on the Activities of Bible Translators* [초기 한글성경번역에 관한 연구특히 성경번역자들의 활동을 중심으로], *Korean Bible and Korean Culture: Encounter between Catholicism and Protestantism* (Seoul: Christian Literature Press 1985), p. 418

This period is usually classified as the "early stage" in the history of Korean biblical translation. The main goal in this series of Bible translations was to "break free from the restraints of Chinese characters and use pure Korean" (순 한글). In 1893, this premise was adopted as the most important policy of Christian missionaries. For example, while Catholics referred to the Christian God as "Ch'ŏnju" (天主), Christians borrowed the pure Korean word "Hananim" (하ᄂ님). "Hananim" was not a new term; it referred to the unique concept of a monotheistic god that had been passed through the language of the common people and the Korean nation (한민족).[40] The meaning inherent to this concept shows that Christian missionaries work had the goal of indigenization and popularization in mind from the beginning of mission.

Let us examine the Ross Edition version of "Christ's Teachings in the New Testament" (Yesusŏnggyojŏnsŏ or 예수성교전셔),[41] which was translated by Ross and Seo Sang-Ryun. When one examines the book, one clearly notices the distinct and unique form of translated words.[42] Seo Sang-Ryun was obtained from Uiju in North Pyongan Province. For this reason, his translation contains many words from the North Pyongan dialect as well as purely Korean words in place of Sino-Korean words, also called "Chinese characters". Let us look at the following examples:

Figure 2 Translations of Mark 1:1-2

Ross Edition (Korean)
1)하나님의 아달 예수 키리쓰토 복음의 처음이라 2) 션지 이사야 써사되 보라 늬가 늬의 사쟈를 너희 압페 보늬여 너희 길을 에비ᄒ며 (마가복음 1장 1~2절)[43]

40 ake-Bu Chun (전택부), *A Historical Essay on the Concepts of God and Tenchu: Focusing on the 18th and 19th Centuries* [하나님 및 텬쥬라는 말에 관한 역사 소고-18세기와 19세기를 중심으로]. *Korean Language Bible and Korean Culture: Encounter between Catholicism and Protestantism* (Seoul: Christian Literature Press, 1985), 591-638.

41 John Ross (존 로스), Lee Eung-Chan (이웅찬), Baek Hong-Jun (백홍준), Seo Sang-Ryun (서상륜), Lee Seong-Ha (이성하), Kim Jin-Gi (김진기). *Christ's Teachings in the New Testament* [예수성교젼] (Korean Bible Society, 1887), accessed May 2, 2023, https://www.bskorea.or.kr/data/pdf/bible_1887b.pdf.

42 Chang-Hai Park (박창해), *Korean Grammar Structures in John Ross's "Yesu Seonggyo Jeonso (New Testament)"* [로스 (예수성교전셔), 에 쓰인 한국어의 문법구조]. *The Korean Bible and Korean Culture: Encounter between Catholicism and Protestantism* (Christian Literature Press, 1985).

43 Ross, Eung-Chan, Hong-Jun, Sang-Ryun, Seong-Ha, Jin-Gi, *Christ's Teachings in the New Testament.*

Sarah Mack's Translation of the Ross Edition
1) The good news about the Son of God Jesus Christ 2) starts with the words of the prophet Isaiah: "Look! I send your messenger in front of you to prepare your path." (Mark 1:1-2)

King James Version (KJV)
1) The beginning of the gospel of Jesus Christ, the Son of God; 2) As it is written in the prophets, Behold, I send my messenger before thy face, which shall prepare thy way before thee. (Mark 1:1-2)

New International Version (NIV)
1)The beginning of the good news about Jesus the Messiah, the Son of God, 2) as it is written in Isaiah the prophet: "I will send my messenger ahead of you, who will prepare your way." (Mark 1:1-2)

New Living Translation (NLT)
1) The Good News of Jesus Christ, the Son of God, 2) begins with the words of the early preachers: "Listen! I will send My helper to carry the news ahead of you. He will make the way ready." (Mark 1:1-2, NLV)

Figure 3 Word-By-Word Translation of Mark 1:1-2

Ross	Modern Korean	English	Etymology	Note
하나님	하나님	God	Pure Korean	하나 (one) + 님 (honorific), "The One"
의	의	of	Pure Korean	Possessive particle
아달	아들	Son	Pure Korean	Pyongan dialect
예수	예수	Jesus	Loan Word	From Galilee Hebrew "Yeshu" or " יֵשׁוּ "
그리쓰토	그리스도	Christ	Loan Word	
복음	복음	the gospel	Sino-Korean	福 (blessing, fortune) + 音 (sound, message), "The Good News"
처음	처음	the beginning	Pure Korean	
이라	이라	it is	Pure Korean	
션지자	선지자	prophet	Sino-Korean	先 (first) + 知 (know) + 者 (person, one who), "Person who knows first"
이사야	이사야	Isaiah	Loan Word	
써사되	써서되	spoke, saying	Pure Korean	
보라	보라	Look	Pure Korean	informal imperative
늬가	내가	I	Pure Korean	informal

너의	너의	your	Pure Korean	informal
사쟈	사자를	messenger	Sino-Korean	使(send, utilize) + 者 (person, one who), "Person who sends [a message]"
룰	를		Pure Korean	direct object marker
너희	너희	your	Pure Korean	informal
압페	앞에	in front	Pure Korean	Pyongan dialect
보닉여	보내어	send	Pure Korean	
너희	너희	your	Pure Korean	informal
길	길	way	Pure Korean	
을	을		Pure Korean	direct object marker
에비ᄒ며	예비하게	prepare	Sino-Korean	豫 (prepare) + 備 (equip), "prepare"

Meanwhile, Lee Soo-Jeong, who came from a scholarly background, accompanied students who were studying abroad as a member of the Susinsa diplomatic corps in September 1882 but ended up translating the Bible. His translation contains many Sino-Korean "Hanja" words.

Figure 4 Translations of Matthew 1:23

Lee Soo-jeong Edition[44]
"회당에 계실제 흔 스람이 잇셔 몹쓸 귓것시 들녀 웨여 왈업다. 拿撒勤(나쟈레트) 사람 耶蘇(예수쓰)야 우리와 무슴 싱괸이 있관닉……."(마가복음 1장 23~)[45]
Sarah Mack's Translation of the Lee Soo-jeong Edition
23)There was one person there at the synagogue who had been possessed by an evil ghost cried out, 24 "O, Jesus the Nazarene, what relation have you to us?" (Matthew 1:23~)
King James Version (KJV)
23) And there was in their synagogue a man with an unclean spirit; and he cried out, 24 saying, Let us alone; what have we to do with thee, thou Jesus of Nazareth? (Matthew 1:23~)
New International Version (NIV)
23) Just then a man in their synagogue who was possessed by an impure spirit cried out, 24 "What do you want with us, Jesus of Nazareth? (Matthew 1:23~)
New Living Translation (NLT)
23) Suddenly, a man in the synagogue who was possessed by an evil spirit cried out, 24 "Why are you interfering with us, Jesus of Nazareth? (Matthew 1:23~)

44 이수정 역, 『마가전복음셔』, 삼, accessed May 2, 2023, https://www.bskorea.or.kr/data/pdf/Mark_188

Figure 5 Word-by-Word Translation of Matthew 1:23

Lee	Modern Korean	English	Etymology	Notes
회당	회당	synagogue	Pure Korean	會 (assembly) + 堂 (hall, place) = "meeting place"
에	에	at	Pure Korean	location marker
계실제	계실 때	when at	Sino-Korean	Formal
흔	한	one	Pure Korean	
스람이	사람이	person	Pure Korean	
잇셔	계셔	was there	Sino-Korean	
몹쓸	악독한	very bad	Pure Korean	몹 (very, extremely) + 쓸 (bad, evil) = "extremely evil"
귓것시	귀신이	ghost	Sino-Korean	鬼 (evil ghost, spirit) + 神 (spirit, god)
들녀	들어	entered	Pure Korean	
웨여	외치다	screaming	Sino-Korean	
왈업다	말씀하옵니다	says	Sino-Korean	Honorific expression. 索 (speak)
拿撒勤 (나쟈레트)	나사렛	Nazareth	Loan Word	
사람	사람	person	Pure Korean	
耶蘇 (예쑤스)	예수	Jesus	Loan Word	From Latin "Iesus"
야	야	O	Pure Korean	Alt: "O Jesus"
우리	우리	Pronoun "us"	Pure Korean	Alt: "we"
와	와	with		
무슴	무슨	what	Pure Korean	
상관	상관	relation	Sino-Korean	相 (mutual, together) + 關 (gate, point of connection) = "connection [with us]"
이	이		Pure Korean	topic marker
있관녀	있나이까	do you have?	Pure Korean	Alt: "is there?"

As seen in Lee Soo-Jeong's 1885 mixed-script version of the New Testament Gospel of Mark (신약마가젼복음셔언히), post-Ross Bibles began to use the

5b.pdf.

45 Soo-Jeong Lee (이수정), "The Gospel of Mark," accessed May 2, 2023, https://www.bskorea. or.kr/data/ pdf/Mark_1885b.pdf.

Hangul script exclusively. Hangul also became the national script of Korea. After, Hangul was disparaged as a "vernacular script" for more than 400 years. The change was the result of early translators opting to use Hangul, which was used by the masses, rather than Chinese characters, which were the common script of the literate ruling and scholarly classes.[46] The spelling and writing conventions of early Korean biblical texts can also be considered contributions to Korean literature.

Two key features emerge during the translation process. One is the phenomenon of parallel or mixed use of both Hangul and Chinese characters. This enabled the texts to be read by all regardless of social status. The other is the role of literate scholars and intellectuals. The fact that it was possible to translate the Bible into Hangul from Manchuria or Japan at all was only possible because scholars had accepted the Gospel early on.[47]

As modern Western Europe developed into an industrialized capitalist mass production system, writing and knowledge spread among workers in the process of modern state formation. The medium that spread common language in this process was print media such as newspapers. Some say that the spread of printed materials in regional vernaculars, as opposed to the language of the elite that could be used and enjoyed only by privileged classes, is what made possible the formation of modern nations and nationalities.[48] Considering the significance of early biblical translations in Manchuria and Japan, the fact that these translations were carried out in specific regional languages for the local people implies that the Bible facilitated communication between anonymous individuals who otherwise did not know each other.

What, then, was the impact of the dissemination of printed books with content about "consciousness" on Koreans throughout the journey of modern Korean history? To confirm its role in the formation of "national consciousness", it is necessary to investigate this phenomenon from the Enlightenment Period

---

46 Young-Taik Chun (전영택), "Christianity and the Korean Script [基督教와 朝鮮文字]," *Hangul* 4, no. 8 (1936): 2.

47 Ryu, Dae-Young et al. (류대영 외), *History of the Korean Bible Society, Volume II* [대한성서공회사 I · II]. Korean Bible Society, 1994, pp. 46.

48 See Gellner, *Nations and Nationalism.*

(1876-1905) to Japan's annexation of Korea and, in particular, around the year 1904. This is because the year 1904 marked a turning point in both Korean society and the history of the Korean Bible, with several factors intertwined. On a national level, there was the Russo-Japanese War, and on in regards to Christianity in Korea, there was the emergence of a collaborative organization branch called the Korean Bible Society (KBS) and a newly revised translation of the New Testament. Here, we will examine this topic, focusing on the mixed-script publication of the New Testament that was published in both Hangul and Chinese characters between 1904 and 1906.

4. Biblical Nationalism and the 1904 and 1906 Editions of the New Testament

1) The 1904 and 1906 Editions of the New Testament

Missionaries were surprised that Koreans such as Seo Sang-Ryun and Lee Soo-Jeong had translated the Bible into versions written in Korea before missionaries even entered the country. In response, they organized a missionary-centered biblical translation committee and published a single-volume version of the New Testament in 1900.[49] The Korean New Testament underwent its first incomplete provisional translation in 1900 and included three types of scripts and two new terms.

In 1904, a revised 3rd edition known as the "Authorized Version" (공인역) was printed in Japan. However, this version of the manuscript faced significant issues, as it contained more than 1,000 errors. Despite facing such problems, the 1904 edition of the "New Testament" spanned 785 pages and published 15,000 copies.[50] Surprisingly, it sold out within six months, even amid the turmoil of the Russo-Japanese War. This shows that there was tremendous demand for the Bible among Koreans. Subsequently, on February 15, 1905,

---

49 Ryu, Dae-Young (류대영 외), *History of the Korean Bible Society, Volume II* [대한성서공회사 I·II]. Korean Bible Society, 1994, pp. 52-61.

50 The Board of Official Translators (성경번역자회), *the New Testament in Korean 1904* (The Korean Bible Society) accessed May 2, 2023, https://www.bskorea.or.kr/data/pdf/bible_1904_NTb.pdf.

the New Testament entered a year-long revision process to address the discovered errors. After 240 reading sessions were conducted over 12 months, the final version of the manuscript was completed on February 14, 1906. This 1906 edition of the "Authorized Version" New Testament is known as "the Complete Text of the New Testament [Written in] the National Script and Han [Chinese] Characters" (新約全書 國漢文)[51] and features a mixed script of Hangul and Chinese characters.[52]

What, then, is the reason for this shift from the previous primary principle of Bible translation — the exclusive use of the Hangul Korean script — to a mixed script of Korean and Chinese? First, the answer becomes clear when we analyze the background of the early Korean church's members. As is widely known, a large number of scholars and educated classes converted to Christianity in the Korean church between 1902 and 1903. This began when many political prisoners, including Syngman Rhee, Lee Sang-jae, Lee Won-Geun, and Yoo Sung-Jun, converted to Seoul Prison (監獄署). After being released in 1904, they attended the Yeondong Church or spread the Christian faith movement through the Hwangseong Christian Youth Association (YMCA).[53]

Even before the individuals above were converted, there was no shortage of yangban (educated elites) within the Korean church. However, they were more comfortable with classical Chinese than with Hangul and preferred the Bible written in Chinese characters. Lee Soo-Jeong's 1885 mixed-script translation of "The Gospel According to Mark in the New Testament" (약마가전복음셔언히) and the continuous provision of the Classical Chinese Bible known as the

---

51 The Board of Official Translators (성경번역자회), *the New Testament in Korean 1906* (The Korean Bible Society) accessed May 2, 2023, https://www.bskorea.or.kr/data/pdf/bible_1911_NTb.pdf.

52 Ryu et al., *The History of the Korean Bible Society*, 61-70.

53 The conservative faction within the government created several political incidents to eliminate reformist forces such as the Independence Association, starting with the arrest of Syngman Rhee (이승만) who had led the All-Nation Congress in January 1899. Until early 1904, individuals such as Yi Sang-jae (이상재) Lee Won-kyung (이원경), Yu Sung-jun (유성준), Hong Jae-gi (홍재기) Ahn Guk-seon (안국선), Kim Jeong-sik (김정식), Lee Dong-nyeong (이동녕), Shin Heung-woo (신흥우), and Lee Seung-in (이승인) were imprisoned. They underwent religious conversion through Christian books in the prison library and the preaching of figures like Bunker, Underwood, and Gale. See: Gwang-Rin lee, "Conversion of Confucian Scholar-offcials to Christian Faith in the Late Choson Dynasty Korea [구한말 옥중에서의 기독교신앙]," *The Issue of Ancestral Tablets in Korean Modernization* (Ilchokak, 1986).

"Wenli New Testament" (文理新約全書) after Seo Sang-Ryun distributed 212 copies in 1886 and the publication of Sino-Korean diglot Bibles such as Fenwick's 1891 translation of "The Gospel of John" (요한복음젼) all occurred out of consideration for the class of churchgoers that preferred Chinese characters. However, as Ross argued, the Bible had to be translated into the language of the people to be easily accessible to all social strata. With the implementation of the Nevius Method, where the focus of the mission was determined to be the common people, Bibles written primarily in Hangul became mainstream.

In the process of the New Testament being bound into a single volume in 1900 and the provisional New Testament being prepared in 1904, literate groups within the church who preferred the Classical Chinese script once again demanded a Sino-Korean mixed script version of the New Testament. This was significantly influenced by the fact that most documents at the time were still in a Sino-Korean mixed script format. It was easier for the literate class to understand and clearly comprehend the meaning when the important vocabulary in sentences was written in Chinese characters. However, the point when "the Complete New Testament in the Korean/Chinese Mixed Script" (新約全書 國漢文) was requested coincided with the period when conversions were occurring within prisons. At the same time, the missionaries who favored the church's request for a mixed-script version and supported its translation were Underwood and Gale, who were involved in prison evangelism. Therefore, it can be inferred that there is a mutual correlation between the publication of the mixed script New Testament and the conversion and baptism of the literate elite in prison.

Second, the context for the republication of the New Testament in a mixed Sino-Korean script involved active participation and financial burden-bearing by Koreans. Koreans interested in this matter expressed their intention to Gale and Underwood to finance publications out of their own pockets. Many missionaries, under the belief that a mixed script version would impede the use of the vernacular, defined it as a 'competing version' and opposed its publication. However, Miller, who had been in Korea the longest, agreed with Gale and Underwood's opinion that the Hangul and mixed-script Bibles could coexist. He believed that, from a price perspective, this could not be a competing version because the mixed-script version's price of 50 sen per volume was significantly greater than that of the Hangul version. If it did become popular, he thought it would be because it was a mixed-script version.

This "Complete New Testament in the Korean/Chinese Mixed Script" was published in two versions, the 4th and 5th editions, in April 1906. The translation particularly gained fame because of its dedication to Emperor Gojong. Missionaries Underwood, Dr. Evison, and Secretary Miller presented two volumes of the Sino-Korean mixed-script New Testament to Emperor Gojong on April 25th. Inside, the covers were inscribed with the message, "The Word of God Presented to His Majesty, The Emperor of Korea."

This event is highly important not only because it shows that a Bible that was financed and edited by Korean Christians was being presented to Gojong but also because it concretely demonstrated that the Bible and Christianity were now truly accepted in Korea, even by the king.

This mixed-script version is said to have targeted the educated class. At that time, the use of Hangul in Seoul gradually increased, and several newspapers were published exclusively in Hangul. Supporters of the mixed-script version argued that its dual use of Hangul and Chinese characters would actually familiarize the literate class with Hangul, thus leading to a cessation of the use of Classical Chinese. In brief, one can see that the mixed-script version, which blended traditions, was in some ways more popular and representative of the national spirit than was the Bible written purely in Hangul, which was aimed at common people.

During this period, a patriotic enlightenment movement was being carried out in the country as part of an educational initiative to reclaim the nation. This movement was developed mainly around the Christian communities in Northwest Korea. The movement aimed to gradually recover national sovereignty by establishing schools, publishing newspapers and magazines, promoting industries, etc., particularly around the time of the Eulsa Treaty. Missionaries saw the Russo-Japanese War as awakening the Korean intellectual and religious communities. The growing demand for books, particularly the surge in acceptance of books on geography, history, economics, and Christian literature, was attributed to the national education movement and religious awakening in Korean society.[54]

Such phenomena, which occurred in Christian and Western civilizations, were sought as realistic solutions to Korea's national crisis after the Russo-Japanese War. This led to an explosive increase in demand for books, particularly for the Bible. The New Testament published after the Russo-Japanese War in 1904 and 1906 was distributed rapidly. This phenomenon was closely related to the Great Revival Movement of 1907. The following table shows the changes in the Bible distribution between 1904 and 1906, when the 4th and 5th editions of the New Testament were published.

Figure 6 Bible Distribution from 1904 to 1907[55]

Year	Full-Text Bible	New Testament	Individual Bible Books	Total
1904	325	3,669	48,009	52,003
1905	733	16,076	81,689	98,498
1906	962	25,323	100,984	127,269
1907	721	54,551	95,958	151,230

As shown in the table above, demand for Bibles skyrocketed after the Russo-Japanese War in 1905. This was due to the publication of a mixed-script version of the Bible, the change in the method of selling books from direct sales to sales through distribution centerscentres or churches, and the opening of bookstores to supply Bibles and Christian literature.

The sudden drop in demand for complete Bible or individual Bible books in 1907 after an increase in 1906 could be interpreted as a shift in preference to the New Testament. This was because the text was written in a mixed-script version rather than at the price. The mixed-script version's price of 50 sen per volume was significantly greater than that of the Hangul version; hence, the mixed-script version could not be a competing version from a price perspective. Therefore, mixed-script translations were not popular *despite* but rather *because* they were written in both Hangul and Chinese characters. This new script system could encompass both commoners and students and would have instilled new ideas. In addition, apart from a few novels, almost no books

54 Ryu et al., *The History of the Korean Bible Society*, 310.

55 Ibid., 254.

were written in Hangul, so for those who wanted to read books in Hangul, the Bible was an excellent textbook.[56] This also contributed to the increase in demand for the mixed-script version of the New Testament.

2) Biblical Nationalism

Let us examine the relationship between the Bible and nationalism in the historical context of Korea during the late Chosun era. As we have previously shown, the demand for books increased as part of the national enlightenment movement, especially the movement to save the nation through education (Kyoyuk-kuguk, 교육구국). Among the books disseminated at the time, the Bible was central. Moreover, it was evident that those leading the education-based national salvation movement were predominantly from the Christian community in Northwest Korea.

More importantly, the New Testament, translated after the Russo-Japanese War, experienced explosive demand. Despite being more expensive than the Hangul version of the Bible, it was written in a mixed script of Korean and Classical Chinese, making it accessible to both commoners and scholars. These findings show that the Bible, printed in standard Korean, gained more popularity than any other book at the time. The act of reading and reciting verses from the Bible, printed in the same script regardless of social status, at worship or in public places, ultimately led to a shared identity as biblical Christians and a sense of nationhood. This was an embodiment of egalitarian ideas and practices transcending the barriers of the hierarchical society.[57]

According to Benedict Anderson's explanation of nations and nationalism, print capitalism plays a significant role in initially imagining a "national community."[58] Given that Protestantism would have been impossible without books during the Reformation, the number and speed of dissemination of

---

56 Ibid., 358-9.

57 Ian Green, *Print and Protestantism in Early Modern England* (New York: Oxford University Press, 2002).

58 Benedict Anderson, *Imagined Communities: Reflections on the Origin and Spread of Nationalism* (London: Verso Editions, 1983). Note: Translated into Korean by Hyung-Suk Yoon (윤형석), *상상의 공동체* (서울: 나남, 2002), ch. 3.

those who could access the Bible in the Late Chosun era allows us to gauge the impact of national consciousness through the Bible.

Second, we can read a narrative of nationhood in the content of the Bible. During the European Reformation, biblical faith and political ideals were not separated. This was particularly the case in the newly established Protestant nations; they identified their national identities with the "new Israel." The power to make such a claim came from the vocabulary and discourse of "nationhood" in the Bible.

When the Netherlands waged an independence war against Spanish oppression to create a new Dutch nation and when the Church of England declared its independence from the Roman Catholic Church during the reign of Henry VIII, the discourse they drew from the Bible was the narrative of the "chosen people" and "New Israel."[59] The Netherlands succeeded in the war of independence with such justifications, and when they established the Dutch Republic in 1581, they described themselves as the people of God ("Godts volck". They adopted the Biblical model of nationhood as the official program for their actions while establishing a national identity where religious and political matters were inseparable.[60]

In the late Chosun era of Korea, we can speculate that the Bible, which was translated and distributed mainly among Korean Christians, may have integrated these individuals' religious beliefs with their political ideals. If the main narrative flowing throughout both the Old and New Testaments is the idea of a covenant, then the concept of the covenant — the promise of salvation and liberation for Israel in a state of oppressed slavery — was similar wouldto the hardships faced by Koreans. Furthermore, perhaps even more than the other lessons in the Bible, early Korean Christians would have learned through the story of Israel about the idea of the covenantal nation — a community

---

59 Anthony D. Smith, *Chosen Peoples* (Oxford: Oxford University Press, 2004).

60 Refer to the following: Alastair Duke, *Reformation and Revolt in the Low Countries* (London: Hambledon Press, 1990); Joshua Dunkelgrün, "'Neerlands Israel' Political Theology, Christian Hebraism, Biblical antiquarianism, and Historical Myth," in *Myth in History, History in myth*, eds. Laura Cruz and Willem Frijhoff (Leiden: Brill, 2009); Craig Harline, *Pamphlets, Printing, and Political Culture in the Early Dutch Republic* (Dordrecht: Martinus Nijhoff, 1987); Simon Schama, *The Embarrassment of Riches; an Interpretation of Dutch Culture in the Golden Age* (Berkeley: University of California Press, 1988); Appelbaum, *Biblical nationalism and the sixteenth*, 329.

bound by a shared destiny.

As mentioned earlier, the Russo-Japanese War awakened the Korean spiritual and religious community. This means that movements such as the educational national salvation movement, which was led primarily by the Christian community in the Northwest, and the Great Revival Movement of 1907 had the character of national movements with religious awakenings and active real-life participation. On the other hand, nationalists established the concept of nation and nationalism as ideological resistance against Western and Japanese imperialism, emphasizing historical, cultural, and ethnic community aspects.

Third, the Bible provided a model of societal and institutional nationhood in its external form. This was not limited to the Bible's lexicon or narratives. There is a receptacle for encapsulating narratives and discourses of homogeneous nationhood. Put differently, the Bible enabled the capture of nationhood within shared structures. One significant characteristic was that the Bible translations were conducted in indigenous regional languages. Around the 1600s, in the early modern period in Europe, translations of the New Testament were made into German, Italian, French, Spanish, Polish, Czech, Hungarian, Welsh, Irish, Basque, Romansh, and a South Slavic language similar to present-day Croatian and Slovenian. By the end of the 17th century, all portions of the Bible were published in more than 50 languages.[61] Such propagation and proliferation of a standard language served to dismantle linguistic barriers between one nation and others, as well as among various dialects within a single nation, initially in written form and later in spoken form, thereby contributing to the unification of the region where it was used.[62] The gradual standardization of language superseded regional dialects with national norms in the realm of print and written communication.[63]

During the late Chosun period, Korean Christians were divided into two linguistic realms: one centeredcentred around Chinese characters and the other

---

61 Stanley Lawrence Greenslade, *The Cambridge History of the Bible, vol. 3, The West from the Reformation to the Present Day* (Cambridge: Cambridge University Press, 1963).

62 Peter Burke. "Nationalisms and Vernaculars, 1500–1800." in *The Oxford Handbook of the History of Nationalism*, ed. John Breuilly (Oxford: Oxford University Press, 2013), 29.

63 Ibid., ch. 2.

around Hangul. This starkly highlighted the distinct social divisions that exist in Korean society. However, through the process of translating the Bible, these two separate worlds started to converge and interact. It became evident that the mixed-script Bible, which incorporated both Hangul and Chinese characters, was more widely embraced and resonated with the Korean people, reflecting a sense of national identity.

Through this, we can witness how separate social classes, when reading the same Bible, formed a faith community and gradually dismantled the established social hierarchy. That is, just by being able to read the same text, they could have fostered a sense of homogeneous community consciousness, regardless of their social status. Additionally, it is inferred that the teachings of the Bible, stating that everyone is a creation in the likeness of God the Creator, must have instilled in Koreans the ideas of equality and dignity. Furthermore, the frequent use of the term "nation"[64] in the Bible, along with the narrative of the Israelite people, would have instilled in the readers a new consciousness of nationhood.

Finally, several aspects of the Bible appear to exemplify modern nationalism. Biblical Israel possesses egalitarian elements reminiscent of modern civic nationalism. The Bible speaks of nations enjoying their sovereignty in justice and equality, implying that there are no hereditary privileged aristocracies or priesthoods. The temple does not own land; instead, the land is divided among tenant farmers, with a sophisticated system in place to support the poor.[65] Rituals exist for all farmers to recite their national history when they bring their first fruits to the national temple, which includes the authority to study Israel's history and laws and teach them to their children (Deuteronomy 26:1-11;

---

64 Upon verifying the original texts of the early versions of the Bible, it has been found that the English word "nation" in the Bible's original texts was translated as "paeksŏng" (빅셩), literally "the hundred names" or "the common people," and "nara" (나라), which means "country" in the Ross Edition, Lee Su-Jeong's translation, the "New Testament" (1904), the "Old Testament" (1911), and the "Gospel of John" (1913). The translation for "nation" as "minjok" (민족) first appears in the "Revised Version of the Bible" (1938). Currently, "nation(s)" in the New and Old Testament is translated as "minjok," and this term can be found in a total of 246 Bible verses. accessed May 2, 2023, https://www.bskorea.or.kr/bbs/content.php?co_id=subpage2_3_3_4

65 Joshua Berman, *Created equal: How the Bible broke with Ancient Political Thought* (Oxford: Oxford University Press, 2008). Appelbaum, *Biblical nationalism and the sixteenth*, 322-3.

11:19).

Moreover, the rights of the Israelite people — or the elders who can represent them — to establish and renew covenants, institutionalize monarchy against God's advisement (1 Samuel 8), and crown Josiah (2 Kings 21:24) unfolded fundamental premises of nationalism. This conveys a political doctrine defined by the idea that "a distinct and unique nation exists" and that because this nation has the right to preserve its 'interests and values,' the nation has the right to acquire "political sovereignty."[66]

Such characteristics suggest that the story of the nation of Israel shares aspects with the modern concept of a political nation. This discourse on biblical nationhood came as a new revelation to modern individuals who previously had limited access to the Bible. Those who hoped to find their own spiritual salvation in the Bible discovered a model for societal reform within it, which ultimately appeared in the form of nationhood. The reformation manifested in reality as practical nationalism, or "biblical nationalism." The translation of the Bible during the late Chosun period played a role internally as a practical programme for societal reform and externally as a protective programme for national resurgence against the invasions of foreign powers.

The biblical narrative of nationhood became a catalyst for the Christian national movement. The translation of the Bible — which made sharing this narrative possible — and the widespread dissemination of those translations played significant roles. From these points, we can identify the characteristics of Biblical nationalism.

5. Conclusion

This article examines the influence of the narrative of nationhood in the Bible on the formation of modern nation-states in Europe, focusing particularly on the role and significance of the early Bible translations on the emergence of the concept of nationhood in late Chosun Korea. When examining early

---

66 John Breuilly, *Nationalism and the state* (Chicago: University of Chicago Press, 1993[1982]), 2.

Korean Bible translations, including the 1882 Ross Edition, Lee Su-jeong's 1885 translation, the 1904 New Testament (신약전서), the 1911 Old Testament (구약전서), and the 1913 Gospel of John (요한복음), the English term "nation" is translated into Korean as "paeksŏng" (빅성) or "nara" (나라). The translation of "nation" as "minjok" (민족) first appeared in the Korean Revised Edition (Sŏnggyŏnggaeyŏk or 성경개역) in 1938.

In the early Bible translations, the terms "paeksŏng" (백성) and "nara" (나라) were eventually replaced with "minjok" through early work on the Bible revision in 1938. This shows that the corresponding Korean term for the English word "nation" was revised to "minjok" (민족), a concept that was widely used at the time. In 1938, Japan's oppressive colonial rule reached its peak, corresponding to a time of militarization and genocidal rule following the outbreak of the Second Sino-Japanese War in 1937. Korean resistance movements exploded in response. As a result, the concept of "minjok" became popular.

Accordingly, the term "minjok" came to acquire the meaning of "aejok" (애족 or 愛族), meaning "love of the nation" or "love of [one's] people." This embedded a sense of anti-colonial resistance into public consciousness. It is generally accepted that this widespread adoption was also reflected in Bible translations. Through such examination, this paper sought to investigate why early Bible translations contributed to the formation of nationhood in terms of its form and substance during the late Chosun period. This series of investigations ultimately aimed to define the characteristics and concept of biblical nationalism, which emerged throughout the process.

During the late Chosun period, as the Chosun Dynasty faced instability due to the encroachment of the West, there was a growing sense of crisis and instability within the kingdom. The impending downfall of the nation was perceived as a threat to the Korean people, and this ignited a sense of national consciousness and awakening. It was during this time that the concept of 'nation' began to take root in the collective consciousness. The emergence and widespread availability of books played a significant role in challenging traditional thinking with modern Western ideas. Notably, Christian-related books, especially translated bibles, dominated the publishing landscape of that era. It is important to recognize that the Bible translation project gave birth to new ideologies, shaping the zeitgeist and cultivating a unique form of nationalism known as "biblical nationalism."

First, the distribution of translated texts provided a societal and institutional model of nationhood. The most in-demand translated Bible was written in a "Kuk'anmun" mix of Korean and Chinese characters and encompasses both commoners and scholars. For this reason, the Bible was able to gain popularity at the time by being printed in standard language more than any other book. The process of reading and reciting the Bible printed in the same script gradually dismantled long-standing systemic barriers of social status, eventually leading to the formation of a sense of unified consciousness of nationhood. In other words, during the period of early Bible translations, Christians started to recognize and unify their national identity in the process of gradually standardizing language barriers between classes.

Second, biblical nationalism serves as an example of modern nationalism. In other words, Biblical Israel exhibits egalitarian aspects that evoke the principles of modern civic nationalism. The Bible portrays righteous nations enjoying equal sovereignty. It articulates a political doctrine that defines a "a nation with a distinct and unique character" and recognizes the nation's right to preserve its interests and values, thereby asserting its "entitlement to political sovereignty." Hence, the modern notion of national identity was understood as the identity adopted by the "people" as a "nation." Under this interpretation, all members of the "people" are perceived as inherently homogeneous residents, with their status and class distinctions being considered superficial. It is believed that during the late Chosun period, Koreans also started to recognize themselves as fellow "compatriots," forming a homogeneous community of citizens as class divisions gradually eroded.

Third, the role of Christianity in the late Chosun period is considered significant in terms of its contribution to the narrative of nationhood found in the Bible, which was then linked to narratives of social reform and resistance against foreign influences, thereby connecting it to the nationalist movement. The recognition of the concept of the covenant, which promised the liberation of Israel from foreign oppression, infused a sense of motivation and legitimacy into the acts of resistance against foreign powers during the Late Chosun period. Amidst the encroachment of Chosun's sovereignty by both the Qing and Japanese empires, as well as Western powers, the Korean people developed a heightened sense of national sovereignty. It can be inferred that Christians may have aligned their religious beliefs with their political ideals, merging them into a unified framework. This can be referred to as covenant nationalism.

Therefore, it would be appropriate to label the outcome of the translation of the Bible by Protestant Christians during the Late Chosun era as "biblical nationalism." This concept encompassed an internal call for social reform and an external program of resistance against foreign powers, all aimed at revitalizing the nation.

Metamorphosis of Seoul:

Visual Representations of the Korean Capital at the Turn of the 20th Century

MECSI Beatrix

1. Introduction

Korea, the "Hermit Kingdom" opened its ports to the outside world in the 1880s and with the introduction of photography around the same time, the capital city[1] as a symbol of Korea received an increased visibility. The city – that was seen by foreign travellers, diplomats, writers who usually spent a few days here during their travels around the world –, made a long-lasting impact on them, and these experiences were recorded not only in their diaries, and travelogues, but also in their drawings, paintings and through the lens of their cameras. So far, most researchers interested in photographic images of Korea have focused on extracting insights into the everyday life of Koreans, viewing them as historical documents of the era. However, by adopting a different approach and examining images of the capital created by both foreigners and Korean photographers and artists across various media at the turn of the century, we can discern deliberate or unintentional choices in their use

---

[1]   What we call now Seoul, had several names in the past: it was first called Yangju (양주, 楊州), then Namgyeong (남경, 南京), and Hanyang (한양, 漢陽). Then, with the beginning of the Joseon dynasty, in 1395 when it was chosen as the capital, it was called Hanseong (한성, 漢城), but at the same time it was also called as Hanyang, Gyeongdo (경도, 京都). After the annexation to Japan, it was named as Gyeongseong (경성, 京城). (Na 2008:5)

of subjects, angles, and compositions. Analysing these images from a visual standpoint provides valuable insights into the various perceptions of the evolution of the Joseon capital into the modern Korean Empire, followed by the Japanese occupation marked by a transition towards consumerist entertainment and tourism. Furthermore, delving into these images helps us grasp the changing visual portrayal of Seoul as a symbol of Korea.

This paper aims to juxtapose the painted and printed depictions of the city from earlier periods in the Joseon era, primarily intended for local use (e.g., images of palaces), with the newly emerging photographic images from the 1880s. These photographs were predominantly captured by foreigners but later also by Koreans, including the Korean photographer Hwang Cheol. By doing so, it seeks to contextualize the visual recordings of Seoul by Hungarian visitors such as Ferenc Hopp, an optician, and Dezső Bozóky, a naval doctor, alongside earlier and contemporary perspectives offered by other foreigners such as the American Percival Lowell in 1883 and the French Pierre Loti in 1901, as well as a local Korean approach to the city in the year 1915 by the painter An Jungsik.

2. Representations of Seoul in the Joseon era

Yi Seonggye (1335-1408, r. 1392-98), known under the posthumous title of Taejo established Joseon dynasty in 1392 and proclaimed Seoul[2] the site of his new capital in 1394. Ruling according to the Neo-Confucian (Seongnihak) principles, the influence of Buddhism disappeared and gave visibility to the Confucianism-related buildings and structures. New palaces were constructed during this time, with the first being the Gyeongbok Palace, serving as both the government headquarters and the royal residence of the new dynasty. Its location was chosen based on geomantic principles, being shielded by Mount Bugak to the north, Naksan Mountain to the east, and Inwangsan Mountain to the west, while facing the Han River to the south.[3] During the fifteenth

---

2   The indigenous Korean word for 'capital'.

3   The following passage includes information about the Seoul palaces taken from the chapter "Ritual

century, the Eastern Palaces, namely Changdeokgung and Changgyeonggung, were constructed. These palaces were destroyed during the Japanese invasions in the sixteenth century, along with Gyeongbok Palace. However, they were later rebuilt and served as both the government seat and royal residence until the late nineteenth century. It was during this time that Gyeongbok Palace was also reconstructed.

Two large court paintings, created between 1826 and 1830, depict Seoul during the time when the Eastern palaces served as the government headquarters.[4] These paintings offer a bird's-eye view of the palace area, surrounded by mountains and hills. They are comprised of sixteen long sheets of paper, each folded accordion-style into six leaves. To view the entire image, all sixteen units must be unfolded and arranged side by side. Otherwise, each unit resembles a small book that could be stored in a library. This format functions like a foldable map, with the names of important buildings written in Chinese characters next to their painted images. The accuracy of these representations has even allowed modern restorers to gather valuable information from them.

For residents of Seoul and visitors to the capital city, Gyeongbok Palace symbolized Korea's seat of power. As such, its depiction can be seen as a portrayal of Korea itself. By studying images of this palace, we can understand how those who created visual representations perceived Korea. The early twentieth century marks a significant period for visual representations, with the emergence of photography in the 1880s. However, examining depictions of the palace and its surroundings in other forms of media is also valuable. Comparing these images not only from the same time period but also in a chronological sequence, starting from the late 19th century until 1915 when significant changes occurred during Japanese colonial rule (1910-1945) is very meaningful. Sections of the Gyeongbok Palace were demolished then to make room for the Joseon Product Exposition's temporary exhibition halls, followed by the construction of a Western style building a year later to serve as the

and Splendor: Chosŏn Court Art" by Jungmann, Burglind 2020:344-348.

4   Paintings made ca. 1830. Ink on paper and silk. Dimensions: The painting in the Korea University Museum: width of 583 cm and a height of 274 cm; the other painting in the Dong-A University Museum: width of 576 cm and a height of 273 cm.

seat of colonial power administered by the Japanese Governor-General. Between 1926 and 1945, this building became the largest government structure in East Asia. After restoration efforts following the Korean War, the building housed the government of South Korea from 1962 and became the National Museum of Korea in 1986. The Gyeongbok Palace site, seen as a symbol of Korea, with a new building constructed on it, was not only seen as a symbol of Japanese colonial oppression but also believed to disrupt the geomantic balance of the palace and the country. This building was torn down, and the area was restored to its original state from 1995.

3. Representations of Seoul by Foreigners

Painting

Western painters like Henry Landor (1865-1924) from the United Kingdom, the Dutch American Hubert Vos (1855-1935), and Constance Tayler (1868-1948) from Scotland were the first foreign painters who were granted audiences with the Joseon king. They could paint Western-style portraits of royal family members and court officials, as well as created many sketches depicting common people and local scenery.[5]

Hubert Vos in Seoul (1897-1900)

One of the earliest Western painters to serve the Joseon court was Hubert Vos. He worked as a painter in Paris and Brussels before gaining recognition in various European exhibitions, including the Royal Academy of London, where he opened his studio in 1888. Vos became known for his portrait paintings. In 1893, he represented the Netherlands at the World's Columbian Exposition in Chicago. After marrying Hawaiian princess Kaikilani in November 1897,[6] Vos travelled the world with her until 1900 when the World Exposition in

---

5   Jungsil Jenny Lee, "Modern Korean Art in the Japanese Colonial Period," in *A Companion to Korean Art*, 1st edition, edited by J. P. Park, Burglind Jungmann, and Juhyung Rhi (New Jersey: Wiley&Sons, 2020), 407-408.

6   'A Romantic Marriage', New York Times, 7 November 1897. Horlyck 2017: 18.

Paris began. In 1898, he visited Korea and stayed there for about two years.[7] His *Landscape of Seoul*, painted in 1899, depicts the city as seen from what was then the U.S. Legation (presently the U.S. ambassador's residence) in Jeong-dong, facing the Gyeongbok Palace.[8] In this oil painting, the mountains, especially Bukhan Mountain, play a central role. Only a small portion of the royal palace's gate and pavilions are visible just above the horizon. In the foreground, there are tile-roofed houses and a blossoming fruit tree nearby. Hubert Vos emphasized this aspect in a letter to his friend in 1911, describing Korea as one of the most fascinating countries in the world, with beautiful flowers growing everywhere. He noted that the people, belonging to one of the oldest races, always wore white clothes and moved quietly, creating a dreamlike atmosphere.[9] To underscore the tranquillity of the city, a lone human figure was portrayed on the left side of the houses.

Photography

Following the invention of photography in the 1840s, this technology was soon used to document anthropological and archaeological work in the recently acquired colonial territories by colonial powers.[10] Photography was introduced to China and Japan in the 1860s, but Korea didn't adopt the technology until it opened its ports for foreign trade with Japan in 1876, and with the USA and China in 1882.[11] In the early 1900s, people worldwide, and various industries like newspapers, engineering, architecture, transportation, and tourism, widely embraced photography. They used it extensively to document geography, natural resources, historical sites, indigenous cultures, and artworks. This served both to inform their own citizens and to display their discoveries to the colonized populations. The visual knowledge they produced could have been interpreted

---

7 국립현대미술관 (National Museum of Modern and Contemporary Art, Korea) https://www.mmca.go.kr/engN/pop/exhibition/2012/05/detail1_eng.html (accessed March 18, 2024).

8 *Scenery of Seoul*, 1899, oil on canvas, 31 × 69 cm. Museum of Modern and Contemporary Art, Seoul.

9 국립현대미술관, Ibid.

10 Hyung Il Pai, "Visualizing Seoul's Landscapes: Percival Lowell and the Cultural Biography of Ethnographic Images," *The Journal of Korean Studies* 21, no. 2 (Durham: Duke University Press, 2016), 366.

11 Jeehey Kim, *Photography and Korea* (London: Reaktion Books, 2023), 18-19.

and reframed accordingly, and the seemingly objective genre was sometimes used to formulate distinct meanings just by choosing the angles and frames of their photo shots. The rise of photography around the world happened alongside advancements like steamships, transcontinental railways, and postal services. These developments fuelled a growing desire for new images of different cultures and landscapes among publishers, readers, consumers, and travellers.[12] In the 1860s, with the availability of portable cameras to amateurs, a new form of travel and documentation emerged, now known as "photojournalism".[13] Photojournalists focused on creating and selling souvenir albums featuring panoramic views of popular destinations. The progress of photography and anthropological fieldwork ran alongside empire expansion, international travel, and the rise of commercial media. This significantly influenced the subjects and individuals captured through the camera lens, thereby shaping visual representations.[14] During the early 1900s, photography was not commonly practiced in Korea. Most of the photographers at that time came from abroad, and the majority were travellers, diplomats, army officers, or war correspondents.

Seoul's palaces, gardens, and gates as landmarks attracted visitors symbolized Korean national identity, both domestically and globally. Monuments and their images on postcards (invented around the 1870s and spread worldwide), posters, and dioramas were cherished as tangible connections to the lasting traditions of the Joseon dynasty, and as must-visit places for tourists.[15]

4. Foreign Photographers

Percival Lowell in Seoul (1883-1884)

Out of the numerous foreign photographers active in Seoul at the beginning of the 20th century, Percival Lowell (1855-1916), an early American photographer

---

12 Pai, "Visualizing Seoul's Landscapes," 366.

13 Important representatives were Francis Firth (1822-1898), William Stillman (1828-1901), Roger Fenton (1819-1869), and Felice Beato (1832-1909). Ibid., 366.

14 Ibid., 366.

15 Ibid., 366.

who worked in Korea in the 1880s is an important case because he possesses one of the oldest and most complete photographic collections of Korea.[16] Additionally, his book titled *Chosön, the Land of the Morning Calm*, published by Ticknor and Company in Boston, with twenty-five original photographs, is recognized as the first detailed firsthand account of Korea,[17] therefore his photographs might have served as an example for the later visualisations of the city. Percival Lowell, an astronomer, mathematician, traveller, and diplomat, spent four months in Seoul from December 1883 to March 1884. During his stay in Japan from 1883 to 1893, he likely had access to various photographs depicting Japanese culture and customs, which may have influenced his own photography of Korean culture. His photographs of Korea targeted foreigners, showcasing exotic landscapes and people. Lowell was the first American diplomat to use a camera, capturing portraits of King Gojong, palace scenes, and daily life in Seoul. His collection of sixty photographs is preserved at the Boston Museum of Fine Arts, providing insights into the Joseon Dynasty era. Lowell's royal patronage allowed him access to restricted areas of Gyeongbok and Changdeok palaces, capturing unique images. He introduced the Korean capital in detail in his book, showing a deep understanding of the court's culture and the symbolism of its art and architecture. Lowell's photographs depict the deserted yet grand Gyeongbok Palace, highlighting its unique features like the Gyeonghoeru Banquet Hall. His strategic arrangement of figures in his photographs enhanced the architectural grandeur, earning widespread recognition in foreign media. Lowell's images are invaluable for studying palace architecture, as they depict the original layout before significant changes occurred in the palace grounds.

Pierre Loti in Seoul (1901)

Pierre Loti (1850-1923), a French naval officer and writer,[18] is an interesting example for recording the visual appearance of Seoul, not only through his

---

16 About Percival Lowell, information here is summarized from Pai, Ibid., 355-384.

17 Percival Lowell, *Chosön, the Land of the Morning Calm*. (Boston. Ticknor and Company, 1885), Library of Congress website, https://www.loc.gov/item/04016695 (accessed March 22, 2024.)

18 His original name Julien Viaud.

photography, but also with his literary works and visually strong descriptions of the city.

He interrupted his journey from China to Japan to spend only a few days in Korea, between 17 and 26 June 1901. This short period of time provided him with enough material for his literary work, which, in addition to his diary entries,[19] is also recorded in one of his novels[20] and photographs of the capital. The now almost forgotten writer was very popular at the turn of the century, not only in his homeland but also abroad, including Hungary. His most successful novels were inspired by his experiences as a professional naval officer. His first literary texts were written in the form of a diary, and from these lines grew his short stories, novels and longer travelogues. Loti's documentary approach is most interesting for the present subject, the representation of Seoul at the turn of the century, because the writer, who also had a fine art talent, reproduces the places, people and street scenes he sees as sensually as possible.

Here, too, his writing, which is considered impressionistic, is expressed in the emphasis on personal impressions and, with them, on colours that express emotions and suggest a painterly vision. For him Seoul is best characterised by the colour grey: "Early in the morning, the sunlight floods the vast grey city, enclosed in grey mountains. Straight grey streets, four kilometres long and a hundred metres wide, run between low, grey cottages. And the city, beyond the fortifications, is surrounded by a ring of grey, blackened, bare, spiky, tiger-ridden mountains, like some monumental city wall."[21] The author finds the rocky, stony countryside around the capital peaceful but melancholic.[22] The pervading grey is broken up by a crowd of passers-by dressed in white, a few babies in bright red swaddling clothes and golden-yellow hoods,

---

19 Pierre Loti, *Journal, IV* (1896-1902) (Paris: Les Indes savantes, 2016), 574-580.

20 Pierre Loti, *La Troisième jeunesse de madame Prune* [The third youth of Lady Plum], (1905) La Tour-d'Aigues, Éd. de l'Aube, 2010. See: XL. chapter (À Séoul [in Seoul]): I. Dans la rue [On the street], II. À la cour [At the court], 187-208.

21 Loti, *Journal*, 575.

22 Ibid., 580. For Loti's melancholic, nostalgic sense of life in the Far East, see: Cseppentő, István, "Discours d'exilé, discours de voyageur", in Maár, J. – Lefebvre, A. (eds.), *Exils et transfert cuturels dans l'Europe moderne*, Paris, L'Harmattan, Cahiers de la Nouvelle Europe, 21, 2015, 291.

and a woman of a certain social caste wearing a green coat: a sea of colour in a sea of grey.

Loti's descriptions are known for their attention to the minutest details, reflecting a style and mood reminiscent of the 18th-century French Rococo tradition.[23] There is a direct allusion to this in the description of Seoul: the appearance and facial expressions of the dancers performing in the imperial palace remind Loti of 18th century France,[24] most typically of the dolls of Louis XVI.[25] Indirectly, however, there are also adjectives often used by Loti, such as "grotesque", "small", "clumsy", etc., which belong to the concept of the Rococo aesthetic. The bizarre, yet playful atmosphere is well combined with a melancholic, almost morbid sense of life, also in the spirit of the Rococo aesthetic: "When you climb up one of the black towers over the gates of Seoul, adorned with granite monsters, the whole city spreads out like a vast graveyard beneath your feet: the roofs of every house are like a series of tortoise-shell tombstones, made of grey potsherds. And on the wide, straight avenues, among the multitude of tombstones, pass the crowds of passers-by in white muslin dress."[26]

This personal, almost poetic testimony of early 20th century Seoul sets Pierre Loti apart from most travel writers. However, like other contemporary travellers to Korea, such as the Hungarian Péter Vay, Ferenc Hopp, Dezső Bozóky, and the American Percival Lowell, Loti is an important source.[27] His approach and the visually detailed descriptions of perceiving the city of Seoul is a distinct way of how a foreign observer react to the visuality of the capital, evoking feelings and elements drawn from his own country's art and history as a reference point.

---

23 István Cseppentő, "Galantéria, nosztalgia, keleti egzotikum. A rokokó 'turquerie' irodalmi továbbélése Pierre Loti *A kiábrándultak* című regényében", in: Bartha-Kovács Katalin – Fórizs Gergely (eds.), *A rokokó arcai. Tanulmányok egy tünékeny fogalom történetéhez* (Budapest: Reciti, 2022), 71-81.

24 Loti, *Journal*, 578.

25 Loti, *La Troisième jeunesse de madame Prune*, 206.

26 Loti, *Journal*, 576.

27 For a selection of these, see: Quella-Villéger, Alain – Vercier, Bruno, *Pierre Loti photographe*, Saint-Pourçain-sur-Sioule, Éd. Bleu autour, 2012, 322-331.

Hungarian Photographers of Seoul: Ferenc Hopp and Dezső Bozóky

Two archive photographic collections in the Ferenc Hopp Museum of Asian Art in Budapest are particularly important as they reflect the different approaches of a globetrotter (Ferenc Hopp) and a naval doctor (Dezső Bozóky) to the city. Hopp (1833-1919), an optician and later the founder of the Museum of Asian Arts in Budapest, travelled to Korea in 1903, while Bozóky (1842-1919), a naval doctor, visited five years later, in 1908. Both collected photographs during their visits, including ones they took themselves and others they acquired locally. Their personal photographs reflect their unique styles and characters, offering insights into life in Korea just before the Japanese occupation through their own personalities and backgrounds. The existing photographs of Korea by Bozóky and Hopp are just fragments of their larger collections. These surviving photos are particularly valuable, offering us a chance to view Korea through the eyes of two distinct European perspectives.[28] Centering on depictions of the Korean capital, I have chosen images captured by Hopp and Bozóky during their time in Seoul. By situating these images alongside those of contemporary foreign and local photographers, we can discern their photographic interests and compositional approaches in the city.

Ferenc Hopp in Seoul (1903)

Hopp, a well-to-do optician, made five trips around the world between 1882 and 1914.[29] In 1903, at the age of seventy, he made his third trip to Korea out of a total of five journeys he undertook. He was a lifelong learner who continuously sought to expand his knowledge and experiences by living abroad. Apart from spending two years in Vienna and four years in New York, he

---

28 Tatjána Kardos, "Old Korean Photographs in the Archives of the Hopp Museum," in Fajcsák and Mecsi, *The Land of the Morning Calm* (2012), 9-11; Beatrix Mecsi, "Two Hungarian Hobby Photographers in Old Korea: Ferenc Hopp and Dezső Bozóky," in Andreas Schirmer (ed.), *Koreans and Central Europeans. Informal Contacts up to 1950* (Vienna: Praesens, 2020), 115-128.

29 The following information about Hopp and Bozóky's photography collections is based on the chapters written by Tatjána Kardos, 2012:9-11;26-37;141-166 and by Mária Ferenczy 2012:12-25;141-166 in the volume *The Land of the Morning Calm. Korean Art in the Ferenc Hopp Museum of Eastern Asiatic Arts*, Budapest. and from Csoma Mózes, Kardos Tatjána, Látogatás a Hajnalpír Országában Dr. Bozóky Dezső koreai fotográfiái = Visit to the Land of Morning Calm: Dr. Dezső Bozóky's Korean photographs./조용한 아침의 나라 방문기: 보조끼 대죠의 사진. Ferenc Hopp Museum of Asiatic Arts and the Embassy of Hungary, Seoul, 2020.

was fluent in several languages and excelled in various fields. This expertise proved beneficial when he successfully revitalized the Calderoni firm, making it the leading supplier of optical and educational materials for schools in Hungary following the 1870 educational reforms. These reforms mandated that every elementary school in the country be equipped with top-notch learning resources. Hopp's company also advertised and sold photographs and photographic instruments, leading to significant success.[30]

By the time he reached his fifties, Hopp could afford both pleasure and business travel. He toured Mediterranean countries, visited Central Africa to see the Congolese railway, and embarked on five global ventures. His correspondence with friends provides valuable insights into his experiences. He wrote about his travels and spoke publicly about them as an invited speaker. Over time, he developed a strong interest in East Asian art, particularly Asian lacquer works. Hopp passed away on September 7, 1919, in Budapest. In his will, he left his collection of over 4,500 artifacts, mostly from East Asia, as well as his villa and garden on Andrássy Street, to the Hungarian government. His intention was to establish a museum of East Asian art.

In the summer of 1903, Ferenc Hopp embarked on his third trip around the world, accompanied by a wealthy friend who was a merchant. They journeyed to Korea by crossing the Atlantic Ocean, travelling by train across the United States, sailing across the Pacific, and spending a month in Japan. They arrived at the port of Busan on July 28th, having sailed from Nagasaki. Two days later, they sailed to Chemulp'o and reached the capital, Seoul, by train where they stayed for a week.[31] Hopp's detailed travel diary documents their time in Korea. Upon returning, Hopp lectured about his travels at a meeting of

---

30 Béla Kelényi, "A Calderoni kirakatja" [The shop window of Calderoni], in Györgyi Fajcsák and Zsuzsanna Renner, eds., *A Buitenzorg-villa lakója. A világutazó, műgyűjtő Hopp Ferenc (1833-1919)* [The man of Buitenzorg Villa: Ferenc Hopp, globe-trotter and art collector (1833-1919)] (Budapest: Ferenc Hopp Museum of Asiatic Arts, 2008), 55-62.

31 Inv. No.: A 1718.10. Railway station, Seoul, 1903. Albumen print, half stereo contact, 8,5 x 8 cm. (On the backside of the photo, written with an unknown hand: "1432 Eisenbahn Train /in Sëaul"). The photograph appears to have been captured shortly after Hopp disembarked from the train. The presence of the train divides the scene, resulting in empty spaces at the bottom and top right of the image. On the left side, two Korean gentlemen dressed in white robes and wearing horsehair hats can be seen walking, while a young man in Western attire strides by, gazing at the foreigner behind the camera.

the Hungarian Geographic Society in Budapest on March 24, 1904. He used 170 photographs as illustrations, and the lecture was later published with 47 illustrations in the Society's Geographic Proceedings. Hopp's published travel journal also includes his observations of Korea, focusing more on history and experiences rather than poetic descriptions. Although Hopp was an active photographer, his collection mainly consists of photographs that he purchased rather than ones he took himself.

As the number of foreign travellers to Korea grew, small photographic studios began producing photos of Korean landscapes, traditional customs, and portraits to meet the rising demand for souvenirs. Ferenc Hopp bought photos in Korea showing city views, town gates, streets, and scenes of both aristocratic and peasant life. Unfortunately, most of Hopp's photos did not survive. During his third trip around the world, he took around 17,000 pictures, but only about fifty are known today, with fewer than eight taken in Korea. Although Hopp purchased hundreds of photos during his travels, only twenty-two of them from Korea have been preserved.[32]

Even though this collection is small, it demonstrates Hopp's interest in and appreciation for this distant country and its people. As we browse through his photographs, it becomes clear that Ferenc Hopp was a considerate individual who aimed to respect local customs and sensitivities. For example, many of his photographs lack a prominent subject in the foreground.[33] Hopp's photographic subjects were limited because monasteries and palaces were not accessible to visitors, and according to Hopp, the main attractions in the capital were the town gates. Only one of the surviving pictures was taken during a visit to a shrine or palace garden, where Hopp's travel companions posed

---

32 Kardos, Ibid., 9-11; 26-37.

33 Inv. No.: A 1718.15. Ferenc Hopp: The main street in Seoul. 1903. Collodion print, half-stereo contact. Embossed with mark. 8 x 8 cm. The photograph was captured from the tram, evident from the clearly visible rails on the right side. In the empty foreground, shadows of local people can be seen. On the left, there is a row of ground-floor houses.; Inv. No.: A 1718.16. Ferenc Hopp: Seoul, main street with a row of one-story buildings with open shopfronts. 1903. Albumen print, half stereo contact Signed. 8 x 8 cm. Like the previous photo, this one depicts the right side of the street, also featuring an empty foreground.; Inv. No.: A 1718.04. A street scene at the fuel market. 1903. Albumen print, half stereo contact, 8 x 8 cm. (On the margin the serial number of the glass negative is visible: 1435) Here we also observe the empty foreground, with people walking in from the edges.

for him.[34] Hopp described Seoul as a "big village" and a "strange capital" that seemed incomplete to European visitors, lacking typical town features like gardens, parks, restaurants, theatres, and hotels. He also noted the scarcity of churches and anticipated that the city would undergo significant changes with advancements in government. Therefore, in his approach the anticipation of a modernized city appears, comparing Seoul to the cities he saw in Europe and during his travels.

Dezső Bozóky in Seoul (1908)

For two years, Dezső Bozóky served as a doctor on an Austro-Hungarian naval ship. During his time in the navy, he travelled to various places. In 1905, he visited Constantinople, then, in 1907, he sailed to Singapore and worked on the cruiser Franz Joseph I until the end of 1908. Bozóky boarded the cruiser in Colombo on March 31, 1907. The ship stopped in various ports, including Tienjin, Yokohama, Vladivostok, Qifu, and Hong Kong, before sailing to Japanese waters in May. The cruiser spent some time in Yokohama for maintenance, during which Bozóky might have visited Korea. Finally, the ship departed for Pula, the main Austro-Hungarian naval base, where Bozóky arrived on December 16, 1908. He visited Korea aboard this ship in the summer of 1908.[35]

There are 689 hand-coloured glass slides, seven photo albums containing approximately 1,400 photographs, and 380 stereophotographs documenting Bozóky's travels in East Asia that have survived.[36] Dezső Bozóky's collection of photographs encompasses a wide range of photographic mediums that were popular during that time. This collection includes albums, stereophotographs,

---

34 Inv. No.: F 2012.30. Tourists and local people in a garden. Seoul, Korea 1903. Gelatin silver print, half stereo contact, 8 x 8 cm. The image depicts three foreigners alongside Korean individuals, with one of them holding an umbrella and wearing a long vest, likely identified as Mr. Chin-Soo, a teacher known for his ability to speak German. Notes from Ferenc Hopp mention Mr. Chin-Soo's kindness in guiding him and his companions around the city. Similar to other photographs by Hopp, the composition shows an empty foreground.

35 Kardos, Ibid.

36 Dénes Mirjam and Sebestyén Ágnes Anna, "Egy magyar utazó Japán-olvasata a századfordulón: Bozóky Dezső fotográfiái," Doma Petra and Takó Ferenc (eds.): „Közel, s Távol" V., Az Eötvös Collegium Orientalisztika Műhely éves konferenciájának előadásaiból 2015 (Budapest: Eötvös Collegium, 2016), 11-34.

and slides. Bozóky captured these images with the intent of sharing his experiences with friends, acquaintances, and the general public upon his return home. He also published some of these photographs in his book *Two Years in East Asia*.[37] The purchased photographs shed light on how locals portrayed themselves to Western travellers and how Bozóky selected from the numerous available images. His personal photographs illustrate how he documented and interpreted his experiences through his unique perspective and written accounts. It is intriguing to explore the extent of his impartiality or subjectivity as a mediator and what his main focus was. We can notice his approach to the places he visited that he usually tried to catch an overview of the whole city by climbing up to higher spots and taking pictures of the scene, usually showing human figures in the foreground.[38] Thanks to his approachable demeanour and professional background as a medical doctor, he often established closer connections with local people than many other photographers in Korea.

His photographs showcased not only the prominent tourist sites like the city gates and trams,[39] but primarily focused on capturing the diverse activities

---

37 Dezső Bozóky, *Két év Keletázsiában* [Two years in East Asia], vol. 1 (Published by the author, 1911).

38 Inv. No.: F 2004.654. Dezső Bozóky: Panorama of Seoul with three men in the foreground. 1908. Hand-coloured glass slide. 6 x 7 cm. View of the city from the hills on the right. Working on the hillside, under the crooked pines, are probably surveyors.; Inv. No.: F 2004.655. Dezső Bozóky: Seoul, 1908. hand-coloured glass slide, 8 x 8 cm. Panorama of Seoul, with one man under a tree.; Inv. No.: F 2004.656. Dezső Bozóky: Seoul. The Japanese quarter, with a Japanese person in the foreground. 1908. hand-coloured glass slide, 8 x 8 cm. View of the city from the hills on its right. The view includes houses of the Japanese quarter, as well as thatched Korean homes at the foot of the hill. In the distance stand the hills that protect the city. A Japanese man stands in the foreground, with a parasol. "The district spreading beneath our feet is already completely Japanese, with little left of the old Seoul, only a few small isles, here and there, of the thatched houses pressed close together". (Bozóky 1911, I. 511).

39 Inv. No.: F 2004.657. Dezső Bozóky: Seoul. Dongdaemun (Heunginji-mun) with a tram in front of the gate, and people of different nationalities and clothes, 1908. hand-coloured glass slide, 8 x 8 cm. Built in 1396, the Eastern Gate (Heunginji-mun, "Gate of Rising Benevolence"), was given to look visible in the picture during the 1869 reconstruction. Visible through the opening of the gate is the outer wall. On the left, a tram car can be seen. Trams were put in service in Seoul in 1899, and they ran along the east-west main road, the Jong-no, and along the way, passed under the Eastern Gate. The photo also bears evidence to how diverse Seoul's population had become by the time of Bozóky's visit: alongside the locals, men in Japanese and European clothes can also be seen around the gate.; Inv. No.: F 2004.658. Dezső Bozóky: Seoul. Namdaemun (Sungryemun)1908. Hand-coloured glass slide, 8 x 8 cm. There were four large and four smaller gates in the wall that surrounded Seoul. The Southern Gate (Sungye-mun, "Gate of Honouring Propriety") was erected in 1396, and was rebuilt several times during the 15th century. Also visible in the picture are the

of people dressed in various attire. When photographing the streets of Seoul, he intentionally framed the images to highlight the bustling activities, such as a rickshaw,[40] an elderly man tending to children near advertisements,[41] and three elegantly dressed women in front of a basket weaver's shop.[42] He captured images of the Wongudan temple, which was demolished shortly after his visit.[43] Bozóky also photographed another renowned tourist spot, the marble pagoda in Tapgol Park, in two different versions.[44] However, the majority

construction works that were carried out around the partially demolished city wall: "From the city walls, already pulled down in part, they have already cut out the stone gate, which has a beautiful, double curved roof, and a tall arch. The old city gate will subsequently stand in the middle of a circular square, on its own, as an interesting monument, and will be bypassed, left and right, by wide roads of granite cobbles. The gate itself is now also carefully restored." (Bozóky 1911, I. 502).

40 Inv. No.: F 2004.660. Dezső Bozóky: Seoul. Rickshaw.1908. Hand-coloured glass slide, 8 x 8 cm. On the main street of Seoul (Jongno Street, a rickshaw puller, the distinguished gentleman in the rickshaw, two men in hats running behind the rickshaw, the South Gate and the tram in the distance). A rickshaw is approaching on the Jongno, with a well-off passenger and two escorts (one of whom is covered by the vehicle). Open shops line the road, in front of which, a couple moving away can be seen, as well as onlooking small girls. In the distance, the city gate can be seen at the end of the road, as well as a tram. Rickshaws had been in use in Seoul since the middle of the 1880s. In 1884, during the Gapsin Revolution, protesters set fire to all of them, as vehicles of Japanese origin. In the next decade, however, they appeared again in the streets of Seoul, and in 1899 there were enough rickshaw men to protest against the introduction of the tram service for fear of losing their jobs.

41 Inv. No.: F 2004.661. Dezső Bozóky: Seoul. Koreans, 1908. Hand-coloured glass slide, 8 x 8 cm. In the street, an elderly Korean man watches over two children. Behind them, a fence displays bilingual Korean Japanese advertisements. One of the posters, written vertically, advertises a tooth powder named Lion.

42 Inv. No.: F 2004.662. Dezső Bozóky: Three cloaked ladies in front of a basket weaver's shop. Seoul, 1908. Hand-coloured glass slide, 8 x 8 cm. "Three women wrapped in their aprons approach in the strong headwind on the Jongno. On the right, a basket maker's offer is on view. (⋯) And the women of Seoul wear, almost all of them, light green aprons on their heads, with the two empty sleeves hanging by their ears, and red, crimson or violet ribbons on their chests". (Bozóky 1911, I. 501-502)

43 Inv. No.: F 2004.670. Dezső Bozóky: Seoul. The "Yellow Temple" in Seoul, 1908 Hand-coloured glass slide, 8 x 8 cm. From beyond the fence, one can see the Wongudan temple, which contained the Altar of Heaven and Earth. Above the fence, the polygonal roof of the Altar of Heaven, the white marble balustrades encircling its circular terraces, and the multi-tiered roof of the octagonal pavilion, known as the Hwanggungu, where sacrifices were made, are visible.

44 Inv. No.: F 2004.671. Dezső Bozóky: The marble pagoda in Seoul, 1908, Hand-coloured glass slide, 8 x 8 cm. The originally ten-storey Wongaksa Pagoda in Tapgol Park, built in 1468.; The top three stories, which collapsed during the Japanese invasion from 1592 to 1598, are visible behind the man wearing a dark coat. Bozóky's fellow officers are seen approaching from the direction of the pagoda. In the distance, the curved roof marking the entrance to the park, along with its fence, can be observed. Additionally, some of the bare mountains encircling Seoul are visible in the background.; Inv. No.: F 2004.672. Dezső Bozóky: Seoul. Seven storey marble Pagoda, in Tapgol Park, 1908.

of the photographs preserved in his collection feature Gyeongbok Palace, which was accessible to special visitors at that time.[45]

5. Korean Photographers of Seoul

The introduction of photography changed how people saw the world. It is intriguing to examine how photography and modernity are interconnected, as well as how photography impacted and was affected by portrait and landscape

Hand-coloured glass slide, 8 x 8 cm. Tapgol Park was the first public park in Seoul. Constructed in 1895-1896 based on a design by McLevy Brown, who served as the chief inspector of the customs office, the park occupies the former grounds of one of Seoul's largest Buddhist monasteries, Wongaksa, built in the 15th century. By the 16th century, all that remained of the monastery was the marble pagoda depicted in the picture, along with a stone stela commemorating the monastery's foundation.

45 Inv. No.: F 2004.663. Dezső Bozóky: Seoul. Entrance of the Former Imperial Palace. 1908. hand-coloured glass slide, 8 x 8 cm. Dezső Bozóky's fellow officers stroll toward the entrance of the former imperial palace, on the ceremonial stage known as the woldae. One of the gates is open, with a soldier standing guard.; Inv. No.: F 2004.664. Dezső Bozóky: Seoul.1908. hand-coloured glass slide, 8 x 8 cm, Gyeongbok Palace: Geungjeong-jeon (Hall of Audiences), Published in 1911. The ruler no longer resides here, and you can see the stone pillars that once marked the locations of the ministers. When the photo was taken, the palace had been empty for over ten years. The monarch, Gojong, fled with his son in February 1896 and never returned. Signs of neglect are evident throughout: grass grows between the paving stones, and the paper on the doors is torn in multiple places. Inv. No.: F 2004.665. Dezső Bozóky: Seoul. Hyangwon-jeong (Pavilion of Distant Fragrances) in the Imperial Park, 1908. hand-coloured glass slide, 8 x 8 cm, 1908. Constructed in the 15th century, the resting pavilion sits on a small island, connected by a wooden bridge. Dezső Bozóky believed that Min, the queen with pro-Russian leanings, was killed here in 1895, and her body was burned. However, she was actually attacked in a separate building within the palace complex, specifically in her own set of rooms.; Inv. No.: F 2004.666. Dezső Bozóky: The Gyeonghoeru (Hall of Joyful Ensemble) in Gyeonbok Palace. The pavilion in Gyeongbok Palace was constructed in the 15th century for hosting envoys and conducting official ceremonies. Bozóky describes the scene in his book in the following way: "A vast Chinese tiled roof rests on twenty-four cylindrical, thick columns, and is also supported along its circumference by rectangular stone pillars. This airy pavilion is as large as a four-storey palace, with large stone slabs covering its floor, and red lacquered stairs rising in the centre, leading up to the upper floor, which is open all around. Pale pink lotuses, the size of babies' heads, open on the surface of the lake. A beautiful forest lies on the other bank, above which the bare, black rocks that form the boundary of Seoul rise majestically". (Bozóky 1911, I. 508); Inv. No.: F 2004.667. Dezső Bozóky: Seoul. Gyeonghoe-ru (Pavilion of Joyous Meeting) 1908. Hand-coloured glass slide, 8 x 8 cm. Two of Bozóky's fellow officers stand by the railing.; Inv. No.: F 2004.668. Dezső Bozóky: Seoul. Gyeonghoe-ru (Pavilion of Joyous Meeting) 1908. hand-coloured glass slide, 8 x 8 cm. One side of Gyeonghoeru (Hall of Joyful Ensemble) is shown, along with the stone bridge leading to it. Stone lions adorn the railing corners, while lotus patterns decorate the balusters. Bugaksan mountain is visible in the distance. One of Bozóky's fellow officers stands by the railing.; Inv. No.: F 2004.669. Dezső Bozóky: Seoul. Gyeonghoe-ru (Pavilion of Joyous Meeting) 1908. hand-coloured glass slide, 8 x 8 cm, Dezső Bozóky is standing at the railing.

painting. The Korean royal family was among the earliest supporters of photography, and their engagement profoundly shaped early photographic practices, particularly in portraying the royals as an imperial power transitioning into the Japanese ruling family during colonialism.[46]

To early Korean photographers, the idea of depicting their people and surroundings was not self-evident. It was mainly the concern of foreigners who visited the country, and the photo studios ran by Japanese served these needs mostly. Between the years 1883-84, the first three Korean-owned photo studios to open in Seoul belonged to Kim Yong-Won (1842-1891), Ji Un-Yeong (1852-1935), and Hwang Cheol (1864-1930), all of whom had once worked as bureaucrats in the Foreign Office or as court painters endorsed by the crown.[47] They learnt photography in China or Japan. Among these Korean photographers I focus on Hwang Cheol who also took photos of the capital city. He was an aristocrat's son, bought a German camera and photographic materials in Shanghai and learned how to take photographs there. Back in Seoul in 1883, he converted part of his residence into a photography studio, where he specialized to making portrait photographs, and we know that he suggested to King Gojong that the system of court painting be replaced with photography.[48] He photographed royal palaces, major buildings and famous sites in Seoul, but he made portraits of high officials as well. Some high officials mistook Hwang's photography for espionage because he was suspected of selling the images to foreigners. Between 1896 and 1906 he was in Japan, and after coming back to Korea he taught the Imperial Prince Uichin (Prince Yi Kang, 1877-1955), the fifth son of King Gojong calligraphy, painting, and photography. He was practicing photography until 1906, but again left for Japan in 1910, when Korea was colonized.[49]

In the late 1880s, while Hwang was photographing the urban scape of Seoul, Percival Lowell and other foreign photographers also documented the capital in travelogues and souvenir photography. Comparing Hwang's

46 Jeehey Kim, *Photography and Korea* (London: Reaktion Books, 2023), 15.

47 Pai, Ibid.

48 Kim, *Photography and Korea*.

49 Ibid., 20.

photograph of Gyeongbok Palace at the centre of Seoul[50] with images made by foreign photographers such as Ogawa Kazumasa (Japanese, 1860-1929) and Percival Lowell, one notices that Bugaksan Mountain, situated behind the palace, was visualized differently. For Ogawa and Lowell, the scale of the mountain is the overwhelming feature, while for Hwang, the contours of the palace gate and a sculpture of the legendary creature *haetae* take precedence over Bugaksan's presence. As Kim Jeehey analyses these differences, she assumes that Hwang sought to capture the essential elements of Korean royal heritage, foregrounding the monumentality of the palace over its surrounding landscape.[51] Instead of referring to the traditional painting style of the literati, giving the mountains an important role in the imagery, he probably was making a more objective approach to the city scape, in accordance with the new genre called "View", in which visual records serve to provide information and objective knowledge.

6. New Images of Seoul in the era of Photography

An Jung-sik, an artist active from 1861 to 1919, blended Western linear perspective and photographic elements with traditional East Asian painting aesthetics in his depictions of Gyeongbokgung Palace in Seoul during the summer and autumn of 1915, five years after Joseon Korea became part of the Japanese Empire.[52] Both paintings share a similar composition, featuring Mt. Baegak prominently with the palace and Gwanghwamun Gate below. The serene landscapes add mystery to the palace's buildings, drawing attention to Gwanghwamun Gate. An adopted one-point perspective for the pathways leading to the palace gate and utilized the "seonyeom" technique to blend the palace into the mountain surroundings.[53] Despite the title "Spring Dawn", An likely

---

50 Hwang Cheol, *Gwangha Gate, Gyeongbok Palace,* 1880s, published in: Kim, Ibid., 27.

51 Ibid., 24-25.

52 An Jungsik (1861-1919), *Spring Dawn at Mt. Baegak ("Summer" Version),* 1915, ink and light colours on silk, 129.5 × 50.0 cm, Registered Cultural Heritage 485; An Jungsik, *Spring Dawn at Mt. Baegak ("Fall" Version),* 1915, ink and light colours on silk, 126.1 × 51.9 cm, Registered Cultural Heritage 485 (The National Museum of Korea).

53 Seung-ik Kim, "An Jungsik, Spring Dawn at Mt. Baegak," The National Museum of Korea, in

envisioned the palace during the prosperous Joseon period rather than its state in 1915, expressing a longing for Korea's glorious past.

The Japanese Government-General of Korea started demolishing the palace in 1910 to construct the Western-style Government-General Building, aiming to weaken local authority and promote 'progress'. Demolition began in 1912, and by 1915, marking its fifth year of colonial rule, the government held the Joseon Product Exhibition on the palace grounds. This resulted in the destruction of most major structures, replaced by eighteen Western-style temporary exhibition halls. Thus, Gyeongbokgung Palace, once the heart of the Joseon Dynasty, became a venue for promoting Japanese colonial rule.

The paintings, titled "Spring Dawn", reflect An's nostalgia for the Joseon Dynasty era and his hope for a brighter future for Korea. The pictures, looking at them in sequence, capture viewers' attention with elements suggesting Korea's diminished status, such as the disappearance of the second haetae figure and the less palace roofs from the autumn scene and the empty street and obscured palace features. Created by An Jungsik, a prominent Korean traditional painter of the early 20th century, these paintings offer insights into the artist's perception of reality during the Japanese colonial era with these symbolic elements.

7. Conclusion

Around the turn of the 20th century, foreign painters and photographers, including Hungarian visitors, depicted Seoul in different ways. This paper focuses on photographs taken by two Hungarian travellers. Ferenc Hopp, a wealthy globetrotter, viewed Seoul as a tourist interested in modernization. He captured famous landmarks like the main gates, but he was longing for the typical modern cityscape with theatres and hotels. His photos lacked engagement with locals. On the other hand, Bozóky, a medical doctor, took a more open approach, including locals in his photos, offering a broader view of the city from higher, strategic points.

Smarthistory, August 4, 2022 https://smarthistory.org/an-jungsik-spring-dawn-at-mt-baegak/ (accessed March 24, 2024).

It is intriguing to observe whether the representations included people or deliberately omitted human presence. In the 19th century, Korean court painters typically excluded human figures from their map-like depictions, and An Jungsik followed suit in his paintings depicting the main palace gate area in 1915. Despite the bustling reality of the time, with the palace neighbourhood always teeming with people, An Jungsik's painting notably lacks any human figures, suggesting a deliberate choice with a specific purpose. In the late 1890s and early 1900s, the serenity of the city was captured in Hubert Vos's oil painting, depicting only a solitary figure in the scene. Additionally, Pierre Loti's personal descriptions paint a picture of Seoul with its grey tones and tranquil, melancholic atmosphere.

Creating images while adhering to the East Asian traditions of landscape painting presents a unique blend of approaches in representing the city. While Percival Lowell and Japanese photographers focused on the literati landscape genre, emphasizing mountains, local photographer Hwang Cheol adopted the "View" genre, prioritizing objective depictions of buildings over surrounding landscapes. An Jungsik uniquely fused these traditions, blending classical literati style with objective representation of buildings, imbuing the cityscape with symbolic meaning during a crucial period of Seoul's history. As the historically significant Gyeongbok Palace was demolished to make room for colonialism's advancement, Korean symbols of authority were diminished, serving as mere entertainment props for modernization. However, in a symbolic epilogue to this narrative, recent restoration efforts have revived the "woldae" ritual stage in front of Gyeongbok Palace's Gwanghwamun gate. Historically used for public rituals during the Joseon Dynasty, this terrace, absent during Japanese occupation, has been restored nearly a century later. This restoration symbolizes a return to the heyday of Joseon Korea, reconnecting the city's metamorphosis with its royal past.

Reconstruction of the Power System in the 1950s between Colonial Heritage and the Pressure of the Aid Economy

OH Sunsil

1. Introduction

Historically, there has often been a perceived disconnection between the 1950s and the post-1960s. The former era represents a continuation of the late Japanese imperial era, when systems of total mobilization for development were retained, while the latter era was characterized by rapid industrialization. The period following Korea's liberation in 1945, its division into North and South, and the Korean War were marked by ongoing political chaos. From the aftermath of the war until 1960, a significant portion of aid funds were wasted, leading to serious inflation that the government struggled to control. Consequently, South Korea struggled to achieve industrialization. In the early stages, capital accumulation relied heavily on aid funds. Scholars studying Korea's contemporary history, particularly the United States' aid policy toward South Korea, highlight this situation as clear evidence of the priority placed on maintaining order in South Korea by policy-makers in Washington. It was an essential part of their strategy to reshape the East Asian order.[1]

---

1   To learn more about the nature of US economic aid to Korea and its influence, refer to: Jung-Gi No (노중기), "An Examination of the Impact of Foreign Aid on Korean Society in the 1950s [1950년대

However, while scholars have focused primarily on the reasons behind the United States' decision to provide substantial aid to South Korea and its impact on Korean society, they have paid relatively little attention to the internal factors within Korean society that contributed to change. Woo Jung-en suggests that within the realm of these internal factors, the Syngman Rhee government displayed a certain level of rationality in its pursuit of import-substitution industrialization, despite resistance from Washington. Pak Tae-gyun argues that although the U.S. held an advantageous position in the U.S.-ROK relationship during the 1950s, South Korea's positions and responses could influence the terms of the relationship, and these experiences served as a crucial foundation for the creation of economic development plans in the 1960s.[2] In addition, Lee Hyun-jin asserts that U.S. policy toward South Korea was not only planned but also modified and implemented through the establishment of the Combined Economic Board (CEB), which was tasked with managing aid to South Korea.[3]

During the 1950s, numerous reform attempts took place within Korean society. Among these plans, the Power Development Plan (전원개발계획) aimed at rebuilding the electricity grid, which served as the cornerstone for industrialization and the foundation of growth. Remarkably, this plan underwent ten revisions. However, the 1950s were marked by political turmoil, a scarcity of capital and goods, and a series of unsuccessful implementation attempts. Nevertheless, these documented failures provide vivid insights into the diverse array of actors engaged in these plans, the objectives they aimed to achieve, and the conflicts that arose among them.

한국 사회에 미친 원조의 영향에 대한 고찰]," Capital Accumulation and People's Livelihood in Modern Korea [현대한국의 자본축적과 민중생활], *Literature and Intellectual History* [문학과 지성사], 1989; Daegun Lee (이대근), *Economy in the Post-Liberation 1950s: Industrialization's Personal Background* [해방후 1950년대의 경제—공업화의 사적 배경 연구] (Seoul: Samsung Economic Research Institute, 2004); Jong-Won Lee (李鍾元), *The East Asian Cold War and Korean-American-Japanese Relations* [-東アジア冷戦と韓美日關係-] (Tokyo: University Press [東京大學出版會], 1996).

2   See the following: Jung-En Woo, "A Method to His Madness: The Political Economy of Import-Substitution Industrialization in Rhee's Korea," in *Race to the Swift: State and Finance in Korean Industrialization*, ed. Eric Charry (Columbia: Columbia University Press, 1991), 545-573; T'ae-Gyun Pak (박태균), *Origins of Won-yong: Korea's Economic Development Plan* [원용과 변용: 한국 경제개발계획의 기원] (Seoul: Seoul National University Press, 2007).

3   Gabrielle Hecht, *The Radiation of France: Nuclear Power and National Identity after World War II* (Cambridge, MA and London: The MIT Press, 1998).

There is a growing body of scholarly work that examines the extensive discussions surrounding the reconstruction of South Korea's electrical grid in the 1950s. Notably, Lee Hyunjin has observed that the reconstruction of the grid was a prominent item on the agenda of the Combined Economic Board (CEB), as evident from its agendas and activities during that period. Yim Song-ja's analysis of the Korean government's electricity policies during this time highlights the complete dependence on aid for postwar reconstruction, which limited the ability of both the Syngman Rhee government and its successor, the Democratic Party government, to prioritize the development of the country's electricity capacity.

On May 14, 1948, North Korea decided to cut off its electricity supply to the South, as the majority of the peninsula's power-generating facilities were located in the North. This led to a severe power shortage in South Korea, which was attributed to fuel supply issues. Jeong Dae-hun, whose work focuses on the process of developing the 1953 Power Development Plan, notes that while South Korea and the United States shared a similar understanding of ground realities, they proposed different solutions, which hindered the implementation of a concrete resolution. No Sang-ho further argues that the state-managed energy system, established during the late Japanese colonial regime of general mobilization, was restored and further industrialized but remained a closed, state-owned industrial system.[4] Overall, this body of literature examines various challenges faced by South Korea's actual electrical network during reconstruction. However, the underlying issue of why U.S. and South Korean engineers struggled to find a rational solution to the reconstruction problem has not been adequately explained.

This article traces the goals and direction of comprehensive power

---

4 See the following: Hyunjin Lee (이현진), *US Policy on Economic Aid to Korea, 1948-1960* [*미국의 대한경제원조정책, 1948-1960*] (Seoul: Hye-an, 2009), 152-213; Song-Ja Yim (임송자), "Electric Power Policy and Power Sources Development Policy of the Past Governments from the Mid 1950s to the Early 1960s [1950년대 중·후반기~1960년대 전반기, 역대 정부의 電力對策과 電源開發政策]," *Sarim* [*사림*] 56 (2016): 51-53; Dae-Hoon Jeong (정대훈), "The Countermeasure of the Electric Power Shortage in 1948~1953 – Focusing on the Establishment of the Three-Year Plan for Development of Power Resources [1948-1953년의 남한 전력수급대책 – 전원개발계획의 수립과정을 중심으로]," *Sarim* [*사림*] 74 (2020): 51-53; Sangho No (노상호), "Emergence of 'Electricity System' and State-Owned Power Companies in the 1940s-1950s [1940-50년대 '전기체제'와 국영전력사업체의 등장]," *The Korean Cultural Studies* [*한국문화연구*] 33 (2017): 63-92.

development sought by South Korea's electrical engineers from the immediate postliberation period up to the submission of the final Power Development Plan to the Syngman Rhee government — the product of politics within the engineering community.[5] Beginning with the small-scale hydroelectric power plant plan in 1951, the Power Development Plan went through twelve drafts, while South Korea's electrical engineers, officials from the Ministry of Commerce and Industry, the Ministry of Restoration, and U.S. aid officials, who each held different positions on the aims and direction of the plan, gradually reached a consensus. South Korean electrical engineers clashed with U.S. aid officials who aimed to quickly restore the electrical network through the construction of coal-fired power stations. In contrast, South Korean electrical engineers argued that the network should be reconstructed with a focus on hydroelectric plants. Their unwavering adherence to a policy of 'water [hydroelectricity] leads, fire [coal] follows' (수주화종 or 水主火從) reflected the colonial experience. Engineers witnessed the construction of large hydroelectric power plants and a high-voltage transmission network in the northern part of the peninsula in the 1930s and 1940s had resolved the country's power issues and even surpassed Japan proper.[6] Their memory and experience gave rise to a shared understanding that hydroelectric power should serve as the foundation of the network, even though the division and war resulted in the loss of facilities for such a network. Their joint efforts at independent study further reinforced this perspective. Under opposition from U.S. aid officials, they ultimately could not accomplish their objectives. However, they had the opportunity to familiarize themselves with the most up-to-date coal-fired power station technology, acquire

---

5   According to technology historian Gabrielle Hecht, the introduction and diffusion of technology, as well as choices, take place within a "techno-political regime," which is a complex network of relationships involving specific institutions, the people within those institutions, the myths and ideologies they adhere to, the artifacts they create, and the technological politics they pursue. Understanding these processes of "techno-politics" involving various actors is useful in explaining why a particular society prefers a specific form of technological system and how technology choices and society intertwine and coevolve. See: Hecht, *The Radiation of France.*

6   Regarding the construction of large-scale hydroelectric power plants and the growth of the power system in the 1930s, refer to: Sun-Sil Oh (오선실), "Transition of the Power System in Colonial Korea during the 1920-30s: Emergence of Large-scale Hydropower Plants for Industrial Use and Establishment of Power Grid System [1920-30년대, 식민지 조선의 전력 시스템의 전환: 기업용 대형 수력발전소의 등장과 전력망 체계의 구축]," *The Korean Journal for the History of Science [한국과학사학회지]* 30 (2008): 1-52.

new knowledge, and make alternative technical decisions.

Tracing the process through which consensus was reached between these two distinct groups allows us to move beyond the prevailing focus of much research on U.S. aid policy toward South Korea, which has predominantly emphasized aims alone. This article aims to demonstrate how diverse voices within South Korea's aid-dependent economy in the 1950s played a role in shaping U.S. aid policy toward the country. The Combined Economic Board (CEB) delayed or canceled development projects not only under the influence of the U.S. but also because South Korean economic officials prioritized social stability. However, officials from the Ministry of Commerce and Industry advocated for active development, including projects such as the construction of hydroelectric power plants, and they also embraced U.S.-style technical systems and utilized them as technical resources. Ultimately, the 1950s Power Development Plan served as a bridge between the colonial era and the state-led power development of the 1960s. South Korea's electrical engineers, who came of age during the colonial era, were shaped by the experiences of war and reconstruction, and they effectively utilized the technical resources provided by the U.S. Foreign Operations Administration (FOA). This served as a stepping stone for the growth of South Korean electrical technology in the subsequent period.

2. Division of the Electrical Grid and the Formation of the South Korean Electrical Eengineering Community

Until the end of the colonial era, the Korean peninsula's electrical grid relied on large hydroelectric power stations located in the north. These power stations were interconnected through high-voltage power lines passing through Pyongyang, Seoul, and Daejeon in a north-to-south direction. The power supply was highly dependable and advanced and comparable to that of any country in East Asia or even the world.[7]

---

[7]   For the hypothesis of the 220 kV high-voltage transmission network and the hypothesis of the North–South terminal transmission network, refer to pp. 32-37 of Oh Sun-sil's article mentioned

In 1943, as the Pacific Theater of World War Two reached its final stages, the colonial government consolidated all the companies involved in generating and transmitting electrical power, as well as those responsible for constructing hydroelectric power plants in the northern part of the country, including the Jangjin and Heocheon Rivers. These were merged into the Korean Power Corporation (a stock company).[8] However, this consolidation excluded the company that operated the Yalu River Hydroelectric Company (Amnok River) jointly with Manchukuo.

Figure 1. Map of Korea's electrical grid, with North and South connected. (RG469, Entry422, Box 4a).

above. For information about the construction of Supum Dam, refer to the following: Sun-Sil Oh (오선실), "The Largest Power Plant in the East Asia on the Amnok River: Formation of the Supum Dam and Dongisa Technical System [압록강에 등장한 동양 최대의 발전소, 수품댐과 동이시아 기술체계의 형성]," *The Journal of Humanities and Social Sciences [인문사회과학연구]* 21-1 (2020): 269-294; An-Ki Joung (정안기), "A Study of the Chousen Amnokgang Waterpower Corporation, a Chousen Special-Purpose Company Active in the 1930s [1930년대 조선형 특수회사, 조선압록강수력 발전(주)의 연구]," *Chung-Ang Saron [중앙사론]* 47 (2018): 5-57.

8   At that time, the Japanese Government-General of Korea tried to absorb and integrate the existing power companies into the largest Chosun Electric Company and convert it into a state-owned company, but it was not successful. "Official Gazette of the Government-General of Korea [朝鮮總督府官報]," Issue 2932, October 27, 1939; The Research Institute for Ethnic Issues [朝鮮總督府遞信局(民族問題研究所 編), "Various Aspects of National Control over Electric Power [電力國家統制ニ關スル諸要網]," Office of Communications, Government-General of Korea, in the Series of Policy History during the Period of Japanese Imperial Rule [日帝下 戰時體制期 政策史科叢書]," Volume 82, (Korean Studies Information Co., Ltd. [한국학술정보(주)], 2001).

Table 1. Power Output on the Korean Peninsula, April 1944 – March 1945.

Power Station Name	Capacity	Average Output (1944.4-1945.3)	Percentage of National Output
Above 38th Parallel	kW	kW	%
Supung Hydro	600,000	412,662	42.0
Jangjin River Hydro	371,444	196,458	20.0
Bujeon River Hydro	223,000	80,466	8.0
Heocheon River Hydro	394,000	217,682	22.0
Hwacheon Hydro	60,000	17,102	2.0
Bunyeong Hydro	35,800	9,137	1.0
Geumgang River Hydro	12,970	8,775	1.0
Subtotal	1,697,214	942,282	96.0
Below 38th Parallel	kW	kW	%
Cheongpyeong Hydro	44,000	18,793	1.8
Chilbo Hydro	16,000	3,945	0.4
Unam Hydro	6,400	1,603	0.2
Seomjin River Hydro	3,900	836	0.1
Yeongwol Coal	125,000	17,343	1.60
Danganri Coal	28,125	-	-
Busan Coal	17,500	-	-
Subtotal	240,925	42,520	4.0
Total	1,938,139	984,802	100.0
Hydroelectric	1,767,514	967,459	98.0
Coal-fired	170,625	17,343	2.0

To reduce electricity production costs, the Korean Power Corporation minimized the operations of coal-fired power stations in the southern region. Instead, it supplied cheap and abundant power generated by hydroelectric plants in the North throughout the entire colony. The output of these hydroelectric plants was substantial enough to meet demand, eliminating the need to operate coal-fired plants in the southern region. Consequently, the majority of the electrical production facilities, totaling 198,700 kW, ceased to provide power after liberation. The exceptions were the Cheongpyeong Dam in the Han River water system, the Seomjin River dam, which also served agricultural purposes in the southern region, the Unam Dam, and the Yeongwol thermal power station, which is situated in a coal-producing area.[9]

Following the division of the Korean Peninsula, the five electricity companies that had been in operation prior to liberation came under the control of either Soviet or U.S. military administrations in the northern and southern regions of the country, respectively. The Bukseon [Northern Line] Electrical Company (북선전기회사), which had handled the provision of power to Hamgyeong Province, fell under Soviet control, while the Kyongseong Electric Company (경성전기), which supplied energy to the entirety of Gyeonggi Province, and the Namseon [Southern Line] Electrical Company (남선전기), which supplied energy to regions south of Gyeonggi, fell under U.S. administration. The Seoseon [Western Line] Electrical Company (서선전기회사), which supplied energy to Pyeongan Province, Gaeseong, and a part of Gangwon Province, was divided between the two sides, with the part of the company's facilities, located in the U.S.-occupied region, coming under the management of the Kyongseong Electric Company. The Korean Electric Company (조선전업), also known as KECO, was the only firm with integrated electricity generation and transmission services, headquartered in Seoul. KECO came under U.S. control, but its power plants on the northern side came under Soviet control.

However, the power system itself was not divided. Power transmission from the North continued. Just like it had during the colonial period, KECO was able to distribute and sell this electricity to companies through two distribution companies, namely, the Kyongseong Electric Company and the Namseon Electrical Company. Prior to liberation, the power consumption in the southern region was approximately 100,000 kW, but with the closure of many factories following liberation, it significantly decreased to approximately 60,000 kW.[10]

---

9   During that period, the total maximum electricity generation capacity of the entire Korean Peninsula was 1,722,700 kilowatts (kW), and only 11.5% of this capacity was situated in the southern region.

10 Generally, industrial use accounts for a large proportion of electricity demand. However, in

Even though this small demand for power could be met by southern power facilities, KECO chose the familiar method of receiving cheap electricity from the North while the local situation was lacking various materials, funds, and electrical engineers and demanding considerable fuel costs and separate operating engineers to operate the thermal power facilities in the South. While power transmission from the North continued, the southern power companies recovered from the chaos and confusion in the void created by the simultaneous departure of Japanese senior electrical engineers and reorganized the power supply system without much difficulty.[11] Yun Il-jung, a high-level engineer who served as the director of the Heocheon River dam, was appointed president of KECO, and restarted transmission work. Lee Tae-hwan, also an electrical engineer, was appointed head of Kyongseong Electric and was able to rehabilitate and expand its transmission facilities. In addition, at Namseon Electric, which had a comparatively high number of Korean staff, Chang Taek-sang, a large landowner and major shareholder in the company, was appointed president, and the company's operations rapidly normalized.[12]

postliberation Korea, most factories were closed, resulting in a reversal of the ratio between industrial and household use, with household use accounting for 80% and industrial use accounting for 20%. The Korean Electric Power Corporation (조선전업주식회사), *10-year History of The Korean Electric Power Corporation [조선전업주식회사10년사]* (Seoul: The Korean Electric Power Corporation, 1955), 60-64.

11 During that time, a group of American electrical engineers invited by the U.S. military government played a crucial role in providing assistance. Around ten experts from Chosun Electric Company were sent to support the maintenance, operation, and reconstruction of power facilities in South Korea. This information is documented in Shin Ki-jo's book, *Off the Beaten Path: 57 Years of Electric Power,* a book he self-published in 2005 (see pp. 77-80). Shin Ki-jo, born in Hwanghae Province in 1923, graduated from Kyongsong High School of Industry in 1943 and began his career as an electrical engineer at Chosun Electric Company shortly before liberation. After Japanese senior electrical engineers, who occupied most positions in Chosun Electric Company, returned to Japan, Shin Ki-jo assumed the role of a power distribution supervisor. In 1947, at the young age of 27, he was promoted to the position of a power supply manager, highlighting the shortage of highly skilled Korean electrical engineers at the time. Later, Shin Ki-jo served as the director of Cheongpyeong Hydroelectric Power Plant and Hwacheon Power Plant, taking charge of the power facility restoration. After filling significant roles in The Korea Electric Company, he retired as a deputy general manager in 1974.

12 Yun Il-jung (尹日重, 1892-1981) graduated from the Electrical Engineering Department of Sendai Technical High School in 1917. After working briefly as an operator at Mapo Power Plant in Gyeongseong (now Seoul), he returned to Japan because Koreans were only given lower-level technical positions. He worked as an engineer at Tokyo Electric Power Company for eight years. He then participated as a Korean engineer in the construction of Bujeon River, Jangjin River, and Heocheon River power plants. He also served as the director of Heocheon River Power Plant during the colonial period. After liberation, he served as the president of Chosun Electric Company, followed by the director

1) The May 14 Power Outage and the Division of the Electrical System

The rapid decrease in electricity consumption immediately after liberation gradually increased as people's lives stabilized and industries recovered. By the end of 1947, consumption had increased to 110,000 kW, surpassing that of the southern regions just before liberation, but the southern region still did not invest much in power generation and transmission facilities; instead, it relied on power transmitted from the north.[13]

Immediately after liberation, GARIOA (Government and Relief in Occupied Areas), operated by the U.S. military government, focused on stabilizing political turmoil and people's lives in South Korea rather than industrial recovery. GARIOA aid funds were mainly used in a nonplanned manner to restore urgent transportation and communication networks and to provide food, clothing, and housing. With the continuous influx of aid funds without the expansion of production means, Korean society inevitably became engulfed in severe inflation.[14] Electricity companies also had difficulties due to the sharp rise in prices. They raised electricity fees several times, but due to regulations on public charges, they could not keep up with soaring prices; as a result, there were often situations where it was difficult to even maintain power supply facilities. KECO complained that the electricity fee was too low to even fundamentally maintain service levels or completely repair the "legacy of the Japanese rule" and managed to perform only urgent repairs. The company urged the U.S. military government to invest aid funds in power facilities, which are important parts of national infrastructure. However, despite the

---

of the Electric Department at the Ministry of Commerce and Industry from 1948, and the director of the Electric Testing Institute at the Ministry of Reconstruction from 1951. He founded the "Korean Electric Society" after liberation and served as its inaugural chairman, later serving as the chairman for the 3rd, 4th, 5th, and 6th terms until 1965. Little is known about Lee Tae-hwan.

13 The demand for household lighting gradually increased. In response, Kyeongsung Electric Company distributed a large quantity of "American-made light bulbs" through public auctions. *Dong-a Ilbo*, January 19, 1947.

14 At that time, the total amount of aid provided by GARIOA was 49.394 million dollars, which accounted for approximately 10.6% of the total aid given to Korea until 1960. For the goals and execution of the U.S. military government's rule in South Korea, see: Yong Wook Chung (정용욱), *US Policy on Korea before and after Liberation [해방 전후 미국의 대한정책]* (Seoul: Seoul National University Press, 2003), 469-470.

difficulties faced by these electricity companies, cheap electricity continued to be supplied from the North, and southern Korean society was able to maintain their usual levels of immediate power usage without much interruption.[15]

However, the integrated power system between the South and the North that had continued since the colonial period began to fall apart in 1946 and 1947, when issues of unpaid electricity charges arose between the U.S. and Soviet military administrations and between the U.S. and North Korea.[16] This was a highly unusual situation: — since the division, exchanges between the North and South had ceased, yet the North continued to supply the South with power. After several fierce disputes between North Korea and the U.S. military government, the negotiations eventually broke down, and the North began to limit power transmission and openly announced power cuts. Only then did the U.S. military government hastily begin to prepare several countermeasures.

First, on December 16, 1947, the U.S. military government promulgated a new Electricity Consumption Law, Administrative Order No. 9 (전기 소비법, 행정명령 9호). This established an Emergency Electricity Contingency Committee and issued Electricity Order No. 1, which was essentially a generation and transmission plan. In the following January, a national industrialist meeting was held, and a South Korean Electricity Development Contingencies Committee (남한 전력 개발 대책위) was organized.[17] However, power-saving policies could be only temporary measures, as there was a need to increase power generation to meet the shortage of demand. At this time, the U.S. military government chose to introduce power ships from the U.S. instead of constructing new

15 Korea Electric Power Corporation (한국전력공사), *A 100-year History of the Korea Electric Power Corporation [한국전력100년사]* (Seoul: Korea Electric Power Corporation, 1989), 119-122.

16 According to Ryu Seung-ju, a series of incidents related to the supply of electricity between North and South Korea were the result of complex political dynamics between the Soviet Union and the United States, as well as between the North and the United States. As negotiations became tense, the issue of electricity payment was not straightforward, and, above all, when the establishment of a separate government in South Korea became certain, inter-Korean power transmission was discontinued. Seungju Ryu (류승주), "Power Supply Negotiations between North and South Korea, 1946-1948 [1946-48년, 남북한 전력수급교섭]," *Quarterly Review of Korean History [역사와 현실]* 40 (2001): 51-53.

17 "Emergency Order No. 2, Determining the Priority of Electricity Use" [비상명령제2호, 전력사용우선순위 결정], *Seoul Sinmun*, Dec. 18, 1947.

power plants. The U.S. military government anchored the *Jacona*, a 20,000 kW ship, and the *Electra*, a 6900 kW ship, in Incheon Port and Busan Port, respectively, to start power generation. These two ships soon became responsible for the basic power that was consumed in the South.[18] Bringing in existing power ships had the advantage of offering a rapid and flexible response to electricity shortages, but it was not a long-term investment in power facilities to build the network in the South that electric companies had been requesting.[19]

The North suddenly ceased supplying electricity to the South at noon on May 14, 1948, four days after the South Korean general election on May 10. According to the memoirs and personal records of electrical engineers, this outage was expected. KECO, Kyongseong Electric, and Namseon Electric closely monitored changes in the North's situation and managed the power supply and demand situation in the South. When the outage began, KECO immediately started a previously retired Danginri generator and was able to satisfy the demand for electricity within Seoul to power trams and lighting within two hours of the power cut. At the time, newspapers reported that "the South responded quickly to North Korea's sudden stoppage of power and as a result there has been no big cost."[20]

However, the reality on the ground was different. Although KECO started operating previously idle thermal power plants by injecting expensive imported fuel and coal oil, the power generation costs were high, making it difficult to maintain in the long term, and the power generation facilities were also old. Most importantly, however, existing facilities could not satisfy domestic

---

18 *Dong-A Ilbo*, April 16, 1948.

19 During that time, the operating funds for the Jacona and Electra power lines were included as part of economic aid. During the U.S. military government period, they were covered by GARIOA aid funds, after the establishment of the government, they were supported by ECA funds, and during the exhibition, CRIK funds were used. The operation and management of the power barges were initially under the Ministry of Commerce and Industry and then transferred to Chosun Electric Company in April 1949. In September 1949, a formal contract was signed between Korea and ECA. The technical aspects of the power lines were handled by the American company Gilbert, while the expenses for imported goods and American personnel were covered by ECA, and expenses for domestic goods and Korean personnel were borne by Chosun Electric Company. See the following: Korea Electric Power Corporation, *A 100-year History,* 406-408; *Choson Ilbo*, December 19, 1947; *Seoul Sinmun*, March 9, 1948.

20 *Dong-A Ilbo*, December 19, 1947.

demand. Even with all the power-generating ships provided by the U.S. in operation, the power supply dropped by more than half, and eventually, the supply to industry was rationed on a rotating basis. Factories began working on a two-shift rotation and were supplied with only up to four hours of electricity for every eight-hour shift and sometimes as little as one hour. As a result, factory capacity utilization fell to 10-20% of prior levels. Due to the shortage of electricity during the planting and dry seasons, food production fell onlyin Pyeongtaek and Bucheon alone by 552,000 seok (石 koku).[21]

The construction of power plants, which was delayed due to problems such as lack of funds, emerged as an urgent issue, and KECO started the expansion of the Seomjin River Dam in June. The Ministry of Commerce and Industry began to take over and manage the Yeongwol power plant, and the Ministry of Agriculture and Forestry started to manage the Boseong River power plant. Power generation was integrated under the special presidential order the following year, with KECO taking control of both plants and beginning construction and maintenance work on them. The position of the American aid organization, which had little interest in the reconstruction of Korea's industrial facilities, also changed, largely due to the realization of the North–South confrontation after the establishment of the Korean government. As early as January 1948, the argument that economic aid was needed "to prevent economic collapse" was put forward by Arthur C. Bunce, an economic advisor to the U.S. military government, but the U.S. Department of State, generally passive about economic support for developing countries, reacted negatively. However, the atmosphere reversed soon after the victory of the Communist Party in the Chinese civil war became certain, and South Korea was recognized as a front line in the Cold War. The argument was that substantial U.S. support,

---

21 Refer to the following: "Factories in Incheon Area Paralyzed by Power Outage" [단전으로 인천 일대 3백 여 공장 마비상태], "Operations at Samcheok Industrial Zone Halted" [삼척공업지대 조업 마비], "Expected Water Shortage in Gimhae Plain" [김해평야 감수 예상], *Choson Ilbo*, May 29, 1948; Jun. 1, 1948; Jun. 22, 1948; Ki-Jo Shin (신기조), *Off the Beaten Path: 57 Years of Electric Power [전력 외길 57년]* (Seoul: Self-Published, 2005), 68-72; Korea Electric Power Corporation, *A 100-year History*, 365-369. In addition, the production of incandescent bulbs was discontinued, and a ban was imposed on the use of light bulbs over 60 watts. Furthermore, to promote energy conservation, the use of residential heaters was prohibited. *Choson Ilbo*, May 22 and 24, 1948; *Dong-A Ilbo*, May 25, 1948.

namely, aid for economic development, was needed to establish a "united and democratic government" in South Korea that could "resist aggression from North Korea or other military forces."[22]

The aid goal of the U.S. State Department was partially realized when the Economic Cooperation Administration (ECA), an American aid organization that focused mainly on the reconstruction of Europe, emerged as a new aid organization for Asia, including Korea, and started full-scale planned aid. The ECA initially allocated 2.7% of the total aid funds ($59,043,000) to power generation and transmission facilities.[23] This funding laid the foundation for the resumption of construction on the Seomjin River Dam. The project, which had faced continued problems with a lack of construction materials, including cement, and a lack of expertise, began to show signs of progress after the Gukje Tokeon Construction Company (국제토건회사) concluded an agreement with the ECA to take over construction. The ECA also sent technical survey teams to Korea twice, once in 1949 and once in 1950, to examine where electricity generation facilities could be developed. The team, having looked broadly across the country, proposed a plan to start constructing thermal power plants with capacities of 30,000 kW in Gyeonggi-do's Deokso and 15,000 kW in Gangwon-do's Samcheok and to complete them by the following year. The ECA also submitted a report suggesting that 52 locations nationwide, including in the northern and southern parts of the Han River and the Geumgang River, could be developed as potential hydropower plant sites in the long term. Although this power survey did not immediately lead to the construction of new power plants, it is important because the report was written by American technicians trusted by aid organizations and continued to be used afterward. Moreover, to alleviate the power shortages, the U.S. aid authorities installed a medium oil power plant (5,000 kW) in Mokpo, which soon went into operation.[24]

---

22 United States Department of State, "General political policies of the United States toward Korea and Appeal to the United Nations General Assembly [한국에 관한 미국의 입장에 대한 NSC의 보고]," in *Foreign Relations of the United States, 1948: The Far East and Australasia, Volume VI*, eds. John G. Reid and David H. Stauffer General eds. S. Everett Gleason and Frederick Aandahl (Washington: United States Government Printing Office, 1974). 1163-1169.

23 Lee, *Economy in the Post-Liberation 1950s*.

24 Several records state that the Mokpo Jungyu Power Plant was constructed with funding from the U.S. Foreign Operations Administration (FOA). However, considering that FOA was established

2) Establishment of the "Korean Electricity Studies Association" and Hydroelectric Centrism

The sudden division of the electrical grid on the Korean Peninsula united South Korea's electrical engineers and pushed them to find new alternatives with an insufficient base. Like scientists and engineers in other fields postliberation, Korea's electrical engineers established the Korean Electrical Studies Association (KESA) in July 1947, with Yun Il-jung, KECO's president, instrumental to its development. At the time, the membership credentials required for the KESA broadly included:

(1) Individuals with significant experience teaching electrical studies or electrical engineering;

(2) Individuals with significant experience researching electrical technology or proficiency in electrical equipment;

(3) Individuals with significant experience closely related to electrical studies or electrical engineering;

(4) Individuals with significant academic achievements and responsibilities pertaining to electrical engineering for more than three years;

(5) Individuals with significant experience of five years learning electrical engineering in middle or higher education.[25]

The membership of the KESA was not only open to those with academic

---

in 1953, there are issues with those records. There may be other sources of funding. Namseon Electric Company (남선전기주식회사), *Status of Namseon Electric Company [남선전기주식회사현황]* (Seoul: 1958), 97; The Korean Electric Corporation, *10-year History of The Korean Electric Power Corporation*, 371-372.

25 The Korean Electricity Studies Association was later renamed as the "Korean Institute of Electrical Engineers" and became more focused on academic research when it revised its membership qualifications in 1972, shifting its center from technicians to engineers. The Korean Institute of Electrical Engineers (대한전기학회), *25-year History of Electrical Society [전기학회 25년사]* (Seoul: 1973). Yun Il-jung organized a separate organization called the "Korean Association of Electrical Engineers" in 1963 exclusively for electrical engineers. This organization was later renamed as the "Korean Association of Electrical Technicians" and then converted back to the (Registered) Korean Association of Power Technology Professionals in 1996. This organization has made efforts to improve the welfare and rights of electrical professionals while enhancing the qualifications of electrical technicians. Korea Electric Power Engineers Association (韓國電力技術人協會編), "A Decade History of the Korea Electric Power Engineers Association: 43 Years since the Establishment of the Association of Chief Electric Technicians of Korea [韓國電力技術人協會 10年史: 대한전기주임기술자협회 창립 이후 43년-]," 2007.

expertise in electrical engineering but also expanded to include those who had acquired electrical technology-related expertise through experience. Hence, the KESA included technicians and engineers engaged in electricity-related activities and those who were involved in practical electrical work. This membership policy reflected the reality that there were very few high-level electrical engineers who had received proper electrical engineering education on the Korean Peninsula immediately after liberation. The College of Engineering at Kyongsong Imperial University (an Imperial University of Japan that existed in the area that is now Seoul between 1924 and 1946 and was also known as Keijō Imperial University or 京城帝國大學), which established a preparatory department in 1938, did not open any engineering-related departments. Hence, unless students traveled abroad, they had no opportunity to acquire an engineering education in colonial Korea.

Moreover, it was difficult for Koreans to reach the only school that offered coursework related to engineering, namely, Kyongsong Technical High School (경성고등공업학교). Thus, the electrochemistry department of the school admitted only two to three Korean students per year out of a class size of 30. However, the number of electrical engineers, when expanded to those practicing in the field, was far from small. After the 1930s, due to the specialization of the industrial structure of colonial Korea around electrochemical industries, there was considerable demand for technicians who could help maintain and repair generators and transmission facilities. Technical schools such as the Euljung Technical School (을종기술학교) and the Kyongsong Electrical School (경성전기학교) alone produced approximately 240 graduates each year in the 1940s. Most of the students at these lower technical schools were Koreans, and after graduation, they could easily obtain jobs in electronics-related professions as intermediate technicians or "Gongsu" (工傭). Moreover, toward the end of the Pacific War, as most young Japanese technicians were conscripted into military service, opportunities and space for Korean technicians to hone their skills greatly expanded. In other words, by liberation, although there were few high-level technicians on the Korean Peninsula, lower-level technicians were able to form a substantial foundation for growth.[26]

KESA members, who initially numbered just over 100, rapidly increased to over 1,000 by the end of the 1950s. This included a small number of professors from engineering colleges, electric engineers from the three major power companies, and bureaucrats from the Ministry of Commerce and Industry who worked in the electronics industry. The KESA became a practical forum for sharing opinions on how to overcome the power situation in South Korea and how to create a shared vision for the future. In particular, starting in 1948, the KESA published a journal titled *Electrical Engineering* (전기공학 or EE), which introduced the latest foreign electrical engineering theories and development trends while initiating concrete discussions on long-term power development prospects in South Korea. Lee Jong-il, a professor at Seoul National University at the time, asserted through "Electrical Engineering" that Korea was a "world-class resource area". In response, KECO engineer Choe In-seong released research indicating that there were many sites suitable for hydroelectric power generation south of the 38th parallel.

Lee Jong-il, in particular, cited the colonial government's "Hydroelectric Power Resource Survey Reports" (수력자원 조사보고서), which included four editions, indicating that there was 10 million kW of potential hydroelectric power on the Korean peninsula. Although most of these were located in the north, he noted that there were also viable hydroelectric power areas in the southern region, including the Han River, North Han River, and South Han River. Moreover, he argued that thermal power generation was not efficient due to poor coal quality, and since coal was also needed in other industries, hydroelectric power was the more favorable power source. Based on this, he proposed a five-year plan and urged the government to promote power development from a long-term perspective.[27]

---

26 See the following: Shin, *Off the Beaten Path*, 27-30. For a detailed analysis of Kyongsong High Industrial School, refer to: In Kyung Jeong (정인경), "The Foundation and Management of Kyongsong Highter Technical School under the Japanese Imperialism [일제하 경성고등공업학교의 설립과 운영]," *The Korean Journal for the History of Science* [한국과학사학회지] 16-1 (1994): 31-65; Geun-Bae Kim (김근배), "Emergence of Modern Science and Technology Personnel in Korea [한국 근대과학기술인력의 출현]," *Literature and Intellectual History* [문학과 지성사], 2005.

27 Lee Jong-il (李宗日, 1905-1978) graduated from the Department of Electrical Engineering at the Imperial University of Tokyo (동경제국대학) in 1932. Afterward, he worked in the Civil Government General of Korea as a technical officer. After the liberation, he served as the Chief of the Electrical Department in the U.S. Military Government Office, and in 1946, he assumed a professorship at the College of Engineering in Seoul National University. In 1950, Lee was appointed as the Director of the Electrical Division in the Ministry of Commerce and Industry and later returned to Seoul National University. In 1953, he achieved the first-ever doctoral degree in the field of electrical engineering

The discussions on long-term power development prospects on the Korean Peninsula conducted within the KESA quickly became government policy. Since there were few groups of experts who could manage power policies after liberation, it was common for the Electrical Bureau of the Ministry of Commerce and Industry (MCI) to borrow not only academics but also senior technicians from electric companies and appoint them as bureaucrats. Therefore, the contents discussed in the Korean Institute of Electrical Engineers could naturally be submitted as the government's power policy.

For example, Yoon Il-jong, who had been the president of KECO, was appointed as the head of the MCI's Electrical Bureau in 1948 for five months, while Seoul National University Electrical Engineering Professor Lee Jong-il also served as the head of the bureau beginning in 1950.[28]

In other words, until then, the academy, industry, and government had been undifferentiated in the electricity sector. Rather than having their own separate interests, they shared the goal of establishing a new electrical grid in South Korea. The KESA was their forum for discussing the tasks involved in realizing this goal. In early 1950, Yun Il-jong was entrusted by the MCI's Electrical Bureau to submit a policy proposal to the National Assembly that, on the basis of the discussions and consensus reached within the KESA, emphasized the importance of establishing a grid centered on hydroelectric power.

According to Yun, beginning early on, Korea had excellent experience building an electrical grid, including the construction of large-scale hydroelectric power plants. In particular, Yun argued that "coal is needed in other industries

---

after the establishment of the nation with his dissertation titled "3-Phase 2-Wire Transmission System Utilizing the Earth (대지) as a Ground." Jongil Lee (이종일), "Power Resources and the 5-Year Plan in South Korea [한국의 전력자원과 5개년계획]," *Electrical Engineering [전기공학]* 3-4 (1950): 2, 3-36; Jaesook Lee (이재숙), "Urgency of Hydropower Resource Development [수력자원개발의 긴급성에 대한]," *Electrical Engineering [전기공학]* 3-4 (1950): 41-58; In-Seong Choe (최인성), "On Hydropower Development in Sam Pal's Southern Region [삼팔 이남의 수력전원개발에 대하여]," *Electrical Engineering* [전기공학] 3-4 (1950): 59-64; Sung-Rae Park et al. (박성래 외), "A Study on the Formation of Korean Scientists and Technologists [한국 과학기술자의 형성 연구]" (research report of the Korea science foundation [한국과학재단 연구 보고서], 1995), 88; Nate Korean Studies Person Search [네이트 한국학 인물검색], http://koreandb.nate.com/history/people/detail?sn=2546.

28 Such personnel exchanges continued throughout the 1950s. In 1958, Shin Ki-jo was also seconded to the Ministry of Commerce and Industry as the head of the equipment division (機材 과장) but returned to the company after only one year. Shin, *Off the Beaten Path*, 159-162.

too, and I believe that deposits would not last 100 years as a source of electricity";
hydroelectric power must be used as a baseline source of power – under the
principle of "water [hydroelectricity] leads, fire [coal] follows" or "hydro as
master, coal as subordinate" (水主火從).[29]

Such power development prospects and plans by electrical engineers were
the first experiences that Korean engineers had in reviewing Korea's resources
and creating long-term power development plans, which became important
foundational assets for planning power development in the future. The plan
to draw up in support of hydroelectric power was created with reference to
the colonial-era electrical grid. In other words, the stable electrical grid based
on large-scale hydroelectric power plants that had been built by the colonial
government and Japanese firms in the 1930s-1940s served as the basis for
their goals postliberation.

In particular, the top-tier engineers who played the leading role in the
production of policy by the KESA were colonial-era large-scale hydroelectric
power plant engineers or other officials from the colonial government whose
knowledge and experience made them most accustomed to large-scale
hydroelectric plants and high-voltage electricity transmission. The division of
the electrical grid between the North and South meant that few colonial-era
electrical power plants remained. However, within the plans that these engineers
who came of age in the colonial era developed could be seen technical ideals
created within a technical discourse that sought to maintain a hydropower-
centered system.

3. Learning through Reconstruction and the Strengthening of Hydropower Centrism

The Korean War effectively undid all prior efforts to establish an electricity

---

29 Iljoong Yoon (윤일중), "Review of National Basic Industries; Electricity [국가기본산업재검토;
전력]," *National Assembly Review* [국회보 통권] 2 (1950): 51-53. Note: Considering the fact that
the aforementioned paper by Lee Jong-il was written during his tenure at the Ministry of Commerce
and Industry, it is highly likely that it was originally written as a policy proposal for the ministry.

system. In particular, indiscriminate aerial bombings over a short period of time turned the physical assets of the Korean Peninsula, including power facilities, into ashes. The existing power plants in South Korea, such as the Yeongwol Thermal Powerplant, the Boseong River Plant, and the Seomjin River power plants, suffered significant damage. Even worse, the power ship *Electra*, which had been anchored in Incheon Harbor, was destroyed, and the Mokpo thermal power plant, which was had been only recently built, was burned to the ground. In addition, the transmission and distribution facilities throughout the country were cut off and damaged, leading to the collapse of the national power system.

In this situation, the U.S. military quickly introduced four 2,500 kW power ships and stationed them at major ports for the purpose of conducting the war. Subsequently, the U.S. military added the 30,000 kW large power ship *Impedance* and the small power ship *Saranac* to supply power. The power supplied by these power ships accounted for 56.4% of the total power supply in South Korea at that time.[30]

Thus, efforts continued to provide a minimum amount of electricity amid continued war. Electric companies each organized "Electricity Restoration Groups." Even in situations where the occupation forces were alternating and power lines were fluctuating, these groups carried out work to repair broken power facilities and connect severed power lines. After 1951, as the front stabilized to some extent, South Korea's power system could gradually be rebuilt. In May 1951, the Yeongwol Thermal Powerplant and the Chilbo Hydroelectric Powerplant began generating electricity, allowing for the supply of power for irrigation in the Honam region, which was entering the farming season.[31]

1) Learning through the Restoration of Hydroelectric Power Plants

The Hwacheon Hydroelectric Powerplant, which was incorporated into the South following the demarcation of the new ceasefire line after the war, brought about significant changes to the South Korean power system. Located upstream of the Bukhan River, the Hwacheon Hydroelectric Powerplant was initially

---

30 Korea Electric Power Corporation, *A 100-year History*, 378-386, 407.

31 Ibid., 387.

planned and built by the Han River Hydroelectric Power Plant during the colonial period, along with the Cheongpyeong Hydroelectric Power Plant below.

While Hwacheon was smaller than the large power facilities built in the north, such as the water dam, the Jangjin River power plant, and the Heocheon River power plant, it was equipped with facilities capable of producing 60,000 kW and 44,000 kW of electricity, respectively. After liberation and the subsequent division at the 38th parallel, the Hwacheon power plant fell under North Korean control, and Cheongpyeong fell under the South. The Cheongpyeong power plant was a crucial asset for South Korea, which severely lacked power facilities, and was responsible for the base load power during summer. The Hwacheon Hydroelectric Power Plant also had a significantly greater generation capacity than did the other power plants in South Korea, and its recovery was significant because it maximized the generation efficiency of the Cheongpyeong power plant located downstream.

Above all, during the war, electrical engineers had the opportunity to grow into professionals while carrying out the restoration of the two hydroelectric power plants using only the insufficient levels of capital and technology available in South Korea at the time. Restoration of the Cheongpyeong power plant began immediately in March 1951, when the war situation was somewhat stabilized. The Cheongpyeong power plant was severely damaged due to two rounds of evacuation and recovery, but it was judged restorable because the expensive generator was not damaged. KECO dispatched fifty engineers led by Shin Ki-jo, who was the director of the Cheongpyeong power plant, to inspect the damage and start to restore what could be repaired immediately. It was not easy to deliver materials during the war, so the engineers completed the restoration by completely disassembling the two generator facilities, gathering usable parts, and reassembling them into one.[32] Gaining confidence from the successful restoration of the second unit, which was less damaged than the first, the engineers hastened the restoration of the first unit. The first was badly damaged, and there was a need to build a new power station because

---

32   Shin Ki-jo reflected, "Just as doctors learn excellent medical skills through clinical experiments, technicians could become mature professionals by dismantling and reassembling machine components in the field." Shin, *Off the Beaten Path*, 121.

they had used all the spare parts they had available for the second, but it was possible to obtain supplies from Japan, and the restoration was comparatively easy. The Cheongpyeong power plant was able to reopen with a large ceremony in May 1952.[33]

The following year, the Hwacheon No. 2 Power Plant was also restored. Originally, the Hwacheon power plant restoration was planned to use airlifted equipment from overseas with aid funds from the United Nations Korean Reconstruction Agency (UNKRA). However, funding was not provided in time, and it was necessary to use the funds and technology that could be rapidly mobilized domestically, with all equipment and tools repaired and produced domestically.[34]

In the process, construction had to be halted occasionally due to the lack of funds for power plant restoration, but even amidst such scarcities, Korean engineers were able to gain technical experience in fabricating and installing power facilities. Finally, on October 9, 1954, the completion ceremony was held at the Hwacheon No. 2 Power Plant. At this event, President Syngman Rhee lauded the Hwacheon Power Plant as the "inspiration for self-reliance, independence, and reconstruction."

Indeed, the Hwacheon Power Plant was a product of a test of strength by approximately 200 Korean electrical engineers under the pressure of scarce funds and resources, mobilizing all the technical resources and energy they could muster. It generated an average of approximately 54,000 kW of electricity to all of South Korea. This accounted for approximately 50% of the total power supply.[35]

33 Refer to the following: "Seoul Families Brighten as Two-Day Power Restriction for Homes and Factories is Abolished [밝아지는 서울 가정, 공장 2부제 철폐]," *Choson Ilbo*, Mar. 14, 1953; "Power Supply Improving, Suspension of Thermal Power Operation [전력호조로 화력은 조업 중지]," *Choson Ilbo*, Mar. 22, 1953; "Power Situation Improving [전력 사정은 호전일로]," *Choson Ilbo*, Apr. 11, 1953; Korea Electric Power Corporation, *A 100-year History*, 388-390.

34 For this purpose, other planned construction and maintenance projects, such as the dam height work for the Seomjin River Power Plant, the canal reinforcement work for the Cheongpyeong Power Plant, and the construction of the No. 2 generator at the Sogye Gokbosung River, were all canceled, and all funds were concentrated on Hwacheon. Ibid., 398.

35 See the following: *Choson Ilbo*, June 15; July 2; August 3; October 11; 1954. The Korean Electric Corporation, *10-year History of The Korean Electric Power Corporation*, 269-300; Shin, *Off the Beaten Path*, 127-139.

As a result, the Korean War gave engineers the opportunity to improve their technical skills. They learned how to make the most of the little they had by taking apart and putting back together damaged generators, and from this base, they were able to master higher-level skills that they could not acquire from the short education received during the colonial or postliberation period. Engineers acquired the ability to build and operate hydroelectric power plants on their own and further expanded the groundwork for the technical sharing of preferences surrounding hydropower. Furthermore, with the restoration of the Hwacheon Hydroelectric Power Plant, South Korea's power situation temporarily stabilized, strengthening the belief that large hydroelectric power plants similar to those used during the colonial period were the solution to South Korea's power problem.

2) The Creation of an Independent Electrical Development Plan Centered on Hydroelectricity

In the midst of the war, the Ministry of Commerce and Industry saw the need for an independent long-term power development plan to meet immediate power requirements for the war effort and postwar power supply. The "Small Valley Electricity Development Plan" (소계곡전원개발계획) submitted in 1951 was part of such long-term planning. Particularly in war conditions where funds and materials were scarce, small hydropower plants constructed in both large and small valleys were seen as an appropriate solution to quickly secure electricity at low cost. Although small in scale, the ability to distribute and develop power across the nation was also considered an important advantage.

To this end, the MCI and the KECO organized a joint investigation team and announced three final candidate locations, the Gwisan, Cheongyang, and Boseong riversRivers, after investigating approximately ten strong candidate sites nationwide by October of that same year. It appeared that the small valley power plant construction plan would be complete by the following year, after geological surveys and designs completedwere finished, but the plans to develop Cheongyang were found to be lacking measures to address flooding and were ultimately excluded from consideration in the National Assembly's budget deliberations. Additionally, the funds to be used for the development of the Boseong River were redirected to the recovery costs of the Hwacheon Power Plant. Thus, only the construction of the Gwisan Power Plant began in 1952 — and barely began at that time.[36]

In 1952, when the construction of small hydropower plants was not successful, the MCI unveiled a "New Power Generation Development Plan" (신규발전원개발계획). This plan included proposals for a number of new facilities, including a 2,800 kW thermal power plant on Jeju Island, a 13,850 kW Seomjin River facility, a 50,000 kW Chungju hydropower plant, and another 50,000 kW hydroelectric power plant at Yeoju. These location choices were on the Economic Cooperation Agency (ECA) list of potential locations and were comparatively large in scale. However, due to poor planning and a lack of funding at home, these projects were not even attempted. Thus, South Korea's electricity development had made little progress up to the armistice in 1953.[37]

Discussions on US economic assistance to Korea for postwar recovery began, and the reconstruction of the power system was given top priority. However, it was clear from the first stages of negotiations that Seoul and Washington had different plans. Starting in 1952, the Korea-US Power Consultation began with the participation of the UN Korean Reconstruction Agency (UNKRA) and the Korean government. However, they failed to reach any conclusion. It was not until the fifth meeting of the following year that UNKRA reached a mutual agreement to invest $7.1 million in the power sector, including transmission and distribution facilities, out of a total aid fund of $70 million.

At this point, the South Korean government said it would allocate all reconstruction funds in the form of counterpart funds but demanded that $6 million be disbursed rapidly as aid funds. Moreover, all restoration had to be handled by Korean engineers, and all materials and equipment that could be acquired domestically were not to be imported — i.e., only what had to be imported could be. This demand reflected the Korean government's expectation that power recovery operations would not only be limited to a few power plants or strengthen transmission and distribution facilities but also aim at growing Korea's power system itself using Korean labor and materials.

---

36 Korea Electric Power Corporation, *A 100-year History,* 417.

37 Ibid., 418-421.

Moreover, reducing technical costs and ensuring that aid funds are~~were~~ not recycled back into the U.S. economy in the form of fees for technology and inputs were practical measures. In response, UNKRA refused because after considering Korea's production technology, a considerable portion of the equipment needed for recovery had to be imported from foreign countries and because Korea's technical ability was insufficient to fully take charge of the recovery work.

Eventually, the Korean government and UNKRA agreed to purchase necessary materials from foreign countries, excluding some materials that Korea already had and that the aid country would support the training of Korean engineers. Furthermore, as UNKRA funds were disbursed, the total amount of funding available was halved, with the rash construction of a large-scale power plant during war cited as the reason. With the exception of the new construction of the Jeju Oil Power Plant, all of the original plans were abandoned, including the construction of the Hwacheon No. 3 Power Plant and the resumption of construction on the Seomjin River Power Plant.

As negotiations with the aid countries encountered difficulties, the South Korean government once again sought to establish its own power development plan. In November 1953, the MCI formed a new Electricity Committee. This committee brought together a wide range of individuals, including senior bureaucrats from various government offices, high-level technicians from the three major power companies, and academics.[38] Over the course of multiple discussions, they drew up plans to develop four sites within the South Han River water system and to continue to develop Hwacheon and Seomjin, creating 330,000 kW of new generating capacity and 80,000 kW of thermal generation capacity when water levels were too low for sufficient power generation. If this plan, which was expected to take three years to implement, was to be

---

[38] At that time, the Rural Development Committee appointed Sanggongbu Director Ahn Dong-hyuk as the chairman and appointed Yun Il-jung, Lee Jong-il, Choi Kyung-yeol, Lee Hee-joon, and Yang Jae-ui as specialized committee members. In addition, it included key industrial bureau chiefs from the Ministry of Commerce and Industry, the Electricity Bureau, the Gwangmu Bureau, the Industry Bureau, the Construction Bureau, as well as comprehensive representation of economic bureaucrats, including the Agricultural Bureau, the Water Management Bureau, and the Economic Planning Bureau Director. Korea Electric Power Corporation, *A 100-year History*, 420-421; Jeong, "The Countermeasure of the Electric Power Shortage in 1948~1953," 24-30.

realized, it was expected to create a stable generation capacity of 367,000 kW, sufficient to support South Korea's industrialization.

The electrical engineers, officials and scholars who were involved in the planning process of the Electrical Committee considered it important to rely primarily on hydroelectric power but also to have coal play a subordinate role (the principle of 'hydro as master, coal as subordinate'). The places with significant potential for development were identified by the ECA and KECO in its survey of potential hydroelectric power plant sites in 1950. Hence, even if construction costs were high, hydroelectric power was taken as being obviously preferable because after construction was over, electricity could be produced without fuel costs.[39]

Engineers held firm to the hydro-first principle because they believed that an independent nation-state would need to be self-reliant and self-sufficient in the natural resources it consumed. South Korea's electrical engineers and technical officials sought to allocate resources efficiently, and by reconstituting the country's electrical grid, they hoped to construct a rational industrial state.[40] However, the main reason why the country's electrical engineers, technicians, and technical officials all looked to hydroelectricity as the principal source of power was, as we have seen above, because the KESA brought them together with a common goal and aims and shared a set of policy tasks.

Furthermore, since the 1940s, the country's thermal power plants had not functioned properly, and their equipment hads aged. Since the late colonial period, KECO had utilized a small number of large hydroelectric plants in the northern part of the peninsula to supply electricity to the entire country, while thermal plants were mothballed. As a result, few engineers had experience running such plants in the southern half of the peninsula. Young engineers, in particular, had no experience with them because as they were being trained, the plants had stopped running. This meant that they did not see such facilities as an alternative major source of power in the construction of a new grid

---

39 Survey reports on water resources in the Korean region conducted until the fourth period of the colonial era and the ECA power plant survey reports have frequently been cited as prominent evidence in arguments that Korea was suitable for hydropower generation even after that period. Korea Electric Power Corporation, *A 100-year History*, 422-424.

40 Ministry of Reconstruction (부흥부), *White Paper on Revitalization [부흥백서]* (Seoul: 1958), 59.

but as a supplement to hydropower.

4. US Aid Policy toward Korea and Reconstituting Electricity Development Plans

Following the armistice, efforts to overcome the scars of war continued throughout the 1950s. The most powerful group in postwar reconstruction was inevitably the U.S. aid authorities who held the funds. The distribution of aid funds was decided around a negotiation table between the Korean government and U.S. aid authorities, such as the Combined Economic Board (CEB), known as the 합동경제위원회 in Korean. However, on many issues, US influence was strong, which meant that plans for both postwar reconstruction and the direction of South Korea's subsequent industrialization were subordinated to US strategic considerations in East Asia.

Even during the war, U.S. aid authorities began to consider power augmentation and power development plans for postwar reconstruction. In 1952, the Nathan Report, written by Robert R. Nathan, was part of such research and review efforts.[41] This report optimistically projected that with about three years of aid, South Korea would enter a highly favorable developmental trajectory. In particular, the report argued that by 1957-58, the country would need to increase its electricity capacity to 150,000 kW or above to ensure smooth reconstruction and economic development, given that electricity was essential for industrial growth. To this end, the authors suggested building hydroelectric power plants despite considerable initial construction costs per unit of power generation, fuel procurement, and depreciation.

South Korean anthracite is a low-quality fuel and is not even available

---

[41] Robert R. Nathan (1908-2001) was an American economist who worked in the U.S. Department of Commerce during World War II and formulated industrial policies for the exhibition industry. After the war, he founded the Nathan Associates and engaged in economic advisory activities. The Nathan Report was commissioned by the UN Korean Reconstruction Agency to the Nathan Associates to establish Korea's reconstruction plan. The Nathan Associates submitted an interim report in December 1952 and a final report in February 1954. Korea Development Institute (한국개발연구원), *Policy Documents on the Korean Economy: Half a Century of Korean Economic Development [-한국경제 반세기 정책자료집-]* (1995), 152.

in plentiful amounts. The Nathan Report thus suggested building as many hydroelectric power plants as possible within the budget of power restoration funds and building thermal power plants minimally to prepare for dry seasons.[42] Many of the contents of the Nathan Report were reflected in the Taska Report, which was written the following year. The Taska Report team had little time, so they made ample use of the many materials that the UN had to offer, relying in particular on the Nathan Report for reconstruction planning. According to Lee Hyeon-jin, while the Nathan Report saw the need for military augmentation for stable reconstruction in Korea, the Taska Report proposed a reconstruction program aimed at augmenting the Korean military.

The latter report, officially titled "Strengthening the Korean Economy", was submitted to the National Security Council (NSC) to facilitate dialogue between the U.S. President and federal agencies in June 1953 and became the basis for the 'Paik-Wood Agreement' signed between Seoul and Washington in December of the same year.[43]

After four months of deliberation, the Paik-Wood agreement was reached on December 14, 1953, predicated on the assumption that the economic reconstruction of Korea would be impossible without assistance from the United Nations and the United States. The Paik-Wood Agreement broadly specified the direction of economic stabilization in Korea, stipulating that while the aid program was in operation, Korea must establish a price policy through the stabilization of fiscal policy and a unified exchange rate while also implementing measures to construct a free enterprise system. In particular, the Paik-Wood agreement explicitly stated that funds obtained from the sale of aid materials should be accumulated as counterpart funds, and the consent of the Combined Economic Board (CEB) was required to use these funds. This allowed the aid authorities to directly manage the use of Korean funds.[44]

---

42 National Assembly Library (국회도서관 입법 조사국), *Nathan Reports [네이산 보고서]* (Seoul: National Assembly Library, 1965), 780-817.

43 Lee, *US Policy on Economic Aid.*

44 The Counterpart Fund is the fund created by the recipient country's government to deposit an equivalent amount of the aid in local currency into a special account when utilizing foreign aid funds provided by the United States as part of post-World War II external assistance. Ibid., 190-200.

According to the Taska Report, if the electricity output was 100 in 1953, it could rise to 222 by 1956 with the assistance of aid programs. Using the Nathan Report and the Economic Cooperation Agency (ECA) as its base, the Taska Report stated that it would be possible to construct thermal plants at Samcheol and in Seoul and hydro plants at Chungju (Yeosu), the Seomjin River, the Boseong River, and the Gwisan. A fourth colonial-era power station was also planned before a plan to expand the Hwacheon facility with another generator was considered more seriously.[45]

While these reports, which were written on the ground in South Korea, suggested positive assessments of Korea's industrialization and economic growth potential and hinted at the possibility of increasing investments in Korea, the U.S. Department of State, which had the decision-making authority over the funds of the actual aid organization, viewed the priority of aid to Korea as mainly military supplementation and civilian stabilization. In other words, military and economic aid was a strategic tool for maintaining U.S. hegemony in East Asia. for maintainingThe U.S. was in a position to change its South Korea-related aid policies in accordance with how the Cold War developed. This meant that the aid agreements between Seoul and Washington could be read differently by the two signatories, and the size and way aid was used under the agreement could also differ depending on the circumstances.[46]

---

45 According to a report compiled by the UN Korean Civil Affairs Division, Korea had experience building a stable power grid after the colonial period, although it suffered significant damage due to division and war. There were considerable potential hydropower sites, and the presence of basic infrastructure such as railways provided a significant potential for rural development. The report proposed a five-year plan for immediate postwar recovery, increased agricultural productivity, and industrial development, suggesting the development of two thermal power plants (36,000 kW) and five hydropower plants (78,000 kW) in addition to the restoration of damaged power plants. This report was prepared based on the 1949 ECA report and the opinions of the Korean government and the Ministry of Commerce and Industry. Ibid., 1953.

46 The United States' aid policy toward Korea was implemented as part of its East Asia policy, which focused on building a Japan-centered security bloc. Therefore, it differed from the assistance programs implemented by the United States in countries like Vietnam and Indonesia as part of broader social engineering and democracy promotion projects. While those countries implemented long-term dam construction projects to expand power facilities, Korea preferred to rapidly strengthen its power supply through thermal power generation. For information on the East Asia security bloc, refer to: Jong-Won Lee (이종원), *Cold War in East Asia and Korean-American-Japanese Relations* [東アジア冷戰と韓美日關係] (Seoul: Tokyo University Press, 1996). The implementation of aid programs was decided through agreements in the Joint Economic Committee, but the U.S. position generally prevailed. There were instances where aid programs were altered without going through

1) Construction of the 100,000 kW Tthermal Pplant by the FOA and Reeducation Programs

After the Paik-Wood Agreement was established in December 1953, US economic aid to Korea began in earnest in 1954. With the direct handling of aid by the Foreign Operation Administration (FOA), the amount of aid increased significantly, and more importantly, facility investments for economic recovery were aggressively pursued. Expanding the electrical grid was an important priority for major industrial planning. The MCI took the three-year electricity development plan drawn up by Korean engineers and officials the previous year, revised and expanded it, and used it as the basis for seeking support from the FOA for electrical development. However, the construction of hydroelectric power plants promoted by the Korean government was indefinitely postponed before it even began, as the FOA was reluctant to provide funding.

The FOA agreed with Korean electrical engineers and technical bureaucrats on the need for new power plants for Korea's postwar recovery and industrial revitalization, but they had different opinions on the choice of power sources. In particular, the FOA suggested that the construction of hydroelectric power plants proposed by South Korea was not suitable for Korean society, which urgently needed a power supply, as hydroelectric plants took longer and were more expensive to construct than thermal power plants. They argued that if a thermal power plant using Korean anthracite as fuel was constructed, there would not be the excessive dependency on imported resources that Korean engineers were concerned about.

However, separate from such surface-level reasoning, communications between the U.S. State Department and aid officials at the time indicate that they sought to use U.S. aid to South Korea – a state on the frontlines of the Cold War – as leverage to realize something else. Correspondence with aid officials responsible for South Korea indicates that they were skeptical

---

the Joint Economic Committee, and even if the execution was approved, the U.S. could delay the approval of aid programs to the point where the fiscal year had passed, resulting in the implementation being neglected. Ibid., 173-213; Pak, *Origins of Won-yong*, 109-129.

about whether South Korea needed to construct hydroelectric power plants, as the aid officials expected thermal power plant(s) to quickly help stabilize the economy (and military); moreover, such thermal power plants could provide technological contracting opportunities for Bechtel, a US firm. The U.S. officials thus considered how to persuade South Korean President Syngman Rhee to adopt thermal power sources instead.

In other words, the U.S. wanted aid to Korea to help not only stabilize the Korean economy but also the U.S. economy. The aid policy was designed to encourage Koreans to "buy American", employ American engineers dispatched to Korea, and thus see funds returned to the U.S. economy.[47] As the executing agency of aid funds, the FOA preferred a method of power production that could quickly achieve results at a low cost and help the U.S. economy. The answer was thermal power, a technological form that could be moved quickly and where American electric companies had competitive advantages.[48] Of course, they also had practical difficulties in pursuing long-term plans that required significant funding and time, such as the construction of hydroelectric power plants, since the aid plan and execution by the aid authorities, including the FOA, had to be made anew annually in line with the U.S. fiscal year. Using the constraints of this system, the United States often thwarted plans by postponing the execution of aid funds that the aid authorities and the Korean government had agreed on to the next fiscal year.

As a result of the collision between the Ministry of Commerce's long-term power development plan and the FOA's plan, involving differing views on total power generation and demand forecasting, as well as the choice of power sources, the FOA's proposal ultimately prevailed.[49] During this process, the

---

47 Furthermore, the United States considered it important to form an East Asia bloc centered around Japan to maintain military stability in the region and sought to connect the Korean economy with the Japanese economy. To achieve this, despite the resistance from Koreans, they even imported some aid materials from Japan. "FOA Cablegram From Seoul Wood/No; TOFOA 530, 1 April 1954", RG 469, Entry 422, box4a.

48 For information on the development of the electric power industry and electrical technology in the United States, refer to: Richard F Hirsh, *Technology and Transformation in the American Electric Utility Industry* (Cambridge and New York: Cambridge University Press, 1989).

49 The execution of aid funds requiring the involvement of the Joint Economic Committee (CEB) could not be decided solely by the Korean government, and the U.S. pressured Korea by indefinitely postponing the execution of aid funds if an agreement was not reached. Delays in the execution

American aid authority and Bechtel, the U.S. electricity technology firm that was to manage the construction of the thermal power plant, continued negotiations with those in charge of power-related matters such as the MCI and KECO, which still prioritized the construction of hydroelectric power plants. They also directly met with President Syngman Rhee to explain the benefits of constructing thermal power plants and sought to reinforce their position.

The president of Bechtel, along with the head of the FOA, met with President Rhee, claiming that if they were to take charge of the construction of thermal power plants, they could secure a large amount of power generation in a short period. Amidst the continuous news of power shortages causing political and economic difficulties, President Rhee welcomed Bechtel's argument. He ordered them to coordinate with aid authorities and build themthese thermal plants as quickly as possible, promising full support. There was a difference in opinion regarding long-term electricity generation development plans and the choice of power sources within the South Korean government itself. While the bureaucrats in the Ministry of Commerce were striving to implement a long-term power development plan centered on hydroelectric power, President Rhee and economic bureaucrats, including Paik Too-chin, prioritized swift forms of public welfare over growth objectives. According to Jeong Jin-a, they presumed that without U.S. aid funds, the economy would not grow and sought first and foremost to use such funding to control runaway inflation.[50]

In the end, in 1954, the FOA invested all of its $3 million in expanding power facilities into the construction of new thermal power plants. In charge of constructing the thermal power plant, Bechtel installed four 25,000 kW generators with the same design in Masan (two units), Samcheok, and Dangjin, securing a total power generation of 100,000 kW. As thermal power plants began construction in three areas in 1954, after smooth construction, total

of aid funds would have significant economic consequences, so eventually the Korean government had no choice but to follow the U.S. position. Ibid., 192.

50 Jin-A Jeong (정진아), "War Inflation and the 'Baekjaejeong' Economic Planning Board [전쟁 인플레이션과 '백재정']," "The Korean History Society Modern History Research Division [한국역사연구회 현대사분과 편]" in *Interpreting the Korean War from the Perspective of History: From Facts to Comprehensive Understanding* (Humanist, 2010), 648-649.

power generation in Korea rapidly increased to 280,000 kW by 1958.

The FOA's new thermal power plant construction funds also included wage costs for engineers and operators involved in running the plant. The American engineers dispatched to Korea for power plant construction remained in Korea for several years even after the construction was finished. These engineers took charge of overall power plant operation, including operation, maintenance, and repair of the power plants, together with Korean engineers, thereby naturally transferring overall technology related to thermal power plant operation to Korean engineers. This process helped to prepare Korean engineers, who are were thus far accustomed to hydroelectric power generation, for use inoperating thermal power plants. This experience allowed them to update their knowledge of thermal power, which had not been updated to that point.[51] This experience served as an opportunity for Korean electric engineers, who had perceived thermal power plants as outdated technology, to recognize them as the latest technology.

In addition to direct technology transfer in Korea, the FOA also operated a program to support overseas training for Korean electrical engineers in the U.S. Primarily conducted as retraining for skilled Korean workers, U.S. training provided opportunities to directly experience "advanced technology." According to Shin Ki-jo, who was part of the technical training team, they inspected power plants and power grid operations in various parts of the U.S. and then received additional technical training in their chosen fields. In particular, during this period in the U.S., an intense program for training engineers to operate newly built thermal power plants was implemented. Despite the short training period of approximately six months to a year, after learning various matters for power plant operation, visiting power plants, and learning practical skills, they were able to act as responsible engineers for each thermal power plant upon their return.[52]

---

51 The thermal power plants constructed by Bechtel were soon acquired by the Korea Electric Company (KECO) after completion. KECO paid the construction costs to the Korean government. *Kyunghyang Shinmun*, September 25, 1957.

52 In 1955, a total of 12 technicians went to the United States for training along with Shin Ki-jo. The list can be found in the "Technical assistance and service request," RG 469, series 23, Office of Engineering. Han Jin-geum argues that the technical training provided by the United States not

As the number of engineers with such experience rose, perceptions of thermal power generation also began to gradually shift gradually. Articles and news reports published in KESA's journal, *Electrical Engineering*, offer a glimpse of such a shift in mood. From around this time, the journal began to regularly publish writings and interviews with engineers who had gone on training trips to the U.S. Many of them contained claims about what they had learned, and their experiences with thermal power indicated that the U.S. electricity system was well developed and robust.[53] In addition, academics also expressed that thermal power could be a new alternative, introducing recent trends in the field of power technology based on their own training experiences. Notably, Kim Jae-shin, a professor at Seoul National University's College of Engineering, introduced the recent developments in thermal power technology based on his training in West Germany, claiming that large-scale, efficiency-enhanced thermal power plants could be a good choice for Korea, where the urgent resolution of power shortages was needed.[54]

2) Negotiation and Ccompromise toward an Electricity Development Plan Iinvolving "Hhydrothermal Ccoexistence"

As such, with the construction of thermal power plants at the start of the power system reconstruction project under the influence of American aid,

---

only had the effect of acquiring advanced technology but also played an important role in creating pro-U.S. forces. Shin, *Off the Beaten Path*, 140-150; Geum Han Jin (한진금), "Research on the Technical Assistance and Training Plan of US Aid Institutions in the 1950s [1950년대 美國 원조 기관의 對韓 技術援助訓練計劃 연구]" (Master's thesis, Seoul National University, 2010).

53 See the following: Chan-Yong Seong (성찬용), "A Visit to the Electrical Industry in the United States [미국 전기계 방문기]," *Electrical Engineering [전기공학]* (1953): 26-28; Editorial Board (편집부), "An Interview with Engineers Who Visited the United States and Returned: Insights into the Power Industry [전력계소사: 미국을 시찰하고 돌아온 기술자 인터뷰기]," *Electrical Engineering [전기공학]* (1958): 1-7.

54 According to an electrical engineering website accessed online, Kim Jae-sin's article is classified as published in the December 1948 issue. However, the content of the article discusses the situation after 1953. It would be more accurate to consider this article as published around the time when there was a shift in perception toward thermal power generation, which occurred after 1953. Jae-Shin Kim (김재신), "Trends in Modern Thermal Power Plants [근대식 화력발전소의 추세]," *Electrical Engineering [전기공학]* (1948): 15. See link: http://ocean.kisti.re.kr/IS_mvpopo212L.do?method=list&poid=kiee&kojic=DHJGBB&sVnc=v1n2&sFree=

it became difficult for Korean electrical engineers and technical bureaucrats to insist solely on the construction of hydroelectric power plants. Above all, there was a concern that if they continued to insist on the construction of hydroelectric power plants alone, despite repeated setbacks in the new hydroelectric power plant construction plans agreed upon in the Korea–US Joint Power Committee, the negotiations themselves could fail, and overall power development could be delayed. The only hydroelectric power plant construction agreed upon in the Korea-U.S. Joint Power Committee that was actually realized was the third unit of the Hwacheon Hydroelectric Power Plant (27,000 kW), which was believed ready to secure a large amount of power generation with little investment, as the groundwork had already been laid during the period of relief.[55]

During this time, KECO completed the Gwisan Hydroelectric Power Plant without the support of an aid agency. In 1951, the MCI invested the little capital it had in the 'little valley electrical resource development plan' to meet immediate electricity needs. The Gwisan facility was limited to only 2100 kW in generation capacity, but it was significant as it was planned by South Korean engineers in accordance with the needs of the country and funded by domestic capital alone.[56] As the new hydroelectric facility was designed with plans that considered long-term projections, the acquisition of planning capacity, and technical breakthroughs with equipment, it was worthy of becoming a model for future development in the industry.

However, by the time it was finished, South Korea lacked a potential alternative for resolving its power issues. Considering the basic land and funds required for power plant construction, the power production of Gwisan was too low, and the economic feasibility was poor. Furthermore, the electrical engineers who witnessed the drastic increase in power production in the process of

55 The construction of the Hwacheon Hydroelectric Power Plant Unit 3 received a total of $13,517,000 in aid from FOA from 1954 to 1957, and Morrison-Knudsen was responsible for the construction. An additional power generation capacity of 27,000 kW was added.

56 The construction of the Goseong Hydroelectric Power Plant required a total cost of 1,531,226,000 won. Of this, 311,220,000 won was provided as government subsidy, and the remaining 1,220,000,000 won was financed through bank loans. The Korean Electric Company (조선전업주식회사), *Construction Site of Goseong Hydroelectric Power Plant [괴산 수력발전소 건설 공사지]* (1958), 6.

recapturing the Hwacheon Power Plant decided that constructing large-scale power plants was more advantageous than constructing small-scale power plants in terms of resource use efficiency and power stability.[57]

In 1957, four new thermal power plants built with aid funds from the FOA temporarily stabilized Korea's power system and proposed new possibilities for power development. For a while they managed to escape chronic power shortages and implement "unlimited transmission." The 100,000 kW of electricity provided by the four thermal power plants supplied a solid base load to Korean society, serving as the fundamental driving force for growing other industries. This was a new experience for Korean electrical engineers who had hitherto regarded thermal power plants as outdated technology.[58]

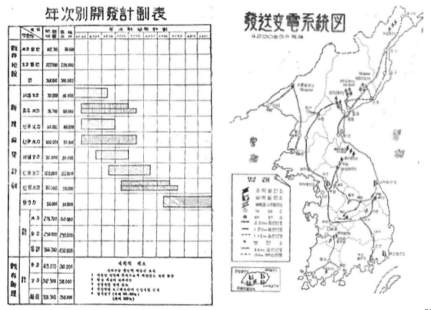

Figure 2. Five-Year Plan for Power Development, Power Supply Network Diagram, May 1958.[59]

57 See the following: The Korean Electric Corporation, *10-year History of The Korean Electric Power Corporation*.; Korea Electric Power Corporation, *A 100-year History*, 417.

58 However, even at this time, officials from the Ministry of Commerce and Industry argued that the reason the long-term power development plan and the principle of self-sufficiency in resources failed was that "the biggest problem in plan implementation was the reliance on aid funds as the source of construction funds." Ministry of Commerce and Industry (상공부), *Government Administration in Commerce [상공행정계관]* (Seoul: 1958).

Ultimately, the South Korean government and the MCI abandoned their principle of 'hydro as master, coal as subordinate'. Instead, they adopted the principle of 'hydro-thermal coexistence'. This was the result of compromises with the aid authorities, but from another perspective, it also reflected shifting views among Korean electrical engineers about the validity of thermal power as a choice in long-term planning of power sources. It was also the result of learning how to persuade American aid authorities through a long process of failed compromise and how to gain what they wanted. While establishing the 1958 long-term power development plan, the Korean government reduced the target of hydropower to 45% and increased the target of thermal power to 55%, thereby devising a plan to quickly push forward the construction of thermal power plants, which could easily satisfy the United States, instead of delaying the construction of hydropower plants during difficult negotiations with US aid authorities.

Additionally, the Korean government included nuclear power at the end of the 1958 plan to secure new technology by gaining cooperation from aid authorities. The sudden inclusion of nuclear power as a new power source was primarily a result of the United States' attempt to maintain control of nuclear power technology, as the peaceful use of nuclear power began to be openly discussed both worldwide and subsequently in Korea.[60] However, on the other hand, Korean electrical engineers and technical bureaucrats may have understood nuclear power as a new cutting-edge technology that extended the discourse from existing hydropower-centric technology. Nuclear power shares the characteristics of the power system that Korean engineers aimed for, such as large-scale power generation and high-voltage transmission, in addition to being a cutting-edge technology that follows the general technological development trajectory. Additionally, at that time, nuclear power was recognized

59 It can be confirmed that nuclear power development was included. In addition, in 1957, the integration of the power systems between North and South Korea was still being considered.

60 See the following: Seong-Jun Kim (김성준), "Formation and Changes in the Technological Regimes of the Nuclear Program in South Korea, 1953-1980 [한국 원자력 기술 체계의 형성과 변화, 1953-1980]" (Ph.D. dissertation, Seoul National University [서울대학교], 2012), 24-27; John Dimoia, "Atoms for Sale?: Cold War Institution-Building and the South Korean Atomic Energy Project, 1945-1965." *Technology and Culture* 51 (2010): 589-618, doi: 10.1353/tech.2010.0021.

as nearly free energy that could produce infinite energy from a small amount of elements, replacing expensive fossil fuels; this perception coincided with the technological view of large-scale hydroelectric power systems areat.

5. Conclusions

After liberation, increasing power generation and building a power grid were regarded as extremely important preliminary tasks for industrialization in South Korea. However, the long-term power development plans created by the technical bureaucrats of the Ministry of Commerce and Industry (MCI) and electrical engineers, who were at the forefront, faced repeated setbacks, leading to little progress as the 1960s began. These delays were primarily of thedue to conflicts between the hydroelectric power plan pursued by Korean electrical engineers and technocrats at the time and the thermal power plant-centered construction plan proposed by the American aid organization.

South Korea's technocrats and specialists were forced to abandon their 'hydro as master, coal as subordinate' principle and adopt an approach of 'hydro-thermal coexistence'. They complained that the pressure from the U.S. aid authorities meant that they were unable to realize their ideals, but those same ideals were a legacy of the specific colonial context in which they were formed. This kind of intangible legacy was understood by Korea's electrical engineers as a "pure technical logic" and continued to exert greater influence than other colonial legacies.

On the other hand, the thermal power plant-centered policy pursued by the aid authorities in the interest of achieving quick stability pressured the technological orientation of Korean electrical engineers who advocated a hydroelectric power-centered discourse, but it also presented new options. Electrical engineers who encountered the state-of-the-art thermal power plants built by American aid authorities realized that they could also be the answer to the new power system. As a result of these choices, Korean electrical engineers were able to deal with negotiations much more flexibly and had various options. They proposed a plan to build thermal power plants that could be constructed quickly with less money, using aid funds, and to bring in a deputy minister to push for hydroelectric power plants, which require considerable money and time investments. They also set the long-term goal of acquiring nuclear technology from the U.S.

How *Gayo* became K-POP:

International Song Festivals and South Korean Musicians' Sense of the World, 1970-1982

KIM Sunghee

1. Introduction: "The Bulldozer of the Entertainment Industry" and the Beginning of the International Pop Music Festival Era

Lee Bong-jo didn't particularly enjoy Western-style meals. Not just that—he was a quintessential Korean who couldn't eat at all without kimchi. Knowing this, I packed fifty cans of kimchi and brought them along to Greece. While staying in Athens for a month, we cooked rice for the four people in the hotel room and used the kimchi to complete our meals. However, we had to ration the kimchi by tearing it into small, thin pieces and sharing them little by little when we started to run out. Those days are still vividly etched in my memory.[1]

Lee Bong-jo (1931-1987) was the type of person who could not eat a single meal without kimchi. For this reason, when he participated in the Song Olympiad (Ολυμπιάδα Τραγουδιού; Olympiade de la Chanson) held in Athens, Greece, in the summer of 1971, he had no choice but to bring kimchi with him. To be more precise, his partner and fellow musician for the competition, Hyun

---

1   Mee Hyun, *As If Today is the Last Day* [오늘을 마지막 날처럼] (Seoul: Moonhakmaeul, 1997), 250.

Mee (1938-2023), took charge of packing the kimchi for the journey. The group comprised four individuals, including Hwang Jeong-tae (b. 1937), the music director of Tongyang Broadcasting Company (TBC), who accompanied them as a manager, and Chung Hong-taek (b. 1936), an entertainment reporter from *Hankook Ilbo* (Daily Korea), who participated as a judge. Initially, the four of them shared the kimchi. However, after three days, only ten cans remained, and the group conceded the remaining kimchi to Lee Bong-jo.[2]

Although he could not live a day without kimchi, Lee Bong-jo's senses were open to the world, and he harbored ambitions overseas. Renowned as "the bulldozer of the entertainment industry," he was not only an artist but also a shrewd businessman.[3] Lee owned a nightclub,[4] held the position of chair of the Korean Entertainment Association, and served as vice-chair of the "Korea Harmony Club," a gathering of light music performers. These prominent roles solidified his influence within the Korean entertainment industry.[5] A year after the release of his composition "Fog," which garnered a positive response when it was released by Japan's Victor Records in 1969,[6] Lee Bong-jo, along with singer Chung Hun Hi (b. 1952) took part in the inaugural Yamaha World Popular Song Festival in Tokyo, Japan.[7]

---

2   Hong-Taek Chung (정홍택), "Korea's #1 Entertainment Journalist Jeong Hong-Taek Speaks Out, 43: The Greece World Song Festival [한국 연예기자 1호 정홍택의 지금은 말할 수 있다]," *Hankook Ilbo*, Jan. 20, 2009, https://www.hankookilbo.com/News/Read/200901200111927560.

3   "Lee Bong-jo Wants to Enrich His TV Show 'Lee Bong-jo Hour' and Opens a Nightclub Enriches Himself and Opens a Nightclub [李鳳祚아워 充実 꾀해 自己 나이트클럽]," *Chosun Ilbo*, May 19, 1970.

4   "Mr. Lee Bong-jo Elected [李鳳祚씨 뽑아]," *Chosun Ilbo*, Mar. 24, 1970; "Gil Okyun Elected as Chair [会長에 吉屋潤씨]," *Chosun Ilbo*, Jan. 20, 1970. The Chair of the Korea Harmony Club was Gil Okyun.

5   "Popularity of the Japanese Music Album 'Fog' Rises [「안개」 日音盤 人氣]," *Kyunghyang Shinmun*, Sep. 20, 1969. To be precise, the Japanese singer Tashiro Miyoko (田代美代子) released a cover of "Fog" in Japanese. According to the article, the French singer Yvette Giraud, who had previously visited Korea, suggested to Miyoko Tashiro that she cover the song. Tashiro held a release event for the new song dressed in hanbok, at the Korean-style restaurant Hien (祕苑) in Ginza (銀座), where Patti Kim, the most popular female singer in 20th century Korea, was in attendance.

6   Yamaha Music Foundation, "The 1st Tokyo International Popular Song Festival (Renamed to World Popular Song Festival from the 2nd Festival Onwards) [in Japanese, 'Dai 1-kai Tōkyō Kokusai Kayō Ongakusai (Dai 2-kai yori 'Sekai Kayōsai' ni meishō henkō)']," *The World Popular Song Festival*, https://www.yamaha-mf.or.jp/history/e-history/wpsf/.

Note: In this paper, the festival will be referred to as the "Yamaha World Popular Song Festival" to distinguish it from other world song festivals (e.g., TBC World Song Festival).

Among the 580 songs submitted to the competition, "Fog" was placed in the top ten and received a prize.[8] This marked the beginning of the international song festival era in Korean popular music history. As Hyun Mee recalled in the quoted passage above, Lee Bong-jo went to Athens, Greece in July 1971, then back to Tokyo in November, and then to Athens and Tokyo again in 1972.[9] Lee Bong-jo, the "bulldozer" of the Korean entertainment industry, broke new ground and ushered in the era of international song festivals. After nine years as a contestant, Lee Bong-jo took a seat at the judges' table at the first TBC World Song Festival[10] in 1979.[11] Not satisfied with simply participating, Lee Bong-jo led the hosting of international song festivals at TBC with Hwang Jung-tae, who had traveled the world with him.

This study highlights the history of Korean international song festivals inaugurated by Lee Bong-jo. Commencing with Lee Bong-jo and Chung Hun Hi, eminent songwriters such as Gil Okyun (1927-1995) and Kim Kee-ung (1936-2013), alongside accomplished and renowned vocalists, including Hyun Mee, Park Kyung-hee (1951-2004), Hye Eun-Yi (b. 1954), Yoon Sinae (b. 1952), Min Haekyung (b. 1962), and Yang Soo Kyung (b. 1965), ventured into the realm of international song festivals. Patti Kim (b. 1938), Cho Yong-pil (b. 1950), and Kim Yon Ja (b. 1959) also displayed their prowess and popularity by participating in these global events. The spectrum of festivals they engaged

---

7 The English title of "Fog" (안개) was officially translated as "Foggy" in the Yamaha World Popular Song Festival, while the Japanese title was "Kiri no machi" (霧の街: A foggy street), which was released by Japan's Victor Records. "Fog" has been covered by other singers and used in films several times. Notably, this song was featured in Park Chan-Wook's film "Decision to Leave" (2022).

8 The competition awarded one grand prize winner and nine runner-up prize winners through the selection process.

9 "'Fog' Combo Participates in the Argentine World Song Festival [아르젠틴 世界歌謠祭에 「안개」 콤비 參加]," *Dong-A Ilbo*, Feb. 22, 1971. Although invited to the international pop music festival held in Argentina, Lee Bong-jo was unable to participate in the event. Chung (정홍택), "Korea's #1 Entertainment Journalist Chung Hong-Taek." At the time, Chung Hong-Taek, a reporter for the *Hankook Ilbo*, attempted to participate in the Viña del Mar International Song Festival with Lee Bong-jo in the spring of 1971, but he recalled that the event was canceled due to a change in Chile's government. It appears that he confused Chile with Argentina. Chile's government had not changed at the time, but Argentina's had in March 1971.

10 The TBC World Song Festival was only held in 1979 and 1980. The third festival was held by KBS in 1981 after the Chun Doo-Hwan government forcibly integrated TBC into KBS. However, KBS no longer hosted the World Song Festival after the third festival.

11 See Table 2.

in spanned across the world. These included the Yamaha World Popular Song Festival, the TBS Tokyo Music Festival, Chile's Viña del Mar International Song Festival (Festival Internacional de la Canción de Viña del Mar), the World Song Festival in Hawaii,[12] the Los Angeles Song Festival,[13] the Pacific Song Contest in New Zealand, and the Asia-Pacific Broadcasting Union (ABU) music festivals, notably the ABU Popular Song Contest (1985-1987) and the ABU Golden Kite World Song Festival (1989-1991). These musicians also took part in festivals hosted within South Korea, such as the MBC Seoul International Song Festival and the TBC World Song Festival.

Although many Korean singers, composers, and other musicians have participated in numerous popular music festivals, the reality is that research on Korean international song festivals inevitably becomes a study of how Korean popular music was influenced by that of Japan.[14] This era began with Lee Bong-jo's participation in the Yamaha World Popular Song Festival, and it ended with the discontinuation of the Yamaha World Popular Song Festival and the TBS Tokyo Music Festival. In this sense, this study contributes to East Asian popular music studies by identifying and analyzing "cross-border practices" and "forgotten lines of exchange and intersection", with a focus on Japan and Korea.[15]

However, the history of Korean international song festivals cannot be solely explained by their relationship with Japan or Asia. While a centripetal force

---

12 The Hawaii World Song Festival was held for the first time in 1982. The contest featured twelve singers from nine countries, including the United States, Italy, the United Kingdom, Japan, Hong Kong, and South Korea. Yoon Bok-Hee, a Korean singer, won the Grand Prix with her entry song, "I'll Follow." However, detailed information about the event is scarce.

13 The Los Angeles World Song Festival was organized by Gu Duhoe (구두회, 1938-2014), a prominent figure in the Korean community in Southern California, particularly in San Diego. However, the festival was relatively short-lived, and as a result, it is difficult to find information about it.

14 Haejoang Cho-Han (조한혜정), *Modernity, Popular Culture and East–West Identity Formation: A Discourse Analysis of Korean Wave in Asia* [글로벌 지각 변동의 징후로 읽는 '한류 열풍」, 『한류와 아시아의 대중문화』] (Seoul: Yonsei University Press, 2003), 24. According to Cho-Han Haejong, the growth of the Korean popular music industry is an extension of the colonial manufacturing industry export. Cho-Han claimed that "Korean pop music" imitates "Michael Jackson and Madonna or imitates Japanese song festivals."

15 Hyunjoon Shin, "The Cultural Politics of K-Pop: A Case Study of Popular Music Crossing Borders [K-Pop의 문화정치(학): 월경(越境)하는 대중음악에 관한 하나의 사례연구]," *Media and Society* 13, no. 3 (2005): 8; Hyunjoon Shin, "Re-Examining Asian Popular Music from an Inter-Asian Perspective [인터아시아 시각에서 아시아 대중음악을 다시 조명하기]," *Hwanghae Culture* 89 (2015): 65.

existed, pulling Korean popular music toward Japan's sphere of cultural influence, there was also a centrifugal force attempting to break away from it. The organizers (MBC, TBC) sought authority from a third party that surpassed their relationships with participants, especially foreign singers and Japan-Korea relationships. Interestingly, the two Korean broadcasting stations sought this transcendent authority from Yugoslavia, a communist country. The International Federation of Festival Organizations (Federation Internationale des Organisations de Festivals: FIDOF), headquartered in Split, Yugoslavia, played a crucial role in the organization and execution of the MBC Seoul International Song Festival and the TBC World Song Festival.

Research on Korea's international song festivals inevitably includes the study of Yugoslavia's FIDOF. This enables researchers to examine Korean popular music, particularly from the 1970s to the early 1980s, not only through an inter-Asian lens but also within the broader context of Cold War cultural history. By delving into international song festivals, we can expand our geographical perspective beyond Asia and encompass the Eurasian landscape.

As highlighted by Shin Hyunjoon, a prominent scholar in Korean popular music studies, the 1970s continue to recede from the present but remain too proximate to be relegated to the realm of history. This temporal positioning has resulted in a noticeable gap in discussions surrounding Korean popular music during this era.[16] Prevailing examinations of Korean popular music from the 1970s and 1980s have predominantly centered around dialogs about youth culture, with a specific emphasis on folk music, characterized by the use of "acoustic guitars", and the genre of "group sound" music. These themes have been explored in connection with subcultures and acts of cultural resistance.[17]

---

16 Hyun-Jun Shin (신현준), "The Issues of Writing Histories of Korean Popular Music in the 1970s and 80s: The Difficulties of Indeterminate Texts and Complex Mediations [1970~1980년대 한국 대중음악사 서술의 쟁점 — 불확정적 텍스트와 복합적 매개의 난점]," *Journal of Popular Music* [대중음악] 15 (2015): 95.

17 Herim Erin Lee (이혜림), "The Formation of 1970s Korean Youth Culture: Focusing on the Cultural Consumption of Popular Music [1970년대 청년문화구성체의 역사적 형성과정 — 대중음악의 소비양상을 중심으로]," *Korean Journal of Social Issues* 6, no. 2 (2005): 7-40; Chang Nam Kim (김창남), "The Cultural Identity of Korean Youth Culture in the 1970s: Focusing on Guitar Music [1970년대 한국 청년문화의 문화적 정체성 — 통기타음악을 중심으로]," *Journal of Popular Music* 2 (2008): 144-65; Ae-Kyung Park (박애경), "An Explore on the Potential of Korean Folk Song as the Urban Song-with a Focus on the Folk Song and Folk Culture in 1970s [한국 포크의 '도시민요'적 가능성 탐색 — 1970년대

While some attention has been given to analyses of song festivals such as the *Daehak gayoje* (Campus Song Festival) (1977-2012) and *Haebyeon gayoje* (Beach Song Festival) (1978), these investigations have also been confined within the broader discourse of Korean youth culture.[18] Consequently, international song festivals in South Korea have remained significantly understudied. Despite once constituting a dominant presence within the popular music landscape, these events have now receded into sporadic mentions within television programs and have yet to assume the status of subjects for scholarly examination.

The temporal proximity of international song festivals is not the only reason why they have not become a subject of academic research; the networks that connected Seoul with other places where festivals were organized and held, such as Yugoslavia, Chile, and Greece, have faded, disappeared, or been forgotten. In particular, little research on the FIDOF has been performed by either scholars in South Korea or popular music scholars in other countries.

This study examines how Korean *gayo* (popular song) musicians, broadcasters, and entertainment industry professionals participated in and organized international song festivals and how they attempted to enter the global music market through these events. Essentially, this paper focuses on producers rather than consumers of Korean popular music. Korean *gayo* producers learned how to communicate with the world beyond Japan through their experiences at international song festivals. This research focuses on *gayo* musicians who learned how to interact with the American and European popular music scenes during the Cold War era, particularly in the 1970s and early 1980s.

포크송과 포크문화를 중심으로]," *Korean Folk Songs* 41, no. 2 (2014): 53-77; Yong-Gyu Park (박용규), "Television and Popular Music in the 1970s: Focusing on Popular Music Programs for Teenagers [1970년대의 텔레비전과 대중음악─청소년 대상 대중음악 프로그램을 중심으로]," *Korean Journal of Journalism and Communication Studies* 51, no. 2 (2007): 5-29; Pil-Ho Kim (김필호), "Group Sound Rock Music of the 1960s-70s - Archaeology of Korean Pop Music [1960-70년대 그룹사운드 록음악 ─ 한국 팝의 고고학]," *Cultural Science* 6 (2005): 211-28.

18 Hyun-Jun Shin, Yong-Woo Lee, and Ji-Seon Choi (신현준·이용우·최지선), *Archaeology of Korean Pop Music 1970 - Korean Folk and Rock, Its Peak and Diversification* [한국 팝의 고고학 1970 ─ 한국의 포크와 록, 그 절정과 분화] (Seoul: HanGilArt, 2005). Lim Hyeong-Soon has been involved in organizing university song festivals and beach song festivals, with a focus on campus bands. Hyeong-Soon Lim (임형순), "Influence of 7080 Campus Bands on Korean Rock Music [7080 캠퍼스 밴드가 한국 록 음악에 미친 영향]," *Journal of Popular Music* [대중음악] 13 (2014): 8-32.

2. From Seoul to Tokyo: The Endeavors of Korean Pop Musicians at the Japanese International Song Festivals

Before Lee Bong-jo won an award in Tokyo in 1970, the *world* of Korean pop musicians was synonymous with the Eighth United States Army. For instance, Yoon Bok Hee (b. 1946), who later won the grand prize at the 1979 MBC Seoul International Song Festival, began her singing career by auditioning for an Eighth Army entertainment production after being told that "with [her] talent, [she] should go to the Eighth Army."[19] Hyun Mee also performed on the Eighth Army stage under the pseudonym "Bella" before gaining domestic popularity with her performance of the song "Night Fog" and participating in the international song contest in Athens, Greece.[20] For these singers, the world became accessible by performing for the U.S. Eighth Army. However, in addition to experiencing the world through the Eighth Army, Hyun Mee testified about how her partner Lee Bong-jo, obtained inspiration and created his songs:

> When Lee Bong-jo was home, it was like he lived with the radio on. His passion for music was extraordinary. He often tuned in to Japanese music broadcasts, and when a melody he liked came on, he would record and sometimes even arrange it. One day, late at night, while listening to the radio, he suddenly sat up from where he had been lying down. It was as if a surge of inspiration had ignited within his heart.[21]

According to Lee Bong-jo's partner Hyun Mee, he always "lived with the radio on" and mainly listened to "Japanese music broadcasts." While doing this, he once heard "It's A Lonesome Old Town" by Nat King Cole on a Japanese radio broadcast and created Hyun Mee's signature song, "Night Fog." Japanese music broadcasts served as a gateway to Western music genres such as jazz

---

19 Bok-Hee Yun (윤복희), *It's Me, Lord* [저예요, 주님] (Seoul: Duranno Seowon Corporation, 2011), 88-9.

20 Hyun (현미), *As If Today is the Last Day*, 100.

21 Ibid., 130.

and blues.[22] For this reason, Lee Bong-jo was criticized by the media in the mid-to-late 1960s as a "*gayo* musician" who created and performed "Japanese-style pop songs."[23] He even had three songs simultaneously banned from Korean broadcasts because they were allegedly "plagiarized" from Japanese songs.[24]

Lee Bong-jo was not alone in facing allegations of plagiarism. Park Chun Seok (1930-2010) and Gil Okyun, who, in addition to Lee Bong-jo, were called "the three major composers of the time," were also criticized for copying Japanese songs.[25] However, while these musicians were criticized for creating Japanese-style *gayo* in the 1960s, by the 1970s, they were perceived as patriots who brought honor to the nation. International song festivals began to take place in Japan, and Korean *gayo* musicians began to participate in these events as representatives of Korea. The first to enter Japan was Lee Bong-jo, the "bulldozer." He submitted his most "original" song, "Fog,"[26] to the first Yamaha World Popular Song Festival.

The Yamaha World Popular Song Festival attracted massive interest from its very first event. While more than 580 songs were submitted to the first competition,[27] only 44 were played at the three-day preliminaries held between November 20 and 22, 1970 at the Nippon Bukodan Hall [日本武道館大ホール]. The scale of the event was even larger than that of the Eurovision Song Contest at the time. The Yamaha Music Foundation [ヤマハ音楽振興会] hosted the event, and there was sponsorship from the Ministry of Foreign Affairs of Japan, the Japanese Government's Agency for Cultural Affairs, and the Tokyo

---

22 "Recorded Music Market: Cutthroat Competition [레코드街 出血경쟁]," *Kyunghyang Shinmun*, Nov. 16, 1963. After Hyun Mee's "Night Fog" became popular, seven different versions of "Night Fog," including the original by Nat King Cole, were allegedly released through five different record companies.

23 "Thirteen Thoughtless *Gayo* Musicians Who Have Gone Crazy for Japan [日本에 미쳤나 소갈머리 없는 13名의 歌謠人]," *Kyunghyang Shinmun*, Aug. 4, 1965. See Footnote 36 for context.

24 Yoon-Hwan Jang (장윤환), "Plagiarism in the World of Popular Music [표절 판치는 歌謠界]," *Dong-A Ilbo*, Jul. 23, 1968.

25 "Plagiarism or Coincidence? The Music Industry Protests against Immorality Judgment [『표절』이다 『偶合』이다 放倫判定과 歌謠界반발]," *Dong-A Ilbo*, Sep. 12, 1968.

26 "Lee Bong-jo's New Song 'Fog' Highly Praised as Original [李鳳祚 新曲 「안개」 獨創的이라고 好評]," *Kyunghyang Shinmun*, Aug. 5, 1967.

27 "Lee Bong-jo and Two Others to Participate in Tokyo World Music Festival [東京 세계歌謠祭에 李鳳祚씨 등 셋參加]," *Dong-A Ilbo*, Nov. 13, 1970.

Metropolitan Government [東京都]. Corporate sponsors included Toyota, Sony, and Shiseido and music-related companies such as King Records [キングレコード], Nippon Columbia [日本コロンビア], Nippon Gramophone/Polydor Records [日本グラモフォン], and Toshiba Music Promotion [東芝音楽振興].[28] The competition mobilized Japan's cultural capabilities. Lee Bong-jo won an award[29] for composing "Fog," which was performed by Chung Hun Hi during the competition. International song festivals almost always needed participants to compete under their national flag. Hence, Lee Bong-jo became the first popular music composer to win an award at an international song festival as a representative of the Republic of Korea.

When Lee Bong-jo won the award, the organizers of song festivals worldwide began to take interest in him. The 1970s was the era of international popular music festivals. Various international pop music festivals were being held around the world. In addition to winning an award at the Yamaha World Popular Song Festival, he received many invitations from international pop music festival organizers. Many of these festivals took place in Europe, including Italy's Sanremo Music Festival [Festival della Canzone Italiana di Sanremo], one of the earliest and most influential of its kind. Among the European festivals, the organizers of the Sanremo Music Festival and the Greek Song Olympiad [Ολυμπιάδες Τραγουδιού] invited Lee Bong-jo to participate in their festivals.[30]

In Korea, Lee Bong-jo received a hero's welcome, similar to that of an athlete returning home with an Olympic medal.[31] From Busan Port all the way to Seoul's Central Hotel, successive welcome parties were held in his honor.[32] Munhwa Broadcasting Corporation (MBC) even aired a recording of his performance at the Yamaha World Popular Song Festival during prime time (8:15 PM).[33] This was before South Korea liberalized access to Japanese media

28 Yamaha Music Foundation, "The 1st Tokyo International Popular Song Festival."

29 The competition awarded one grand prize and nine other awards to the winners.

30 "[Lee Bong-jo] Invited to Italy's Sanremo Music Festival [伊 산 레모 音楽祭 초청받아]," *Joongang Ilbo*, Nov. 27, 1970.

31 "Going to the South America Song Festival with 'Fog' [南美 歌謠祭 가는 「안개」]," *Kyunghyang Shinmun*, Feb. 20, 1971. In early 1971, Lee Bong-jo received a letter of appreciation from the Minister of Culture and Public Information.

32 "Party to Celebrate the Award of 'Fog' at International Song Festival [국제가요제 입상 안개 축하회]," *Kyunghyang Shinmun*, Nov. 25, 1970.

in 1998, so broadcasters were not allowed to air Japanese-language broadcasts on television at the time.[34] These restrictions caused a few problems,[35] but the Yamaha World Popular Song Festival was broadcast multiple times and was a constant topic of discussion.[36] In late 1971, Lee Bong-jo was honored with the Artist of the Republic of Korea award by the Ministry of Culture and Public Information.[37] Once treated as a *gayo* musician with "no sense of national identity" for creating and performing songs with a "Japanese color," Lee Bong-jo was now recognized as a pop musician who represented Korea. For example, he composed a "new *gayo* for the people" called "Song of the Homeland" in preparation for the 1972 Munich Olympics.[38] Lee also took the lead in a government-sponsored campaign promoting "wholesome, healthy" popular music.[39]

Lee Bong-jo's win also led to an increase in broadcasting exchanges. Live broadcasts of Italy's Sanremo Music Festival began airing on Korean radio in 1967.[40] However, for most people, international song festivals were still

---

33 "Exclusive Broadcast of Tokyo International Song Festival (MBC TV at 8:15 pm) [동경국제가요제 독점중계(MBC TV 밤8시 15분)]," *Kyunghyang Shinmun*, Nov. 27, 1970.

34 Prior to 1998, the South Korean government prohibited legal access to Japanese media. However, during the Kim Dae-Jung administration (1997-2002) and subsequent administrations, the legalization of Japanese media has been gradually implemented.

35 "Broadcast Ethics Committee Rebukes MBC TV [放送倫理委員會 MBC TV에 견책]," *Dong-A Ilbo*, Dec. 15, 1970. During a conversation with Chung Hun Hi on MBC's "Im Taek-Geun Morning Show," there was an incident where a part of the song "Fog" sung by Chung Chun Hi in Japanese was broadcasted. As a result, the show received criticism from the Korea Communications Standards Commission for violating broadcasting ethics.

36 Yeog-Il Jeong (정영일), "Culture Recap 1970 Part 12: Broadcasting – Song [文化界決算 70 ⑫ 放送-歌謠]," *Joongang Ilbo*, Dec. 18, 1970. Yeong-Il Jeong, a culture journalist at the *Joongang Ilbo*, regarded the awards received by Chung Hoon Hi and Lee Bong-jo at the 1970 song festival as the greatest issue in the music industry.

37 "Winners of the Culture and Arts Award Decided [文化藝術賞 受賞者 결정]," *Dong-A Ilbo*, Nov. 20, 1971. The Ministry of Culture and Public Information underwent successive changes between 1989 and 2008 and is now known as the Ministry of Culture, Sports, and Tourism.

38 "New National Song 'Song of the Homeland Composed' [새로운 国民 歌謠 「祖国의 노래」 作曲]," *Joongang Ilbo*, Oct. 20, 1971. Park Mok-Wol (박목월), a renowned poet, wrote the lyrics and Hyun Mee was the vocalist.

39 "A Discussion on the Urgent Need for Healthy Songs [노래는 즐겁게 健全歌謠 「육성」이 時急하다 座談会]," *Joongang Ilbo*, Jan. 29, 1972. Lee Bong-jo's position on promoting "healthy" music was not particularly proactive. In one discussion, he even advised not to put too much pressure on pop musicians who are making music to earn a living.

40 "Sanremo Music Festival Special Broadcast on DBS [산·레모 칸소네典 DBS서 特輯放送]," *Dong-A*

211

just distant events in far-off countries, not competitions in which Korean singers had a realistic chance of participating. However, after Lee Bong-jo's win at the Yamaha World Popular Song Festival, public interest in international song festivals skyrocketed.[41] The competitions in which people were most interested included those hosted by Sanremo and Yamaha. As a result, MBC formed a partnership with the Fuji Network System (FNS), the exclusive broadcaster of the Yamaha World Popular Song Festival. In response, Tongyang Broadcasting Company (TBC) partnered with Nippon Television (NTV), and the Korean Broadcasting Corporation (KBS) strengthened their cooperation with the Japan Broadcasting Corporation (NHK) through the Asia-Pacific Broadcasting Union (ABU).[42]

Lee Bong-jo returned to Korea from Greece with Hyun Mee in July 1971. He went to Tokyo in November of the same year to participate in the second Yamaha World Popular Song Festival with his song "Class of Love," performed by the Pearl Sisters." In 1972, he participated in the Greek Song Olympiad in Athens and the Yamaha World Popular Song Festival, where he was accompanied by Chung Hun Hi.[43] Lee Bong-jo and Chung Hun Hi's most significant achievements came from the Viña del Mar International Song Festival, the largest music festival in Latin America. There, they won third place with

Ilbo, Mar. 4, 1967. Beginning in the early 1960s, Dong-A Broadcasting System (DBS) played an important role in introducing and popularizing the Sanremo Music Festival and Canzone in Korea. "Let's Enjoy Canzone [칸조네를 즐깁시다]," *Kyunghyang Shinmun*, May 28, 1964.

41 "Sanremo International Song Festival [「산레모 국제가요제」] (MBC TV, Saturday at 7:50 pm) [MBC TV 土(토) 밤7시50분]," *Kyunghyang Shinmun*, Apr. 17, 1971. The 1971 Sanremo Music Festival was initially broadcast by Dong-A Broadcasting System (DBS) radio, but it generated significant interest from listeners and was subsequently also broadcast on Munhwa Broadcasting Corporation (MBC) television. The winning song of the festival was "Il Cuore E' Uno Zingaro," with the second-place song being "Che Sarà." In South Korea, "Il Cuore E' Uno Zingaro" was covered by Chung Hun Hi, Lee Yong-Bok, and Kim Choo-Ja, while "Che Sarà" was covered by Lee Yong-Bok, Song Chang-Sik, and Cho Yong-Pil.

42 "TV Broadcasts Bring International Partnership and Vitality [TV放送 國際 제휴 活氣]," *Dong-A Ilbo*, May 17, 1971. Both KBS and NHK are the members of the ABU.

43 The 1972 Yamaha Song Festival had preliminary rounds on November 17th and 18th, and the final round was held on the 19th. In the preliminary rounds held on the 17th, the Swedish group ABBA also participated under the name Benny and Bjorn alongside Chung Hun Hi. As you can tell from the group name, ABBA at the time consisted of male members Benny Andersson and Bjorn Ulvaeus as the lead vocalists, and the female members provided the chorus. This is possibly why ABBA failed to qualify in the preliminary rounds.

the song "Deserted Island" in 1975 and took home the Best Vocal Performance Award with "In the Flower Garden" in 1979.[44]

Lee Bong-jo, Chung Hun Hi, and Hyun Mee's achievements inspired other composers and singers. Gil Okyun and Kim Gang-seop (1932-2022) provided songs to Patti Kim[45] and Kim Sang Hee (b. 1943), respectively, to participate in the TBS Tokyo Music Festival. This festival, which began in 1972, was an international song festival organized by the "Tokyo Music Festival Association Foundation [東京音楽祭協会]," which was an affiliate of the TBS (Tokyo Broadcasting System). By the mid-to-late 1970s, it was even more famous than the Yamaha World Popular Song Festival. The Yamaha Foundation obtained the commercial rights to distribute, sell, and license any songs played as part of the Yamaha World Popular Song Festival, while the TBS Tokyo Music Festival did not infringe on the commercial interests of the participants. As a result, the TBS competition attracted more interest from overseas singers and songwriters.[46] However, Korean musicians frequently participated in international music festivals held in Japan both for commercial purposes and to enhance Korea's international prestige. Therefore, Koreans viewed the Yamaha World Popular Song Festival as comparable to the TBS Tokyo Music Festival in terms of importance.

In 1974, Park Kyung Heuy participated in the Yamaha World Popular Song Festival with a song composed by Kim Kee-ung. In 1975, Jeong Mijo (b. 1949) participated in the festival with a song written by Song Chang-sik (b. 1947). In 1977, Hye Eun-Yi performed "I Love You Only," which was composed by Gil Okyun, in Tokyo. In 1978, Jeong Mijo participated again with a song by Kim Kee-ung. In 1980, Jeong Jae-eun (b. 1964), who is now known as Cheuni and is the daughter of Lee Mi-ja (b. 1941), one of the most popular singers in Korea in the 1950s-1970s, participated in a contest with a song by Jang Sei Yong. Moreover, following the footsteps of Patti Kim

---

44 Chung Hun Hi sang the song in Spanish at Viña del Mar with the title "Un Día Hermoso Como Hoy," (A Beautiful Day Like Today), while its Korean title is "꽃밭에서" (In the Flower Garden).

45 "Patti Kim Wins Third Place at Tokyo International Song Festival [패티金 3등 入賞 東京 국제歌謠祭]," *Kyunghyang Shinmun*, Jul. 1, 1974.

46 Akira Yamaguchi, "Festivals, A Shot at the Spotlight," *Billboard*, Apr. 30, 1977, 67.

and Kim Sang-Hee, the vocalist Lee Sung-ae (b. 1952)[47] participated in the TBS Tokyo Music Festival in 1977, followed by Park Kyung Heuy in 1978, Seonu Hye-kyung (b. 1957) in 79, and Yoon Sinae in 1981. The table below summarizes the participation of Korean musicians in Japanese international song festivals, including the Yamaha World Song Festival and the TBS Tokyo Music Festival, from 1972 to 1981.

Table 1. Korean Participation in Japanese International Song Festivals, 1972-1981

Year	Host	Song	Composer	Singer
1972	TBS	Lover Forever (사랑은 영원히)	Gil Okyun (길옥윤)	Patti Kim (패티 김)
1976	TBS	Joyful Arirang (즐거운 아리랑)	Kim Gang-seop (김강섭)	Kim Sang-Hee (김상희)
1974	Yamaha	"The Bright Light in the Flower" (저꽃속에서 찬란한 빛이)	Kim Kee-ung (김기웅)	Park Kyung Heuy (박경희)
1975	Yamaha	"Bul Kot/Fireworks" (불꽃)	Song Chang-sik (송창식)	Jeong Mijo (정미조)
1977	Yamaha	"Dangshin manool sarang hae/I Love You Only" (당신만을 사랑해)	Gil Okyun (길옥윤)	Hye Eun-Yi (혜은이)
1977	TBS	Dawn, Fly! (夜明けよ、翔べ)		Lee Sung-ae (이성애)
1978	Yamaha	"Oh! My Love" (아 사랑아)	Kim Kee-ung (김기웅)	Jeong Mijo (정미조)
1978	TBS	"Even If I Don't Know Where You Are" (머무는 곳 그 어딜지 몰라도)	Kim Kee-ung Cho Yong-ho (Lyric, later the director of the 1980 TBC World Popular Song Festival)	Park Kyung Heuy (박경희)
1979	TBS	"You Don't Know" (君は知らず)		Seonu Hye-gyeong (선우혜경)

47 "Lee Sung-Ae Faces Criticism [비난받는 李成愛양]," *Chosun Ilbo*, Jun. 26, 1977. Lee Sung-Ae rose to popularity in the early 1970s and was recognized as one of the top ten singers on MBC. She showcased her proficiency in Japanese by singing a Japanese cover version of Nam Jin's chart-topping song "Heartbreaking" (가슴 아프게). Additionally, she performed in Japanese during her participation in the TBS Tokyo Music Festival. However, she faced criticism from the Korean media, who accused her of lacking a sense of national identity.

1980	TBS	"Papa's Cradle Song (父に捧げる歌)		Park Kyung Heuy (박경희)
1980	Yamaha	"I Think Our Love's Something Like That Too"	Jang Sei Yong (장세용)	Jung Jae-eun (정재은)
1981	TBS	"You, Only You" (오직 당신만을)		Yoon Sinae (윤시내)

One significant difference between the two festivals was that the Yamaha World Popular Song Festival placed equal emphasis on both singers and songwriters, while the TBS Tokyo Music Festival focused more on singers. In some ways, Yamaha was more "creator-oriented," while TBS was more "interpreter-oriented." When Korean broadcasters later created their own international music festivals, MBC adopted the former approach, while TBC adopted the latter.

3. From Tokyo to Seoul:
The Korea Song Festival and the Seoul Music Festival

The two international music festivals began in Japan but significantly changed the popular music scene in Korea. As explained in earlier passages, Korean singers' participation in international music festivals was the greatest change. Korean musicians then used this as a steppingstone to take on the Japanese music market themselves. Lee Sung-ae and Jung Jae-eun performed in Japan before and after trying their luck at international music festivals. Soon after, Kim Yon Ja and Kang Susie (b. 1967) entered the Japanese market through the TBS Tokyo Music Festival.

Nonetheless, two changes of equal significance unfolded. The first pertained to the surge in performances hosted in Korea by foreign vocalists who had previously participated in Japanese song festivals. Throughout the 1960s and 1970s, Korea became a regular stage for performances by popular foreign singers. Notably, Anglophone artists such as Patti Page, Nat King Cole, and Cliff Richard, alongside Italian canzone singers such as Claudio Villa, Milva, and Gigliola Cinquetti, held concerts in the 1960s and 1970s.[48] However, a pivotal transformation occurred subsequent to the commencement of international

215

song festivals in Japan — singers who had engaged with these festivals in Japan started making appearances in Korea.

The winners of the 1970 Yamaha World Popular Song Festival, an Israeli duo called Hedva and David, held a concert at Seoul Citizens Hall[49] during the winter of 1971.[50] The show was broadcast by the TBC.[51] An American band called "A Taste of Honey" that had advanced to the Yamaha World Popular Song Festival finals appeared on the MBC's show "Saturday Saturday Night."[52] The Hong Kong native Chelsia Chan also appeared at the 1975 Yamaha World Popular Song Festival and later appeared in two films coproduced by South Korea and Hong Kong, namely, "Chelsia My Love" (1976) and "Rainbow in My Heart" (1977).[53] In 1979, the Welsh-born singer Bonnie Tyler was invited to Korea by the TBC. She had won the Yamaha World Popular Song Festival that year.[54]

As the 1980s approached, performances by two groups could be called significant landmark events. These were performances by the Dooleys and the Nolans from the United Kingdom. The Dooleys, who had taken the Gold Prize (second place) at the TBS Tokyo Music Festival in 1980, performed in Korea in 1981.[55] The Nolans, who had been the grand prize-winning team

---

48 The visits to Korea by the singers listed here were also linked to their visits to Japan. For example, Milva performed in Japan and released a Japanese-language single titled "Una Sera Di Tokyo" [ウナ・セラ・ディ東京] (a remake). The original song was a Japanese hit by the famous twin sister duo called "The Peanuts" [ザ・ピーナッツ]. Milva released several Japanese and Italian-language singles and albums in Japan. She visited Korea for the first time in 1972 and released a live album called "Milva in Seoul" that same year through a Korean record label, Seongeum [성음].

49 Seoul Citizens Hall was destroyed by fire in December 1972. The Sejong Center was subsequently constructed on the same site and opened in April 1978.

50 Chung Hun Hi and Kim Choo-Ja [김추자] later translated Hedva and David's contest-winning song "I Dream of Naomi" [ימענ לע סולוח ינא] was later translated into Korean as "Naomi-ui Kkum" [나오미의 꿈] and performed it in Korean.

51 "TBC TV 1970 Tokyo Music Festival Grand Prix Winners [TBC TV 70年度 東京歌謡祭 그랑쁘리 受賞者]," *Dong-A Ilbo*, Dec. 22, 1971. Hedva later participated in the 3rd KBS World Music Festival in 1981.

52 "Black [Singer] Group Performance [黑人 보컬그룹 出演]," *Joongang Ilbo*, Dec. 14, 1974.

53 "Hong Kong Actress Chen Chow Ha Visits Korea [홍콩여배우 첸추샤 한국에]," *Kyunghyang Shinmun*, May 10, 1977. If classified as a Korean film, "Chelsia My Love," starring Chelsia Chan, was the highest-grossing film of 1976 in Korea.

54 "Film Data [映畵界 자료]," *Chosun Ilbo*, Dec. 17, 1976.

55 Sang-Heon Kang (강상헌), "The Dooleys Come to Korea to Perform [둘리스 來韓公演]," *Dong-A*

at the same competition in 1981, performed at Jamsil Indoor Gymnasium in Seoul in 1982.[56] These performances are viewed as milestones because the two groups significantly impacted the Korean music market during its formative years, both before and after their visits to Korea. In the early 1980s, sales of albums by the Nolans and the Dooleys were massive, comparable to those of the Beatles.[57]

By 1982, MBC Radio "2 O'clock Date" host Kim Ki-deok stated that although Korea's "receptiveness" "to pop music" was still a month behind the United States, it was in sync with Japan.[58] He likely meant to convey that Korea was not lagging behind Japan, but his statement also hinted at Japan's influence on Korea's acceptance of foreign pop music. This was clearly a result of Japan's international song festivals. Metaphorically speaking, Korea's "pop music time zone" was synchronized with Japan Standard Time (JST) due to Japan's international song festivals.

The second significant change brought about by Japan's international song festivals was the hosting of an international song festival in Korea. The first person to envision an international song festival hosted in Korea was likely Chung Hong-taek, an entertainment reporter for the *Hankook Ilbo*.

By chance, [I] had the opportunity to attend the Yamaha World Popular Song Festival in Japan. I was upset, and I felt a sense of frustration in my heart. I asked myself, "Why can't we host such a song festival [in Korea]?" When it came to songs, [a lot of people say that] Koreans sang much better and created better songs than Japanese people. This is something that even Japanese people

---

Ilbo, Feb. 17, 1981. The Dooleys also performed in Korea in 1982, 1983, and 1989.

56 "Pop Fairies the Nolans Come to Korea on April 2, 1982 and Perform [팝의 요정 「놀란스」 來 2일 來韓 공연]," *Kyunghyang Shinmun*, Mar. 25, 1982. "Music," *Chosun Ilbo*, Apr. 13, 1982. On January 20, 2021, Coleen Nolan, the youngest member of the Nolans and a relief presenter on the British talk show "Loose Women," revealed during one of her appearances that the Nolans' concert in Seoul, which had originally been scheduled for three days, had to be shortened due to lead vocalist Bernie Nolan's laryngitis. https://www.youtube.com/watch?v=PNW8kEAQJPo.

57 Yoon-Hwan Jang (장윤환), "What Sells Well in the Recorded Music Market? [레코드街 어떤 것이 잘팔리나]," *Dong-A Ilbo*, Aug. 19, 1981; Hye-Jin Ji (지혜진), "What Kind of Songs Do Korean Pop Music Fans Like? [우리나라 팝송팬 어떤 노래 좋아하나]," *Dong-A Ilbo*, Oct. 14, 1981.

58 Joong-Heon Jeong (정중헌), "Predictions by Three Pop Music Experts for 1982 [팝스'82 전문가 3人의 豫言]," *Chosun Ilbo*, Jan. 1, 1982.

acknowledge. "Is it because of a lack of money?" [I wondered]. So [I said], instead of doing an international song festival from the beginning, let's at least do a domestic song festival. We could do it a few times, build some experience, and then advance to an international scale.[59]

Chung Hong-taek was jealous and frustrated after attending the Yamaha World Popular Song Festival. He believed that Japan's only advantage was its economic capacity and that Koreans' cultural and artistic abilities were superior. As mentioned earlier in this article, Chung had been a judge in the Greek Song Olympiad, where Hyun Mee was a singer, Lee Bong-jo was a composer, and Hwang Jeong-tae was a manager. There, he met an influential figure, Japanese jazz musician Hattori Ryōichi (服部良一, 1907-1993).

Hattori attended Korea's first-ever international music festival, the 1978 MBC Seoul International Song Festival, as an observer. He significantly influenced the early stages of Korea's international song festivals.[60] Hattori was still sitting alongside Chung Hong-taek at the judges' table in Athens in 1971, but by June 1972, he had become the chief judge at the TBS Tokyo Music Festival.[61] This transition, no doubt, added to Chung's sense of "frustration in [his] heart."

Thus, Chung Hong-taek also hosted a song festival. He originally planned to host a domestic song festival and then develop it into an international event. With the approval of Hankook Ilbo's president and chair, Chang Kang-jae (1945-1993) and Chang Ki-young (1916-1977), he hosted the first Popular Song Festival in Korea at the Daehan Theater, then the largest theater in Korea, from September 13 to 15, 1974. He selected a total of sixty judges, including music critics Hwang Mun-pyeong (1920-2004) and Lee Baek-cheon (b. 1933) and composers Lee Bong-jo and Gil Okyun. He allowed anyone to participate, whether they were established composers or novice songwriters. Due to this

---

59 Hong-Taek Chung (정홍택), "Korea's #1 Entertainment Journalist Chung Hong-Taek Speaks Out, 30. The Korean Song Festival [한국 연예기자 1호 정홍택의 지금은 말할 수 있다] <30> 한국 가요제]," *Hankook Ilbo*, Oct. 21, 2008, https://www.hankookilbo.com/News/Read/200810210025501826.

60 "The Seoul International Song Festival Attracts a Large Crowd, Demonstrating the Potential for the Enhancement of Popular Culture [서울 국제가요제 大盛況 "대중문화 高級化의 可能性 보여"]," *Dong-A Ilbo*, Jul. 4, 1978.

61 "Hattori was Chief Judge," *Billboard*, Jun. 3, 1972, 47. Hattori Ryoichi was the chief judge of the TBS Tokyo Music Festival from 1972 to 1984.

low barrier to entry, approximately 300 songs were submitted. The judges determined the winning song through a series of preliminaries and finals that took place over the course of three days. This was the same format used at the Yamaha World Popular Song Festival.

"The Brilliant Light in the Flower," composed by Kim Kee-ung and performed by Park Kyung Heuy, won first place, albeit "by a very narrow margin" in the words of Chung Hong-taek, while Song Chang-sik's song "Pied Piper" came in second.[62] As the winners of this competition, Kim Kee-ung and Park Kyung Heuy earned the right to participate in the Yamaha World Popular Song Festival.[63]

Chung Hong-taek's first competition was also his last. However, Chung's dream was realized by MBC and the *Kyunghyang Shinmun*, which were one company at the time. Three years later, in 1977, they held a competition called the "Seoul Song Festival." The first thing MBC-Kyungyang did to organize this event was strengthen its partnerships with affiliate broadcasting stations in Japan, Hong Kong, and Taiwan. The plan was to develop the Seoul Music Festival into an international song festival centered around Asia. MBC also expanded their "Pops Orchestra" to forty people.[64] Although the use of synthesizers in disco music was popular at the time, orchestras were still important in international music festivals.

The 1977 MBC Seoul Song Festival took place on May 28 at the Munhwa Sports Arena, owned by the company. The underlying motive behind the festival was indeed captivating. The front page of May 27, 1977's *Kyunghyang Shinmun*[65] says that the purpose of the Seoul Song Festival was to "rectify" the reality of "vulgar songs rampant in a disorderly mass-production environment."[66] The discourse of so-called "wholesome music" was inherited as the discourse

62 Chung (정홍택), "Korea's #1 Entertainment Journalist Chung Hong-Taek Speaks Out, 30."

63 They participated in the preliminary round held on November 16, 1974, but did not advance to the final round held on the following day, November 17.

64 "New Energy [Brought] to the Korean *gayo* Industry as Seoul Song Festival Founded [韓國 가요계에 새 活力素 서울歌謠祭 창설]," *Kyunghyang Shinmun*, Jan. 31, 1977.

65 "The 1st Seoul Song Festival [제1회 서울歌謠祭]," *Kyunghyang Shinmun*, Mar. 24, 1977.

66 The exact phrase used was "무질서한 양산(量産) 풍토 속에 지속한 노래가 범람"을 "시정하기 위해서…"

of the music festival.

The grand prize-winning piece of this competition was "Love You, Only," composed of Gil Okyun and sung by Hye Eun-Yi. However, singers invited from abroad also attracted attention. Those invited included the Japanese vocalist Sugawara Yoichi (菅原洋一), the Taiwanese singer Louise Tsuei (崔苔菁), and the Hong Kong musician Michael Lai (黎小田).[67] They came to the Seoul Song Festival through an agreement between MBC and broadcasting stations in their respective home countries.

The festival was a massive success.[68] The quality of the songs was positively evaluated, and the organizers were able to strengthen their cooperation with other Asian broadcasting stations. Taking the success of the Seoul Song Festival as a foundation, MBC-Kyunghyang hosted Korea's first international music festival in 1978.

4. Inter-Asian Perspective and the Global Market: The MBC Seoul International Song Festival and the TBC World Music Festival

The MBC Seoul International Song Festivals of 1978 and 1979 differed significantly from those of 1980 and 1981. The first two Seoul International Song Festivals primarily featured Asian or Asia-Pacific music. However, a challenge arose when the inaugural TBC World Music Festival in 1979, which invited renowned singers from Japan and Europe, demonstrated better organization and received more critical acclaim than did the MBC festival.[69] In response, MBC invited famous European composers to give their competition

---

67 "Organizing the Seoul Music Festival [서울歌謠祭를 마련]," *Joongang Ilbo*, May 26, 1977. They did not participate in the competition category.

68 "Seoul Song Festival with Many Ticket Scalpers [暗票 많았던 서울歌謠祭]," *Dong-A Ilbo*, Jun. 4, 1977.

69 Jung-Heon Jeong (정중헌), "Showmanship Shines...[TBC] World Song Festival [演出 돋보인 쇼····세계歌謠祭]," *Joongang Ilbo*, Dec. 16, 1979; Jung-Heon Jeong (정중헌), "No Special Features at the 1979 [MBC] Seoul International Song Festival ["特性" 없었던 「79서울 국제 가요제」]," *Joongang Ilbo*, Jun. 10, 1979. The Joongang Ilbo's Jeong Jung-Heon (정중헌) gave contrasting reviews for the two song festivals. "International Brief," *Billboard*, Oct. 18, 1980, 60. *Billboard* described the 1st TBC World Music Festival as "a notable success."

some authority. The International Music Festival Federation (FIDOF) played a significant role in this process. Beginning with the 1980 competition, Yugoslavia's FIDOF intervened deeply in the MBC-hosted competition, turning it into a full-fledged international music festival that attracted the participation of composers and singers from Europe and the Americas.

In 1978 and 1979, MBC's Seoul International Song Festival centered around ASEAN countries, Korea, Japan, Taiwan, and Hong Kong.[70] Materials published during this time evoked a sense of strong pride as Asians, arousing anti-Western sentiment and even anti-Americanism. Hwang Mun-pyeong, who was a judge at the time, praised Song Chang Sick's song "Mount Toham" for its "folk sentiment" and "locality" in a column he contributed to the *Kyunghyang Shinmun* after the first Seoul International Song Festival in 1978. In contrast, he harshly criticized Japanese representative participant Simon Masahito (子門真人) for excessively "imitating American pop singer Elton John." Hwang said that this was ultimately a "minus" for Sugiyama Kōichi (すぎやまこういち)'s[71] highly rated work (which eventually won the Best Composition Award at the competition).[72]

It is worth noting that Elton John is a British singer, and the extent to which Simon Masahito emulated him is subject to interpretation. Simon Masahito was a vocalist[73] who sang theme songs for animated films such as "Kamen Rider" (仮面ライダー) and "Science Ninja Team Gatchaman" (科学忍者隊ガッチャマン).[74] Hwang Mun-pyeong seems to have misunderstood the somewhat exaggerated expression of an animated film theme song vocalist as a "mistaken

---

70 "Visit to Southeast Asia for the Work Consultation of the Seoul Music Festival Secretariat [서울 가요제 사무국간사 업무협의차 東南亞 순방]," *Kyunghyang Shinmun*, Feb. 18, 1978. Seoul International Song Festival secretary Kim Woo-Ryong visited each broadcasting station in Southeast Asia four months before the competition to prepare for the event.

71 Composer Sugiyama Kouichi (すぎやまこういち) has made significant contributions in various fields, including film music, commercial music, and television music. In the late 1960s, he composed numerous songs for the group sound (グループ・サウンズ) band, The Tigers (ザ・タイガース).

72 Mun-Pyeong Hwang (황문평), "The [Town] Square of 'Contemporary Music Language': A General Review of the 1978 Seoul International Song Festival [「音樂現代語」의 광장: 78 서울국제가요제 總評]," *Kyunghyang Shinmun*, Jul. 4, 1978.

73 Although Simon Masahito mainly sang anime and movie theme songs, he was also one of the most popular singers in Japan at the time.

74 Translated and broadcast in Korea under the title "Eagle Five Brothers" (독수리 5 형제).

interpretation" caused by the influence of American pop music.

This anti-Western, anti-American sentiment can also be found in an interview between another MBC judge named Choe Gyeong Sik and Antonio Barreiro, the senior vice president of the Association of Philippine Broadcasters, also known as the KBP (Kapisanan ng mga Brodkaster ng Pilipinas). Barreiro mentioned the implementation of a policy that would reduce the proportion of American music broadcasts during Philippine music programs. Aside from saying this, however, he did not express serious concern about the issue of the Americanization of Asian popular music. However, Choe Gyeong Sik continued to emphasize the importance of resisting Americanization and maintaining cultural subjectivity. He argued that the Seoul International Song Festival, unlike the two international festivals in Japan that had become "model markets for American popular music," should be a festival where "East and West meet as equals."[75] This was not merely an argument; MBC awarded the grand prize to Filipino composer Ryan Cayabyab in 1978 and to Yoon Hang Ki and Yoon Bok-hee in 1979, centering the Seoul International Song Festival around Asian countries.

TBC's World Song Festival was organized and conducted in a very different way. Cho Yong-ho,[76] who produced the festival, had many opportunities to learn the system of Japan's international song festivals. He covered the 1971 Yamaha World Popular Song Festival as a journalist alongside Lee Bong-jo and the Pearl Sisters.[77] In 1978, he wrote the lyrics to "Even if I Don't Know Where You Are," which was composed by Kim Kee-ung and sung by Park Kyung Heuy at the 1978 TBS Tokyo Music Festival.[78] TBC's choices in regard

---

75 Gyeong Sik Choe (최경식), "Meeting with Antonio Barreiro, Chief Executive Officer of the Association of Philippine Broadcasters - Seoul Song Festival: A Meeting of East and West [필리핀 大衆음악재단 首席부이사장 안토니오 바레이로씨와 만나― 서울歌謠祭는 東과 西의 만남]," *Kyunghyang Shinmun*, Jul. 1, 1978.

76 Park, "Television and Popular Music in the 1970s," 18. After Hwang Jung-Tae, Cho Yong-Ho became the producer of "Show Show Show" (쇼쇼쇼). Prior to that, he was a producer of youth-targeted variety programs such as "1, 2, 3 Go!" (원투쓰리고). Later, he also served as the executive director of M-Net.

77 "Pearl Sisters and Lee Bong-jo to Participate in 2nd Tokyo Music Festival Starting on the 25th [25일부터 제2회 동경가요제 「펄·시스터즈」·이봉조 참석]," *Joongang Ilbo*, Nov. 20, 1971.

78 "Kim Kee-Ung Song 'Where You Are...' [김기웅씨 작곡 『머무는곳…』] Passes the Preliminary Round of Japanese International Song Festival [일 국제가요제 예선통과]," *Joongang Ilbo*, Apr. 29,

to their song festival were closer to that of TBS than Yamaha.

Meanwhile, MBC took many cues from Yamaha. MBC had signed a contract with Fuji Television. The agreement allowed them to broadcast the Yamaha World Popular Song Festival and hold the Korean preliminaries for the festival. For this reason, the 1978 Seoul International Song Festival's domestic preliminaries featured composers from the Yamaha Foundation. Additionally, the main event featured composers and singers related to Fuji Television at the time. These included Sugiyama Koichi and Simon Masahito.[79]

On the other hand, TBC followed the TBS Tokyo Music Festival system. First, the award system involving rewarding prizes in order from largest to smallest (grand prize, gold, silver, and bronze) was adopted from TBS. MBC only began using this system in 1980. Second, while MBC emphasized the authority of composers, TBC focused on the skill and marketability of singers. This was similar to the TBS strategy used at the time. In other words, MBC emphasized the originality of songs that were created for the competition, similar to Yamaha, while TBC allowed the submission of existing songs, similar to TBS.[80]

Interestingly, this second difference led to an unexpected result: the MBC Seoul International Song Festival underwent a shift toward a predominantly male and composer-centric competition, whereas the TBC World Song Festival transformed into a primarily female and singer-centric contest. Of the twenty participants in the inaugural 1979 TBC World Song Festival, eighteen were female singers. When a competition was oriented toward highlighting singers, it naturally evolved into female-centric competition.

Upon scrutinizing the roster of participants and victors of the TBC World Song Festival, one would discern that a substantial number of them had taken part in analogous events held in Japan. In the inaugural competition held

---

1978.

79 Geon-Hyuk Ahn (안건혁), "Magnificent Opening of the 1978 Seoul International Song Festival Domestic Event on the 27th [78 서울國際歌謠祭 국내大會 27일 華麗한 개막]," *Kyunghyang Shinmun*, May 25, 1978. A composer named Hayashi Masahiko, who was affiliated with the Yamaha Foundation, participated in the 1978 Seoul International Song Festival domestic preliminary round as a judge.

80 For example, the grand prize-winning song "I Can't Help Myself" (어쩔 수 없어요) by Sami Jo Cole at the 3rd competition in 1981 (organized by KBS) was a cover of Eddie Rabbitt's 1977 song.

223

in December 1979, the grand prize was secured by Ohashi Junko (大橋純子) for her rendition of "Beautiful Me." Notably, she performed the same composition at the TBS Tokyo Music Festival held in June of that same year. Similarly, the recipient of the gold award, Gilda Giuliani, had previously clinched the Grand Prix at the Yamaha World Popular Song Festival in 1972 and had also received the Singing Award on the same occasion in 1978. This pattern persisted until the cessation of the World Song Festival in 1981. During this era, Korea did not stand as an independent music market. For foreign musicians contemplating participation in the festival, Korea represented merely a facet of the expansive Japanese market. Consequently, numerous singers and composers found their way to Korea through Japan.

Another noteworthy aspect is that, unlike the 1978 and 1979 MBC International Song Festivals, the TBC World Song Festival did not exhibit any resistance to or desire to overcome American influence. As shown in Table 2, the list of judges for the TBC World Song Festival includes Edward A. Green, the military bandmaster for the United States Eighth Army. Green was one of three judges who participated in the competition in both 1979 and 1980, which he did because the United States military band had provided assistance during the event. Although TBC had the best orchestra in Korea at the time, they invited performers from the U.S. Eighth Army Band to improve the quality of their musical performance.[81] In 1979, the grand prize winner Ohashi Junko (大橋純子) performed better at the TBC World Song Festival on December 9 than she did at the TBS Tokyo Music Festival on June 17 of that year, and the *US-ROK Joint* orchestra's performance played a significant role in this improvement.

---

81 James Wade, "Future Uncertainty of Seoul Music Contest," *Billboard*, Dec. 13, 1980, 70. It is said that they also invited musicians, such as George Greely, from New York.

Table 2. Lists of South Korean International Music Festival Judges

1978 MBC Seoul Song Festival Judge List[82]	
Name	Affiliation & Nationality
Chief Judge: Park Geunsuk	Music Critic (South Korea)
Bruce Weber	Australia
Li Lixiong	Taiwan
Elina Morris	Hong Kong
Iskandar	Indonesia
Masaru Inoshima	Japan
Isabelle de Silva	Malaysia
Eduardo Montilla	Phillipines
Manrat Srikaranoda	Thailand
Yullari Atamel[83]	Turkey
Na Yongsu	South Korea
Yi Kyosuk	Music Critic South Korea
Cho Byeonghwa	Poet (South Korea)
Choe Gyeog Sik	Music Critic (South Korea)
Hwang Munpyeong	Music Critic (South Korea)

1979 TBC World Song Festival Judge List[84 85]	
Name	Affiliation & Nationality
Armando Moreno	Secretary General (FIDOF, Yugoslavia)
Thomas Fundora	Vice President (*Record World*, USA)

---

82 "Kayabiyab (Composer) and Alejandro (Singer) Win Seoul International Song Festival Grand Prize [比 카야비얍(作曲) 알레얀드로 (노래) 조합 서울국제가요제 대상 차지]," *Kyunghyang Shinmun*, Jul. 3, 1978.

83 This person's name "율라리 아타멜" in Korean, but cannot be found in Turkish sources.

225

Takamada Ihara	Director (NTV, Japan)
Tapio Lipponen	Nat. Broadcasting Station YLE (Finland)
William S. Bates	Ambassador to the ROK (United Kingdom)
Edward A. Green	Band Master (Eighth Army, USA)
Lee Sanghoe	Professor (Yonsei University, South Korea)
Kim Baek-bong[86]	Dancer, Professor (Kyung Hee University, South Korea)
Lee Bong-jo	Composer (South Korea)
Hong Du-pyo[87]	Executive (*Joongang Ilbo* & TBC, South Korea)

1980 TBC World Song Festival Judge List[88]	
Name	**Affiliation & Nationality**
Augusto Alguero	Chair (FIDOF, Spain)
George Greely	Pianist (United States)
Tsuda Akira	Director (NTV, Japan)
Robert B. Weiss	Vice President (Cream Records)
Armando Moreno	Secretary General (FIDOF, Yugoslavia)

84 Ibid.

85 "Patti Page Captivates the Audience [청중 사로잡은 패티 페이지]," *Joongang Ilbo*, Dec. 10, 1979.

86 Kim Baek-Bong (1927-2023) was a distinguished dancer credited with the creation of the Buchaechum, also known as the Korean fan dance.

87 Hong Du-Pyo (b. 1935) is a legendary business figure who has held the presidency of numerous esteemed companies and organizations. These include Joong Ang Ilbo & TBC (1980), JTBC (2011-2013), Korea Broadcast Advertising Corporation (1981-1986), Korea Tobacco & Ginseng Corporation (1987-1992), Korean Tourism Organization (1998-1999), and KBS (1993-1998). Particularly noteworthy is his pivotal role in steering KBS to its golden age during the mid-1990s. Presently, Hong serves as the President of TV Chosun.

88 "The 1980 TBC World Song Festival Held [『'80 TBC 세계가요제』 개최]," *Joongang Ilbo*, Oct.

Bernard Follin	Ambassador to ROK (France)
Kim Namjo	Poet (South Korea)
Lee Bong-rae	Chair (Federation of Artistic and Cultural Organizations of Korea)
Edward A. Green	Band Master (Eighth Army, USA)
Lee Bong-jo	Composer (South Korea)
Hwang Jeong-tae	Executive (TBC, South Korea)

1981 MBC World Song Festival Judge List	
Name	Affiliation & Nationality
Lee Zhito	Editor-in-Chief (*Billboard*, USA)
Augusto Alguero	Honorary President (FIDOF, Spain)
Robert Weiss	Vice President, Intl. Div (Cream Records, USA)
Hong Euyeon	Director (MBC, South Korea)

In a 1980 interview with Billboard, TBC producer Cho Yong-ho expressed his ambition to release a live album of the TBC World Song Festival to the North American market.[89] Possibly because of this, the list of judges for the TBC World Song Festival includes the names of figures from the American popular music industry. In 1979, TBC extended an invitation to Thomas Fundora, the senior vice president of *Record World*. At the time, *Record World* was considered one of the top three American music magazines, alongside *Billboard* and *Cashbox*. Then, in 1980, TBC invited Robert Weiss, Vice President of the American record company Cream Records, to the TBC World Song Festival, with the intention of entering the American market.

Although the TBC World Song Festival was Japan-friendly and US-oriented,

---

18, 1980.

89 "International Brief."

it also had connections with Europe. For example, Marie Myriam of France, who won the grand prize at the 1977 Eurovision Song Contest, came to the 1979 TBC World Song Festival as a relatively big-name participant. However, she came to Korea without attending a Japanese international song festival. Päivi Paunu of Finland, who represented her country at the 1972 Eurovision Song Contest and participated in the TBC competition in 1979, also had no experience in Japan. However, the most surprising participant was Alenka Pinterič,[90] a singer hailing from the communist country of Yugoslavia. The International Federation of Festival Organizations (FIDOF) played an important role in recruiting participants from various countries, even those in Eastern Europe.

Armando Moreno (1921-2005), FIDOF's secretary general at that time, attended the TBC World Song Festival as a judge in 1979 and 1980 (see Table 2). FIDOF actively helped in the execution of the 1980 competition, bringing Radojka Šverko, then known as one of the best Yugoslav singers, and Alfi Kabiljo, one of the best composers, to take part in the TBC competition. It is worth noting that Robert Weiss of Cream Records also served as a judge in 1980 and maintained a close relationship with FIDOF, even holding a position within the organization.[91] FIDOF designed everything from event planning and execution to the sale of live recordings in the American and European music markets.

To summarize, the MBC Seoul International Song Festival followed the format of Asia-Pacific song festivals with the help of affiliate broadcasting stations in other Asian countries. Judges Hwang Mun-pyeong and Choe Gyeong Sik were wary of Americanization, Japanization, and commercialism. They hoped that music that expressed the traditional rhythms and emotions of Asian countries would be discovered and performed through the MBC Seoul International Song Festival.

Meanwhile, the TBC World Song Festival, where Lee Bong-jo and Hwang

90 Alenka Pinterič, "Faces of Slovenian Landscapes," *Obrazi Slovenskih Pokrajin*, Jul. 7, 2022, https://www.obrazislovenskihpokrajin.si/oseba/pinteric-alenka/. Alenka Pinterič is a Slovenian singer, actress, and writer (born in 1948). In 2006, she published a book called *The Beatles, Tito, and Me* about the Yugoslavian entertainment industry under the Tito regime.

91 "Join FIDOF Today," *Billboard*, Jan. 31, 1987, 65.

Jung-tae served as judges, actively recruited singers who had participated in Japanese international song festivals. TBC also bolstered their festival's orchestra with the help of the U.S. Eighth Army Band and other American musicians. TBC actively invited figures from the American music industry to the competition in the active pursuit of Americanization. They also successfully brought in singers from Western Europe and even Yugoslavia with the help of FIDOF.

MBC wanted to adapt, so they reached out to FIDOF.

5. The Eurasian Connection: Armando Moreno and the International Federation of Festival Organizations (FIDOF)

The MBC Seoul International Song Festival became a full member of FIDOF in 1979,[92] and it seems likely that the TBC World Song Festival joined FIDOF around the same time. Armando Moreno, the de facto leader and secretary general of FIDOF, visited Korea in December 1979 to attend TBC's song festival as a judge. However, serving on the judges' panel was not Moreno's only objective when he visited Korea. The TBC World Song Festival was held on December 9. However, on December 11, a day before Chun Doo-hwan's *Coup d'état of December Twelfth*, Moreno met with Lee Hwan-ui (1931-2021),[93] then president of MBC-*Kyunghyang Shinmun*.[94] What Moreno and Lee discussed remains unknown, but subsequent events make it possible to infer that they discussed measures to strengthen the cooperation between MBC and FIDOF.

First, FIDOF gave the MBC Seoul International Song Festival its "World Song Festival Award" at its annual conference held by MIDEM (Marché International du Disque et de l'Edition Musicale, or "The International Music and Discography Market" in English).[95] This move signaled that FIDOF would

92 "MBC Joins the International Federation of Seoul International Song Festival as a Full Member [MBC 서울국제가요제 국제연맹 정회원으로]," *Dong-A Ilbo*, Jun. 30, 1979.

93 Lee is also the founder of the Baekam Academy (Paekche College of Arts).

94 "Visit to MBC & *Kyunghyang Shinmun* by Moreno, President of the World Song Festival Federation [世界歌謠祭聯 총장 모레노氏 本社 방문]," *Kyunghyang Shinmun*, Dec. 12, 1979.

95 "Seoul International Song Festival Receives 1979 World Song Festival Award after Competing with 6 Countries [「79세계歌謠祭賞」 수상 「서울국제가요제」, 6국 경합 끝에]," *Kyunghyang Shinmun*,

provide the MBC Seoul International Song Festival with the same level of support as it had given the TBC World Song Festival.

The 1980 MBC Seoul International Song Festival took place on May 24, 1980,[96] and featured the participation of three renowned European composers: Les Reed[97] from the United Kingdom, Fernando Moreno from Spain, and Alfi Kabiljo from Yugoslavia. These composers were accompanied by the singers Marilyn Miller,[98] Betty Missiego[99] (wife of Fernando Moreno), and Krunoslav Slabinac, who each gave their own notable performances. Les Reed won the Grand Prix, while Fernando Moreno and Alfi Kabiljo achieved the Silver (third place) and Bronze (fourth place) Prizes, respectively.[100]

It is worth noting here that Les Reed was once the president of FIDOF. He was elected president of the Federation in 1977 after Augusto Algueró (see Table 2), who also served as a judge during the 1980 TBC World Song Festival.[101] Fernando Moreno also had a close relationship with FIDOF and had participated in Spain's Mallorca Music Festival (or "Festival Musical Mallorca" in Spanish), which Augusto Algueró organized. Last, Alfi Kabiljo was Yugoslavia's most iconic composer. FIDOF Secretary General Armando Moreno was proud of his countryman and wanted to give him a chance to demonstrate his skill on an international stage.

One year later, Les Reed won the Silver Award at the 1981 MBC Seoul International Song Festival, while the grand prize went to Augusto Algueró

Feb. 8, 1980.

96 Meanwhile, in Gwangju, the Chun Doo-Hwan regime brutally suppressed the Gwangju Uprising (May 18-27) by causing the death of at least 165 citizens.

97 He composed songs such as "Delilah" by Tom Jones and "The Last Waltz" by Engelbert Humperdinck. He was awarded the Order of the British Empire (OBE), ranking fourth in the British honours system.

98 The award-winning song "Everytime You Go," sung by Marilyn Miller, was also covered by Lee Junghee as "Seulpeum sogui sarang" (슬픔 속의 사랑 or Love in Sadness.) Later, Marilyn Miller continued her activities under the name Marilyn David.

99 They competed as the Spanish representatives in the Eurovision Song Contest in 1979 and won second place by a narrow margin.

100 Beverly Bremers, representing the United States, secured the Gold Prize (second place) at the 1980 MBC International Song Festival.

101 Nigel Hunter, "FIDOF's Fund Raising Plan Tabled: President Resigned," *Cashbox*, Jun. 18, 1977, 50. Les Reed served as chairperson for one year.

of Spain. This Alguero was not the one featured in Table 2 who served as FIDOF president from 1973 to 1977 and later remained active as FIDOF president or honorary president.[102] Two Augusto Alguerós can be found in *Billboard* and *Cashbox* issues published in the 1970s and early 1980s. One is Augusto Alguero Alguero (1906-1992), while the other is Augusto Alguero Dasca (1934-2011). The Augusto Alguero featured on the list of judges for the 1980 MBC Seoul International Song Festival (See Table 2) is the former, while the grand prize winner was the latter man, Augusto Alguero Dasca.[103] However, the two Augusto Alguerós were not strangers; Augusto Alguero Alguero was the general director of the Festival Musical Mallorca, and Augusto Alguero Dasca was the music director. Most importantly, they were father and son.

In other words, the 1980 MBC Seoul International Song Festival grand prize went to a former FIDOF president (Les Reed). Furthermore, the 1981 grand prize went to the son of FIDOF's honorary president (Augusto Alguero Alguero), who was also a judge.[104] To exaggerate slightly, one could say that the MBC Seoul International Song Festival was organized by and for FIDOF. By today's standards, this may seem strange. However, it is challenging to argue that this negatively impacted the event. The MBC Seoul International Song Festival organizers simply selected the best composers they could quickly mobilize for their own purposes. Perhaps the songs these individuals created fit well with the style of the MBC festival because they were shaping the international song festival style itself.

TBC attracted the attention of American music magazines and involved FIDOF from their first event because TBC officials such as Hwang Jung-tae, Cho Yong-ho, and Lee Bong-jo went to international song festivals in countries

---

102 "Alguero Named President," *Billboard*, Feb. 17, 1973, 54.

103 Augusto Alguero Dasca was one of the most famous pop orchestra conductors in Spain during his time. He participated in the Eurovision Song Contest in 1961 as a composer while still in his twenties. In 1969, he also served as the music director for the Eurovision Song Contest, which was held in Madrid.

104 Despite media reports stating that Augusto Alguero Alguero participated as a judge, it is difficult to confirm whether this was actually true. During the event, the Korean media's attention was primarily focused on *Billboard*'s Editor-in-Chief Lee Zito. There were no reports specifically mentioning Augusto Alguero Alguero during the event. It would be necessary to conduct interviews with relevant individuals from that time to confirm whether he actually participated.

such as Japan to learn how they were organized and operated. In response, MBC, guided by the leadership of Lee Hwan-ui and the collaboration with FIDOF, transformed the Seoul International Song Festival from one centered around Asian countries to one with a more global appeal.

Armando Moreno, originally from Yugoslavia, played a significant role in driving these transformations. Born in Vienna to an Italian immigrant family in 1921, Moreno actively participated in anti-Nazi guerrilla forces during World War II. Following the war, he assumed leadership of the UNICEF branch in Yugoslavia. His involvement with UNICEF stemmed from his participation in a mission to rescue Jewish children from Villa Emma in Italy and transport them to Switzerland during the war. In 1953, Moreno joined the Yugoslav Ministry of Foreign Affairs and was subsequently assigned to Sweden. His primary responsibility was to attract tourists from Northern European countries to visit Yugoslavia. Recognized for his capabilities, Moreno later assumed the responsibility of overseeing the reconstruction of tourist cities in southern Croatia (Dalmatia) that had been devastated by an earthquake. In 1967, Moreno organized an international song festival in the coastal Croatian town of Split to entice tourists visit to the region.[105]

However, Moreno's dreams did not stop at reviving the tourism industry of a single city. His ambition was to connect the world through festivals. When he founded FIDOF, he dreamed of creating international music festivals worldwide and facilitating the travel of singers and composers between them. Importantly, Moreno was not only a socialist bureaucrat but also a businessman. To create a flow of goods and capital that transcended national borders and ideological camps, he created the International Federation of Festival Organizations (FIDOF) in 1966, centering it on MIDEM, which served as an international music and discography market in Cannes, where the eponymous film festival is held to this day.

Moreno appointed Bernard Chevry, MIDEM's chief executive, as the FIDOF's honorary chair and designated Cannes, France, as the meeting place for FIDOF's

---

105 Goran Pelaić, "Zapisi I Sjećanja Gorana Pelaića (15) Armando Moreno: Mir i prijateljstvo kroz glazbenu umjetnost," *Dalmacija Danas*, Feb. 17, 2020, https://www.dalmacijadanas.hr/zapisi-i-sjecanja-gorana-pelaica-15-armando-moreno-mir-i-prijateljstvo-kroz-glazbenu-umjetnost/.

annual gathering of members. The activities of Armando Moreno's FIDOF included the creation of international music festivals in countries around the world, the facilitation of the comings and goings of composers and singers from all over the globe to enter the music and record markets formed through those festivals, and the introduction of musicians to the Western music market through MIDEM.[106] For example, Celine Dion participated in the Yamaha World Popular Song Festival in 1982, went to MIDEM in 1983, and won the Eurovision Song Contest Grand Prix in 1988 as a representative of Switzerland. Celine Dion's path from Canada to Japan, then back to Europe, was carved by FIDOF through MIDEM.

Another important fact is that festivals hosted in Eastern Bloc countries were not excluded from Moreno's network. FIDOF was involved in international music festivals held in Sopot, Poland; Prague and Bratislava in Czechoslovakia; Bucharest (Bucureşti) and Braşov in Romania; and Sunny Beach (Слънчев бряг) in Bulgaria. For example, Alla Pugacheva, later nicknamed "the Diva of Russia," was able to release an album in Japan thanks in part to FIDOF, which provided her with opportunities to perform in Sunny Beach in 1978 and Sopot in 1979.[107]

As mentioned previously, Armando Moreno's International Federation of Festival Organizations transformed Korea's two major international music festivals. FIDOF invited composers and singers from Europe and the Americas and provided an opportunity for their Korean counterparts to compete alongside them. The Federation also brought figures from foreign record industries into Korea. It was FIDOF that brought Cream Records and RCA officials to Korea as judges.[108] The "*Pop Song-ification*" of Korean *gayo*, in which Korean popular music was recorded and released in English during the early 1980s, occurred as a result.

---

106 "Patti Page Captivates the Audience."

107 Alla Pugacheva released an album in 1978 through Japan's Victor Records. In 1983, she released a single titled "Million Roses" (百万本のバラ or Миллион алых роз). This song was later covered by a Korean singer Sim Soo-Bong as "Baekman songi jangmi" (백만 송이 장미).

108 "Participation of 18 Countries Including Italy, England, and Japan [이·영·일 등 18개국서 참가]," *Joongang Ilbo*, Oct. 5, 1981.

233

The export of *Pop Song-ified*[109] Korean *gayo* can be attributed to the international song festivals that took place throughout the 1970s and 1980s. Through these competitions, Korean singers competed with top vocalists from around the world. This led to the reevaluation of Korean artists' skills and abilities. The Korean music industry also secured international sales channels through licensing and distribution deals associated with the festivals. As a result, Korean music producers gained confidence and were encouraged to develop their talents further.[110]

A newspaper article from this era stated that the series of international music festivals in Korea set new expectations about Korean singers and gave confidence to Korean record producers. The international song festivals allowed Korean popular music producers to obtain a sense of the world beyond Japan. This ultimately transformed Korean popular music (*gayo*) into a globalized form: K-pop.

6. Conclusion: Under Dictatorships, within Festivals

In his later years, Armando Moreno expressed his pride in being able to facilitate the participation of Yugoslavian composers and singers in Seoul through FIDO F.[111] Among the notable individuals was Alenka Pinterič, a singer from Slovenia, which was part of Yugoslavia in 1979. Allegedly, she treasures the TBC World Music Festival Best Singing Performance Award she received in Seoul, along with the numerous other accolades she has achieved throughout her career.[112] These Eastern European artists arrived in South Korea during a remarkably

---

109 The newspaper article quoted here uses the term "팝송화 (pop song 化)," which is translated in this article as *Pop song-ification*. In Korea, pop songs are regarded as American and British popular music. Thus, 팝송화 (pop song 化) can also be translated the Americanization and Britianizaiton of Korean *gayo*.

110 Jun-Sik Kim (김준식), "Korean Popular Music Expanding Overseas - Domestic 'Hit' Songs Arranged as 'Pop Songs' [해외로 진출하는 한국 가요 — 국내 「히트」곡을 「팝송」으로 편곡]," *Joongang Ilbo*, Dec. 20, 1980.

111 Pelaić, "Zapisi I Sjećanja Gorana Pelaića (15) Armando Moreno."

112 "Alenka Pinterič, The Faces of Slovenian Provinces" [Obrazi slovenskih pokrajin] https://www. obrazislovenskihpokrajin.si/oseba/pinteric-alenka/

unique period in 1979 and 1980. Their presence allowed Korean audiences to briefly savor popular music from the Eastern bloc, even amidst the tensions of the Cold War.

A *Dong-A Ilbo* report from November 9, 1979 recounts a scene in which Sim Soo-bong was standing on the stage of "Show Show Show," a television show that could aptly be called the final preliminary round of the TBC World Music Festival, performing "with [just] as much dedication as before." Less than two weeks before, on October 26 of that year, Sim had witnessed the violent end to eighteen years of iron-fisted rule while singing at a private party for authoritarian President Park Chung-hee, where he was ultimately assassinated.[113] Despite this, Sim performed on "Show Show Show" in November as usual. The 1971 Athens Song Olympiad, in which Hyun Mee had participated, continued for almost a month. Greek dictator Georgios Papadopoulos wanted the festival to continue, but it was canceled when he was ousted in 1974.

Meanwhile, just a few miles west of Viña del Mar, where Chung Hun Hi had ranked third with her rendition of "Deserted Island" at Chile's 1975 International Song Festival, laid the infamous Valparaiso prison. More than 3,000 people were killed, and 40,000 people were tortured in Chile under the dictatorship of Augusto Pinochet. Many political prisoners were suffering in Valparaiso as the festival took place.[114] Life, festivities, and celebration continued even amid such turbulent and oppressive political situations, and the world was slowly changing. Korean audiences could obtain a sense of the world in fragments by watching international song festivals in Chile, Japan, and Korea on television.

Korean popular musicians were also able to experience the world through international song festivals. Until the early-to-mid 1970s, they mainly did so through Japan. However, through the MBC Seoul International Song Festival, they began to seek popular music in and eventually beyond Asia. They initially discovered the larger world through the TBC World Song Festival. With the

---

[113] "Singer Sim Soo-Bong Passes the Preliminary Round of TBC World Song Festival... [She is] to Appear on the Show Program on the Evening of the 10th [가수 심수봉 TBC 세계가요제 예선통과... 10일밤 쇼프로에]," *Dong-A Ilbo*, Nov. 10, 1979.

[114] Katia Chornik, "When Julio Iglesias Played Pinochet's Prison," *The Guardian*, May 15, 2014, https://www.theguardian.com/music/2014/may/15/julio-iglesias-valparaiso-pinochet-chile.

help of Yugoslavia's FIDOF, the creators of these two music festivals opened channels for communication and interaction with Europe and the Americas. This eventually changed Korean musicians' conception of the world.

Each country has its own popular musical genre: *Schlager* for Germany and Central Europe, *chanson* for France and the Francophone world, *canzone* for Italy, and *kayōkyoku* for Japan. South Korean popular music is known as *gayo*. However, South Korean musicians and record producers transformed *gayo* into a Westernized and globalized form, which was later called K-pop, by participating in and organizing international song festivals in the 1970s and early 1980s.[115] The Cold War era K-pop served as a precursor to the global phenomenon of the Korean Wave in the world of popular music that began in the late 1990s.[116] Nevertheless, the "*Pop song-ified*" Korean *gayo* from that time was the genesis of K-pop.

---

115 The term J-pop emerged in the early 1990s, as aptly described by Michael Bourdaghs. Therefore, it can be concluded that the concept of K-pop was not utilized during the Cold War era, which is the specific time period addressed in this study. Michael Bourdaghs, *Sayonara Amerika, Sayonara Nippon: A Geopolitical Prehistory of J-Pop* (New York, NY: Columbia University Press, 2012), 198.

116 Eun-Young Jung, "New Wave Formations: K-pop Idols, Social Media, and the Remaking of the Korean Wave," in *Hallyu 2.0: The Korean Wave in the Age of Social-Media*, eds. Sangjoon Lee and Abé Mark Nornes (Ann Arbor, MI: University of Michigan Press, 2015), 76.

Part 3.
The Comparison

Parallels of Metamorphosis in the Theatre in Korea and Hungary

BLAHÓ Kata

1. Introduction

The aim of this study is to introduce the theatrical culture at the turn of the 20th century, on the Korean Peninsula and in the Hungarian territories of the Austro-Hungarian Empire, with a special focus on the leading theatre companies in the capitals, Budapest and Seoul; and how we can draw - albeit separated by decades - parallels to the two country's theatrical metamorphoses.

In this study, what I call Western-style, or modern, theatre has two main characteristics. First, modern theatres have permanent theatre buildings that are established to provide a stage specifically for theatre performances. Second, these performances are based on canonized drama texts, that became an important part of the theatrical processes. These restrictions are the best framework that helps us understand the notions of theatre in the historical context of the late stage of the Dual Monarchy and the colonial era on the Korean Peninsula. In this sense, the performances that are based on a loose storyline and feature case-by-case improvisation regarding the dramatic literature, are not considered modern or Western-style theatre.

During the 19th century, theatre all over the world reformed itself, and global imperialism introduced Western-style theatre to places that had vastly different traditions of theatre. Hungary, albeit part of what we understand

239

as the West, had been under the rule of the Habsburg emperor, thus the majority of modern Western theatrical practices, such as a permanent theatre building, or repeated performances of an appointed play, were either nonexistent or were limited to the German-speaking troupes that formed to entertain the German residents living in the cities. Up until the middle of the century, the majority of plays played by Hungarian actors were staged for special occasions in noble courts or played by troupes that toured the country. While the first Hungarian theatre building opened in Kolozsvár, a big city in Transylvania, and later in smaller cities, like Miskolc and Balatonfüred, there was only a German theatre building in Budapest, Pester Stadttheater opened in 1812. The first modern indoor theater building in Budapest opened in 1837 for the company of the Pesti Magyar Theater, the company of the first diet-supported national theatre.[1]

Similarly, the first Western-style theatre came to be on the Korean Peninsula by Japanese settlers, who had been exposed to Western theatre culture for decades prior. Korean performative traditions had three main genres that had narratives and characters that took an active part in forming the storyline, thus fitting the conceptions of theatre-like performances. These three are the following: pansori (판소리), a narrative performed by one artist accompanied by percussion, with both singing and spoken parts; masked dances called *talchum* (탈춤), which are performances made up of multiple, loosely connected scenes with improvised dialogues and characteristic dance moves; and lastly, the Korean puppet plays (한국의 인형극) that had similar storylines to those of masked dances. They were performed on improvised stages usually in the open air (as the pan syllable, which means open air, in the name of pansori suggests), thus these performances fall short of the criteria of permanent theatre buildings. Moreover, neither of these genres had canonized literary texts, the stories were passed down by oral tradition especially in the case of masked dances and puppet plays, often taking the mood and demands of the audience into consideration.[2] The first modern indoor theatre, Hyeomyulsa (협률사)

---

1   György Székely and Ferenc Kerényi, eds., *Hungarian Theatre History I (1790-1873)* (Budapest: Akadémiai Kiadó, 1990), https://mek.oszk.hu/02000/02065/html/1kotet/index.html.

2   Miy He Kim, *Acts and Scenes − Western Drama in Korean Theater* (Seoul: Hollym Corp. Publishers,

established in 1902, but was mostly used as a performance venue until it closed down.[3]

A notable similarity between them is that during their respective era, the beginnings of professional theatre in Hungary and Korea both faced severe censorship by foreign forces. While plays that nurtured national spirit and had Hungarian historical themes were not explicitly forbidden as long as they weren't openly anti-Austrian, staging national stories of Korea often faced severe suppression.

This study is composed the following way: first, I introduce the first and most notable theatre companies of the era in Hungary, then in Korea; and introduce the most characteristic genres they were staging. Then in part III, I will introduce more in detail and compare the work of the Hungarian Thália Company (Thália Társaság, 1904-1908), and the leading companies of the Korean *singeuk* (신극, „new theatre") movement, as they played similar roles in the development of the theatrical culture in the later decades.

2. New Types of Theatre in Hungary at the Turn of the Century

After the Diet decided to fund the establishment of a national theatre in Budapest, baron Frigyes Podmaniczky became the official patron of the new theatre, called Pesti Magyar Theatre, often referred to as the National Theatre. This new theatre focused on opera and dramas, primarily staging contemporary works about the bourgeois. They mostly translated French works into Hungarian, as the German-speaking Pester Stadttheater (City Theatre of Pest) performed most of the German plays. Few classics were staged with moderate success, as these plays received little to no interest from the audience. On the other hand, *népszínmű* ("folks comedy") quickly became the main point of attraction for the theatre. *Népszínmű* was originally created by Ede Szigligeti, the director of the drama department between 1873 and 1878. Népszínmű was based on

2013), 5.

3   Meewon Lee, "The Modernization of Korean Theatre Through the Reception of Western Realism," in *Modernization of Asian Theatres*, ed. Y. Nagata and R. Chaturvedi (Singapore: Springer), 25.

the German – Austrian *Volksstück*, and its main plot is about a pair of lovers who face hardships, usually, there are some criminal elements, music, and dance. Since it originates from the Reformation Era of Hungary, it's more Romantic than modern. The "*nép*" (=folk) in the genre refers to the fact, that characters with diverse social backgrounds appear. It is famous for the stereotypes portrayed. In the late 19th century the opera department and the drama department split up, and in 1884 the Hungarian Royal Opera House opened.[4]

Until the 1860s only the National Theater was granted rights to operate as a theater, and even then, they faced censorship from the state. In 1875, however, a new theatre called Népszínház opened, operated under the supervision of the Committee of Népszínház (Népszínházi Bizottmány), whose members were appointed by the city. The Népszínház became the new home for *népszínmű*, which held its popularity mainly among the lower classes. *Népszínmű*'s primary goal was entertaining the audience, and it became a basis for the star system in the Hungarian theatre world. The other part of the repertoire was formed by operettas, such as the works of Jacques Offenbach. From the 1880s the Népszínház started playing more and more Hungarian operettas, but French and Austrian operettas remained more popular until 1902, when Jenő Huszka's *Bob herceg* premiered. This started the era of the Golden Age of Hungarian Operetta, hallmarked by composers Franz Lehár and Emmerich Kálmán.[5]

The first commercial theatre in Budapest, Vígszínház (Comedy Theatre) opened in 1896. The still active theatre focused its repertoire on contemporary plays, particularly on comedies and farces – as a commercial theatre, it was essential to the founders of Vígszínház to emphasize that the new theater did not wish to pose as a competitor to the National Theatre, but the fact that Vígszínház was built out of self-reliance, and successfully mobilized the

4   György Székely and Tamás Gajdó, eds., "I.1 Az állami színházak [State-supported theatres]" in *Hungarian Theatre History II (1873-1920) [Magyar színháztörténet II (1873-1920)]* (Budapest: Magyar Könyvklub – Országos Színháztörténeti Múzeum és Intézet, 2001), https://mek.oszk.hu/02000/02065/html/2kotet/4.html.

5   György Székely and Tamás Gajdó, eds., "I.2. Új színházi vállalkozások – A Népszínház [New Ventures in Theatre – Népszínház]" *in Hungarian Theatre History II (1873-1920) [Magyar színháztörténet II (1873-1920)]* (Budapest: Magyar Könyvklub – Országos Színháztörténeti Múzeum és Intézet, 2001), https://mek.oszk.hu/02000/02065/html/2kotet/20.html.

bourgeoise was able to change the narrative on the role of the theatre, and paved the way for opening other commercial theatres as well. The opening of Vígszínház also marked an important point in the way of the development of Budapest, as this was the first theatre that was built further away from the city center.[6]

The plays in these theatres were striving to leave the sensational, melodramatic acting of Romanticism behind, and aimed for an acting style based on Realism and Naturalism. As the popularity of the plays of Norwegian playwright Henrik Ibsen rose, the melodramatic and romanticized approaches to dramatic form were rejected, greater focus was put on the dramatic text itself, and the acting aimed to mimic the conversations of everyday life. The goal of the performance was to make the audience forget that they are watching a play, thus the stage set, the costumes, the gestures, and the postures mimicked those from real life. The meaning of the play shifted from the storyline to the feelings, thoughts, and evaluations it evoked in the audience. The modern Realist and Naturalist dramas conveyed the everyday struggles of the strengthening bourgeois, the hero became part of the historical process, where everything that happens is closely intertwined with the exact time and place the drama happens in, which emphasized the individuality of the hero; whereas in Shakespeare's plays for instance, the time and place has almost no significance, thus creating a universal feeling, rather than an individualistic one.[7]

3. The Beginnings of Modern Theatre Tradition in Korea

The development of Western-style theatre had numerous basic conditions that

6   György Székely and Tamás Gajdó, eds., "I.2. Új színházi vállalkozások – A Vígszínház [New Ventures in Theatre – Vígszínház]" in *Hungarian Theatre History II (1873-1920) [Magyar színháztörténet II (1873-1920)]* (Budapest: Magyar Könyvklub – Országos Színháztörténeti Múzeum és Intézet, 2001), https://mek.oszk.hu/02000/02065/html/2kotet/25.html.

7   György Székely and Tamás Gajdó, eds., "II.1. Stílusirányzatok az európai színházművészetben - Drámaírók, drámaelméletek – Henrik Ibsentől a szimbolistákig [Styles in European theatre art – Playwrights and drama theory: From Henrik Ibsen to the symbolists]" in *Hungarian Theatre History II (1873-1920) [Magyar színháztörténet II (1873-1920)]* (Budapest: Magyar Könyvklub – Országos Színháztörténeti Múzeum és Intézet, 2001), https://mek.oszk.hu/02000/02065/html/2kotet/90.html.

together helped to establish and form the theatre culture of today in Korea. Among these conditions there are outer impacts, as well as inner changes; however, it is important to highlight those factors that were essential to the rise of the theatres in the early 20th century in Korea.

The first mentions of Western theatres are from the end of the 19th century. In 1985, Yu Gil-jun (유길준, 1856-1914) described the inner workings and technical background (layout, interior, scenes, makeup, and costumes, etc.) of the theatre, as well as types and genres of plays in his work, *Seoyugyeonmun* (서유견문, *"Observations of travels to the West"*).[8] In 1896, envoy Min Yeong-hwan (민영환, 1861-1905) traveled to Russia for the coronation of Nicholas II. He wrote about his experiences in his report, *Haecheonchubeom* (해천추범, „*To go out in the wide world*"), where he mentions that the Korean representatives were invited to a commemorating play as a part of the ceremony. Due to his bad health, he was unable to participate, however recounts the experiences of other officials that attended the play. In this retelling, he highlights the storyline of the play and the realistic acting.[9] From 1899, numerous newly written textbooks also included the European literary canon, introducing drama as a literary category, separated from the notions of theatre.[10]

Foreign theatre processes also had a lasting effect on the Korean theatre, as the incoming Japanese and Chinese settlers brought their own theatre culture as well. After the Japan - Korea Treaty of 1876 the increasing number of Japanese settlers brought on an increase of Japanese theatre on the peninsula, which attracted even a notable Korean audience.[11] Isabella Bird Bishop, an English traveler visited the Korean peninsula four times between 1894 January and 1897 March, and she recollected her experiences in her book, *Korea, and Her Neighbours*. She describes the Japanese settlement in Namsan, Seoul, mentioning the theatre in the settlement:

---

8 Yeon-ho Seo (서연호), *Korean Theatre History- Modern Period [한국연극사, 근대편]* (Seoul: Yeongeuk-gwa Ingan [연극과 인간], 2003), 35.

9 Ibid., 35-36.

10 Ibid., 43-44.

11 Ibid., 37-38.

On the slope of Nam-San the white wooden buildings, simple and unpretentious, of the Japanese Legation are situated, and below them a Japanese colony of nearly 5,000 persons, equipped with tea-houses, a theatre, and the various arrangements essential to Japanese well-being. There, in acute contrast to everything Korean, are to be seen streets of shops and houses where cleanliness, daintiness, and thrift reign supreme, and unveiled women, and men in girdled dressing-gowns and clogs, move about as freely as in Japan.[12]

Apart from the Japanese, Western missionaries also brought theatrical practices with them. The religious groups kept the sacred-educational role of the theatre that characterized it in Ancient Greece and especially the Middle Ages, where the whole community staged biblical stories. Thus, the missionaries in Korea were able to use these techniques to spread their teaching as well.[13]

In contrast to the Hungarian theatre culture, where each theatre specialized in a few genres, the first theatres of Korea operated more as performance spaces for various troupes and performers, and also as movie theatres. The first theatre building, Hyeomyulsa was established by the royal family for the 40th anniversary of King Gojong ascending the throne, originally as a way to entertain foreign envoys, but backlash from officials and audiences closed the theatre down in 1906.[14] In 1908 Wongaksa Theatre (원각사) opened in Hyeomyulsa's empty building and operated until 1914, when it burned down in a fire.[15] After the establishment the first theatre buildings, it took until 1912 for the first Korean drama. Jo Il-jae's (조일재, 1863-1944) drama, *Three Sick Man* (병자 삼인) was published on the pages of *Maeil Sinbo*, pioneering a stream of playwrights publishing their works in newspapers and magazines.[16]

Since theatre as an institution and the genres of drama separated it is

12 Isabella Bird Bishop, Korea, and Her Neighbours (Fleming H. Revell Company, 1897), 43-44, https://www.gutenberg.org/files/69300/69300-h/69300-h.htm.

13 Seo, *Korean Theatre History- Modern Period*, 38.

14 Meewon Lee, "The Modernization of Korean Theatre Through the Reception of Western Realism," in *Modernization of Asian Theatres*, ed. Y. Nagata and R. Chaturvedi (Singapore: Springer, 2019), 25.

15 Seo, *Korean Theatre History- Modern Period*, 50.

16 Won-jae Jang, "History of the Korean Theatre: Transitional Period Leading to the Modern Theatre 1902-1919," *International Journal of Korean History* 4, no.1 (Aug. 2003), 234-235.

important to mention the most notable genres that defined the beginning of the 20th century on the Korean stage.

The first step towards the modern drama was brought over by Japanese settlers. *Shimpa* (jap. 新派, „new style"; kor. *sinpageuk,* 신파극, "new style drama") was created in an attempt to move forward from Japanese *kabuki* (歌舞伎), that was considered too old-fashioned to reflect the contemporary challenges. Despite this, the sensational and artificial style of *kabuki* remained, and moved over to the peninsula as traveling troupes frequented the Japanese theatres in the settlements.[17] The style influenced actor Im Seong-gu (임성구, 1887-1921) who worked as maintenance in a Japanese theatre. He established the theatre company Hyeoksindan (혁신단), where they played adaptations of Japanese *shimpa* plays. The first production failed, but from the second production, they received immense success. *Sinpageuk* started as political dramas, but developed into military dramas, detective dramas, family tragedies, and *kisaeng* tragedies, which themes were thought to be they were thought to be the main issues of contemporary society.[18] At the beginning of this study, the notion of modern theatre was bound to the following two conditions: a permanent theatre building and canonical drama text. Despite this, *sinpageuk,* similarly to the Italian *commedia dell'arte* was based only on a loose storyline, the dialogues were improvised on stage in each performance. This changed after the laws of censorship changed and the government required a detailed libretto before every performance.[19]

Another notable theatre genre was *changgeuk* (창극), which represented a mix of genres of traditional Korean performances such as pansori, Japanese *shimpa* plays, and Western Realist plays. *Changgeuk* is considered a traditional-like performance, some researchers originate it from staging *pansoris* as theatre plays, but there is no definitive evidence for that.[20] The first recorded *changgeuk* performance was *Silver World* (은세계) by Yi In-jik (이인직, 1862-1916), one

---

17 Ibid., 221-224.

18 Kyeong-hwa Ha, *A Brief Study of Korean Theatre History [한국연극사 소고]* (Seoul: M-Ad [엠-에드], 2008), 41-44.

19 Jang, "History of the Korean Theatre," 230-232.

20 Jan Creutzenberg, "From Traditional Opera to Modern Music Theatre? Recent Experiments in Ch'anggŭk," in *Transactions of the Royal Asiatic Society Korea Branch* 88 (2013), 87.

of the artists who played a role in opening the Wongaksa Theatre. He invited numerous *pansori* singers to stage the dramatic version of his short story with the same title, which had a similar style to *pansori*, but instead of one person narrating the story and playing the different characters, it was mostly based on dialogues.[21] *Changgeuk* plays remained popular with the audience up until the 1950s and received state support during the Park Chung-hee regime.[22]

4. Parallels of Metamorphosis in Korea and Hungary

Perhaps the greatest similarity between the course of development of modern theatre in the two cultures is the self-relied artistic companies that aimed to educate people through and about the theatre.

In Hungary, this role was filled by Thália Társaság (Thalia Company), a company ignited by the passion of modern experimental theatre, that had no roots in Hungary at the time. The young artists aimed to introduce productions to the audience with new, unknown styles with new faces and new acting. Most of the plays chosen by the company were either Realist or Naturalist style, using natural tones, dialogues, and everyday situations, In their journey to the establishment of a modern alternative stage in Budapest, Thália Társaság stood in contrast to the five existing theatres that were tied to specific genres – three of them, Népszínház, Magyar Színház and Király Színház focused on operettas, Vígszínház centered on comedies and farces, and the National Theatre still held onto the conventional, sensational, finicking style of acting, although the playwrights later emphasized by Thália Társaság, such as Henrik Ibsen, Gerhart Hauptmann, and Henry Becque had appeared on the repertoire, without much success. Thália Társaság held its constituent meeting in 1904 and recruited actors who were either amateurs or beginner actors. Their debut focused on contemporary societal plays with great literary value, emphasizing both the

---

21 Andrew Killick, "Korean 'Ch'anggǔk' Opera: Its Origins and Its Origin Myth," *Asian Music* 33, no. 2 (2002), 60-61.

22 Creutzenberg, "From Traditional Opera to Modern Music Theatre?," 88.

literature and the art of acting. On their debut night, the company of Thália Társaság produced several plays, and they planned to release the drama text of the plays they performed as well. Thália Társaság made efforts to be an educational space, planned to open programs with famous literary intellectuals and critics at the same time as being a theatre company. During their four years of operation, Thália Társaság introduced a repertoire vastly different from the general repertoires found anywhere else in the country. By their third year, Thália Társaság was well known among critics for the acting of the young players, which was considered finely developed, and the great synergy between the actors. On the downside, the stage sets and costumes were made by the company members themselves, that failed to complement the literary value of their plays. Despite their successes, the company faced an insurmountable obstacle: they did not have a permanent acting space. From 1904 to 1907 they played on numerous smaller stages in the city, and in the beginning of 1908, they also toured the country with their repertoire, performing forty-six times altogether. After the tour, the company arrived back in Budapest, but by that time the interest of the audience dropped, new members came instead of the original cast, and the passion cooled down so that the company disbanded in 1908. Still, the effect Thália Társaság had on the theatre world in the coming decades remains immeasurable.[23]

On the Korean stage, the student troupes of the New Theatre Movement (*singeuk*, 신극) held a similar role in the establishment of modern theatre as the Thália Társaság in Hungary, albeit with a temporary difference of two decades.

The 1920s opened up new possibilities for Korean students to study at Japanese universities that allowed them to become acquainted with the European literary canon and contemporary scenic discourses. The style with the greatest influence on the Korean student was that of the Realist theatre. During the 1920s and 1930s, the intelligentsia started and promoted the modern theatre

---

23 Székely and Gajdó, "II. 3.The Thalia Company [II. 3. A Thália Társaság (1904-1908)]", in *Hungarian Theatre History II (1873-1920) [Magyar színháztörténet II (1873-1920)]* (Budapest: Magyar Könyvklub – Országos Színháztörténeti Múzeum és Intézet, 2001), https://mek.oszk.hu/02000/02065/html/2kotet/106.html.

movement, and at the same time, the first commercial theatres opened. The movement and the commercial theatres were in interaction with each other: the *singeuk* movement inspired commercial theatres to expand the conventions of acting, meanwhile commercial theatres stimulated the artists of *singeuk* movement to better the quality of their craft and helped them to understand the practical processes of theatre art better.[24]

Singeuk started with Korean university students, introduced the written drama text as a modern literary genre that became the compulsory basis of a theatrical performance, and a realistic acting style that differed from the melodramatic *sinpageuk* and traditional *changgeuk*. They emphasized the importation of Western culture, especially European and American dramas. As they viewed the play as the most essential part of the movement, they made efforts to translate the Western works into Korean as well. The *singeuk* movement was the first theatrical movement organized and run by intellectuals, and as such they rather thought of themselves as cultural activists than artists and considered the theatre an outlet of political faith and patriotic ideals.[25]

Other innovations of the *singeuk* movement were the appearance of actresses in theatrical productions and the start of professional training for actors with the first acting academies, producing talents that became famous later on.[26]

The first student company that actively promoted the *singeuk* movement was called Geukyesulhyeophoe (극예술협회, "The Theatre Arts Association"), started in 1920 and disbanded the next year. Geukyesulhyeophoe was founded by Korean students studying at Japanese universities and counted around 100 members. They focused on play-reading and the study of theatre production. They also became the first student troupe to tour in Korea. The 1921 tour closed with huge success, performing in 25 cities for 40 days. Their success inspired other student troupes to do the same, thus creating a tradition for others to follow.[27]

---

24 Won-jae Jang, "Toward a Modern Society: History of the Korean Theatre in the Modern Period 1919~1940," *International Journal of Korean History* 6 (Dec. 2004), 189.

25 Ibid., 193-195.

26 Lee, "The Modernization of Korean Theatre Through the Reception of Western Realism," 28-29.

27 Jang, "Toward a Modern Society," 195-196.

The next notable company was Towolhoe Theatre Company (토월회, 1922 -1931), founded by Korean students in Japan, studying foreign literature and fine art. They followed the mindset of Geukyesulhyeophoe, and toured Korea, in 1922. This tour resulted in no success; however, their next three tours captivated the audiences on the peninsula, who viewed their production as new and realistic, due to their acting style trained in Realism. They became the first modern Korean theatre company to provide modern drama regularly, and the only *singeuk* company that was notable for paying attention to costumes and stage sets complementing their plays.[28]

Lastly, Geukyesulyeonguhoe (극예술연구회, Theatre Art Research Association, 1931-1939) was founded with the goal of deepening the interest and understanding toward modern theatre among Korean audiences; correcting the convention of commercial theatre, and establishing modern Korean theatre. Similarly to Thália Társaság, they announced their mission to educate the audience through publications and various programs. Through these, they provided introductions, translations, and explanations for their productions. Their educational program that they called *silheom mudae* (실험 무대, "experimental stage") was a three-step process: publishing explanations of the plays performed, the performance itself, and lastly the criticism of the performance. Despite their ideas and ideals, the company lost their initial passion due to the indifference from the general public, and they disbanded in 1939.[29] In 1950, Yu Chijin (유치진, 1905-1974), one of the leading members of Geukyesulyeonguhoe became the first director of the newly opened National Theatre of Korea.[30]

Similar to the Thália Társaság, the companies of the *singeuk* movement had problems with maintaining a permanent stage for themselves,

As we can see, the development of modern theatre in Korea and Hungary shows parallels to each other. Albeit started from different cultural backgrounds, and separated by two decades, the course of growth took a similar path. The

---

28 Ibid., 198-200.

29 Ibid., 200-202.

30 Lee, "The Modernization of Korean Theatre Through the Reception of Western Realism," 37.

basis for modern theatre originated from foreign residents, the Germans in Hungary, and the Japanese in Korea, that had been strongly supported by the state in comparison to the native artists, especially in the beginning, resulting in harsh censorship as well. Despite this, both the Hungarian and the Korean process saw transforming foreign genres into characteristic national works, as we saw in the cases of *népszínmű*, and *sinpageuk*.

The most parallelistic element in the history of both countries' theatre is the activities of the Hungarian Thália Társaság and the *singeuk* movement of Korea. Thália Társaság and the companies of the *singeuk* movement started as self-relied companies led by intellectuals. While commercial theatre saw greater success than the artistic visions of these companies, their emphasis on the literary value of plays and the realistic acting style reformed the theatre world for the next generations. Both fit in the modern theatre movement, which mainly focused on contemporary societal problems, the individual's place in the world, and a goal to educate their audience on these issues. Thus, both the work of Thália Társaság and the *singeuk* movement can be understood as more than theatre, as they aimed to educate and enrich the life of their people. In this sense, it is easy to see why the artists thought of themselves as cultural activists rather than mere actors. They aimed to highlight the importance of the literary work and saw theatre performances as an opportunity to further educate their audience, especially in the case of Geukyesulyeonguhoe and Thália Társaság, both of whom planned further educational programs and publications regarding theatre and literature to help their viewers understand the plays better.

5. Conclusion

This study focused on the changes during the late 19th century and early 20th century that happened in Hungary and the Korean Peninsula in the world of theatre and how we can draw - albeit separated by decades - parallels to the two country's theatrical metamorphoses. This study should not be considered a detailed analysis, but an attempt to overview the processes that lead to the modern theatre culture in Hungary and in Korea respectively.

In Hungary, a wave of theater openings began in the late 19th century, with each theater having a specific genre, such as *népszínmű*, operetta, or farces to perform, mainly so they would not present competition to the state-supported National Theater. We must emphasize the role the short-lived Thalia Company, played in the modernization of the theatre in Hungary and the model it became for the subsequent independent theatre troupes. Thalia Company's purpose was to educate the audience on and off the stage, their focus on works with great literary value and realist acting paved the way for the upcoming generation of actors in the 20th century.

In Korea, the establishment of Western-style theatre began in the 20th century. Theater buildings were considered more as general performance spaces than homes to theatre. The first productions staged by Korean theatre companies were *sinpageuk* performances that they imitated from the Japanese *shimpa* style. The first original Korean genre was *changgeuk*, which evolved from the traditional narrative performance *pansori*. The modernization of theatre is intertwined with the *singeuk* movement in the 1920s and 1930s.

The *singeuk* movement, similarly to the Thalia Company, called for realist acting and emphasized the importance of dramatic texts. Both the *singeuk* movement and the Thalia Company had a lasting effect on the education surrounding the theatre as a notion and as an art form for the following decades.

Image of Korea in Hungarian Encyclopedias:

1833-1930

KIM Jiyoung

1. Introduction

From the early 19th century to the early 20th century, Korea and Hungary had very limited understandings of each other. Hungarians began recognizing Korea and Koreans in the early 19th century, and references to Korea appeared in Hungarian encyclopedias published during that time. However, Korean documents from this period do not mention Hungary.

While it was known that there was a small kingdom called Korea (Chosun) in close proximity to Japan, which was emerging as a powerful nation in Asia at the time, Hungarians knew very little about Korea prior to the modern era. The 19th century marked a period of transition to modernity in Europe, driven by advancements in academia and technology, which resulted in a surge of knowledge and interest in the world. During this period, European interest in non-European areas such as Asia and Africa was primarily focused on the objectives of plunder, exploitation, and occupation, intertwined with the spread of Christianity. This trend intensified with the rise of imperialism. Subsequent advancements in transportation diminished the physical distance between Asia and Europe and facilitated the influx of information about Asia, thereby resulting in a considerable increase in the understanding of Asia among Europeans. The large number of research papers, travelogues, and encyclopedia-style books about Asia published during this period is a reflection of this interest in Asia. Hungary was no exception to this phenomenon.

Many Hungarians believe that their ethnicity originated in Asia, and this belief is not entirely unfounded; research in archaeology, anthropology, and historical comparative linguistics has resulted in the recognition and confirmation of Hungarians' Asian ancestry.[1] However, within Hungary, the popular understanding of the Hungarian Asian lineage is mainly based on romantic assumptions that were prevalent in the era of nationalism than on scientific or academic grounds. Therefore, it is natural for Hungarians to be interested in Asia and their ancestral homeland, and it is undeniable that they have more empathy for Asian cultures and traditions than other Europeans. This self-consciousness led to a high interest in Asian civilizations, such as those in Tibet and China, within the Hungarian academic community. Hungarian researchers have been especially interested in modern Japan. However, the explosive interest in Korea has been relatively recent.[2]

The first encyclopedia that explicitly mentioned Korea by name in Hungarian literature was *Közhasznú esmeretek tára* ("Repository of Knowledge for the Public"), published in 1833.[3] Mentions of Korea began to appear in various books after this year, and various encyclopedias and books featured introductions

1   Sang-Hyup Lee (이상협), *The History of Hungary [헝가리史]* (Seoul: Daehan Textbooks [대한교과서], 1966).

2   Hungary has always shown a very positive stance on matters related to Korea. While it may seem a bit simplistic, the author believes this is evident from various instances such as the following: Hungarian viewership of the Korean drama *Jewel in the Palace* (대장금 in Korena or *A palota ékköve* in Hungarian) recording the highest numbers in Europe upon the series' continental debut.; The fact that Europe's biggest Korean Cultural Center is in Budapest, Hungary's capital.; The Korean Language Department of Budapest's Eötvös Loránd University (ELTE) is one of the most sought-after courses at the university, which is the oldest and largest university in Hungary.; The Hungarian government's proactive response during a 2019 disaster where Hableány (Hungarian for "mermaid"), a tour boat carrying 33 South Korean tourists, sank after colliding with another vessel on the Danube River.

3   On the other hand, the first book that mentioned Hungary in Korea was probably the Korean translation of a Chinese book called *Kalsosa* (갈소사전 or 噶蘇士傳 in Korean) which was published in the 1920s. *Kalsosa* is a Korean phonetic transcription of the Chinese pronunciation of the name Kossuth, who was a Hungarian. There have been multiple studies on *Kalsosa* such as: Soo-Young Park (박수영), Sung-Soon Park (박성순) and et al, "A Study of the Relationship Between Korea and Hungary in Modern Times [근대 한국과 헝가리 관계사 연구: '噶蘇士傳'의 수입과 독립정신의 고취를 중심으로]," *Oriental Studies [東洋學]* 77, (2019): 207-20.

and mentions of Korea by the 1930s.

The Austro-Hungarian Empire established diplomatic relations with the kingdom of Choson on July 23, 1892.[4] However, little is known about the eighteen-year bilateral relationship between the two countries prior to 1910. There are studies on the historical relationship and exchange between the two countries by Fendler Károly,[5] Osváth Gábor,[6] Csoma Mozes,[7] Park Soo Young,[8] and Kim Bogook.[9]

Significant studies on Hungarian figures known in Choson during the Japanese colonial period and on Hungarians who supported Korea's struggle

---

4 On the background of the establishment of relations between Choson and the Austro-Hungarian Empire, please refer to: Jiyoung Kim (김지영), "An Analysis of Austro-Hungarian Diplomatic Documents about Korea 1885~1894 [오스트리아-헝가리 제국의 조선에 대한 외교문서 연구: 1885~1894년 발간문서를 중심으로]," *Oriental Studies [東洋學]* 44, no. 4 (2019): 232-4.

5 Refer to: Károly Fendler, "One Hundred Years of Hungarian-Korean Relations (1892-1992) [A Magyar-Koreai Kapcsolatok száz éve (1892-1992)]," in *A Herman Ottó Múzeum Évkönyve XXXII (32)*, ed. Veres László (Budapest, Miskoic: Herman Ottó Múzeum, 2004), 151-65; Károly Fendler, *One Hundred Years of Hungarian-Korean Relations* (Budapest: Korea Journal 30, 1990), 26-34; Károly Fendler, "Austro-Hungarian Archival Sources of Korean History (1884-1910)", *Journal of the German Morgenländische Gesellschaft* 150, (2000): 299-310; Károly Fendler, "The Korean War (1950-1953) in the Foreign Affairs of Hungary," *Korea Journal 30* 11, (1990): 49-60.

6 Refer to: Gábor Osváth, *Korean Language and Literature - Selected Studies [Koreai nyelv és irodalom - Váogatott tanulmáyok]* (Budapest: Pluralingua Kiado, 2006); Gábor Osváth, *On the Relationship of Korean and Other East Asian Languages [A koreai és más kelet-ázsiai nyelvek viszonyáró]* (Budapest: Intézeti Szemle, 1973); Gábor Osváth, *The Work of Ferenc Mártonfi (1945-1991) in Korean Studies [Mártonfi Ferenc (1945-1991) Koreanisztikai Munkássága* (Budapest: Aspect of Korean Civilization, 2002).

7 Refer to: Mozes Csoma, "A Discussion on Hungarian Korean Peninsula Studies [헝가리 한반도사 연구 시론]," *The Journal of History [역사연구]* 136, (2015): 85-107; Mozes Csoma, "A Study on Hungarian Korean Studies Through the History of Korean-Hungarian Relations [한·헝 관계사를 통해 본 헝가리 한국학에 대한 고찰],' *Journal of Korean Culture* 33, (2016): 7-19.

8 Refer to: Soo Young Park (박수영), "Hungarian Study in Korea and Korean Study in Hungary: Achievements and Problems" (presentation, Korea-Poland-Central Europe. Proceedings of the 2nd International Academic Conference of the Korean Association of East European and Balkan Studies, Chicago, 2002) 147-57.

9 Refer to: Bogook Kim (김보국), "Study on the Process of Establishing Diplomatic Relations between the Republic of Korea and Hungary through the Confidential Documents of the Hungarian Ministry of Foreign Affairs," East *European & Balkan Studies [동유럽발칸연구]* 38, no. 3 (2014): 151-76; Bogook Kim (김보국), "The Development of the Diplomatic Relationship between South Korea and Hungary: A Survey of the Diplomatic Documents of the Two Countries," *Bulgarian Historical Review* 3-4, 143-63; Bogook Kim (김보국), "Political Transition, Hungary, South and North Korea: Based on the National Archival Sources [헝가리의 체제전환시기까지 한국과 헝가리의 교류에 관한 연구: 한국과 헝가리의 외교문서를 중심으로 한국-북한-헝가리의 관계 고찰]," *East European & Balkan Studies [동유럽발칸연구]* 39-2, (2019): 161-89.

for independence have been conducted by Park Sung-soon[10] and Yang Ji-sun.[11] Articles dealing with Korean perceptions of Hungary, including Eastern Europe, after the Korean War include those by Kim Do-min,[12] Kim Jong-su,[13] Nagy Tamás,[14] and Tamara Kiss.[15] In contrast, there seems to be very little research on how Hungarians perceive Korea and Koreans.

The knowledge that Hungarians possessed about Korea was likely very limited. Most would have been acquired from fragmented news reports, brief publications, or books of the travel genre. Under these circumstances, the publication of an encyclopedia that explained Korea in a relatively elaborate manner would have contributed to enlightening Hungarians about Korea and expanding the scope of their awareness. However, it is difficult to deny that such sophisticated information was mostly exclusive to intellectuals, bureaucrats, and the noble class.

10 Park, "A Study of the Relationship," 207-20.

11 JiSun Yang (양지선), "Hungarian Support for the Korean Independence Movement and Its Significance [헝가리인 마쟈르의 한국독립운동 지원과 그 의의]," *Oriental Studies [東洋學]* 77, (2019): 233-40.

12 Refer to the following: Do-Min Kim (김도민), "Perceptions and Reactions of North and South Korea to the 'Prague Spring' of 1968 [1968년 '프라하의 봄'에 대한 남북한의 인식과 반응]," *Historical Criticism [역사비평]* 123, (2018): 72-101; Do-Min Kim (김도민), "A Study on the Diplomacy of South and North Korea toward Neutral Countries from 1948 to 1968 [1948~1968년 남·북한의 중립국 외교 연구]" (PhD diss., Seoul National University, 2020).

13 Jongsoo Kim (김종수), "A Historical Study on Representations of Eastern Europe Described in Korea [한국에서 재현된 동유럽 표상의 역사적 고찰]," *East European & Balkan Studies [동유럽발칸연구]* 42-1, (2018): 3-23.

14 A Hungarian student named Tamás Nagy wrote the following master's thesis on Korean literature. On Pages 3, 4, and 106 there is a brief mention of Hungarians' perceptions of Korea.; Tamás Nagy (너지 더마쉬), "The Translation of Two Korean Modern Short Stories "Obaltan" and "Jangma" to Hungarian, the Problems and Possible Solutions [한국 현대 단편소설 「오발탄」 「장마」의 헝가리어 번역]" (Master's thesis, Kookmin University, 2012).

15 The first systematic study on the perception of Hungary by Koreans is a master's thesis submitted to Seoul National University in 2018 by Tamara Kiss, who came from Hungary to study abroad in Korea. In her master's thesis, Kiss analyzed the image of Hungary among Koreans by studying travel accounts of those who traveled to Hungary and shared their experiences on NAVER blogs. She concluded, "...Koreans have a very positive image of Hungary. According to the analysis of blog posts, Koreans overwhelmingly have a positive image of Hungary's night views, architecture, food, cost of living, and tourist sites. On the other hand, negative opinions can also be found about Hungary's public safety, transportation, accessibility, and service quality. In summary, Koreans have a positive image of Hungary (Budapest) as an Eastern European country with beautiful night views, hot springs, delicious and affordable food, friendly locals, and a rich history..." ; Tamara Kiss, "Analysis of Hungarian Images Reflected in Naver Blogs [Naver 블로그에 반영된 헝가리 이미지 분석]" (Seoul National University Master's thesis, Seoul National University, 2018). 78.

This article aims to examine how Hungarians perceived Korea and Koreans from the early 19th century, when Korea was first mentioned in Hungarian encyclopedias, to the early 20th century. It also seeks to demonstrate what their knowledge about Korea was like, primarily based on the encyclopedias published in Hungary at that time.

2. Oriental Studies and Encyclopedia Publication in Hungary

In the nineteenth-century Europe, it was fashionable to publish encyclopedias that collected knowledge about various countries worldwide. Encyclopedias were considered a treasury of knowledge about the world and essential books that should be present in any intellectual's library. This phenomenon was no different in Hungary. Reflecting the trends of the time, encyclopedias were the most popular type of book in Hungary. Particularly after the establishment of the Austro-Hungarian Empire in 1867, the expansion of national education led to a decrease in illiteracy. The desire to read expanded, and the demand for 'knowledge' about the world notably increased. The main readers of these encyclopedias were intellectuals or educated members of the public.

Prominent European publishing houses dispatched experts and correspondents around the world to gather local information in an effort to create encyclopedias based on accurate facts.[16] Hungarian publishing houses also conducted similar activities. Major Hungarian encyclopedias borne out of this effort include *Közhasznú Esmeretek Tára* (1833), *Egyetemes Magyar Encyclopaedia* (1872), *A Föld és népei* (1880), *Atheneum Kézi Lexikona* (1892), *Pallas Nagy Lexikona* (1895), *Révai Nagy Lexikona* (1915), *Tolnai Új Világ Lexikona* (1927), *Katolikus Lexikon* (1932), *Új Lexikon* (1936), and *Új Idők Lexikona* (1939).[17] While most Hungarian encyclopedias were produced in the model of prestigious English and German encyclopedias, they contained

16 The representative encyclopedia published during this period was the *Encyclopedia Britannica*.

17 Unofficial English titles for these volumes are the *Repository of Knowledge for the Public* (1833), *Universal Hungarian Encyclopedia* (1872), *Athenaeum Pocket Encyclopedia* (1892), *Pallas Great Encyclopedia* (1895), *Revai Great Encyclopedia* (1915), *Tolnai New Encyclopedia* (1927), *Catholic Encyclopedia* (1932), and *Encyclopedia of New Times* (1939), respectively.

abundant content characterizing Hungary, distinguishing them from encyclopedias published in English-speaking and German-speaking territories. The Hungarian-language encyclopedias that described Korea during this period are as follows:[18]

	Language	Title	Year of Publication	Reference(s) to Korea
1	Hungarian	Közhasznú esmeretek tára	1833	Vol. VII, pp. 292
	Korean*	공익지식의 보고		
	English**	Repository of Knowledge for the Public		
2	Hungarian	Egyetemes Magyar Encyclopaedia	1872	Vol. X
	Korean	일반 헝가리 백과사전		
	English	Universal Hungarian Encyclopedia		
3	Hungarian	A Föld és népei	1880	Vol. III, Ch. 10, pp. 240
	Korean	영토와 민족들		
	English	The Earth and its Peoples		
4	Hungarian	Athaeneum Kézi Lexikona	1892	Vol. I, pp. 939
	Korean	아테나움 소백과사전		
	English	Athenaeum Pocket Encyclopedia		
5	Hungarian	Földrajzi Közlemények	1892	Vol. XX, pp. 159-160
	Korean	지리학 보고서들		
	English	Geographical Communications		
6	Hungarian	PALLAS Nagy Lexikona	1895	Online Edition
	Korean	팔러시 대 백과사전		
	English	PALLAS Great Encyclopedia		
7	Hungarian	Révai Nagy Lexikona	1915	Vol. VII, pp. 33
	Korean	리버이 대 백과사전		
	English	Révai Great Encyclopedia		
8	Hungarian	Tolnai Új világ Lexikona	1927	Vol. IX, pp. 104-106
	Korean	톨너이 신세계 백과사전		
	English	Tolnai New Encyclopedia		

18 The author expresses his gratitude to Alexandra Urban for confirming the existence of these Hungarian encyclopedias and sending copies of the necessary sections.

9	Hungarian	Katolikus Lexikon	1932	pp. 118
	Korean	천주교 백과사전		
	English	*Catholic Encyclopedia*		
10	Hungarian	Új Lexikon	1936	pp. 2201-2202
	Korean	신 백과사전		
	English	*New Encyclopedia*		
11	Hungarian	Új Idők Lexikona	1939	pp. 3948
	Korean	신시대의 백과사전		
	English	*The Encyclopedia of New Times*		

*Translator's Note: This and the other Korean titles on this chart are not official Korean translations of the title; they are included for the reader's convenience.
** Translator's Note: This and the other English titles on this chart are not official English translations of the title; they are included for the reader's convenience.

Interest in the East seems to have been relatively high in Hungary during this period compared to curiosity about Asia in other European countries. Amid the transitional period of the end of the 19th century, interest in and awareness among Hungarians of their national identity and roots increased, thus intensifying interest in the East. This phenomenon could be found not only among Hungarian academics and experts but also among the general public.[19]

The study of the East in Hungary began at the University of Budapest, an institution established in 1638,[20] and the Hungarian Academy of Sciences (MTA). Led by Professor Vámbéry Ármin, many Hungarian researchers devoted themselves to Oriental Studies. It is worth noting that the influence of Eastern or Japanese-style artworks, which were popular in the late 19th century,

---

[19] Hungary's perception of the East is considerably different from that of other European countries. The Asian origins of the Hungarian people and the rule of the Ottoman Turks from 1541 to 1686 profoundly influenced the formation of Hungarian culture. Specifically, Hungary was under the influence of the Ottoman Turks in various fields, such as systems, culture, and daily life of nobles and commoners, during approximately 150 years of Ottoman rule. This influence can also be found within traditional Hungarian culture. Refer to this article for more information: Ji Young Kim (김지영), "A Study on the Metamorphoses of Hungarian Culture by the Influence of Ottoman Empire [헝가리의 오스만 문화 수용과 문화적 메타모포시스]," *East European & Balkan Studies [동유랍발칸연구]* 43-3, (2019): 45-70.

[20] Currently, the university is known as Eötvös Loránd University, often abbreviated as ELTE.

contributed to Hungary's Oriental Studies.[21] In this atmosphere, relatively detailed descriptions of each Eastern country began to appear in encyclopedias, and the descriptions of Korea started to increase.

3. Analysis of Korea-Related Content in Hungarian Encyclopedias

1) Repository of Knowledge for the Public
(Közhasznú Esmeretek Tára, 1833)

The first mention of Korea in a Hungarian encyclopedia was in the *Repository of Knowledge for the Public* (Közhasznú Esmeretek Tára), published in 1833. According to Károly Fendler, a Hungarian Korean studies scholar who was the first to conduct research on Korea-related entries in Hungarian encyclopedias, this encyclopedia was based on the English Conversations – Lexicon.[22] The author obtained and checked the online version of this encyclopedia and found that it describes Korea for a total of 23 lines from the bottom of Page 292 to the top of Page 293 (see Figure 1).[23] The encyclopedia broadly explains Korea's location, geography, flora and fauna, people, political system, and administration.

Figure 1. Közhasznú Esmeretek Tára.

---

21 The advent of Art Nouveau in art history was a remarkable event. Currently, Art Nouveau architecture and artworks can be found in various locations throughout European cities. Art Nouveau buildings can be found in countries around Eastern Europe, including Hungary, which had a strong self-consciousness of its Eastern roots.

22 Fendler, "One Hundred Years", 151-65.

23 *Repository of Knowledge for the Public, Vol. 7 [Közhasznú Esmeretek Tára Hetedik Kutet]* (Budapest, 1833), 292-3. https://mek.oszk.hu/14700/14714/pdf/kozhasznu07_2.pdf

The dictionary introduces Korea's geography and natural environment relatively accurately in the introduction. This entry implies that the authors likely adopted the knowledge of natural sciences in the West at the time, as there do not seem to be significant errors in the content. However, Koreans are considered to be a mixture of the Manchu-Tungusic people and the Chinese, and Korean customs and lifestyles are considered similar to those of the Chinese. This is likely because it was difficult for Europeans to accurately understand the anthropological and linguistic characteristics of China and Korea. Notably, the dictionary describes Koreans as a "dignified" people.

It is also noteworthy that the encyclopedia points out that Korea had trade relationships with China and Japan but had no interactions with Europe. In describing the political system, the entry presents Choson as maintaining a vassal relationship with China to which it pays tribute, but Choson is described as ruling over itself independently. The capital is referred to as "Kingkidaou," likely a misrepresentation of "Gyeonggi-do" (경기도). The so-called "famous library managed by a prince" described as being in the capital could not be accurately located, but this fact seems to be a misunderstanding and misrepresentation of a place where a crown prince or other member of the royal family was studying at the time.

The final statement, "The region of Tsu-Szin belongs to the Emperor of Japan," seems to have originated from a misunderstanding of Korean geography. Given that a region named "Tsu-Szin" does not appear in the administrative divisions of Choson or on any map of the time, it is unclear where this region was located. Given only the mention that it is in the southwest, there is a possibility that this region could be Jeju Island, but the statement that this place belongs to the Emperor of Japan can be regarded as entirely incorrect.

Overall, while the encyclopedia provides a rudimentary introduction to Korea, the impression of Koreans can be seen to be quite positive, as indicated by the phrase "dignified people." The specifics recorded in the encyclopedia are as follows:

Korea, a peninsula the Chinese call "Chosian" or "Guali" (7,442 square miles, population of 12 million), geographically lies between China and the Japanese archipelago, sharing a border in the north with the Tatar state (Mongolia) and

Chinese territories of Kwangtung or Liaotung. The other three sides are adjacent to the Sea of Japan, the Yellow Sea, and the China Sea (between 34-43°N and 142-148°E). The northern region is covered with perpetual snow, forests, and grasslands. The south is more fertile and densely populated. Various kinds of grain are produced, the textile industry is active, and there is an abundance of metals. Fisheries are developed, and there are many wild animals.

The people are a mix of Manchu-Tungus (Mandsu-Tunguz) and Chinese. They are very dignified, and their lifestyle is similar to that of the Chinese people. Trade is carried out with China and Japan, but there is no interaction with European countries at all. The ruler is called a king and is a vassal to China, paying tribute to China every year but ruling his country independently and in a very absolute manner. The peninsula is divided into eight provinces, each governed by a representative appointed by the king. The capital is Kingkitao (Gyeonggi-do), the residence of the king. There is a famous library in the capital that is managed by the prince. The Tsu-Szin region in the southwest belongs to the Emperor of Japan.

2) Universal Hungarian Encyclopedia
(Egyetemes Magyar Encyclopaedia, 1872)

An article about Korea also appears in the tenth volume of the *Universal Hungarian Encyclopedia* (Egyetemes Magyar Encyclopaedia) published in 1872 (Figure 2). The overall amount of description is similar to that in the previously mentioned *Repository of Knowledge for the Public* (Közhasznú Esmeretek Tára, 1833), and the content is also similar. In contrast with the *Repository of Knowledge for the Public*, the *Universal Hungarian Encyclopedia* erroneously describes the Korean language as "Mongolian" but correctly identifies

Figure 2. Egyetemes Magyar Encyclopaedia.

the capital of Korea as "Hanyang." Notably, Korea is mentioned as a closed country, and the heavy persecution of Korean Catholics is described. An incorrect description that Korea also pays tribute to Japan is also included. The *Universal*

Hungarian Encyclopedia also describes the martyrdom of 34 French missionaries, the subsequent attempted French invasion (Pyŏnginyangyo),[24] and its results. It neutrally mentions that the French army was unable to invade the Korean mainland and had to retreat.

Although the *Universal Hungarian Encyclopedia* was published approximately 40 years after the publication of the 1833 *Repository of Knowledge for the Public*, there are few differences between the two books. This suggests that knowledge and awareness about Korea did not increase much during the period from 1833 to 1872. However, the neutral recording of the fact that the French fleet was defeated by the Korean navy in 1866 may suggest that Korea was introduced as a subject in international relations in Hungary. The specifics of the Universal Hungarian Encyclopedia are as follows:[25]

Korea is a peninsula stretching from Manchuria (as a kingdom) to the south of the peninsula, located in northeast China. It is a very narrow peninsula with no major rivers. The climate is not mild, with very hot summers and very cold winters. The southern region has abundant fertile farmland. Rice, grain, tobacco, fruit, cotton, and ginseng are produced, and hunting is the main industry in the northern region. There are many wild animals in the forests. Livestock and mining have also been developed. The population is approximately 7-8 million. The people are derived from the Mongols, but their customs are Chinese. The language is Mongolian, but many Chinese expressions are mixed in. The religion is similar to that in China, with Confucianism and Buddhism being practiced.

There are approximately 16,000 believers in Catholicism, but they are suffering greatly from relentless persecution. It is likely that the king pays tribute to China as well as Japan. The king has unlimited power, and all the land is owned by

---

24 Pyŏnginyangyo (병인양요 or 丙寅洋擾), literally "Western disturbance of the Pyŏngin year," refers to an 1866 French military campaign that was undertaken as a retaliatory response to the execution of seven French Catholic missionaries by the Kingdom of Choson. The confrontation centered around Ganghwa Island and lasted for nearly six weeks. Ultimately, the French forces eventually retreated, curtailing French influence in the region.

25 János Török, János Pollák, and Ferenc Laubhaimer, *Universal Hungarian Encyclopedia [Egyetemes Magyar Encyclopaedia]* (Budapest, 1872). https://reader.digitale-sammlungen.de/de/fs1/object/display/bsb11007565_00003.html, https://reader.digitale-sammlungen.de/de/fs1/object/display/bsb11007565_00098.html

the king, which is divided into fiefs. The country is very closed, and trade is mediated through Japanese agents. Korea is divided into eight provinces, and the capital is Hanyang, where the royal palace is also located. A French expeditionary force sent to Korea in 1866 to avenge the death of 34 Catholic missionaries failed to enter the Korean mainland and had no choice but to retreat.

3) The Earth and its Peoples (A Föld és népei, 1880)[26]

In addition to the two previously introduced encyclopedias, the encyclopedia that devotes the most space to Korea and that presents it relatively objectively for encyclopedias published at the end of the 19th century was *The Earth and its Peoples* (A Föld és népei, 1880). This encyclopedia was published in 1894 by the Budapest Franklin Society, who assigned the task of writing to György Aladár. It is a specialized encyclopedia in geography that introduces the geography, peoples, and circumstances of each country in the world. Toward the end of the 19th century, specialized encyclopedias catering to readers seeking expert knowledge were published in addition to more comprehensive or general encyclopedias. *The Earth and its Peoples* was an example of this specialized use. Volume III, Chapter 10 provides a detailed description of the Korean Peninsula across six pages.[27] *The Earth and its Peoples* provides a detailed explanation of Korea's geography, climate, industry, politics, administration, and economic characteristics. Notably, this was the first time that illustrations depicting Korea were included in the encyclopedia. After the publication of this dictionary, photographs and illustrations of the time were frequently provided in Hungarian publications about Korea.

---

26 The original edition of this encyclopedia was published in three volumes in 1880 and was based on the German edition of Hellwald Frigyes's Encyclopedia of Geography, which was compiled into a Hungarian version. A completely revised edition, completely rewritten, was issued in 1894 under the auspices of the Hungarian Franklin Association. As stated in the preface by György Aladár, the primary author of the encyclopedia, the need to compile an entirely new encyclopedia emerged due to the increase in knowledge over the fifteen years since the first edition was published. See: Toldy László, The Earth and its Peoples, Vol. 1 [A Föld és Népei, I] (Budapest, 1880), 5. Budapest: Franklin Society Hungarian Literary Institute and Book Printing House [Franklin Társulat Magyar Irodalmi Intézet és Könyvnyomda].

27 The description of Korea is covered from Pages 269 to 274. The description of Japan is provided from Pages 240 to 268.

Chapter One of Volume III, titled "Asia in General," begins with a description of Asia as "the continent considered the homeland of our (Hungarian) ancestors along with most of the European peoples." This sentence indicates the perception of Hungarians' Asian origins[28] and explicitly refers to the region where their ancestors lived as "Asia", meaning that Europeans, as well as Hungarians, recognized themselves as descendants of Asians. Chapter One also introduces the general situation of Asian countries and describes Korea for the first time as follows. This excerpt shows a somewhat negative perception of Korea:

Figure 3. A Föld és Népei Cover. Volume III of this encyclopedia is titled "Asia and Australia."

> A certain group of East Asian nations closed their doors to foreigners. No one has been able to enter Korea for several decades.[29]

Chapter Ten of *The Earth and its Peoples*, titled "Japan and Korea," describes Korea in detail. The latter part of the chapter explores Korea's international relations, portraying with a somewhat negative perspective the Russian occupation of Wonsan to secure an ice-free port. This description demonstrates the tense relationship between Russia and Hungary and between Russia and Germany at the time. The description is as follows:

> Today, we often remember the Korean Empire in relation to Japan. The Korean Empire was a mysterious country that was not well known until approximately 20 years ago, with three sides of its territory facing the sea as if protecting its land and the other side adjoining the continent. Its border has been cut off from the outside world by a fence hundreds of kilometers long for centuries. Even China, which nominally ruled over [Choson] before the Japanese Empire,

---

28 László, *The Earth and its Peoples*, 1.

29 Ibid.

could only appear in the markets of Korea's border cities for three days a year. In 1876, a few ports were opened to the Japanese and then to the Americans in 1882. As knowledge about the country gradually spread, China and Japan soon waged a war over sovereignty [over Korea], but this was mainly a result of competition between Britain and Russia. Despite Japan's victory in this competition, it led to Korea's independence.[30]

The Earth and its Peoples describes Korea's natural environment and agricultural production with a relatively high accuracy compared to that of other encyclopedias.

> The entire Korean Peninsula is pointed [and sharp] and has large mountains to the west, with the largest plain near the capital. There are no roads, railways, or canals present, and transportation and communication are facilitated by post offices and telegraphs, with market boats scattered here and there. Compared to those in European countries at the same latitude, winters are colder, and summers are warmer. Most of the land is fertile, particularly for producing rice and beans, which are the main foods for residents and which are produced along with cotton, hemp, tobacco, fruit, ginger, and ginseng root. Bamboo is found in southern regions, and timber forests cover vast areas in the central and northern regions. Strawberries and oak trees are also produced..."[31]

The relatively detailed and meticulous description of the anthropological characteristics of Koreans can be seen as reflecting the racial and ethnographic perspectives popular in Europe at the time. Notably, Koreans are characterized as good-looking, courteous, and brave when compared to the Chinese and Japanese people. The book also mentions that the educated class tends to use Chinese characters, and the book offers a relatively objective portrayal of Korea's administrative system, bribery, and religious situation.

> Koreans are a mixture of Chinese and Japanese. There are large reserves of gold

---

30 Ibid., 5.

31 Ibid.

and abundant minerals throughout the country. Korea is known as a closed country, but the mines have been largely exploited by foreigners, leaving most of the capital unavailable for Korea's use. Undoubtedly, Koreans of Mongoloid descent are very different from Japanese people and most similar to the inhabitants of the Ryukyu Islands. They are better looking and taller than the inhabitants of northern China and stronger and better looking than the Japanese people are. Their noses are less blunt, their lips protrude forward, and their eyebrows are straight. They grow beards. Some have splendid beards, but Kaiser-style beards, such as those in Europe, are hard to find. Korean hair is long and black. Unmarried women wear their hair in a braid. In terms of clothing, Koreans favor white. Like in the Chinese population, they wear pants over their shoes and a separate ankle-length outer garment. Wealthy people wear light blue silk overcoats with yellow clothes.

Women wear pleated skirts, often adorn their hair with wood or coral, and their hats are typically very wide. Koreans are clearly distinguishable from the Chinese. Koreans are serious, courteous, polite, and more lively than the Chinese people are. Koreans' love for freedom is so great that they have always fought bravely against their enemies. Koreans are educated in Chinese and still imitate everything. Particularly impressive is the widespread use of Chinese characters (Hanja). As the education level increases, the use of Chinese becomes more prevalent, sometimes to the extent of excluding Korean entirely. Korea's administrative system is similar to that of China, and it coexists with bribery. However, [the fact that Koreans] do not drink tea at all is surprising. The most interesting feature of the Korean culture is that their religious beliefs are divided between Buddhism, which is the dominant belief, and other religions, which are less conspicuous. The clergy barely receive any special respect.[32]

The subsequent description includes notable references to major cities such as Seoul and Chemulpo,[33] as well as the Kabo Reforms[34] and subsequent political

---

32 Ibid.

33 Chemulpo (제물포 or 濟物浦) is another name for Incheon, which was designated as a port of trade in the late Choson period.

34 The Kabo Reforms (갑오개혁 or 甲午改革), also known as the Kabo Restructuring (갑오경장

reforms.

One of the oldest buildings, Tongdosa, one of the country's largest temples, accommodates approximately 400 practitioners. Although Christians have been active here for 300 years, they have hardly conquered [Korea]. Koreans are primarily engaged in rice cultivation and poultry farming, and animal pelts in particular are extensively traded. The port location is near a large city. The road from the capital to the Chinese border can be traveled by an ox-drawn cart. The villages are typically small, and there are approximately eight large cities. The largest city is the capital Seoul, located at the confluence of the Han River, which is navigable by boat. The population of this city is estimated to be approximately 150,000, but in reality, it is a large village with one-story houses made of clay.

The royal palace is located in the city center. The city's streets are quite wide, but they are not paved. Seoul lacks large public buildings, and even well-built churches have impoverished interiors. The king's power is significantly constrained by customs and lineage, and rebellions often arise against the king. However, as the leader of the rebellion is close to the king's wife, the king only nominally has omnipotent power. Among other cities, Chemulpo recently gained high fame as a vibrant port with the most foreigners. In 1890, there were 5,500 Japanese, 10,000 Chinese, 92 European, and 48 American individuals in the whole country, but these numbers are still low. Russians have recently occupied the port of Wonsan on the east coast. They are striving to have a port that does not freeze.[35]

4) Athenaeum Pocket Encyclopedia (Atheneum Kezi Lexikona) and Pallas Great Encyclopedia (Pallas Nagy Lexikona)

Despite its small size, the *Athenaeum Pocket Encyclopedia*, published in 1892, describes Korea in relative detail. According to this encyclopedia, Korea's territory is described as 218,000 square kilometers, with a population of 10.51 million.

---

or 甲午更張), was a series of reforms carried out from July 27, 1894 to July 6, 1895. The reform was initiated by the reformist faction who had fled into exile after the failure of the Kapsin Coup, and upon their return, they sought to emulate Japan's success and implement Japanese-style reforms.

35 László, *The Earth and its Peoples*.

Koreans are described as having a Mongol-Chinese heritage, and their religions are said to include Buddhism, Shamanism, Taoism, and Confucianism. Notably, it describes the land as fertile and as holding a large amount of gold. This encyclopedia was the first to summarize the history of Korea in the 19th century.

The *Pallas Great Dictionary* (Pallas Nagy Lexikona, 1895) describes Korea as Chio-szén, Csao-szien, Szenbi, Kirin, and Szinra and describes it as a country surrounded by islands located between the Yellow Sea and the Sea of Japan. Notably, the northern border is described as the Amur and Tumen River basins of Russia. The territory is described relatively accurately as 223,000 square kilometers.[2] One distinctive feature of this encyclopedia is that it details the history of Korea, correctly identifying the foundation of the Choson in 1392 and describing the powerful monarchy that was in place. The entry also mentions Hamel as the first foreigner to arrive in Choson. The article also describes the Pyŏnginyangyo (병인양요), the Shinmiyangyo (신미양요), and other events, showing that Korea's opening to the world did not take place willingly but under coercion from the major Western powers. It also offers an objective and detailed record of the Tonghak movement[36] and explains the contents of the Kabo Reforms of 1895 (also known as the "Kabo Restructuring," or 갑오경장 in Korean).[37]

The Yi Dynasty rules Korea with infinite power. The whole country is governed by a cabinet that only takes orders from the king, and all ministries are subordinate to it. A foreign affairs ministry was established in 1882. China has recognized Korea's independence and sovereignty since ancient times. Korea is divided into the following administrative regions or "provinces": Hamgyong, Gangwon, Gyeongsang, Jeolla, Chungcheong, Gyeonggi, Hwanghae, and Pyongan. Each "province" is ruled by a governor representing the king. Like in China, people in Korea hold reverence for their ancestors, but religion is not highly important. Temples are absent in Seoul, but they can be found in the countryside, and

---

36 Tonghak (동학 or 東學 in Korean, literally "Eastern learning") was a Neo-Confucian movement founded in 1860 by Choe Je-u. It arose in response to "Western learning" (서학 or 西學) and sought to revive Confucian teachings. It eventually evolved into a religion known today as Cheondoism.

37 Gerő Lajos and Bokor Jozsef et al, PASLLAS Great Encyclopedia [PALLAS Nagy Lexikona] (Budapest, 1895). https://mek.oszk.hu/00000/00060/html/059/pc005973.html#1

the form of religion follows that of China. Christianity has also begun to spread. There are approximately 20,000 Catholic believers, 300 Protestant believers, forty Protestant missionariess and twenty Catholic missionary groups currently active in Korea. The national treasury is primarily derived from land taxes, tariffs, and the ginseng trade. The total tariffs in 1892 were 438,000 dollars. The standing army has 5,000 members, trained by U.S. soldiers, and almost all of these soldiers use Remington rifles. The rest of the national defense forces consist of 500 horseback soldiers in cavalries, several artillery units, and a reserve force consisting of all the men in the country. Since most of the military forces serve as police, transporters, or toll collectors, their actual influence is limited.

History: The first European to be introduced to Korea was the Dutchman Hamel Henrik in 1688. He was shipwrecked [near Korea] in 1654 and held hostage in Korea for thirteen years. Since then, the French, British, and American people have greatly publicized Korea. When the Russian frigate appeared near Korea in 1866, a hatred for foreigners was ignited, and nine (mostly French) Catholic missionaries active in Korea were killed. The French sent Admiral Roze to Korea in retaliation. He struck Ganghwa while crossing the Han River in October 1866. In 1871 and 1872, American ships invaded and threatened Korea. Subsequently, Korea had no choice but to open its ports to the United States and the European powers. Japan was able to use several ports because it recognized Korea's independence in 1876. A Japanese diplomat took up residence in Seoul in 1877.

Since then, Korean intellectuals have been divided, with pro-Chinese and pro-Japanese factions emerging. As a result, a bloody conflict erupted in 1884. The pro-Japanese faction killed seven ministers from the pro-Chinese faction and forced the king to appoint pro-Japanese ministers. In response, the pro-Chinese faction retaliated, leading to the Sino-Japanese War. The war, [which lasted] from 1894 to 1895, was a battle over control of Korea and started when the Japanese invaded Korea and expelled the Chinese. In the peace treaty signed on May 3, 1895, China renounced its sovereignty over Korea. The Korean government under King Gojong first announced a declaration of the country's independence in February 1895. The Chinese people were expelled from all ports except four. The following declaration was made in March 1895:

1. Korea is an independent state.

2. The government and the military should be separated.

3. The government should be operated by the king and ministers, and the queen or other members of the royal family should not interfere.

4. The duties of each ministry should be clearly separated.

5. Only taxes defined by law can be collected.

6. The national budget is the responsibility of the finance minister.

7. The military budget should be reduced.

8. The national budget should be predetermined.

9. Capable young people should be sent abroad to study.

10. The Ministry of Defense needs to be reformed.

11. Laws should be created for food and property stability.

12. From now on, individuals should be selected based on ability rather than lineage.

13. The relationship between the king and the government and the issue of succession to the throne should be controlled by law. (This is because the faction supporting the queen has been trying to thwart reform).

The content of this encyclopedia indicates that lectures on Korea were conducted at Hungarian universities since the early 20th century. According to Pendler's research, the first lecture on Korea at the University of Budapest took place in 1904. At that time, Hungarian geographer Jenő Cholnoky delivered six lectures on East Asia in November and December 1904, in which he mentioned Korea, saying, "Korea is a very important country and it would not be an exaggeration to compare Korea's significance in East Asia to that of Italy in the Mediterranean Sea..."[38]

5) The Révai Great Encyclopedia

The *Révai Great Encyclopedia* (Hungarian: *Révai Nagy Lexikona*) was subsequently published in 1915. This extensive 21-volume encyclopedia not only provided basic information about Korea that was already known but also included detailed information on two millennia of Korean history. Separate

---

38 Fendler, "One Hundred Years", 151-65.

sections on Korean language and literature meticulously document Korean culture. The *Révai Great Encyclopedia* reflects the scientific achievements discovered during that time with a high degree of accuracy and describes shipping routes and telegraph lines between Seoul-Busan, Busan-Japan, and Japan-China. It also describes the 1895 Ŭlmisabyŏn Incident (을미사변 or 乙未事變 in Korean)[39] relatively accurately and explicitly states that the Japanese Embassy was the culprit. The encyclopedia then accurately describes the An Jung-geun incident,[40] the establishment of the Korean Empire, the Russo-Japanese War, The Hague Military Incident, Emperor Gojong's abdication, and Japan's 1910 annexation of Korea. This finding confirmed that Hungary had a relatively accurate understanding of the situation in Korea at that time. The contents of the paper entry are as follows:[41]

> Political system: Since 1392, the Yi (李) Dynasty has ruled Korea with infinite power, similar to China. Korea has recognized China's sovereignty over Korea since ancient times. In 1910, Japan annexed Korea. Since then, a Japanese governor has ruled the country, and it operates under Japanese law. The capital is Seoul. Like China, [Koreans] respect their ancestors, but religion is not important. Christianity is spreading. The form of religion is similar to that in China.
>
> History: In the first century AD, the Manchu people moved south and invaded Korea, occupying the land of the indigenous people. The kingdoms established on the peninsula afterward were influenced by China and Japan. The Mongolians took over Korea in the 13th century, and the Mongolian army set out from Korea to invade Japan. The first king after the Mongolian occupation, Taejo, voluntarily became a vassal to the Ming Dynasty of China in 1392. The king established Seoul, which is the capital today, and his descendants ruled the country from Seoul until 1910. Beginning in 1592, Korean kings paid taxes to Japan as well. Korea remained a vassal to China even during the Manchu Dynasty,

---

39 The Ŭlmisabyŏn incident (을미사변 or 乙未事變 in Korean) is the name of an incident where Korean Queen Min was brutally murdered by a mob of pro-Japanese Koreans and Japanese soldiers.

40 Where An Jung-Geun (안중근) assassinated Ito Hirobumi, the first Prime Minister of Japan and former Resident-General of Korea.

41 Révai Samuel et al, Révai Great Encyclopedia, Vol. 12I [Révai Nagy Lexikona XII] (Budapest, 1915), 33-4.

[which came] after the Ming Dynasty.

The first country to sign such a treaty with Korea was Japan (1876), and thereafter, opportunities opened up for European powers to trade with Korea. In 1885, China and Japan signed the Treaty of Tianjin, which allowed both countries to intervene in Korea. When a revolution against corrupt administration broke out in 1894, Japan invaded Chemulpo [Incheon Port] and Seoul, leading to reforms in the Korean regime. When China protested against this unilateral intervention, the Sino-Japanese War broke out (1894-95). The Japanese people emerged victorious in Pyongyang (September 15, 1894) and took over all of Korea, and China recognized the independence of Korea at the Treaty of Shimonoseki (April 17, 1895). Since then, Japan's influence has become stronger than China's. The Japanese ambassador became the de facto ruler of Korea, and he forced reforms on the Korean government and appointed many Japanese administrators. The queen, who was the biggest enemy of the Japanese, was assassinated in her bedroom on the night of October 7, 1895. The Japanese embassy knew about this.

King Gojong fled to the Russian embassy, where he stayed for more than a year. Then, Russia and Japan signed a treaty concerning Korea in May 1896. According to this agreement, both countries could deploy a small contingent of troops in Korea. Russia obtained rights to railway operations, mining, and forest utilization, while Japan took over the Korean postal and telegraph system and customs handling. King Gojong, following Japan's directives, changed his title to 'Emperor' (October 12, 1897). Subsequently, Korea served as a buffer between the two countries. Both Russia and Japan wished to have full sovereignty over Korea, with Japan being particularly eager to prevent Russia from gaining control over Korea. This led to the Russo-Japanese War, which began in February 1904. Despite heavy casualties, Japan was able to achieve victory.

In the Treaty of Portsmouth signed on September 5, 1905, Russia renounced all claims to Korea. As a result, Japan seized full control over Korea's domestic and foreign affairs. Count Itō [Hirobumi] took direct charge of ruling Korea. The Korean emperor protested against this at The Hague Peace Conference through relatives, and Japan used this as a pretext to force King Gojong to abdicate on July 17, 1907. His son, Yi Ch'ŏk, succeeded him. The Korean army was also disbanded. Korean nationalist parties expressed their anger through several political assassinations (including the killing of Itō in Harbin on October 25, 1909).

In 1910, the Japanese Minister of Defense, Terauchi, took over the administration of Korea. On August 22, he made the Korean emperor sign a declaration surrendering all his powers to Japan. In return, the emperor and his princes were given pensions, and the Korean nobles became Japanese nobles. With this declaration, Korea ceased to be an independent state. It became a Japanese colony under the name Joseon, with the same status as Formóza [Taiwan] and Sakhalin. The Japanese sought to forcibly integrate these new colonies into the Japanese Empire.

6) The Tolnai' New World Encyclopedia (Tolnai Új Világ Lexikona)

The *Tolnai New World Encyclopedia*, published in 1927, provides a detailed introduction to Korea across four pages. Notably, this encyclopedia contains valuable illustrations of the scenery of Korea at the time, which helps us understand the contemporary lifestyle. The content of the encyclopedia is not significantly different from that of previously published entries, but more detailed explanations have been added about specific facts. Notably, there are examples of Namdaemun Gate (남대문 or 南大門, also known as Sungnyemun Gate; 숭례문 or 崇禮門), soldiers, Gyeonghoeru (경회루 or 慶會樓), Gyeongbokgung Palace (경복궁 or 景福宮), and palace officials, which help readers understand upper-class Korean lifestyles at the time (Figure 4-4-5). The description of Korea in the encyclopedia is as follows:[42]

> Korea (Chosen, Csoszen) is an East Asian peninsular country located between the Sea of Japan and the North China Sea. It is separated by the Yalu and Tumen rivers of Manchuria. The east side has fewer islands, while the west side has more. [Korea's] territory [spans] 218,000 square kilometers, and the capital is Seoul. For a long time, Korea was a nation that maintained its independence despite the influence of powerful countries, but it has since experienced rapid economic development.

42 Tolnao, *Tolnai New Encyclopedia [Tolnai Új világ Lexikona]* (Budapest, 1927), 104-6.

Gak-Su-Yang koreai alelnök udvari öltözetben.

Figure 4-1. High-ranking Choson bureaucracy wearing court attire.

Koreai katonák.

Figure 4-2. Korean soldiers.

Koreai lakosok.

Figure 4-3. Korean Royal Family.

Szöul főváros déli kapuja.

Figure 4-4. Namdaemun.

Az uj királyi palota Szöulban: a 40 méternyi hires csarnok és a kőtarató.

Figure 4-5. Gyeonghoeru.

A rég királyi palota kertben.

Figure 4-6. Choson Royal Palace.

It is a mountainous country with many large rivers, particularly in the west and north. As a country affected by monsoons, the weather is characterized by heavy spring rains, dry and long autumns, and cold winters. Although it was originally a forest-rich country, the forest has disappeared completely due to severe deforestation. Currently, beautiful forests can be seen only in the north, away from the main roads. Korea is divided into three strata. Seoul is a basin divided on a north–south [axis]. There are differences in climate, flora, and soil quality between the two regions. The periphery of the peninsula is mostly composed of metamorphic rocks, and there are also many igneous [magmatic] rocks. It is a country rich in mineral resources (gold, silver, iron, coal, and copper, etc.). There are also small amounts of lignite. Unlike in Manchuria, there are no underground mineral resources [in Korea]. Korea's climate and flora and fauna lie between those of southern Japan and Manchuria. These three climates roughly correspond to Korea's three regions. The forests lie between the Kelet-Sziberiai Amur type of East Siberia and the Mediterranean type of the middle region of Japan. Cotton is produced in the southern region all the way up to Seoul. In addition to rice and cotton, beans, tobacco, and herbs are produced in large quantities⋯"

The animals of Korea are horses and cows that are small but strong. The use of land and settlement areas has long been determined for political and geographical reasons. Past history strongly influences the current economy. The population of Korea is 17 million (1920). The population density is 77 people per square kilometer. Of the total population, 346,000 were Japanese and 26,000 were foreigners. As a mixed race, the [Korean] natives have been greatly influenced by Mongolian and Manchurian invasions. There is also considerable influence from the south, from the Ryukyu islands in southern Japan and from Shandong, China. Koreans look similar to the Japanese, but the influences of Mongols, Malays, etc., can be felt (especially those of Mongols), and the culture is of the Chinese style. Unlike the surrounding islands, [Korea] is a country that has been invaded by foreign powers repeatedly (13th, 17th century). The Japanese people attacked Korea from the sea during ancient times and between 1593 and 1598 but suffered great damage. Koreans look more like Japanese than Chinese in appearance, but they are taller and more robust than [the Japanese]. Koreans are hardworking, good at farming, talented in horticulture, and good at raising animals. These characteristics can earn them honors in Russian colonies, in China, and in the United States. However, they are a vindictive and fanatical people, politically unreliable, and have a strong proclivity for extreme passion.

The ancient religion of Korea was characterized by respect for nature and shamanism. This has significantly changed under Chinese influence. Currently, Christian missionaries are more successful in Korea than in China. Although the Korean language contains many words derived from Chinese, it developed its own script in the fifteenth century. However, the literature is entirely based on Chinese literature⋯ [omitted]⋯ Agriculture in the south is focused on the production of rice and cotton, while in the north, various types of grain are grown. Both regions produce wheat, silk, and medicinal herbs. Livestock farming is gaining popularity, and the number of cows increased from 7 million to 13.5 million between 1910 and 1916.

Between 1908 and 1916, mining profits also increased from 76 million USD to 399 million USD. There is an effort to revive old craft industries. The economy of Korea has improved considerably since [the beginning of] Japanese rule. From 1908 to 1916, the area for farming doubled, logging became established as an industry, and major improvements took place in grape and fruit production, silk production, and livestock farming. The old road network has improved, and a new road was built from the Pusan-Seoul-Yalu-Mukden Line to the three ports on the Yellow Sea. They established vocational schools for crafts, modernized the banking system, and improved navigation methods.

The center of navigation is gradually moving from the old port of Chemulp'o to the new ports of Pusan, Wŏnsan, etc., which face Japan. The railway line to be built in the north will be very important. The relationship between Japan and Korea can be understood well by comparing it to the relationship between Ireland and Britain. There is similar political and cultural pressure here as well. Elements such as calligraphic scripts, Buddhism, and some forms of crafts cross from Korea to Japan. Just as Britain suppressed the old culture of Ireland, the Japanese are also suppressing the culture of Korea. Of course, if Korea becomes a strong and independent country, it could pose a risk as a major competitor to Japan. The population of prosperous regions has increased significantly and is expected to double soon. However, the key question is whether Koreans will give up their independence for economic development. The solution to the problems faced by Korea depends on how much Japan can assimilate Korea.

In addition, the Catholic Encyclopedia (Katolikus Lexikon), published in 1932, describes the missionaries, believers, priests, and monasteries dispatched to Korea. Hungarian encyclopedias published in the 19th and 20th centuries contained many inaccuracies and mistakes about Korea, but they offered information that was suitable for the knowledge available at that time. These errors are most often found in parts related to the origins of the Korean nation and language and cultural aspects. The economic part often directly reflects Japan's propaganda.

4. Conclusion

The transition from the end of the 19th century to the 20th century holds significance in various aspects of Hungarian history. By establishing a dual empire with Austria, Hungary's national status and authority were incomparable with their historical status before. Furthermore, actively accepting Austria's advanced education, culture, and arts led to significant advancements in Hungarian academia. Economic growth, the expansion of educational institutions, and reductions in illiteracy rates increased the desire for knowledge among intellectuals and the general public alike. This social atmosphere led to the spread of enthusiasm for reading and a desire to expand knowledge about the world. Austria respected Hungarian culture and acknowledged its uniqueness, promoting an attitude that encouraged the distinct culture and traditions of Hungary, particularly in regardthe formal cultural policies of the Austro-Hungarian Empire. In this context, interest in Asia within Hungary was enhanced by a synergy between the recognition of Hungary's ethnic origins in Asia and contemporary tendencies to assign ethnic significance to this identity.

Hungary has long contemplated its roots and origins since the transition to modernity. In the late 19th century, during a global and epochal period characterized by intense nationalistic thought, Hungary developed a heightened interest in its Eastern origins. Consequently, Hungary expanded its focus to include Turkey, Tibet, China, Japan, and Korea. Encyclopedias played a significant role during this period in Hungary, serving as comprehensive publications encompassing a wide range of knowledge. Some notable encyclopedias published during this time include the *Repository of Knowledge for the Public*, the *Universal Hungarian Encyclopedia*, The *Earth and its Peoples*, the *Athenaeum Pocket Encyclopedia*, the *Pallas Great Encyclopedia*, the *Révai Great Encyclopedia*, and the *Tolnai New Encyclopedia*. These encyclopedias provided relatively accurate depictions of Korea, presenting a relatively fair and friendly perspective on Korea's situation based on the information and knowledge available at the time. Despite some emphasis on Japan's influence, they objectively described significant events such as the Tonghak Revolution (동학혁명 or 東學革命), the Kabo Reforms (갑오경장 or 甲午改革), the Eulmi assassination of Queen Min by Japanese armed forces (을미사변 or 乙未事變),

King Gojong's exile to the Russian legation (아관파천 or 俄館播遷), the Eulsa Japan-Korea Treaty of 1905, which made Korea a "protectorate" of Japan (을사조약 or 乙巳條約), and the Japan-Korea Treaty of 1910 (한일병탄 or 韓日併吞), which formalized the annexation of Korea by Japan. Therefore, encyclopedias published in Hungary between 1833 and the 1930s, although influenced by Japan and the West, can be considered relatively factual accounts of the relationship between Korea and Japan during that time, Japan's policy toward Korea, and the Korean people's response to it.

Bibliography

Indigenization and Metamorphosis
BHANG Won-il

Lectures on Christian Ideas Volume 3. The Christian Literature Society of Korea, 1963.

Bhang, Won-Il (방원일). "Theoretical Consideration on Syncretism: Toward the Description of Religious Encounter [혼합현상에 관한 이론적 고찰]." *The Critical Review of Religion and Culture [종교문화비평]* 33 (2018): 55-89.

Chŏn, Gyŏng-Yŏn. "Can Christian Culture Be Indigenized?" *New World* (New York, NY), Mar. 1963.

____. "Indigenization Means Primitization." *Christian Ideas* 6, no. 4 (1963): 22-8.

Chŏng, Dae-Wi (정대위). "Religious Syncretism in Korean Society [한국사회에 있어서의 종교혼합]." *World of Ideas [사상계]* 80 (1960).

Chŏng, Ha-Ŭn (정하은). "The Origins of Theological Indigenization [신학의 토착화의 기점]." *Christian Ideas [기독교사상]* 6, no. 7 (1963): 14-21.

Cox, Harvey. *Fire from Heaven: The Rise of Pentecostal Spirituality and the Reshaping of Religion in the 21st Century*. Cambridge, MA: Da Capo Press, 2001.

Eliade, Mircea (미르체아 엘리아데). *The Myth of the Eternal Return: Cosmos and History [영원 회귀의 신화: 우주와 역사]*. Seoul: Hyŏndae Sasangsa, 1976.

Han, T'ae-Dong (한태동). "Types of Thought and the Indigenization Problem [사고의 유형과 토착화 문제]." *Christian Ideas [기독교사상]* 6, no. 7 (1963): 14-21.

Hong, Hŏn-Sŏl (홍헌설). "The Possibilities and Impossibilities of Indigenization [토착화의 가능성과 불가능성]." *Christian Ideas [기독교사상]* 6-8, no. 9 (1963): 14-8.

Jung, Hye Kyung (정혜경). "Goethes Plant Morphology: Consideration on Its Linkage with Naturphilosophie and Romantic Characteristics [괴테의 식물형태학: 자연철학과의 밀착성과 낭만주의적 속성을 중심으로]." *The Korean Journal for the History of Science [한국과학사학회지]* 11, no. 4 (2004).

Kang, Don-Gu. "Prelude to New Religious Research [신종교연구 서설]." *Religious Studies Research [종교학연구]* 6 (1987): 202-3.

Kim, Gwang-Sik (김광식). *Missionary Work and Indigenization [선교와 토착화]*. Seoul: Korea Theological Study Institute, 1975.

____. *Indigenization and Hermeneutics [토착화와 해석학]*. Seoul: Korean Christian Publishers, 1987.

Lee, Gyu-Ho (이규호). "The Philosophical Basis of Indigenization [토착화의 철학적 근거]." *Christian Ideas [기독교사상]* 6, no. 10 (1963): 10-20.

Lee, Gwang-Sun (이광선). "Missionary Work and Cultural Acceptance [선교와 문화적 수용]."

Christian Ideas [기독교사상] 35, no. 6 (1991): 71.

Lee, Jŏng-Bae (이정배). *Indigenization Theology and the Problems of Minjung Theology [토착화신학과 민중신학의 제문제]*. Seoul: Chongro Books, 1991.

Lee, Jang-Sik (이장식). "The Indigenization of Christianity is a Historic Task [기독교 토착화는 역사적 과업]." *Christian Ideas [기독교사상]* 6, no. 6 (1963): 36-44.

Lim, Jai Dong (임재동). "The Lyrical Subject in Goethe's Poem [The Metamorphosis of the Plant] [괴테의 시 「식물의 변이」에서 서정적 주체]." *Hess-Forschun [헤스연구]* 7 (2002).

Niles, D.T. (나일스). "The Writings of the Saints and the Indigenization Problem [성서연구와 토착화문제]." In *Lectures on Christian Ideas Volume 3 [기독교사상 강좌 3]*, 279. The Christian Literature Society of Korea, 1963.

Pak, A-Ron (박아론). "Theories of Korean Theology [한국적 신학에 대한 이론]." *Christian Ideas [기독교사상]* 16, no. 8 (1973).

Pak, Bong-Rang (박봉랑). "Christianity and the Tangun Myth: Regarding Professor Yun Sŏng-bŏm's Words, Centering on the Theological Interpretation of the Trinity [기독교의 토착화와 단군신화: 윤성범 교수의 소론과 관련하여, 삼위일체적 해석의 신학적 문제를 중심으로]." *World of Ideas [사상계]* 123 (1963).

_____. "Scripture, the Sole Source of Christian Revelation: Talking about Dr. Yun Sŏng-Bŏm's Response [성서는 기독교 계시의 유일한 소스: 윤성범 박사의 대답에 답함]." *World of Ideas [사상계]* 126 (1963).

Pak, Pong-Bae (박봉배). "The Indigenization of Worship in the Korean Church [한국교회 예배의 토착화]." *Christian Ideas [기독교사상]* 35, no. 6 (1991): 54.

Richards, Robert J. *The Romantic Conception of Life: Science and Philosophy in the Age of Goethe*. Chicago, IL and London: The University of Chicago Press, 2002.

Robin, Nicolas. "Heritage of the Romantic Philosophy in Post-Linnaean Botany Reichenbach's Reception of Goethe's Metamorphosis of Plants as a Methodological and Philosophical Framework." *Journal of the History of Biology* 44, no. 2 (2011): 283-304.

Sim, Il-Sŏp (심일섭). *The History of Indigenization Debates within the Modern Korean Christian Church [현대한국 기독교회의 토착화 논쟁사]*. Seoul: Asia Culture Publishers, 1982.

Sim, Sang-Tae (심상태). *The Prospects for the Indigenization of the Korean Church [한국교회 토착화의 전망]*. Seoul: Sŏngbaoro Publishers,

Smith, Jonathan Z. *Relating Religion: Essays in the Study of Religion*. Chicago, IL: University of Chicago, 2004.

Von Goethe, Johann Wolfgang. *The Metamorphosis of Plants*. Cambridge, MA: MIT Press, 2009.

Yu, Dong-Sik. "Understanding the Indigenization of Christianity [기독교 토착화에 대한 이해]." *Christian Ideas [기독교사상]* 6, no. 4 (1963): 65.

Yu, Dong-Sik (유동식). "Research on the Indigenization of Christianity [기독교 국화에 관한 연구]." *Christian Ideas [기독교 이데아]* 6, no. 4 (1963): 64-8.

_____. "Indigenizing the Gospel and Missionary Tasks [복음의 토착화와 선교적 과제]." In *The Way and the Logos [도와 로고스]*, 48. Seoul: Korean Christian Publishers, 1978.

_____. "Traditional Culture and the Indigenization of the Gospel [전통 문화와 복음의 토착화]." In *The Way and the Logos [도와 로고스]*, 40-66. Seoul: Korean Christian Publishers,

1978.

____. "Special Sit-Down: Assessing the Major Debates of Korean Indigenization Theology and Its Prospects [특집좌담: 한국 토착화신학 논쟁의 평가와 전망]." *Christian Ideas [기독교 사상]* 35, no. 6 (1991): 80.

Yun, Sŏng-Bŏm (윤성범). *Christianity and Korean Thoughts [기독교와 한국 사상]*. Seoul: Korean Christian Publishers, 1964.

____. "Cur Deus Homo' and Indigenization of the Gospel ['Cur Deus Homo'와 복음의 토착화]." *Christian Ideas [기독교사상]* 9, no. 12 (1966): 30.

____. *Korean Theology: The Hermeneutics of the Holy [한국적 신학: 성의 해석학]*: Sŏnmyŏng Munhwasa, 1972.

Metamorphosis of Culture and Im Hwa's *The History of New Korean Literature (Gaeseol shinmunhaksa)*

YOON Young Shil

Bang Min-Ho (방민호). "'What is Literature' and 'Heartless,' Their Logical Structure and Modern Transition of Korean Literature [「문학이란 하오」와 『무정』, 그 논리구조와 한국 문학의 근대 이행]." *Chunwon Research Journal [춘원연구학보]* 5 (2012).

____. "Im Hwa and Hagyesa [임화와 학예사]." *Sanghur Hakbo: The Journal of Korean Modern Literature [상허학보]* 26 (2009).

Beck, Ulrich. *The Metamorphosis of the World*. Cambridge: Polity Press, 2016.

Benjamin, Walter. ""Franz Kafka: On the Tenth Anniversary of His Death," and "Some Reflections on Kafka"." In *Illuminations*, edited by Walter Benjamin, Hannah Arendt, and Harry Zohn. translated by Harry Zohn, 131-138. New York: Schocken Books, 1969.

Bode, Christoph. "Plus Ça Change: Cultural Continuity and Discontinuity and the Negotiation of Alterity." In *Metamorphosis: Structures of Cultural Transformations*, edited by Jürgen Schlaeger. Tübingen: Gunter Narr Verlag, 2005.

Chan-ki, Kim (김찬기). *The Formation and Turn of the Modern Korean Novel [한국 근대소설의 형성과 전]*. Somyeong Publishing [소명출판], 2004.

Cho, Dong-il (조동일). *The History of Korean Literature [한국문학통사] Vol. 1-4*. Knowledge Industrial Publishing [지식산업사], 1989.

Deleuze, Gilles (질 들뢰즈). *Différence et Répétition [차이와 반복]*. translated by Kim Sang-hwan [김상환 역]. Minumsa [민음사], 2004.

Dongjoon, Shin (신동준). "China's Modernization Strategy and Body Usage Debate [중국의 근현대화 방략과 체용 논쟁]." *Culture and Politics [문화와 정치]* 5, no. 1 (2018).

Duara, Prasenjit (프래신짓트 두아라). *Rescuing History from the Nation [민족으로부터 역사를 구출하기]*. translated by Mun Myung-ki and Son Seung-hee [문명기, 손승희 역]. Samin [삼인], 2006.

____. *Sovereignty and Authenticity: Manchukuo and the East Asian Modern [주권과 순수성: 만주국과 동아시아적 근대]*. translated by Han Seok-jung [한석정 역]. Nanam [나남],

2008.

Ho-deok, Hwang (황호덕). "Theory Dis/Count, Theorizing in Asia [이론 디스/카운트, 아시아에서 이론하기]." *Literature and Society [문학과 사회]* 30, no. 3 (2017).

Hwa, Im (임화). *Im Hwa Literary Arts Collection [임화문학예술전집] 1-5,* edited by Shin Duwon et al [신두원 외 편]. Somyeong Publishing [소명출판], 2009.

Hyun-ju, Kim (김현주). *Culture: Total History of Korean Concepts 13 [문화: 한국개념사총사 13].* Sowha [소화], 2019.

Injae, Song (송인재). "The Repositioning of Chinese Learning and Western Learning in the Concept of Zhongtixiyong in Modern China [근대 중국에서 중학, 서학의 위상변화와 중체서용: 장즈둥의 『권학편』을 중심으로]." *Concepts and Communication [개념과 소통]* 6 (2010).

Jae-ryong, Jo (조재룡). *Translating Sentences [번역하는 문장들].* Munji Publishing [문학과지성사], 2015.

Jin-young, Park (박진영). *Birth of the Translator and East Asian World Literature [번역가의 탄생과 동아시아 세계문학].* Somyeong Publishing [소명출판], 2019.

Ki-hyeong, Han (한기형). *Perspectives of the Modern Korean Novel [한국 근대소설의 시각].* Somyeong Publishing [소명출판], 1999.

Kojin, Karatani (가라타니 고진). *Origins of Modern Japanese Literature [일본 근대문학의 기원].* translated by Park Yuha [박유하 역]. Minumsa [민음사], 1997.

Levine, Michael G. "The Sense of an Unding: Kafka, Ovid, and the Misfits of Metamorphosis." In Franz Kafka's *The Metamorphosis (new edition),* edited by Harold Bloom, 117-144. New York: Infobase Publishing, 2008.

Liu, Lydia (리디아 리우). *Translingual Practice [언어횡단적 실천].* translated by Min Jung-Ki [민정기 역]. Seoul: Somyung Publishing [소명출판], 2005.

Mignolo, Walter D (월터 D. 미뇰로). *The Dark Side of Western Modernity: Global Futures and Decolonial Choices [서구 근대성의 어두운 이면 전지구적 미래들과 탈식민적 선택들].* translated by Kim Young-ju [김영주 역]. Hyeunamsa [현암사], 2018.

Moon-seok, Jang (장문석). "Publishing Coordinator Im Wha and Hak-Ye-Sa [출판기획자 임화와 학예사라는 문제틀]." *Journal of Korean Literary History [민족문학사연구]* 41 (2009).

Myung-soo, Lee (이명수). *Thinker Dam Sa-dong, Who Thought Communication and Equality [소통과 평등을 사유한 사상가 담사동].* Sungkyunkwan University Press [성균관대학교 출판부], 2010.

Ovid (오비디우스). *Metamorphoses [변신이야기].* translated by Lee Yoon Ki [이윤기 역]. Seoul: Minumsa [민음사], 1998.

Reinhardt, Koselleck et al (라인하르트 코젤렉 외). *Koselleck's Conceptual History Line 1: Civilization and Culture [코젤렉의 개념사 사전 1: 문명과 문화].* translated by Ahn Sam-hwan [안삼환 역]. Pureun Yeoksa [푸른역사]. 2010.

Ricœur, Paul (폴 리쾨르), *Oneself as Another [타자로서의 자기 자신].* translated by Kim Woong-kwon [김웅권 역]. Seoul: Dongmunseon [동문선], 2006.

Schlaeger, Jürgen. *Metamorphosis: Structures of Cultural Transformations.* Tübingen: Gunter Narr Verlag, 2005.

Sung-jun, Son (손성준). *Translated Hero [중역한 영웅]*. Somyung Publications [소명출판], 2023.

Sweeney, Kevin W. "Competing Theories of Identity in Kafka's The Metamorphosis." In *Franz Kafka's The Metamorphosis (New Edition)*, edited by Herold Bloom, 63-76. New York: Infobase Publishing, 2008.

Tae-jun, Kim (김태준). *The History of Korean Novels [조선소설사]*. Filmak [필맥], 2017.

Taylor, Charles (찰스 테일러). *Modern Social Imaginaries [근대의 사회적 상상: 경제, 공론장, 인민주권]*. translated by Lee Sang-gil [이상길 역]. Ieum [이음], 2016.

White, Hayden (헤이든 화이트). *Metahistory: The Historical Imagination in Nineteenth-Century Europe [메타역사: 19세기 유럽의 역사적 상상력]*. translated by Cheon Hyung-kyun [천형균 역]. Munji Publishing [문지], 1991.

Xun, Lu (루쉰). *Chinese Novel History [중국소설사]*. translated by Jo Kwan-hee [조관희 역]. Somyung Publishing [소명출판], 2004.

Yanabu Akira (야나부 아키라). *A Dictionary of a Word, Culture [한 단어 사전: 문화]*. translated by Park Yang-shin [박양신 역]. Pureunyeoksa [푸른역사], 2013.

Yanabu Akira (야나부 아키라). *Formation of Translated Language [번역어의 성립]*. translated by Kim Ok-hee [김옥희 역]. Maeumsanchaek [마음산책], 2011.

Yong-kyu, Kim et al (김용규·이상현 외). *Translation and Crossing: The Formation and Subject of Korean Translated Literature [번역과 횡단: 한국 번역문학의 형성과 주체]*. Hyonamsa [현암사], 2017.

Young-chae, Seo (서영채). "Korean Literature Studies after the National Study [국학 이후의 한국문학 연구]." In *Thinking Again About Literary History [문학사를 다시 생각한다]*. Somyung Publishing [소명출판], 2018.

Young-min, Kim (김영민). *The Formative Process of Modern Korean Novel [한국근대소설의 형성과정]*. Somyeong Publishing [소명출판], 2005.

Young-sil, Youn (윤영실). "Political Thoughts and Representation of the People in The Silvery World [<은세계>의 정치사상과 인민의 '대표/재현'이라는 문제]." *Kubo Studies [구보학보]* 24 (2020).

____. "World Literature, Korean Literature, and (Un)-Translatability of 'Political Novel'-Focusing on Hwa Im's History of Korean New Literature [세계문학, 한국문학, 정치소설의 번역(불)가능성- 임화의 '개설신문학사'를 중심으로]." *Modern Literature Research [현대문학연구]* 60 (2020).

Cultural Metamorphosis:
From Seohak Ethics to Christian Ethics

OH Jie Seok

Aleni, Giulio (알레니, G.). *Introduction to Western Education in the 17th Century Joseon [17세기 조선에 소개된 서구교육]*. Translated by Kim Gui-sung [김귀성]. Wonmi [원미사], 2001.

Beach, Waldo, Niebuhr H. Richard (비치, W., & 니버, H.R.). *Christian Ethics [기독교윤리학]*. Translated by Kim Jung-gi [김중기]. Korean Christian Publishing House [대한기독교출판사], 1992.

Bononi, Alphonso (바뇨니, 알폰소). *Bononi's Theory of Childhood Education [바뇨니의 아동교육론]*. Translated by Kim Gui-sung [김귀성]. Bookorea [북코리아], 2015.

Cho, Hyun-Bum (조현범). *Civilization and Barbarism - 19th Century Joseon seen from the Perspective of the Other [문명과 야만- 타자의 시선으로 본 19세기 조선]*. Book World [책세상], 2005.

Fryer, John (프라이어, 존). *Understanding Western Etiquette [서례수지 or 西禮須知]*. Edited by Heo Jae-young [허재영]. Kyungjin [경진출판], 2015.

Heo, Jae-Young (허재영). "A Study of the Seoryesuji from the Point of View of Speech Education [화법 교육사 차원에서 본 『서례수지』연구]." *Journal of Rhetoric Research [화법연구]* 29, (2015): 216-219, doi: 10.18625/jsc.2015..29.211.

Kang, Myung-Kwan (강명관). *Hong Daeyong and 1766 [홍대용과 1766년]*. Seoul: Korean Classical Literature Translation Institute [한국고전번역원], 2017.

Kim, Seung-Hye (김승혜). "The Encounter of East Asian Religious Traditions and Christianity [동아시아 종교 전통과 그리스도교의 만남]." *Spiritual Life [영성생활]*, 1999.

Kwak, Shin-Hwan (곽신환). "The Direction and Conflict of Scholars Studying Abroad in the Joseon Dynasty [조선조 유학자의 지향과 갈등]." *Philosophy and Reality [철학과현실사]*.

Lee, Jang-Hyung (이장형). *The Korean Acceptance and Establishment of Christian Ethics [기독교윤리학의 한국적 수용과 정립]*. Bookorea [북코리아], 2016.

Lee, Ki-Ji (이기지 or 李器之). *Il-Am-Yŏn-Ki [일암연기]*. Translated by Cho Yung-hee, Shin Ik-chul, Bu Yu-seop [조융희, 신익철, 부유섭]. Seongnam: The Academy of Korean Studies Publishing [한국학중앙연구원출판부], 2016.

Moon, Si-Young (문시영). *The Story of Christian Ethics [기독교윤리이야기]*. HanDeul [한들], 1997.

Oh, Jie Seok (오지석). "Christian Ethical Thought Transplanted through Western Missionaries [서양선교사를 통해 이식된 기독교윤리사상]." *The Korean Journal of Chiristian Social Ethics [기독교사회윤리]* 44, (2019): 273, doi: 10.21050/CSE.2019.44.10.

_____. "Koreans and Christian Ethical Thought [한국인과 기독교윤리사상]." In *Life Led by Value [가치가 이끄는 삶]*, edited by Kim Hyung-Min et al. Dongyeon [동연], 2013.

_____. "Metamorphosis of Philosophy Education in the Modern Transition of Korea: Focusing on the Experience of Pyeongyang Soongsil [한국 근대전환기 철학교육의 메타모포시스: 평양 숭실의 경험을 중심으로]." *The Journal of Humanities and Social Science 21 [인문사회21]* 11(4).

_____. *Joseon Intellectual Society and the Ethics of Christianity during the Transition Period [조선지식인사회와 전환기의 기독교윤리]*. Blue Territory [푸른영토], 2018.

_____. *Western Christianity's Self-led Assimilation and Transformation: Beyond Conflicts and Criticisms [서양기독교의 주체적 수용과 변용-갈등과 비판을 넘어서]*. Blue Territory [푸른영토], 2018.

_____. "Metamorphosis of Philosophy Education in the Korean Modern Transition Period: Focusing on the Experience of Pyeongyang Soongsil [한국 근대전환기 철학교육의 메타모포

시스: 평양 숭실의 경험을 중심으로]." *Humanities and Social Sciences 21* [*인문사회 21*] 11(4) (2020): 498.

Park, Hae-Nam (박해남). "A Study on the Formation and Characteristics of Protestant Ethics during the Empire of Korea [대한제국기 개신교 윤리의 형성과 성격에 관한 연구]." *News of the Institute of the History of Christianity in Korea* [*한국기독교역사연구소소식*] 81.

_____. "A Study on the Formation and Character of Protestant Ethics during the Korean Empire [대한제국기 개신교 윤리의 형성과 성격에 관한 연구]." *News from the Korean Christian History Research Institute* [*한국기독교역사연구소소식*], no. 81 (2008): 3-16.

Roh, Dae-Hwan (노대환). "Discussion on the Acceptance of Western Records and Western Studies Policies in the Age of King Jeongjo [정조시대 서기 수용 논의와 서학 정책]." In *Thoughts and Scholarship in the Age of King Jeongjo* [*정조시대의 사상과 학문*], edited by Jung Ok-Ja et al. Dolbegae [돌베개], 1999.

_____. *Civilization, Assimilation* [*문명, 소화*], 2010.

Seo, Ho-Soo (서호수). *A Record of Travel in Rehe* [*열하기유 熱河紀遊*]. Translated by Lee Chang-suk [이창숙]. Akanet [아카넷], 2017.

Shin, Ik-Chul (신익철) *Journey to Beijing and the Beijing Cathedral: Compilation of Ritual Records at the Beijing Tianchu Temple* [*연행사와 북경천주당: 연행록 소재 북경 천주당 기사집성*]. Bogosa [보고사], 2013.

_____. "The Encounter of Scholars Going to China in the 18th Century and Western Missionaries [18세기 연행사와 서양 선교사의 만남]." *Journal of Korean Literature in Classical Chinese* [*韓國漢文學研究*] 51, (2013).

_____. *Yan Travelogue and the Beijing Cathedral* [*연행사와 북경천주당*]. Bogosa [보고사], 2013.

Sim, Hyeon-Ju (심현주). *Fundamentals of Christian Social Ethics* [*기독교 사회윤리 기초*]. Bundo Publishing [분도출판사], 2009.

"The Study of Order and Peace Called Erudition: The Study of Investigating Meaning and Principle [修齐治平之学厄弟加者:[譯言察義理之學]." In *Western Studies Outline* [*西學凡*], *The First Compilation of Heavenly Studies* [*天學初函*] 1, 40-41. Taiwan Student Bookstore [臺灣學生書局], 1965.

Won, Jae-Yeon (원재연). "Criticisms of Catholic Doctrine by Cheosa Hong Jeong-ha during the Reign of King Jeongjo and Perceptions of Catholicism [정조대 처사 홍정하의 천주교리서 비판과 천주교 인식]." *The Dongguk Historical Society* [*동국사학*] 64, (2018): 183.

_____. "Yi Kyu-gyeong's External Views and the Perception of Catholic Missionary History in Joseon [오주 이규경의 대외관과 천주교 조선전래사 인식]." *Church History Research* [*교회사연구*] 17, (2001): 143.

Yang, Ilmo (양일모). "A Semantic Change of the Confucian Concept of Yunli in Modern Korea [유교적 윤리 개념의 근대적 의미 전환-20세기 전후 한국의 언론잡지 기사를 중심으로]." *Philosophy and Communication* [*개념과 소통*] 64, 2017.

Red Yongjeong [LONGJING]

Geographical Manifestation of Socialist Ideology of the Yongjeong Movement in the 1920s

QIAN Chunhua

"CK Group Members Also Participate, Kando Redness Plan, Distributing Numerous Leaflets in Yongjeong City and Turning Kando into Redness! Electric Fist Group Case Public Trial [CK 團員도 參加, 間島赤化計劃, 용전시에서 선던문 다수를 배포하고 간도 일대를 적화려든 사건! 電拳團 事件 公判]." *Dong-a Ilbo [동아일보]*, Oct. 7, 1925.

"Communist Party Distributes Proclamations, Three School Students Take a Day Off, Numerous Subversive Propaganda Distributed [共産黨은 檄文配布 三校生은 休校 불온선전문 다수 배포]." *Jungwai Ilbo [중외일보]*, May 6, 1930.

"Confidential No. 174: On the Establishment of the Third International Communist Party Propaganda Department in Korea [機密 제174호: 朝鮮內의 第三國際共産黨 宣傳部 設置에 관한 件]." *Miscellaneous Cases related to Insurgency Group – Koreans' Part - Koreans and Radicals Vol. 4 [不逞團關係雜件-朝鮮人의 部-鮮人과 過激派 4]*, Jun. 6, 1923.

"Confidential No. 210: On the Case of the Insidious Conspiracy of Communist Koreans [機密 제210호: 共産主義 鮮人의 不逞陰謀事件 檢擧에 관한 件]." *Miscellaneous Cases related to Insurgency Group: Koreans' Part, Koreans and Radicals [不逞團關係雜件: 朝鮮人의 部 鮮人과 過激派]*. Jul. 9, 1923.

"Korea Communist Party Sneaking Activity in Longjing, Activity in Various Places in Kando [高麗共産黨 龍井에 潛入活動, 間島 각디에 활동]." *Dong-a Ilbo [동아일보]*, Apr. 1, 1927.

"Longjing May Day Grand, Organized by Various Social Organizations, First Large Demonstration in Kando [龍井메이데이盛大 각사회단톄련합주최로 間島初有의 大示威]." *Jungwai Ilbo [중외일보]*, May 8, 1927.

"Three Students of Dongyang Academy Arrested [東洋學院 生徒 三名 押送]." *Maeil Shinbo [매일신보]*, May 25, 1923: 3.

"Unexpected Police Arrest Interrupts Dongyang Academy's Parade [동양학원순강, 의외의 경찰에 구인되는 화로 중지]." *Dong-a Ilbo [동아일보]*, Jul. 15, 1923: 4.

Ahn, Jang-Won (안장원). "Exploration of the Yongjeong 3.13 Movement [용정《3.13》운동에 대한 탐구]." *The Korean Diaspora Journal [동포논총]* 3 (1999).

Ahn, Mi-Kyung (안미경). "Women's Liberation Movement and Women's Liberation Thought of Park Won-hee in the 1920s [1920년대 박원희의 여성해방운동과 여성해방사상]." *Journal of Studies on Korean National Movement [한국민족운동사연구]* 74 (2013): 176-8.

Baek Min-Sung (백민성). "The May 30 Riot [5.30폭동]." In *Yuseo deep Haeran River [유서 깊은 해란강반]*, 27. Yanbian People's Publishing House [연변인민출판사], 2001.

Chae, Young-Guk (채영국). *Armed Struggle against Japanese Imperialism in the Late 1920s in Manchuria [1920년대 후반 만주지역 항일무장투쟁]*. Cheonan: Independence Memorial Hall, Research Institute for Korean Independence Movement History [독립기념관 한국독

립운동사연구소], 2007.

Cho, Kyu Tae (조규태). "National Movement of Cheondogyo and Cheondoists in North Gando, 1920~1925. [1920년대 전반 북간도의 천도교와 민족운동]." *The Korea Journal of Donghak Studies [동학학보]* 57 (2020).

Choi, Byungdo (최병도). "Organization of the Joseon Communist Party Manju Chongguk Dongmanguyeokguk and the Frist Round of Gando Communist Party Incident [朝鮮共産黨 滿洲總局 東滿區域局 조직과 제1차 間島共産黨事件]." *Journal of Studies on Korean National Movement [한국민족운동사연구]* 90 (2017).

Choi, Moon-Sik (최문식). "The Peak of Armed Anti-Japanese Independence Struggle: 1920 [반일 무장 독립 투쟁의 고봉: 1920]." *Journal of Humanities [인문논총]* (1996).

CPPCC Ethnic Korean Autonomous Prefecture Committee, Cultural and Historical Data Committee [政協延邊朝鮮族自治州委員會 文史資料委員會]. *Yanbian Cultural and Historical Data 5-6,8: Complete Collection of Educational Historical Materials [延邊文史資料5~6,8: 教育史料全集*. Longjing, China: Longjing Government Printing Press [中國 龍井: 龍井市機關印刷廠], 1988.

Cui, Fenglong (최봉룡). "Korean Social Movements and Religions in 1920~30s' Manchuria –focused on understanding of religions [1920~30년대 만주지역 한인사회주의운동과 종교]." *Journal of Studies on Korean National Movement) [한국민족운동사연구]* 62 (2010).

Eunjin Middle School Alumni Association (은진중학교 동문회). *Enjin 80-Year History: The Morning Star of Bungando Island [恩眞 80年史: 北間島의 샛별*. Seoul: Kormadeo [코람데오], 2002.

Han, Gyu-Moo (한규무). "Trends of Christian Churches and Nationalist Movements in Seoul in the 1900s [1900년대 서울지역 기독교회와 민족운동의 동향]." *Journal of Studies on Korean National Movement [한국민족운동사연구]* 19 (1998).

Han, Saeng-Cheol (한생철). "26 Years of Wind and Cloud Change: Eunjin Middle School [26년의 풍운변화: 은진중학교]." In *Yanbian Literature and History Materials [연변문사자료]* Vol. 6, 45. Yanbian, China: Yanbian People's Publishing House [연변인민출판사], 1988.

Han, Saeng-Cheol (한생철). "A Place of Learning Boiling with Revolutionary Zeal: Daesung School [혁명적 열의로 들끓던 배움터: 대성학교]." In *Yanbian Literature and History Materials [연변문사자료]* Vol. 6, 28. Yanbian, China: Yanbian People's Publishing House [연변인민출판사], 1988.

Hwang, Min-Ho (황민호). "Trends of Korean Socialist Movements and the Eastern Manchuria Youth Federation in the 1920s [1920년대 재만한인 사회주의운동의 동향과 동만청년총연맹]." *Journal of Studies on Korean National Movement [한국민족운동사연구]* 40 (2004).

Im, Gyeong-Seok (임경석). *The Origins of Korean Socialism [한국 사회주의의 기원]*. Goyang: Historical Critique Publishing [역사비평사], 2014.

Im, Jong-Myeong (임종명). "The Recalling and the Representation of Jiandao May 30 of 1930 and their Instabilities in Post-Colonial South Korea [종전/해방 직후 남한에서의 간도 5·30 소환과 표상, 그리고 불안정성]." *Chonnam Historical Review [역사학연구]* 77 (2020).

Jang, Seyoon (장세윤). "Expansion of Gwangju Student Independence Movement to

North-eastern Area of China (Manchuria) and Responses of Korean Students·
Independence Movement Groups [광주학생독립운동의 중국 동북(만주)지역 확산과 한인
학생·민족운동 세력의 호응]." *Journal of Korean Modern and Contemporary History* [*한국
근현대사연구*] 94 (2020).

Jeon, Kwang-Ha (Editor) (전광하 편저). *Ryongjeong in the Passage of Time* [*세월속의 룡정*].
Yanbian, China: Yanbian People's Publishing [연변인민출판사], 2000.

Jin, Taiguo (김태국). "The Social and Cultural Conditions and the Movements of Establishing
Middle School in LongJing in 1920's [1920년대 용정의 사회 문화 환경과 중학교 설립운동]."
The Historical Association for Soong-Sil [*숭실사학*] 25 (2010).

Jun, Myung-Hyuk (전명혁 全明赫). "Life and National Liberation Movement of Gyea Kwang
Kim [解光 金思國의 삶과 민족해방운동]." *Journal of Korean Modern and Contemporary
History* [*한국근현대사연구*] 23 (2002).

Jun, Myung-Hyuk (전명혁 全明赫). "Bang Han-Min's Media, Education Movement and
National Liberation Movement under the Japanese Imperialism Occupation [일제하 方漢
旻의 언로-교육운동과 민족해방운동]." *Sarim* [*사림*] 44 (2013).

Kim, Bang (김방). *Yi Dong-hwi: The First Prime Minister of the Provisional Government of
the Republic of Korea* [*이동휘: 대한민국임시정부의 초대 국무총리*]. Seoul: Historical Space
[역사공간], 2013.

Kim, Chang-Soon (김창순). "The May 30th Riot in Kangdō and the CCP's Manchuria
Detachment [간도 5·30폭동과 중공당의 만주유격대]." *Journal of North Korean Studies*
[*북한학보*] 13 (1989).

Kim, Joo Yong (김주용). "The Characteristics of Student Movements in the Northern Gando
Region in the Early 1920s [1920년대 전반기 북간도지역 학생운동의 양상]." *Journal of
Korean Modern and Contemporary History* [*한국근현대사연구*] 51 (2009).

Kim, Seungtae (김승태). "Canadian Presbyterian Mission to Korea and It's Medical Works
at Yongjeong in Manchuria [캐나다 장로회의 의료선교: 용정 제창병원을 중심으로]."
Yonsei Journal of Medical History [*延世醫史學*] 14, no. 2 (2011).

Kim, Young-Sub (김영섭). "Alliance Suspension and Anti-Japanese Movement [동맹휴학과
항일운동]." In *Eunjin, A 80-Year History* [*은진80년사*], 115. Eunjin Middle School Alumni
Association [은진중학교동문회], Kormadeo [코람데오], 2002.

Lee Jong-Hong (리종흥). "The Road Walked with Many Ups and Downs: Dongheung Middle
School [파란곡절을 걸어온 길: 동흥중학교]." In *Yanbian Literature and History Materials*
[*연변문사자료*] Vol. 6, 3. Yanbian, China: Yanbian People's Publishing House [연변인민출
판사], 1988.

Lee, Bong-Gu (리봉구). "On the Difficult Path of National Education: Yeongsin Middle School
[민족교육의 어려운 길에서: 영신중학교]." In *Yanbian Literature and History Materials*
[*연변문사자료*] Vol. 6, 63. Yanbian, China: Yanbian People's Publishing House [연변인민출
판사], 1988.

Mun, Baek-Ran (문백란). "Mission Work of the Canadian Missionaries for the Korean People
in Yongjung, East Manchuria and the Ministry of the Rev. Chairin Moon after the
1920s [1920년대 이후 용정 주재 캐나다 선교사들의 활동과 문재린 목사]." *The Dong
Bang Hak Chi* [*동방학지*] 180 (2017).

Nakamura, Gentō (中村玄濤). Visiting the Villages of Longjing Island: *Mourning the Weakness of Diplomacy towards China* [間島龍井村地方を視察して: 對支外交の軟弱を悲しむ]. Japan: Tairiku No Nihon Hachi-Sha [大陸之日本八社], 1931.

Pan, Byung-Ryul (潘炳律). "Reinterpretation of the 150,000 Won Incident in Kangdō (Gando) [간도(間島) 15만원 사건의 재해석]." *Journal of History and Culture* [역사문화연구] 12 (2000).

Park, Ju-Shin (박주신). *History of the Ethnic Education Movement of Korean Residents in Japan* [간도한인의 민족교육운동사]. Seongnam: Asia Culture Publishing [아세아문화사], 2000.

Park, Kye-Joo (박계주). *Park Kye-joo Literature Collection 3: Love and Passion, Virgin Land* [박계주문학전집3: 애로역정, 처녀지]. Samyoung Publishing House [삼영출판사], 19756, 67-8.

Park, Sun-Seob (박순섭). "Shifts in Anti-Japanese Struggles by Korean Socialists in the 1920s [1920년대 재만한인사회주의자들의 항일투쟁 노선 변화]." *Journal of Studies on Korean National Movement* [한국민족운동사연구] 90 (2017).

Seo, Dae-Suk (서대숙). *The Pioneer of the Ethnic Movement in North Manchuria, Mr. Gyeyam Kim* [북간도 민족운동의 선구자 圭巖 金躍淵先生]. Seoul: Historical Space [역사공간], 2017.

Seo, Gung-Il (서긍일). "Nationalist Movements and Christianity in the Japanese-occupied Northern Gando Region (1906-1920) [일제하 북간도지역 민족운동과 기독교(1906~1920)]." *The Korean Nationalist Movement in the Northern Gando Region* [북간도지역 한인민족운동] (2008).

Seo, Gwang-Il and Jae-Hong Kim (서긍일·김재홍). *Kim Yeok-Yun: The Leader of the Korean Independence Movement in Manchuria* [김약연: 간도 민족독립운동의 지도자]. Seoul: Goryeo Publishing [고려글방], 1997.

Shin, Ju-Baek (신주백). "The Korean socialist Anti-Japanese move-ment in the 'Kan-Do(間島)' region, 1926~1928 [1926~28년 시기 간도지역 한인 사회주의자들의 반일독립운동론]." *The Journal of Korean History* [한국사연구] 78 (1992).

Shin, Ju-Baek (신주백). *History of the Ethnic Movement of Korean Residents in Manchuria, 1925-1945* [만주지역 한인의 민족운동사; 1925~1945]. Seongnam: Asia Culture Publishing [아세아문화사], 1999.

Yang, So-Jeon et al. (양소전 외 4명 저, 김춘선-김철수-안화춘 옮김). *History of the Revolutionary Struggle of the Chosonjok in China* [중국조선족혁명투쟁사]. Yanbian, China: Yanbian People's Publishing House, 2009, 280.

Yoon, Byung-Seok (윤병석). "The 3 - 13 Movement in Yong-Jung, Yon-Byon, and 「The Declaration of Chosun Indenpendent」 [북간도 용정 3.13운동과 조선독립선언서포고문]." *Korean History Review* [사학지] 31 (1998).

Korean Transformation of Western Christian Nationalism: Biblical Nationalism in Modern Korea at the Turn of the 20th Century

MA Eunji

로스, 매킨타이어, 이응찬, 서상륜 외, 『예수성교누가복음젼서』, 문광서원, 1882년. Accessed May 2, 2023. https://www.bskorea.or.kr/data/pdf/bible_1882b.pdf.

로스, 매킨타이어, 이응찬, 백홍준, 서상륜, 이성하, 김진기 외, 『예수성교젼서』, 문광서원, 1887년. Accessed May 2, 2023. https://www.bskorea.or.kr/data/pdf/bible_1887b.pdf.

이수정, 『신약마가젼복음셔언해』, 1885년, 대한성경공회. Accessed May 2, 2023. https://www.bskorea.or.kr/data/pdf/Mark_1885b.pdf.

성경번역자회, 『신약젼서』, 1904년, 대한성경공회. Accessed May 2, 2023. https://www.bskorea.or.kr/data/pdf/bible_1904_NTb.pdf.

성경번역자회, 『신약젼서』, 1906년, 대한성경공회. Accessed May 2, 2023. https://www.bskorea.or.kr/data/pdf/bible_1911_NTb.pdf.

Anderson, Benedict. *Imagined Communities: Reflections on the Origin and Spread of Nationalism.* London: Verso Editions, 1983. Note: Translated into Korean by Yoon, Hyung-suk (윤형석), [상상의 공동체, 서울: 나남, 2002.].

Baek, Dong-hyeon (백동현). *Discussions on Nationalism and State Ideologies during the Period of the Great Korean Empire [大韓帝國期 民族談論과 國家構想].* Research Institute of Korean Studies, 2010.

Bell, David. *Cult of the Nation in France: Inventing Nationalism,* 1680-1800. Cambridge: Harvard University Press, 2001.

Billig, Michael. *Banal Nationalism.* London: Sage, 1995.

Breuilly, John. *Nationalism and the State.* Chicago: University of Chicago Press, 1993[1982].

_____. "Dating the nation." In *When is the Nation; Towards an Understanding of theories of nationalism*, edited by Atsuko Ichijo and Gordana Uzelac. Abingdon: Routledge, 2005a.

_____. "Changes in the political uses of the nation: Continuity or discontinuity." In *Power and the Nation in European History*, edited by Len Scales and Oliver Zimmer. Cambridge: Cambridge University Press, 2005b.

_____. *The Oxford Handbook of the History of Nationalism.* Oxford: Oxford University Press, 2013.

Burke, Peter. "Nationalisms and Vernaculars, 1500-1800." In *The Oxford Handbook of the History of Nationalism*, edited by John Breuilly, 21-35. Oxford: Oxford University Press, 2013.

Chang, Mun-seok (장문석). The Taming of Nationalism [민족주의 길들이기]. Seoul: Knowledge Landscapes, 2007.

Cho, Hong-sik (조홍식). "Reflections on the Concept of Nation: A Political Sociology Approach [민족의 개념에 관한 정치사회학적 고찰]." *Korean Political Science Review* 39, no. 3 (2005): 129-45.

Chun, Bok-hee (전복희). "The Racism of Progressive Korean Intelligentsia in the Late 19th

Century [19세기말 진보적 지식인의 인종주의적 특성 —독립신문과윤치호일기를 중심으로]." *Journal of Korean Political Science* 29, no. 1 (1995).

Chun, Taek-pu (전택부). *A Historical Essay on the Concepts of God and Tenchu: Focusing on the 18th and 19th Centuries [하나님 및 텬쥬라는 말에 관한 역사 소고-18세기와 19세기를 중심으로]. Korean Language Bible and Korean Culture: Encounter between Catholicism and Protestantism* Seoul: Christian Literature Press, 1985.

Chun, Young-taik (전영택). "Christianity and the Korean Script [基督教와 朝鮮文字]." *Hangul* 4, no. 8 (1936).

Duke, Alastair. *Reformation and Revolt in the Low Countries*, London: Hambledon Press, 1990.

Dunkelgrün, Tirtsah. "'Neerlands Israel' Political Theology, Christian Hebraism, Biblical antiquarianism, and historical myth." In *Myth in History, History in Myth, edited by* Laura Cruz and Willem Frijhoff, 201-36. Leiden: Brill, 2009.

Eckette, Carter. *Offspring of Empire: The Koch'ang Kims and the Colonial Origins of Korean Capitalism.* Seattle: University of Washington Press, 1996. Note: Translated into Korean by Ju, Ik-Jong (주익종). *제국의 후예 고창 김씨와 한국 자본주의의 식민지 기원 1876~1945.* 서울: 푸른역사, 2008

Em, Henry (헨리 임). *The 'Nation' as a Modern and Democratic Construct: Shin Chae-ho's Historical Narrative [근대적·민주적 구성물로서의 '민족': 신채호의 역사 서술].* Samin, 2006.

Gellner, Ernest. *Nations and Nationalism.* Ithaca: Cornell University Press, 1983.

Green, Ian. *Print and Protestantism in Early Modern England*, New York: Oxford University Press, 2002.

Greenfeld, Liah. *Nationalism: Five Roads to Modernity*, Cambridge: Harvard University Press, 1992.

Greenslade, Stanley Lawrence. *The Cambridge History of the Bible, vol. 3, The West from the Reformation to the Present Day.* Cambridge: Cambridge University Press, 1963.

Grosby, Steven. *Biblical Ideas of Nationality: Ancient and Modern*, Winona Lake: Eisenbrauns, 2002.

Guibbory, Achsah. *Christian Identity, Jews, and Israel in Seventeenth-Century England.* Oxford: Oxford University Press, 2010.

Ha, Young-Sun (하영선). *A History of Social Science Concepts in Korea: From Tribute to Informatization [근대한국의 사회과학 개념 형성사].* Changbi Publishers, 2009.

Han, Myoung-keun (한명근). *Publication of New Books and Its Characteristics in the Enlightenment Era (1876-1905) [개화기(1876~1905), 신서적 발간과 그 특징].* Soongshil University Historical Society, 2007.

Han, Young-Woo (한영우). *Shin Chae-ho's Historical Consciousness in the Korean-Japanese Relationship [한말에 있어서의 신채호의 역사인식].* Danjae Shincheaho Commemorative business Association, 1980.

Harline, Craig. *Pamphlets, Printing, and Political Culture in the Early Dutch Republic.* Dordrecht: Martinus Nijhoff, 1987.

Hastings, Adrian. *The Construction of Nationhood: Ethnicity, Religion and Nationalism.*

Cambridge: Cambridge University Press, 1997.

Helgerson, Richard. *Forms of Nationhood: The Elizabethan Writing of England*. Chicago: University of Chicago Press, 1992.

Hill, Christopher. *The English Bible and the Seventeenth-Century Revolution*. New York: Penguin, 1993.

Hobsbawm, Eric J. *Nations and Nationalism Since 1780*. Cambridge: Cambridge University Press, 1990. Note: Translated into Korean by Kang, Myeong-Se (강명세), 1780이후의 민족과 민족주의. 서울: 창작 과비평사, 1994.

Houston, Rab A. *Literacy in Early Modern Europe: Culture and Education*, 1500-1800. Harlow: Longman, 2002.

Jeong, Changnyeol (정창렬). *The Political and Economic Nature of the Late Joseon Reform Movement [한말 변혁운동의 정치·경제적 성격]. Theory of Korean Nationalism*. Changbi Publishers, 1982.

Jo, Seongyun (조성윤). "Outer Sol (oe-sol), and Linguistic Nationalism: From the World of Chinese Characters to the World of Hangul [외솔과 언어 민족주의: 한문의 세계에서 한글의 세계로]." *The Korean Association of Humanities and the Social Sciences, Phenomenon and Cognition* 18, no. 3 (1994).

Kang, Man-gil (강만길). *The Historical Significance of the Creation of Hangul [한글창제의 역사적 의미]*. Changbi Publishers, 1977.

Kim, Bong Hee (김봉희). *A Study on the Book Culture of the Korean Enlightenment Era [한국개화기 서적문화 연구]*. Seoul: Ewha Womans University Press, 1999.

Kim, En Joong (김인중 외). *The Encounter of Current Civilizations [이제문명의 조우이다]*. Seoul Economic Management, 2009.

Lee, Deok-Ju (이덕주). *A Study on Early Translations of the Korean Bible: With a Focus on the Activities of Bible Translators [초기 한글성경번역에 관한 연구-특히 성경번역자들의 활동을 중심으로], Korean Bible and Korean Culture: Encounter between Catholicism and Protestantism*. Christian Literature Press, 1985.

Lee, Gwang-Rin (이광린). "Christian Faith in Late Joseon Imprisonment [구한말 옥중에서의 기독교신앙]." *Ilchokak, The Issue of Ancestral Tablets in Korean Modernization*, 1986.

Lee, Peter. *Sourcebook of Korean Civilization, vol. 2*. New York: Columbia University Press, 1998.

Lee, Soo-jeong (이수정). *Explanation of the New Testament Gospel of Mark [신약마가전복음셔언해]*. The Korean Bible Society, 1885. Accessed May 2, 2023. https://www.bskorea.or.kr/data/pdf/Mark_1885b.pdf.

Lim, An-Sup (임안섭). "Let's return to 'Bible Christianity' [성경 기독교로 돌아가자]." *News & Joy*, Jun. 22, 2016.

Ma, Eun-Ji (마은지). "Nationalism in France [프랑스 민족주의]." *Soongshil University Historical Society* 20 (2007): 78-80.

____. *Rediscovering the Nationalism of Maurice Barrès [민족주의의 재발견: 바레스의 민족주의]*. Seoul: Samin, 2016.

Oak, Sung-Deuk (옥성득). *Major Controversies in the Translation of the Korean Scriptures, 1877-1939] [초기 한글성경 번역에 나타난 주요 논쟁 연구(1877~1939)*. Presbyterian

University and Theological Seminary, 1993

Pang Kie-Choong (방기중). "A Study on Paik Nam Woon's Scholarship and His Political Economic Thought in 1930's and 1940's [한국근대사상사 연구]." *Critical Review of History* (1992).

Park, Chan Seung (박찬승). *The Formation Process of 'Minjok' Concept in Korea [한국에서의 '민족 개념의 형성] Concept and Communication.* Hallym Academy of Sciences, Hallym University, 2008.

____. *Nation and Nationalism* [민족·민족주의]. Seoul: Sohwa, 2010.

Park, Chang-Hai (박창해). *Korean Grammar Structures in John Ross's "Yesu Seonggyo Jeonso (New Testament)" [로스 (예수성교젼서), 에 쓰인 한국어의 문법구조]. The Korean Bible and Korean Culture: Encounter between Catholicism and Protestantism.* Christian Literature Press, 1985.

Park, Chung-Shin (박정신). *A New Understanding of Korean Christian History [한국 기독교사 인식].* Hyean, 2004.

Pastreich, Eman-Uel (이만열 / 李萬烈). *History of the Christian Cultural Movement in Korea [한국기독교 문화운동사].* The Christian Literature Society of Korea, 1987.

____. "The Formation Process of National Consciousness among Korean Christian Converts [한말 기독교인의 민족의식 형성과정]." *Journal of Korean History* 2 (1973).

Ross, John (존 로수), McIntyre (매킨타이어), Lee Eung-chan (이응찬), Seo Sang-ryun (서상륜) et al. *St. Luke's Gospel [수성교누가복음젼].* Mun'gwangsŏwŏn Publishing House [문광서원], 1882. Accessed May 2, 2023. https://www.bskorea.or.kr/data/pdf/bible_1882b.pdf.

Ross, John (존 로스), Lee Eung-Chan (이응찬), Baek-Hong-jun (백홍준), Seo Sang-ryun (서상륜), Lee Seong-ha (이성하), Kim Jin-gi (김진기) et al. *Korean New Testament [예수성교젼].* Mun'gwangsŏwŏn Publishing House [문광서원], 1887. Accessed May 2, 2023. https://www.bskorea.or.kr/data/pdf/bible_1887b.pdf.

Ryu, Dae-Young (류대영 외). *History of the Korean Bible Society I & II [대한성서공회사 I·II].* Korean Bible Society, 1994.

Schama, Simon. *The Embarrassment of Riches: An Interpretation of Dutch Culture in the Golden Age.* Berkeley: University of California Press, 1988.

Schmid, Andre. *Korea Between Empires, 1895-1919.* New York: Columbia University Press, 2002. Note: Translated into Korean by Chung, Yeo-Wool (정여울), 제국, 그 사이의 한국. 정여울 옮김. 서울: 휴머니스트, 2007.

Shin, Gi-Wook, and Michael Robinson (신기욱·마이클 로빈슨 엮음). *Colonial Modernity in Korea* [한국의 식민지 근대성]. Translated by Do Myeon-hoe. Seoul: Samin, 2006.

Shin, Gi-Wook. *Ethnic Nationalism in Korea: Genealogy, Politics, and Legacy.* 2006. Note: Translated into Korean by Lee, Jin-Jun (이진준), *한국 민족주의의 계보와 정치.* 이진준 옮김. 서울: 창비, 2010.

Shin, Ki-Young (신기영). "The Emergence of Christian Nationlism in Colonial Korea [일제하 한국 기독교 민족주의의 형성]." *Tonghap Yeongu* 8, no. 1 (1995).

Smith, Anthony D. *The Ethnic Origins of Nations.* New York: Blackwell, 1986.

____. *The Oxford Handbook of the History of Nationalism.* Oxford: Oxford University Press, 2013.

____. *Chosen Peoples*. Oxford: Oxford University Press, 2004.

____. *Ethno-Symbolism and Nationalism: A Cultural Approach*. London & New York: Routledge, 2009. Note: Translated into Korean by KIm, In-Joong (김인중), [족류상징주의와 민족주의] 서울: 아카넷, 2016

____. *The Nation Made Real: Art and National Identity in Western Europe 1600-1850*. Oxford: Oxford University Press, 2013.

The Board of Official Translators (성경번역자회). *The New Testament in Korean [신약젼셔] 1904*. The Korean Bible Society. Accessed May 2, 2023. https://www.bskorea.or.kr/data/pdf/bible_1904_NTb.pdf.

____. *The New Testament in Korean [신약젼셔], 1906*. The Korean Bible Society. Accessed May 2, 2023. https://www.bskorea.or.kr/data/pdf/bible_1911_NTb.pdf.

The Capital Gazette [황성신문]

The Christian Advocate [죠션 크리스도인 회보]

The Christian News [그리스도 신문]

The Daehan Maeil Shinbo [대한매일신보]

The Independence Newspaper [독립신문]

Tsukihashi Datsuhiko (쓰키하시 다쓰히코). "Exploration of Methods in East Asian Humanities and National Studies: Focusing on 'Modernity' in Korean History Research [동아시아 인문학국학 방법의 모색-한국사 연구에 있어서의 '근대'를 중심으로]." *The Journal of Korean Studies* (2007).

Yu, Geun-Ho (유근호). "Formation Process of Korean National Consciousness [한국 민족의식의 형성과정]." *Cultures and Ethics* no. 12 (1982): 4.

Metamorphosis of Seoul:
Visual Representations of the Korean Capital at the Turn of the 20th Century

MECSI Beatrix

Bennett, Terry. *Korea: Caught in Time*. With an Introduction by Martin Uden. Reading: Garner, 1997.

Bishop, Bird Isabella. *Korea and Her Neighbors*, New York Chicago Toronto: Fleming H. Revell Company, 1898. [Available at: http://anthony.sogang.ac.kr/Bird/IsabellaBird.pdf]

Bozóky, Dezső. *Két év Keletázsiában* [Two years in East Asia]. Vol. 1. Published by the author, 1911.

Cseppentő, István. "Discours d'exilé, discours de voyageur." In: Maár, J. – Lefebvre, A. (eds.), *Exils et transfert cuturels dans l'Europe moderne*. Cahiers de la Nouvelle Europe 21, Paris: L'Harmattan, 2015, 287-293.

Cseppentő, István. "Galantéria, nosztalgia, keleti egzotikum. A rokokó *turquerie* irodalmi továbbélése Pierre Loti *A kiábrándultak* c. regényében." [Gallantry, nostalgia, oriental exoticism. The literary survival of the rococo *turquerie* in Pierre Loti's novel *The Disillusioned*]. In: Bartha-Kovács, K. – Fórizs, G. (eds.) *A rokokó arcai. Tanulmányok egy tünékeny fogalom történetéhez* [The faces of the Rococo. Studies in the history of a disappearing concept]. Budapest: Reciti, 2022, 71-81.

Csoma Mózes, and Tatjána Kardos. Látogatás a Hajnalpír Országában Dr. Bozóky Dezső koreai fotográfiái = Visit to the Land of Morning Calm: Dr. Dezső Bozóky's Korean photographs. 조용한 아침의 나라 방문기: 보조끼 데죠의 사진. Ferenc Hopp Museum of Asiatic Arts and the Embassy of Hungary, Seoul, 2020.

Dénes Mirjam, and Sebestyén Ágnes Anna. "Egy magyar utazó Japán-olvasata a századfordulón: Bozóky Dezső fotográfiái." Doma Petra and Takó Ferenc (eds): „Közel, s Távol" V. Az Eötvös Collegium Orientalisztika Műhely éves konferenciájának előadásaiból 2015, Eötvös Collegium, Budapest, 2016, 11-34.

Fajcsák, Györgyi, and Mecsi, Beatrix. *The Land of the Morning Calm: Korean Art in the Ferenc Hopp Museum of Eastern Asiatic Arts*. Budapest: Ferenc Hopp Museum of Asiatic Arts, 2012a.

____. *A hajnalpír országa. Koreai Művészet a Hopp Ferenc Kelet-ázsiai Művészeti Múzeumban*. Budapest: Hopp Ferenc Kelet-ázsiai Művészeti Múzeum, 2012b. [Note: Hungarian translation of the English version, Fajcsák and Mecsi 2012a.]

Fajcsák, Györgyi, and Renner, Zsuzsanna. eds. *A Buidenzorg-villa lakója. A világutazó, műgyűjtő Hopp Ferenc (1833-1919)* [The man of the Buitenzorg villa: Ferenc Hopp, globe-trotter and art collector (1833-1919)]. Budapest: Ferenc Hopp Museum of Asiatic Arts, 2008.

Felvinczi-Takács, Marianne. "Hopp Ferenc." *Keletkutatás* (Autumn 1994): 7-24.

Felvinczi-Takács, Zoltán. *A Hopp Ferenc Keletázsiai Művészeti Múzeum* [The Ferenc Hopp Museum of Eastern Asiatic Arts]. Budapest: Hungarian National Museum of Fine Arts, 1923. Exhibition catalog.

Fendler, Károly. "Austro-Hungarian Archival Sources of Korean History (1884-1910)." *Seoul Journal of Korean Studies* 20 no.2 (2007): 221-235.

Ferenczy, Mária, and Kardos, Tatjána. "A Descriptive Catalogue of the Archive Korean Photographs of the Ferenc Hopp Museum of Eastern Asiatic Arts." In: Fajcsák and Mecsi, *The Land of the Morning Calm*, 141-174, 2012.

Ferenczy, Mária, and Kincses, Károly. *Mandarin öszvérháton. Hopp Ferenc fényképei* [Mandarin on a Mule: Ferenc Hopp and Hungarian photography]. Budapest: Hungarian Museum of Photography and Ferenc Hopp Museum of Asiatic Arts, 1999.

Ferenczy, Mária. "Korean art in the Ferenc Hopp Museum, The Antecedents." In: Fajcsák and Mecsi, *The Land of the Morning Calm*, 12-25, 2012a.

____. "Koreai művészet a Hopp Múzeumban. Előzmények." [Korean art at the Hopp Museum. History] In: Fajcsák and Mecsi, *A hajnalpír országa*, 12-25, 2012b.

Hopp, Ferenc. "Hopp Ferencz utazása a Föld körül, Szibírián át." [Ferencz Hopp's journey around the world through Siberia]. [Offprint from] *Földrajzi Közlemények* [Geographic Proceedings] 33 no. 5 (June and July 1904): 48.

Horlyck, Charlotte. *Korean Art from the 19th Century to the Present*. London: Reaktion Books, 2017.

Jaisohn, P. *My Days in Korea and Other Essays*. Seoul: Yonsei University Press, 1999.

Jungmann, Burglind. *Pathways to Korean Culture. Paintings of the Joseon Dynasty 1392-1910.*

London: Reaktion Books, 2014.

_____. "Ritual and Splendor: Chosŏn Court Art." In *A Companion to Korean Art*, First Edition, edited by J. P. Park, Burglind Jungmann, and Juhyung Rhi. New Jersey: Wiley & Sons, 2020.

Kardos, Tatjána. "Old Korean Photographs in the Archives of the Hopp Museum." In: Fajcsák and Mecsi, *The Land of the Morning Calm*, 9-11, 2012a.

_____. "Ship's Doctor with a Camera. Dezső Bozóky's Photo Collection on Korea." In: Fajcsák and Mecsi, *The Land of the Morning Calm*, 26-37, 2012b.

_____. "Hajóorvos fényképezőgéppel: Bozóky Dezső fotógyűjteménye Koreáról." [Ship's doctor with a camera: Dezső Bozóky's photo collection on Korea]. In Fajcsák and Mecsi, *A hajnalpír országa*, 26-37, 2012c.

Kelényi, Béla. "A Calderoni kirakatja." [The shop window of Calderoni]. Györgyi Fajcsák and Zsuzsanna Renner, eds., *A Buitenzorg-villa lakója. A világutazó, műgyűjtő Hopp Ferenc (1833-1919)* [The man of Buitenzorg Villa: Ferenc Hopp, globe-trotter and art collector (1833-1919)]. Budapest: Ferenc Hopp Museum of Asiatic Arts, 2008, 55-62.

Kim, Jeehey. *Photography and Korea*, London: Reaktion Books, 2023.

Kim Seung-ik. "An Jungsik, Spring Dawn at Mt. Baegak," The National Museum of Korea, In *Smarthistory*, August 4, 2022. Accessed March 24, 2024. https://smarthistory.org/an-jungsik-spring-dawn-at-mt-baegak/

Lee, Jungsil Jenny. "Modern Korean Art in the Japanese Colonial Period." In *A Companion to Korean Art*, 1st edition, edited by J. P. Park, Burglind Jungmann, and Juhyung Rhi. New Jersey: Wiley & Sons, 2020.

Loti, Pierre. *La troisième jeunesse de madame Prune*. 1905. La Tour-d'Aigues: Éditions de l'Aube, 2010.

_____. *Journal*, IV (1896-1902). Paris: Les Indes savants, 2016.

Lowell, Percival. *Chosön: The Land of the Morning Calm*, 2nd ed. Boston: Ticknor and Company, 1888. https://www.loc.gov/item/04016695 1886

Mecsi, Beatrix. "Two Hungarian Hobby Photographers in Old Korea: Ferenc Hopp and Dezső Bozóky". *Koreans and Central Europeans. Informal Contacts up to 1950*. Ed. by Andreas Schirmer, 115-128. Vienna: Praesens, 2020.

Na Gak-sun. "Seoul jimyeong ui byeoncheon gwa teukjing," *Seoul gwa yeoksa* 72 (October 2008): 5-17.

Nahm, C. Andrew. *Korea – Tradition and Transformation. A History of the Korean People*. New Yersey–Seoul: Hollym, 1988.

Pai, Hyung Il. "Visualizing Seoul's Landscapes: Percival Lowell and the Cultural Biography of Ethnographic Images." *The Journal of Korean Studies* 21, no.2 (2016): 355-384.

Park Eun-suk, "Gaehang hu (1876-1894) Seoul ui jabon juui dosihwa wa gong-gan jaepyeon," *Hyangto Seoul*, no. 74 (October 2009): 86-87.

Quella-Villéger, Alain and Bruno Vercier. *Pierre Loti photographe*. Saint-Pourçain-sur-Sioule: Bleu autour, 2012.

Sonne, Wolfgang. *Representing the State: Capital City Planning in the Early Twentieth Century*. Munich; London: Prestel, 2003.

Reconstruction of the Power System in the 1950s between Colonial Heritage and the Pressure of the Aid Economy

OH Sunsil

Choe, In-Sung (최인성). "On Hydropower Development in Sam Pal's Southern Region [삼팔 이남의 수력전원개발에 대하여]." *Electrical Engineering* [전기공학] 3-4 (1950): 51-53.

Chung, Yong Wook (정용욱). *US Policy on Korea before and after Liberation [해방 전후 미국의 대한정책]*. Seoul: Seoul National University Press, 2003.

Dimoia, John. "Atoms for Sale?: Cold War Institution-Building and the South Korean Atomic Energy Project, 1945-1965." *Technology and Culture* 51 (2010): 589-618, doi: 10.1353/tech.2010.0021.

Editorial Board (편집부). "An Interview with Engineers Who Visited the United States and Returned: Insights into the Power Industry [전력계소사: 미국을 시찰하고 돌아온 기술자 인터뷰기]." *Electrical Engineering [전기공학]* (1958): 1-7.

Han, Jin Geum (한진금). "Research on the Technical Assistance and Training Plan of US Aid Institutions in the 1950s [1950년대 美國 원조 기관의 對韓 技術援助訓練計劃 연구]." Master's thesis, Seoul National University, 2010.

Hecht, Gabrielle. *The Radiation of France: Nuclear Power and National Identity after World War II*. Cambridge, MA and London: The MIT Press, 1998.

Hirsh, Richard F. *Technology and Transformation in the American Electric Utility Industry*. Cambridge, MA and London: Cambridge University Press, 1989.

Hong, Seon-Kyu (홍성유). *Korean Economy and US Aid [한국경제와 미국 원조]*. Seoul: Pakyoungsa, 1960.

Institute of Asian Culture Studies, Hallym University [한림대학교 아세아문화연구소]. *HQ USAFIK Intelligence Summary Northern Korea: 1947.4.1 – 1948.3.31*, Vol. 2. 1998.

Jeong, Dae-Hoon (정대훈). "The Countermeasure of the Electric Power Shortage in 1948~1953 — Focusing on the Establishment of the Three-Year Plan for Development of Power Resources [1948-1953년의 남한 전력수급대책 – 전원개발계획의 수립과정을 중심으로]." *Sarim [사림]* 74 (2020): 51-53.

Jeong, In Kyung (정인경). "The Foundation and Management of Kyongsong Highter Technical School under the Japanese Imperialism [일제하 경성고등공업학교의 설립과 운영]." *The Korean Journal for the History of Science [한국과학사학회지]* 16-1 (1994): 31-65.

Jeong, Jin-A (정진아). "War Inflation and the 'Baekjaejeong' Economic Planning Board [전쟁 인플레이션과 '백재정']." *The Korean History Society Modern History Research Division [한국역사연구회 현대사분과 편]* 51-53.

Joung, An-Ki (정안기). "A Study of the Chousen Amnokgang Waterpower Corporation, a Chousen Special-Purpose Company Active in the 1930s [1930년대 조선형 특수회사, 조선압 록강수력 발전(주)의 연구]." *Chung-Ang Saron [중앙사론]* 47 (2018): 5-57.

Kim, Geun-Bae (김근배). "Emergence of Modern Science and Technology Personnel in Korea [한국 근대과학기술인력의 출현]." *Literature and Intellectual History* [문학과 지성사] (2005).

Kim, Seong-Jun (김성준). "Formation and Changes in the Technological Regimes of the Nuclear Program in South Korea, 1953-1980 [한국 원자력 기술 체계의 형성과 변화, 1953-1980]." Ph.D. dissertation, Seoul National University [서울대학교], 2012, 24-27.

Korea Electric Power Corporation (한국전력공사). *A 100-year History of the Korea Electric Power Corporation [한국전력100년사]*. Seoul: Korea Electric Power Corporation, 1989.

Korea Electric Power Engineers Association (韓國電力技術人協會編). "A Decade History of the Korea Electric Power Engineers Association: 43 Years since the Establishment of the Association of Chief Electric Technicians of Korea [韓國電力技術人協會 10年史: 대한전기주임기술자협회 창립 이후 43년-]." 2007.

Lee, Daegun (이대근). *Economy in the Post-Liberation 1950s: Industrialization's Personal Background [해방후 1950년대의 경제—공업화의 사적 배경 연구]*. Seoul: Samsung Economic Research Institute, 2004.

Lee, Hyunjin (이현진). *US Policy on Economic Aid to Korea, 1948-1960 [미국의 대한경제원조정책, 1948-1960]*. Seoul: Hye-an, 2009.

Lee, Jaesook (이재숙). "Urgency of Hydropower Resource Development [수력자원개발의 긴급성에 대한]." *Electrical Engineering [전기공학]* 3-4 (1950): 51-53.

Lee, Jong-Won (이종원). *Cold War in East Asia and Korean-American-Japanese Relations [東アジア冷戰と韓美日關係]*. Seoul: Tokyo University Press, 1996.

____. *The East Asian Cold War and Korean-American-Japanese Relations [-東アジア冷戰と韓美日關係-]*. Tokyo University Press [東京大學出版會], 1996.

Lee, Jongil (이종일). "Power Resources and the 5-Year Plan in South Korea [한국의 전력자원과 5개년계획]." *Electrical Engineering [전기공학]* 3-4 (1950): 51-53.

Ministry of Commerce and Industry (상공부). *Government Administration in Commerce [상공행정계관]*. Seoul: 1958.

Ministry of Reconstruction (부흥부). *White Paper on Revitalization [부흥백서]*. Seoul: 1958.

Namseon Electric Company (남선전기주식회사). *Status of Namseon Electric Company [남선전기주식회사현황]*. Seoul: 1958.

National Assembly Library (국회도서관 입법 조사국). *Nathan Reports [네이산 보고서]*. Seoul: National Assembly Library, 1965.

No, Sangho (노상호). "Emergence of 'Electricity System' and State-Owned Power Companies in the 1940s-1950s [1940-50년대 '전기체제'와 국영전력사업체의 등장]." *The Korean Cultural Studies [한국문화연구]*: 51-53.

Oh, Sun-Sil (오선실). "The Largest Power Plant in the East Asia on the Amnok River: Formation of the Supum Dam and Dongisa Technical System [압록강에 등장한 동양 최대의 발전소, 수품댐과 동이사아 기술체계의 형성]." *The Journal of Humanities and Social Sciences [인문사회과학연구]* 21-1 (2020): 269-294.

____. "Transition of the Power System in Colonial Korea during the 1920-30s: Emergence of Large-scale Hydropower Plants for Industrial Use and Establishment of Power Grid System [1920-30년대, 식민지 조선의 전력 시스템의 전환: 기업용 대형 수력발전소의 등장과 전력망 체계의 구축]." *The Korean Journal for the History of Science [한국과학사학회지]* 30 (2008): 1-52.

Pak, T'ae-Gyun (박태균). *Origins of Won-yong: Korea's Economic Development Plan [원용과*

변용: 한국 경제개발계획의 기원]. Seoul: Seoul National University Press, 2007.

Park, Sung-Rae et al. (박성래 외). "A Study on the Formation of Korean Scientists and Technologists [한국 과학기술자의 형성 연구]." *Research report of the Korea science foundation* [한국과학재단 연구 보고서], 1995, 88.

Ryu, Seungju (류승주). "Power Supply Negotiations between North and South Korea, 1946-1948 [1946-48년, 남북한 전력수급교섭]." *Quarterly Review of Korean History* [역사와 현실] 40 (2001): 51-53.

Seong, Chan-Yong (성찬용). "A Visit to the Electrical Industry in the United States [미국 전기계 방문기]." *Electrical Engineering* [전기공학] (1953): 26-28.

Shin, Ki-Jo (신기조). *Off the Beaten Path: 57 Years of Electric Power* [전력 외길 57년]. Seoul: Self-Published, 2005.

The Korean Electric Company (조선전업주식회사). *10-year History of Joseon Electric Industry* [조선전업주식회사10년사]. Seoul: 1955.

The Korean Institute of Electrical Engineers (대한전기학회). *25-year History of Electrical Society* [전기학회 25년사]. Seoul: 1973.

United States Department of State. "General political policies of the United States toward Korea and appeal to the United Nations General Assembly." In *Foreign Relations of the United States, 1948: The Far East and Australasia, Volume VI*, edited by John G. Reid and David H. Stauffer. General edited by S. Everett Gleason and Frederick Aandahl. Washington: United States Government Printing Office, 1974.

Woo, Jung-En. "A Method to His Madness: The Political Economy of Import-Substitution Industrialization in Rhee's Korea." In *Race to the Swift: State and Finance in Korean Industrialization*, edited by Eric Charry, 545-573. Columbia: Columbia University Press, 1991.

Yim, Song-Ja (임송자). "Electric Power Policy and Power Sources Development Policy of the Past Governments from the Mid 1950s to the Early 1960s [1950년대 중·후반기~1960년 대 전반기, 역대 정부의 電力對策과 電源開發政策]." *Sarim* [사림] 56 (2016): 51-53.

Yoon, Iljoong (윤일중). "Review of National Basic Industries; Electricity [국가기본산업재검토; 전력]." *National Assembly Review* [국회보 통권] 2 (1950): 51-53.

How *Gayo* became K-POP:
International Song Festivals and South Korean Musicians' Sense of the World, 1970-1982

KIM Sunghee

"The 1st Seoul Song Festival [제1회 서울歌謠祭]." *Kyunghyang Shinmun*, Mar. 24, 1977.

"Thirteen Thoughtless Gayo Musicians Who Have Gone Crazy for Japan [日本에 미쳤나 소갈머리 없는 13名의 歌謠人]." *Kyunghyang Shinmun*, Aug. 4, 1965.

"The 1980 TBC World Song Festival Held [『'80 TBC 세계가요제』 개최]." *Joongang Ilbo*, Oct. 18, 1980.

"Alenka Pinterič, The Faces of Slovenian Provinces" [Obrazi slovenskih pokrajin] https://www.obrazislovenskihpokrajin.si/oseba/pinteric-alenka/

"Alguero Named President." *Billboard*, Feb. 17, 1973.

"Black [Singer] Group Performance [黑人 보컬그룹 出演]." *Joongang Ilbo*, Dec. 14, 1974.

"Broadcast Ethics Committee Rebukes MBC TV [放送倫理委員會 MBC TV에 견책]." *Dong-A Ilbo*, Dec. 15, 1970.

"A Discussion on the Urgent Need for Healthy Songs [노래는 즐겁게 健全歌謠 「육성」이 時急하다 座談会]." *Joongang Ilbo*, Jan. 29, 1972.

"Exclusive Broadcast of Tokyo International Song Festival (MBC TV at 8:15 pm) [동경국제가요제 독점중계 (MBC TV 밤8시 15분)]." *Kyunghyang Shinmun*, Nov. 27, 1970.

"Film Data [映畵界 자료]." *Chosun Ilbo*, Dec. 17, 1976.

"'Fog' Combo Participates in the Argentine World Song Festival [아르젠틴 世界歌謠祭에 「안개」 콤비 參加]." *Dong-A Ilbo*, Feb. 22, 1971.

"Gil Okyun Elected as Chair [会長에 吉屋潤씨]." *Chosun Ilbo*, Jan. 20, 1970.

"Going to the South America Song Festival with 'Fog' [南美 歌謠祭 가는 「안개」]." *Kyunghyang Shinmun*, Feb. 20, 1971.

"Hattori was Chief Judge." *Billboard*, Jun. 3, 1972.

"Hong Kong Actress Chen Chow Ha Visits Korea [홍콩여배우 첸추샤 한국에]." *Kyunghyang Shinmun*, May 10, 1977.

"International Brief." *Billboard*, Oct. 18, 1980.

"Join FIDOF Today." *Billboard*, Jan. 31, 1987.

"Kayabiyab (Composer) and Alejandro (Singer) Win Seoul International Song Festival Grand Prize [比 카야비압(作曲) 알레얀드로 (노래) 조합 서울국제가요제 대상 차지]." *Kyunghyang Shinmun*, Jul. 3, 1978.

"Kim Kee-Ung Song 'Where You Are...' [김기웅씨 작곡『머무는곳…』] Passes the Preliminary Round of Japanese International Song Festival [일 국제가요제 예선통과]." *Joongang Ilbo*, Apr. 29, 1978.

"Lee Bong-jo and Two Others to Participate in Tokyo World Music Festival [東京 세계歌謠祭에 李鳳祚씨 등 셋參加]." *Dong-A Ilbo*, Nov. 13, 1970.

"Lee Bong-jo Want to Enrich His TV Show 'Lee Bong-jo Hour' and Opens a Nightclub [李鳳祚아워 充実 꾀해 自己 나이트클립]." *Chosun Ilbo*, May 19, 1970.

"[Lee Bong-jo] Invited to Italy's Sanremo Music Festival [伊 산 레모 音楽祭 초청받아]." *Joongang Ilbo*, Nov. 27, 1970.

"Lee Bong-jo's New Song 'Fog' Highly Praised as Original [李鳳祚 新曲 「안개」 獨創的이라고 好評]." *Kyunghyang Shinmun*, Aug. 5, 1967.

"Lee Sung-Ae Faces Criticism [비난받는 李成愛양]." *Chosun Ilbo*, Jun. 26, 1977.

"Let's Enjoy Canzone [칸조네를 즐깁시다]." *Kyunghyang Shinmun*, May 28, 1964.

"MBC Joins the International Federation of Seoul International Song Festival as a Full Member [MBC 서울국제가요제 국제연맹 정회원으로]." *Dong-A Ilbo*, Jun. 30, 1979.

"Mr. Lee Bong-jo Elected [李鳳祚씨 뽑아]." *Chosun Ilbo*, Mar. 24, 1970.

"Music." *Chosun Ilbo*, Apr. 13, 1982.

"New Energy [Brought] to the Korean gayo Industry as Seoul Song Festival Founded [韓國

가요계에 새 活力素 서울歌謠祭 창설].” *Kyunghyang Shinmun*, Jan. 31, 1977.

“New National Song ‘Song of the Homeland Composed’ [새로운 国民 歌謠 「祖国의 노래」 作曲].” *Joongang Ilbo*, Oct. 20, 1971.

“Organizing the Seoul Music Festival [서울歌謠祭를 마련].” *Joongang Ilbo*, May 26, 1977.

“Participation of 18 Countries Including Italy, England, and Japan [이·영·일 등 18개국서 참가].” *Joongang Ilbo*, Oct. 5, 1981.

“Party to Celebrate the Award of ‘Fog’ at International Song Festival [국제가요제 입상 안개 축하회].” *Kyunghyang Shinmun*, Nov. 25, 1970.

“Patti Kim Wins Third Place at Tokyo International Song Festival [패티金 3등 入賞 東京 국제歌謠祭].” *Kyunghyang Shinmun*, Jul. 1, 1974.

“Patti Page Captivates the Audience [청중 사로잡은 패티 페이지].” *Joongang Ilbo*, Dec. 10, 1979.

“Pearl Sisters and Lee Bong-jo to Participate in 2nd Tokyo Music Festival Starting on the 25th [25일부터 제2회 동경가요제 「펄·시스터즈」·이봉조 참석].” *Joongang Ilbo*, Nov. 20, 1971.

“Plagiarism or Coincidence? The Folk Music Industry Protests against Immorality Judgment [『표절』이다 『偶合』이다 放倫判定과 歌謠界반발].” *Dong-A Ilbo*, Sep. 12, 1968.

“Pop Fairies the Nolans Come to Korea on April 2, 1982 and Perform [팝의 요정 「놀란스」 來 2일 來韓 공연].” *Kyunghyang Shinmun*, Mar. 25, 1982.

“Popularity of the Japanese Music Album ‘Fog’ Rises [「안개」 日音盤 人氣].” *Kyunghyang Shinmun*, Sep. 20, 1969.

“Recorded Music Market: Cutthroat Competition [레코드街 出血경쟁].” *Kyunghyang Shinmun*, Nov. 16, 1963.

“Sanremo International Song Festival [「산레모 국제가요제」] (MBC TV, Saturday at 7:50 pm) [MBC TV 土(토) 밤7시50분].” *Kyunghyang Shinmun*, Apr. 17, 1971.

“Sanremo Music Festival Special Broadcast on DBS [산·레모 칸소네典 DBS서 特輯放送].” *Dong-A Ilbo*, Mar. 4, 1967.

“The Seoul International Song Festival Attracts a Large Crowd, Demonstrating the Potential for the Enhancement of Popular Culture [서울 국제가요제 大盛況 “대중문화 高級化의 可能性 보여”].” *Dong-A Ilbo*, Jul. 4, 1978.

“Seoul International Song Festival Receives 1979 World Song Festival Award after Competing with 6 Countries [「79세계歌謠祭賞」 수상 「서울국제가요제」, 6국 경합 끝에].” *Kyunghyang Shinmun*, Feb. 8, 1980.

“Seoul Song Festival with Many Ticket Scalpers [暗票 많았던 서울歌謠祭].” *Dong-A Ilbo*, Jun. 4, 1977.

“Singer Sim Soo-Bong Passes the Preliminary Round of TBC World Song Festival... [She is] to Appear on the Show Program on the Evening of the 10th [가수 심수봉 TBC 세계가요제 예선통과... 10일밤 쇼프로에].” *Dong-A Ilbo*, Nov. 10, 1979.

“TBC TV 1970 Tokyo Music Festival Grand Prix Winners [TBC TV 70年度 東京가요祭 그랑쁘리 受賞者].” *Dong-A Ilbo*, Dec. 22, 1971.

“TV Broadcasts Bring International Partnership and Vitality [TV放送 國際 제휴 活氣].” *Dong-A Ilbo*, May 17, 1971.

"Visit to MBC & Kyunghyang Shinmun by Moreno, President of the World Song Festival Federation [세계歌謠祭聯 총장 모레노氏 本社 방문]." *Kyunghyang Shinmun*, Dec. 12, 1979.

"Visit to Southeast Asia for the Work Consultation of the Seoul Music Festival Secretariat [서울 가요제 사무국간사 업무협의차 東南亞 순방]." *Kyunghyang Shinmun*, Feb. 18, 1978.

"Winners of the Culture and Arts Award Decided [文化藝術賞 受賞者 결정]." *Dong-A Ilbo*, Nov. 20, 1971.

Ahn, Geon-Hyuk (안건혁). "Magnificent Opening of the 1978 Seoul International Song Festival Domestic Event on the 27th [78 서울國際歌謠祭 국내大會 27일 華麗한 개막]." *Kyunghyang Shinmun*, May 25, 1978.

Bourdaghs, Michael. *Sayonara Amerika, Sayonara Nippon: A Geopolitical Prehistory of J-Pop.* New York, NY: Columbia University Press, 2012.

Choe, Gyeong Sik (최경식). "Meeting with Antonio Barreiro, Chief Executive Officer of the Association of Philippine Broadcasters - Seoul Song Festival: A Meeting of East and West [필리핀 大衆음악재단 首席부이사장 안토니오 바레이로씨와 만나 — 서울歌謠祭는 東과 西의 만남]." *Kyunghyang Shinmun*, Jul. 1, 1978.

Cho-Han, Haejoang (조한혜정). *Modernity, Popular Culture and East-West Identity Formation: A Discourse Analysis of Korean Wave in Asia* [글로벌 지각 변동의 징후로 읽는 '한류 열풍」, 『'한류'와 아시아의 대중문화』]. Seoul: Yonsei University Press, 2003.

Chornik, Katia. "When Julio Iglesias Played Pinochet's Prison." *Guardian*, May 15, 2014. https://www.theguardian.com/music/2014/may/15/julio-iglesias-valparaiso-pinochet-chile.

Chung, Hong-Taek (정홍택). "Korea's #1 Entertainment Journalist Jeong Hong-Taek Speaks Out, 30. The Korean Song Festival [한국 연예기자 1호 정홍택의 지금은 말할 수 있다] <30> 한국 가요제]." *Hankook Ilbo*, Oct. 21, 2008. https://www.hankookilbo.com/News/Read/200810210025501826.

_____. "Korea's #1 Entertainment Journalist Jeong Hong-Taek Speaks Out, 43: The Greece World Song Festival [한국 연예기자 1호 정홍택의 지금은 말할 수 있다]." *Hankook Ilbo*, Jan. 20, 2009. https://www.hankookilbo.com/News/Read/200901200111927560.

Hunter, Nigel. "FIDOF's Fund Raising Plan Tabled: President Resigned." *Cashbox*, Jun. 18, 1977, 50.

Hwang, Mun-Pyeong (황문평). "The [Town] Square of 'Contemporary Music Language': A General Review of the 1978 Seoul International Song Festival [「音樂現代語」의 광장: 78 서울국제가요제 總評]." *Kyunghyang Shinmun*, Jul. 4, 1978.

Hyun, Mee. *As If Today is the Last Day [오늘을 마지막 날처럼].* Seoul: Moonhakmaeul, 1997.

Jang, Yoon-Hwan (장윤환). "Plagiarism in the World of Popular Music [표절 판치는 歌謠界]." *Dong-A Ilbo*, Jul. 23, 1968.

_____. "What Sells Well in Recorded Music Market? [레코드街 어떤 것이 잘팔리나]." *Dong-A Ilbo*, Aug. 19, 1981.

Jeong, Jung-Heon (정중헌). "No Special Features at the 1979 [MBC] Seoul International Song Festival ["特性" 없었던 「79서울 국제 가요제」]." *Joongang Ilbo*, Jun. 10, 1979.

_____. "Showmanship Shines...[TBC] World Song Festival [演出 돋보인 쇼⋯세계歌謠祭]." *Joongang Ilbo*, Dec. 16, 1979.

_____. "Who Will Win the Grand Prix? [그랑프리 누구에게 갈까]." *Chosun Ilbo*, May 15, 1981.

Jeong, Joong-Heon (정중헌). "Predictions by Three Pop Music Experts for 1982 [팝스'82 전문가 3人의 豫言]." *Chosun Ilbo*, Jan. 1, 1982.

Jeong, Yeog-Il (정영일). "Culture Recap 1970 Part 12: Broadcasting‐Song [文化界決算 70 ⑫ 放送‐歌謠]." *Joongang Ilbo*, Dec. 18, 1970.

Jung, Eun-Young. "New Wave Formations: K-Pop Idols, Social Media, and the Remaking of the Korean Wave." In *Hallyu 2.0: The Korean Wave in the Age of Social-Media*, edited by Sangjoon Lee and Abé Mark Nornes, 73-89. Ann Arbor, MI: University of Michigan Press, 2015.

Kang, Sang-Heon (강상헌). "The Dooleys Come to Korea to Perform [둘리스 來韓公演]." *Dong-A Ilbo*, Feb. 17, 1981.

Kim, Chang Nam (김창남). "The Cultural Identity of Korean Youth Culture in the 1970s: Focusing on Guitar Music [1970년대 한국 청년문화의 문화적 정체성―통기타음악을 중심으로]." *Journal of Popular Music* 2 (2008): 144-65.

Kim, Jun-Sik (김준식). "Korean Popular Music Expanding Overseas - Domestic 'Hit' Songs Arranged as 'Pop Songs' [해외로 진출하는 한국 가요―국내 「히트」곡을 「팝송」으로 편곡]." *Joongang Ilbo*, Dec. 20, 1980.

Kim, Pil-Ho (김필호). "Group Sound Rock Music of the 1960s-70s - Archaeology of Korean Pop Music [1960-70년대 그룹사운드 록음악―한국 팝의 고고학]." *Cultural Science* 6 (2005): 211-28.

Lee, Herim Erin (이혜림). "The Formation of 1970s Korean Youth Culture: Focusing on the Cultural Consumption of Popular Music [1970년대 청년문화구성체의 역사적 형성과정―대중음악의 소비양상을 중심으로]." *Korean Journal of Social Issues* 6, no. 2 (2005): 7-40.

Lee, Seong-Soo (이성수). "What Kind of Songs Do Korean Pop Music Fans Like? [우리나라 팝송팬 어떤 노래 좋아하나]." *Dong-A Ilbo*, Oct. 14, 1981.

Lim, Hyeong-Soon (임형순). "Influence of 1970-1980 Campus Bands on Korean Rock Music [1970-1980 캠퍼스 밴드가 한국 록 음악에 미친 영향]." *Journal of Popular Music* [*대중음악*] 13 (2014): 8-32.

Park, Ae-Kyung (박애경). "An Explore on the Potential of Korean Folk Song as the Urban Song‐with a Focus on the Folk Song and Folk Culture in 1970s [한국 포크의 '도시민요'적 가능성 탐색―1970년대 포크송과 포크문화를 중심으로]." *Korean Folk Songs* 41, no. 2 (2014): 53-77.

Park, Yong-Gyu (박용규). "Television and Popular Music in the 1970s: Focusing on Popular Music Programs for Teenagers [1970년대의 텔레비전과 대중음악―청소년 대상 대중음악 프로그램을 중심으로]." *Korean Journal of Journalism and Communication Studies* 51, no. 2 (2007): 5-29.

Pelaić, Goran. "Zapisi I Sjećanja Gorana Pelaića (15) Armando Moreno: Mir i prijateljstvo kroz glazbenu umjetnost." *Dalmacija Danas*, Feb. 17, 2020. https://www.dalmacijadanas.

hr/zapisi-i-sjecanja-gorana-pelaica-15-armando-moreno-mir-i-prijateljstvo-kroz-glazben u-umjetnost/.

Shin, Hyunjoon. "The Cultural Politics of K-Pop: A Case Study of Popular Music Crossing Borders [K-Pop의 문화정치(학): 월경(越境)하는 대중음악에 관한 하나의 사례연구]." *Media and Society* 13, no. 3 (2005): 7-36.

Shin, Hyun-Jun. "Revisiting Asian Popular Music from an Inter-Asian Perspective [인터아시아 시각에서 아시아 대중음악을 다시 조명하기]." *Hwanghae Culture* 89 (2015): 51-66.

Shin, Hyun-Jun, Yong-Woo Lee, and Ji-Seon Choi (신현준 · 이용우 · 최지선). *Archaeology of Korean Pop Music 1970 - Korean Folk and Rock, Its Peak and Diversification [한국 팝의 고고학 1970 — 한국의 포크와 록, 그 절정과 분화].* Seoul: HanGilArt, 2005.

Shin, Hyun-Jun (신현준). "The Issues of Writing Histories of Korean Popular Music in the 1970s and 80s: The Difficulties of Indeterminate Texts and Complex Mediations [1970~1980년대 한국 대중음악사 서술의 쟁점 — 불확정적 텍스트와 복합적 매개의 난점]." *Journal of Popular Music [대중음악]* 15 (2015): 93-112.

Wade, James. "Future Uncertainty of Seoul Music Contest." *Billboard*, Dec. 13, 1980.

Yamaguchi, Akira. "Festivals, A Shot at the Spotlight." *Billboard*, Apr. 30, 1977.

Yamaha Music Foundation. "The 1st Tokyo International Popular Song Festival (Renamed to World Popular Song Festival from the 2nd Festival Onwards), [in Japanese, 'Dai 1-kai Tōkyō Kokusai Kayō Ongakusai (Dai 2-kai yori 'Sekai Kayōsai' ni meishō henkō)']." *The World Popular Song Festival.* https://www.yamaha-mf.or.jp/history/e-history/wpsf/.

Yun, Bok-Hee (윤복희). *It's Me, Lord [저예요, 주님].* Seoul: Duranno Seowon Corporation, 2011.

Parallels of Metamorphosis in the Theatre in Korea and Hungary

BLAHÓ Kata

Bird Bishop, Isabella. *Korea, and Her Neighbours.* Fleming H. Revell Company, 1897. [Online] Available: https://www.gutenberg.org/files/69300/69300-h/69300-h.htm

Creutzenberg, Jan. "From Traditional Opera to Modern Music Theatre? Recent Experiments in Ch'Anggŭk." *Transactions of the Royal Asiatic Society Korea Branch* 88 (2013): 87-102. [Online] Available: https://www.academia.edu/7361419/From_Traditional_Ope ra_to_ Modern_Music_Theatre_Recent_Experiments_in_Ch_angg%C5%ADk

Ha, Kyeong-hwa. *A Brief Study of Korean Theatre History [한국연극사 소고].* Seoul: M-Ad [엠-에드], 2008.

Jang, Won-jae. "History of the Korean Theatre: Transitional Period Leading to the Modern Theatre 1902-1919." *International Journal of Korean History* 4, no. 1 (Aug. 2003): 213-237. [Online] Available: https://ijkh.khistory.org/upload/pdf/06_History_of_the_Korean_ Theatre. pdf

Jang, Won-jae. "Toward a Modern Society: History of the Korean Theatre in the Modern Period 1919~1940." *International Journal of Korean History* 6 (Dec. 2004): 189-209.

[Online] Available: https://ijkh.khistory.org/upload/pdf/6_07.pdf

Jeon, Kyung-wook. *Traditional Performing Arts of Korea*. Seoul: Korea Foundation, 2008.

Killick, Andrew. "Korean 'Ch'anggŭk' Opera: Its Origins and Its Origin Myth." *Asian Music* 33, no. 2 (2002): 43-82. [Online] Available: http://www.jstor.org/stable/834345

Kim, Miy He. *Acts and Scenes – Western Drama in Korean Theater*. Seoul: Hollym Corp. Publishers, 2013.

Lee, Meewon. "The Modernization of Korean Theatre Through the Reception of Western Realism." In *Modernization of Asian Theatres*, edited by Nagata, Y., Chaturvedi, R., 23-39. Singapore: Springer, 2019. [Online] Available: https://doi.org/10.1007/978-981 -13-6046-6_3

Seo, Yeon-ho (서연호). *Korean Theatre History– Modern Period [한국연극사; 근대편]*. Seoul: Yeongeuk-gwa Ingan [연극과 인간], 2003.

Székely, György and Gajdó, Tamás, eds. *Hungarian Theatre History II. (1873-1920) [Magyar színháztörténet II. (1873-1920)]*. Budapest: Magyar Könyvklub – Országos Színháztörténeti Múzeum és Intézet, 2001. [Online] Available: https://mek.oszk.hu/02000/02065/html/2kotet/index.html

Székely, György and Kerényi, Ferenc, eds. *Hungarian Theatre History I. (1790-1873) [Magyar színháztörténet I. (1790-1873)]*. Budapest: Akadémiai Kiadó, 1990. [Online] Available: https://mek.oszk.hu/02000/02065/html/1kotet/index.html

Image of Korea in Hungarian Encyclopedias: 1833-1930

KIM Jiyoung

Reports of the Austro-Hungarian Monarchy's Embassy in Tokyo, Vienna Archives [Osztrák Magyar Monarchia Tokiói Nagykövetségének jelentései, Bécsi levéltár].

Repository of Knowledge for the Public, [Közhasznú Esmeretek Tára Hetedik Kutet]. Budapest, 1833.

"From the Editors of Neves Folyóirat [Neves Folyóirat Szerkesztőitől Eredt]." *Encyclopedia of New Times [Új Idők Lexikona]*. Budapest, 1939.

Acsády, Ignác. *Athaeneum Pocket Encyclopedia [Athaeneum Kézi Lexikona]*. Budapest, 1892.

Balanyi, Bangha and et al. *Catholic Encyclopedia [Katolikus Lexikon]*. Budapest, 1932.

Berei, Andor. *New Lexicon [Új Lexikon]*. Budapest, 1936.

Cholnoky, Jenö. *The Earth and its Life [A Föld és Élete]*. Budapest, 1936.

Csoma, Mozes. "A Discussion on Hungarian Korean Peninsula Studies [헝가리 한반도사 연구 시론]." *The Journal of History [역사연구]* 136 (2015): 85-107.

Csoma, Mozes. "A Study on Hungarian Korean Studies Through the History of Korean-Hungarian Relations [한·형 관계사를 통해 본 헝가리 한국학에 대한 고찰]." *Journal of Korean Culture* 33 (2016): 7-19.

Fendler, Károly. *One Hundred Years of Hungarian-Korean Relations*. Budapest: Korea Journal

30, 1990, 26-34.

Fendler, Károly. "The Korean War (1950-1953) in the Foreign Affairs of Hungary." *Korea Journal 30* 11, (1990): 49-60.

Fendler, Károly. "Austro-Hungarian Archival Sources of Korean History (1884-1910)." *Journal of the German Morgenländische Gesellschaft* 150, (2000): 299-310.

Fendler, Károly. "One Hundred Years of Hungarian-Korean Relations [A Magyar-Koreai Kapcsolatok száz éve (1892-1992)]." In *A Herman Ottó Múzeum Évkönyve XXXII (32)*, edited by Veres László, 151-65. Budapest, Miskoic: Herman Ottó Múzeum, 2004.

Ferenc, Gáspár. *Forty Thousand Miles by Sail and Steam [Negyvenezer Mérföld Vitorlával és Gőzzel].* Budapest, 1893.

Győző, Temesy and Pécsi Márton. *Geographical Communications [Földrajzi Közlemények].* Budapest, 1892.

Kim, Bogook (김보국). "The Development of the Diplomatic Relationship between South Korea and Hungary: A Survey of the Diplomatic Documents of the Two Countries." *Bulgarian Historical Review*, 3-4, 143-63.

Kim, Bogook (김보국). "Study on the process of establishing diplomatic relations between the Republic of Korea and Hungary through the confidential documents of the Hungarian Ministry of Foreign Affairs." *East European & Balkan Studies [동유럽발칸연구]* 38, no. 3 (2014): 151-76.

Kim, Bogook (김보국). "Study on the Process of Establishing Diplomatic Relations between the Republic of Korea and Hungary," *Bulgarian Historical Review* 3-4, (2014), 143-63.

Kim, Bogook (김보국). "Political Transition, Hungary, South and North Korea: Based on the National Archival Sources [헝가리의 체제전환시기까지 한국과 헝가리의 교류에 관한 연구: 한국과 헝가리의 외교문서를 중심으로 한국-북한-헝가리의 관계 고찰]." *East European & Balkan Studies [동유럽발칸연구]* 39-2 (2019): 161-89.

Kim, Do-Min (김도민). "Perceptions and Reactions of North and South Korea to the 'Prague Spring' of 1968 [1968년 '프라하의 봄'에 대한 남북한의 인식과 반응]." *Historical Criticism [역사비평]* 123 (2018): 72-101.

Kim, Do-Min (김도민). "A Study on the Diplomacy of South and North Korea toward Neutral Countries from 1948 to 1968 [1948~1968년 남·북한의 중립국 외교 연구]." PhD diss., Seoul National University, 2020.

Kim, Jongsoo (김종수). "A Historical Study on Representations of Eastern Europe Described in Korea [한국에서 재현된 동유럽 표상의 역사적 고찰]." *East European & Balkan Studies [동유럽발칸연구]* 42-1, (2018): 3-23.

Kim, Jiyoung (김지영). "An Analysis of Austro-Hungarian Diplomatic Documents about Korea 1885~1894 [오스트리아-헝가리 제국의 조선에 대한 외교문서 연구: 1885~1894년 발간문서를 중심으로]." *Oriental Studies [東洋學]* 44, no. 4 (2019): 232-4.

Kim, Jiyoung (김지영). "A Study on the Metamorphoses of Hungarian Culture by the Influence of Ottoman Empire [헝가리의 오스만 문화 수용과 문화적 메타모포시스]." *East European & Balkan Studies [동유럽발칸연구]* 43-3, (2019): 45-70.

Kiss, Tamara. "Analysis of Hungarian Images Reflected in Naver Blogs [Naver 블로그에 반영된 헝가리 이미지 분석]." Seoul National University Master's thesis, Seoul National University,

2018.

Lajos, Gerő, and Bokor Jozsef et al. *PASLLAS Great Encyclopedia [PALLAS Nagy Lexikona]*. Budapest, 1895.

László, Toldy. *The Earth and its Peoples [A Föld és Népei]*. Budapest, 1880.

Lee, Sang-Hyup (이상협). *The History of Hungary [헝가리史]*. Seoul: Daehan Textbooks [대한교과서], 1996.

Osváth, Gábor. *On the Relationship of Korean and Other East Asian Languages [A koreai és más kelet-ázsiai nyelvek viszonyáró]*. Budapest: Intézeti Szemle 1973.

Osváth, Gábor. *The Work of Ferenc Mártonfi (1945-1991) in Korean Studies [Mártonfi Ferenc (1945-1991) koreanisztikai munkássága]*. Budapest: Aspect of Korean Civilization, 2002.

Osváth, Gábor. *Korean Language and Literature - Selected Studies [Koreai nyelv és irodalom - Váogatott tanulmáyok]*. Budapest: Pluralingua Kiado, 2006.

Park, Soo-Young (박수영), Sung-Soon Park (박성순) and et. al. "A Study of the Relationship Between Korea and Hungary in Modern Times [근대 한국과 헝가리 관계사 연구: '噶蘇士傳'의 수입과 독립정신의 고취를 중심으로]," *Oriental Studies [東洋學]* 77 (2019): 207-20.

Park, Soo Young (박수영). "Hungarian Study in Korea and Korean Study in Hungary: Achievements and Problems." Presentation at the Korea-Poland-Central Europe. Proceedings of the 2nd International Academic Conference of the Korean Association of East European and Balkan Studies, Chicago, 2002. 147-57.

Samuel, Révai et al. *Révai Great Encyclopedia [Révai Nagy Lexikona]*. Budapest, 1915.

Tamás, Nagy. "Hungarian Translations of Korean Modern Short Stories 'Obaltan' and 'Jangma' [한국 현대 단편소설 '오발탄', '장마'의 헝가리어 번역]." Master's thesis, Kookmin University, 2011.

Tamás, Nagy (너지 더마쉬). "The Translation of Two Korean Modern Short Stories "Obaltan" and "Jangma" to Hungarian, the Problems and Possible Solutions [한국 현대 단편소설 「오발탄」 「장마」의 헝가리어 번역]." Master's thesis, Kookmin University, 2012.

Tolnao. *Tolnai New Encyclopedia [Tolnai Új világ Lexikona]*. Budapest, 1927.

Török, János, János Pollák, and Ferenc Laubhaimer. *Universal Hungarian Encyclopedia [Egyetemes Magyar Encyclopaedia]*. Budapest, 1872.

Vay, Péter G. *Emperors and Empires of the East [Kelet Császárai és Császárságai]*. Budapest, 1906.

Yang, JiSun (양지선). "Hungarian Support for the Korean Independence Movement and Its Significance [헝가리인 마쟈르의 한국독립운동 지원과 그 의의]." *Oriental Studies [東洋學]* 77 (2019): 233-40.

Index

A

acculturation 3, 4, 10, 12, 13, 15, 16
A Föld és népei 257, 258, 264
Algueró (Algueró), Augusto 231
Algueró (Dasca), Augusto 231
An Jungsik 144, 160~162
Anthony D. Smith 116
archetypal plant 4, 20, 22
archetype 21
Aristotle 56, 67, 71, 72
Aristotle's ethics 56
Asia 253, 254, 259, 265, 271, 278
Atheneum Kézi Lexikona 257
Austro-Hungarian 155
Austro-Hungarian Empire 239
Austro-Hungarian monarchy 11

B

Baek Hong-Jun (백홍준) 125
Balatonfüred 240
Barbarians 53, 54, 57~59, 64, 74, 81
Bechtel 193~195
Beijing (or Yanjing) 59, 62~64
Benedict Anderson 135
Benjamin, Walter 46
BFBS 123
Bible 107, 108, 110, 111, 113~116, 119~125, 127, 129~142
Biblical narratives 107
biblical nationalism 111, 130, 135, 139, 140~142
biblical translation 116, 124, 125, 130
Billboard 227, 231

Bob herceg 242
Book Publishing 119
Bozóky, Dezső 144, 151, 152, 155~158, 161
Budapest 151~154, 239~243, 247, 248
Buddhism 144
Bukhan Mountain 147

C

Carl Gustav Jung 21
Carl von Linné 17
Catholic ethical theology 56, 66
Chang-Soon Kim 103
Changdeokgung 145
changgeuk (창극) 246, 247, 249, 252
Changgyeonggung 145
Chemulp'o 153
Cheongpyeong dam(Cheongpyeong Hydroelectric Power Plant) 169~171, 183, 184
Chil-guk 60
China 254, 261, 262, 263, 265~267, 269, 270, 272, 273, 276, 278
Cho Yong-ho 214, 222, 227, 231
Cho Yong-pil 204, 212
Choe Gyeong Sik 222, 228
Chosun Dynasty 112, 113, 140
Chosön, the Land of the Morning Calm 149
Chŏn Gyŏng-yŏn 6, 9, 12, 14
Chŏng Dae-wi 15
Christian ethics 53, 56~58, 67, 68, 70, 72, 76, 78~82
Christianity 110, 118~123, 130, 131, 133,

141, 253

Christian nationalism   110

Christian national movement   113, 139

Chujakarye   58

Chung Hong-Taek   203, 204, 217~219

Chung Hun Hi   203, 204, 210, 212, 213, 235

civic nationalism   138, 141

colonial era   239

Combined Economic Board (CEB)   164, 165, 167, 189, 190

commedia dell'arte   246

Confucian intellectual tradition   56

covenant nationalism   116, 142

Csoma Mozes   255

Cui Fenglong   87, 89

cultural metamorphosis   28, 33, 38, 41, 51

D

Daesung   85, 90~97, 99, 100, 101, 104, 105

demythologization   11, 12

Dion, Celine   233

Dong-A Ilbo   97

Dongheung   85, 91~95, 100, 104, 105

Dongman Youth Federation   88

Dongyang Hakwon   89, 96~100, 105, 106

Dual Monarchy   239

Duara, Prasenjit   31, 32

E

Economic Cooperation Administration (ECA)   176

Egyetemes Magyar Encyclopaedia   257, 258, 262

Electrical Engineering   171, 177~180, 196

Electrical Grid   165, 167, 177, 180, 181, 188, 192

ethical propriety (예의 or 禮義)   56, 57

Ethnic Nationalism   113, 117

ethnie   110, 111

etiquette   54, 75, 76, 81

Eunjin Middle School   86, 90, 92~96, 99

Europeans   253, 254, 261, 265

F

Fendler Károly   255

Foreign Operation Administration (FOA)   192

Franz Joseph I   155

G

Gando Communist Party Incident   88, 100

GARIOA (Government and Relief in Occupied Areas)   172

Gayo   202, 207, 209, 211, 234, 236

genuineness (誠)   8, 16

Geo-Ga-Jap-Bok-Go (居家雜服攷)   54

Gerhart Hauptmann   247

German residents   240

German-speaking troupes   240

Geukyesulhyeophoe (극예술협회, The Theatre Arts Association)   249, 250

Geukyesulyeonguhoe (극예술연구회, Theatre Art Research Association)   250, 251

Gil Okyun   204, 209, 213, 214, 218, 220

Goethe, Johann Wolfgang von   3, 4, 17~22

Gojong   149, 158, 159

Gwangmyeonghui   85

Gyeong-Seok Im   94

Gyeongbok Palace   144~147, 149, 158, 160, 162

H

Habsburg emperor   240

Hangul   57, 63, 113, 117, 118, 121, 122, 129~135, 138

Hankook Ilbo   203, 204, 217, 218

Han River   144

Hanyang   262, 264

Harvey Cox   16

Hattori, Ryōichi   218

Henrik Ibsen   243, 247

Henry Becque   247

Henry Landor   146

Hermit Kingdom   143

Hopp, Ferenc   144, 151~155, 161

Hungarian Geographic Society   154

Hungarian operettas   242

Hungarian Royal Opera House   242

Hungary   150, 153, 239, 241, 242, 247, 248, 250~254, 256~259, 263, 265, 272, 278, 279

Huszka, Jenő   242

Hwacheon dam(Hwacheon Hydroelectric Power Plant)   169, 171, 182~187, 191, 198

Hwang Cheol   144, 159, 162

Hwang Jeong-tae   203, 218, 227

Hwang Min-ho   87, 88

Hwang Mun-pyeong   218, 221, 228

hybrid   13

hybridity   28, 30, 31, 33, 37, 51

hydro as master, coal as subordinate   181, 188, 199, 200

hydropower-centered system   181

Hyeoksindan (혁신단)   246

Hyeomyulsa (협률사)   240, 245

Hyun Mee   202, 204, 208, 212, 213, 218, 235

I

ible   123

Il-Am-Yŏn-Ki   55, 60

Im Hwa   23, 24, 27, 28, 32~38, 43, 44, 48~51

Im Seong-gu (임성구)   246

Independence Newspaper (독립신문)   122

Indigenization   3~17, 20, 21, 22

indigenization debates   4

Indigenization theology   3~5, 8~14, 16, 17, 20, 22

International Federation of Festival Organizations (Federation Internationale des Organisations de Festivals: FIDOF)   206, 232, 233

International Federation of Festival Organizations (FIDOF)   228, 229

Inwangsan Mountain   144

J

Japan   244, 245, 250, 253, 254, 261~263, 265, 266, 269, 270, 272~279

Japanese   144~146, 149, 152, 155, 159~162

Japanese settlers   240, 244, 246

Jechang Hospital   90

Jeong Jaeyoon   100

Jesuits   58, 72

Ji Un-Yeong   159

Jo Il-jae's (조일재)   245

John Ross   123, 124

Joo Yong Kim   90

Joseon   144, 146, 148, 149, 160~162, 274

Joseon Product Exposition   145

Ju Si-Gyeong   117, 118

K

K-pop   234, 236

Kabiljo, Alfi   228, 230

kabuki (歌舞伎)   246

kaehwap'a   118

Kafka's The Metamorphosis   45, 46, 47

Kando   85, 87~90, 96, 97, 100, 101, 103~105

Kando Daily   86

Kando Shinbo   86

Katolikus Lexikon   257, 259, 277

Kim Bogook   255

Kim Do-min   256

Kim Jin-Gi (김진기)   125

Kim Jong-su   256

Kim Tae-jun   26, 33, 44

Kim Yong-Won   159

Kim, Patti   204, 213~215

kisaeng   246

Kolozsvár   240

Korea   143~156, 159~162, 241, 244, 245, 247, 249~258, 260~265, 267~279

Korean Bible   122, 123

Korean Bible Society   123, 125, 129

Korean Christian History   110

Korean culture   56

Korean Electric Company (조선전업)   170, 197

Korean Electricity Studies Association

311

(KESA) 177

Korean Empire 144, 265, 272

Korean national identity 112, 148

Korean New Testament 130

Korean Peninsula 239, 240, 244, 251

Korean puppet plays (한국의 인형극) 240

Kukcho Oryeui 58

Kyongseong Electric Company (경성전기)
    170

Kyunghyang Shinmun 219, 221, 229

Kyŏngguk Taejŏn 58

Kálmán, Emmerich 242

Közhasznú Esmeretek Tára 254, 257, 258,
    260, 262

L

Landscape of Seoul 147

Lee Bong-jo 202~205, 208~213, 218, 222,
    226, 227, 228, 231

Lee Eung-Chan (이응찬) 124, 125

Lee Jong-il 179~181, 187

Lee Sang-jae 131

Lee Seong-Ha (이성하) 125

Lee Soo-Jeong 127, 128, 130, 131

Lehár, Franz 242

logos 11

Loti, Pierre 144, 149~151, 162

Lowell, Percival 144, 148, 149, 151, 159,
    160, 162

M

Maeil Shinbo 97, 112

Maeil Sinbo 245

Manchu-Tungusic 261

Manchuria 85, 88, 89, 94, 103, 104, 123,
    124, 129, 263, 275

Manmul Jinwon 60

manners (rye; 禮) 57~59

manners-based governance (예치 or 禮治)
    58

Marché International du Disque et de
    l'Edition Musicale, or "The International
    Music and Discography Market" 229

Matteo Ricci 14

Metamorphosis 3, 4, 17~22

Min Sheng Bao 86, 87, 103

Min-Sung Baek 103

Ming-Qing 53, 59

minjok 111~113, 138, 140

Minjung Theology 8

Mircea Eliade 21

Miskolc 240

missionaries 54, 57~60, 64, 65, 76, 78, 79,
    81

modern Korea 117, 121, 126, 129

modernity 23, 25, 27, 30, 31, 34, 35, 38,
    42, 47, 49~51

Moreno, Armando 225, 226, 228, 229, 230,
    232~234

Mount Bugak 144

Munhwa Broadcasting Corporation (MBC)
    210, 212

Museum of Asian Arts 152

mutual bonds (강상 or 綱常) 56

Myeongshin 85, 86

N

Nagy Tamás 256

Naksan Mountain 144

Nathan Report 189, 190, 191

Nation 111

nation 107~119, 133, 135~142

national identity 108, 112, 118, 136, 138,
    141

national studies movement 120

nationalist movement 108, 119, 141

nationhood 107~111, 114~117, 119, 135~
    137, 139~141

Neo-Confucianism 56, 58

Népszínház 242, 247

népszínmű (folks comedy) 241, 242, 251,
    252

O

of Northern Learning (北學) 54

Ogawa Kazumasa (Japanese) 160

Ohashi Junko 224
Osváth Gábor 255
Ovid's Metamorphoses 44, 46

P

Paik-Wood Agreement 190, 192
Pak A-ron 9
Pallas Nagy Lexikona 257, 258, 268, 269
Pan-Asianism 112, 113
pansori (판소리) 240, 246, 247, 252
Park Chung-hee 247
Park Gyu-su (朴珪壽) 54, 81
Park Kyung Heuy 213~215, 219, 222
Park Soo Young 255
Park Sung-soon 256
Pester Stadttheater 240, 241
Pesti Magyar Theater 240
Phillip Jaison (서재필) 122
photographic images 143, 144
Pinterič, Alenka 228, 234
Plutarch 13
pocket gospel booklets 121
Pop Song-ification of Korean gayo 233
Power Development Plan 164~167, 181, 185, 187, 189, 193, 194, 198~200
Power ship(Jacona, Electra, Impedance, Saranac) 173, 174, 182
Practical Learning (實學) 54
print capitalism 112, 135
Protestant Christians 142
Protestant ethics 56, 57, 63, 78, 81
Protestant nations 107, 114, 136
Pyŏnginyangyo 263, 269

Q

Qing Dynasty 59, 62

R

Reed, Les 230, 231
Reformation 107, 110, 114, 135, 136
reformation 139
Ross Edition 124~126, 138, 140
Rudolf Bultmann 11

Russo-Japanese War 109, 130, 133~135, 137
Révai Nagy Lexikona 257, 258, 271

S

Sanremo Music Festival [Festival della Canzone Italiana di Sanremo] 210, 211
Schlaeger, Jürgen 29, 30
Second Vatican Council 4, 6
Sejong Sillok 58
Seo Sang-Ryun (서상륜) 125, 130, 132
Seongnihak 144
Seoul 144~146, 148~153, 155, 157~162, 239, 244
Shimpa (jap. 新派, „new style"; kor. sinpageuk, 신파극, "new style drama") 246, 252
Shin Joo-baek 87, 88
Shin Ki-jo 171, 180, 183, 195
Shin, Ju-Baek 87
silheom mudae (실험 무대, experimental stage) 250
Silver World (은세계) 246
Simon, Masahito 221, 223
Sin Chae-Ho 112, 117, 118
singeuk (신극, „new theatre") 241, 248~252
singularity 28, 30~33, 36, 51
Sinocentrism 53, 56, 57
Small Valley Electricity Development Plan 185
socialism 87, 88, 94, 96
soil 3~5, 10, 11, 15, 17, 20, 21
Song Olympiad (Ολυμπιάδα Τραγουδιού; Olympiade de la Chanson) 202, 210, 212, 218, 235
Sun Woo Il 86
Swallen (蘇安論) 55, 80, 82
syncretism 13~17, 20, 22
Syngman Rhee government 164~166
Szigligeti, Ede 241
Sŏsedongjeom 57
Šverko, Radojka 228

T

Taejo 144
Taiguo Jin 90, 95
talchum (탈춤) 240
Tamara Kiss 256
Tan Sitong (譚嗣同) 41, 42
Tangun 7
Tapgol Park 157, 158
Taska Report 190, 191
Tayler, Constance 146
TBS Tokyo Music Festival 205, 213~216, 218, 222~224
The History of New Korean Literature (Gaeseol Shinmunhaksa) 23, 28, 33~35, 43~45, 48, 50
The Korean War 163, 181, 185, 256
The May 14 Power Outage 172
The Metamorphosis of Plants 18
the Ministry of Commerce and Industry 166, 167, 172, 174, 175, 179~181, 185, 187, 198, 200
the Royal Academy of London 146
the U.S. military government 171~175, 179
the U.S. State Department 176, 192
theatre 239~252
theatrical metamorphoses 239, 251
thermal power plant 174, 176, 182, 188, 190~196, 198~200
Thomism 56
Three Sick Man (병자 삼인) 245
Thália Company (Thália Társaság, 1904-1908) 241
Tolnai Új Világ Lexikona 257, 258, 274
Tongyang Broadcasting Company (TBC) 203, 212
Towolhoe Theatre Company (토월회) 250
tradition 25, 26, 35, 37~40, 51
transplantation 24, 26~28, 34~38, 44, 51
Transylvania 240

U

Új Idők Lexikona 257, 259
Új Lexikon 257, 259

United Nations Korean Reconstruction
Agency (UNKRA) 184
universality 28, 33, 51
University of Budapest 259, 271
US Aid Policy 189

V

Vay, Péter 151
Viña del Mar International Song Festival (Festival Internacional de la Canción de Viña del Mar) 204, 205, 212
Volksstück 242
Vos, Hubert 146, 147, 162
Vígszínház (Comedy Theatre) 242, 243, 247

W

Western Christian ethics 56, 82
Western ethics 56, 71, 72, 79, 81
Wongaksa Theatre (원각사) 245
Wongudan temple 157
World's Columbian Exposition 146

X

Xavier-Ehrenbert Fridelli 60

Y

Yamaha World Popular Song Festival 203~205, 209~213, 215~219, 222~224, 233
Yanabu Akira 25, 39
Yang Ji-sun 256
Yangi(洋夷 ; 양이) 54
Yeon-hang-sa 55, 59~62
Yi In-jik (이인직) 40, 42, 246
Yi Kang 159
Yi Seonggye 144
Yon-Byon 87
Yongjeong 85~91, 93~106
Yongjeong 3.13 Movement 87
Yoon Bok-hee 205, 222
Yu Chijin (유치진) 250
Yu Dong-sik 5, 6, 8, 9, 11, 14, 15
Yugoslavia 206, 207, 221, 225, 226, 228~230,

Index

232, 234, 236
Yun Il-jung   171, 177, 187
Yun Sŏng-bŏm   5, 7~10, 14~16, 20, 22
Yŏn-haeng-il-lok   60

other
20th century   148, 151, 161